Nina's North Shore Guide

THIRD EDITION

Nina's North Shore Guide
Big Lake, Big Woods, Big Fun

THIRD EDITION

Nina A. Simonowicz

Illustrations by Betsy Bowen

Nina A Simonowicz

2004

UNIVERSITY OF MINNESOTA PRESS
Minneapolis • London

MINNESOTA

First published in 1996 by Many Blankets, Grand Marais, Minnesota

Published by the University of Minnesota Press
111 Third Avenue South, Suite 290
Minneapolis, MN 55401-2520
http://www.upress.umn.edu

Simonowicz, Nina A.
    Nina's North Shore guide : big lake, big woods, big fun / Nina A. Simonowicz ; illustrations by Betsy Bowen. – 3rd ed.
        p.   cm.
    Includes bibliographical references and index.
    ISBN 0-8166-4440-3
    1. Superior, Lake, Region – Guidebooks. 2. Duluth Region (Minn.) – Guidebooks. I. Bowen, Betsy, ill. II. Title. III. Title: North Shore guide.
    F612.S9S56   1999
    917.74'90443 – dc21   99-12102

Printed in the United States of America on acid-free paper

The University of Minnesota is an equal-opportunity educator and employer.

12 11 10 09 08 07 06 05 04   10 9 8 7 6 5 4 3 2 1

To all the amazing, lovely, independent, contentious, kind, funny, encouraging, creative folks who live along this Big Lake and in these Big Woods,

Thanks!

You've made writing this book an absolute treat and living here intriguing, unpredictable, and home.

IT IS FORTUNATE, PERHAPS, THAT NO
MATTER HOW INTENTLY ONE STUDIES THE
HUNDRED LITTLE DRAMAS OF THE WOODS
... NO ONE CAN EVER LEARN ALL THE
SALIENT FACTS ABOUT ANY ONE OF THEM.

Aldo Leopold, *A Sand County Almanac*

Contents

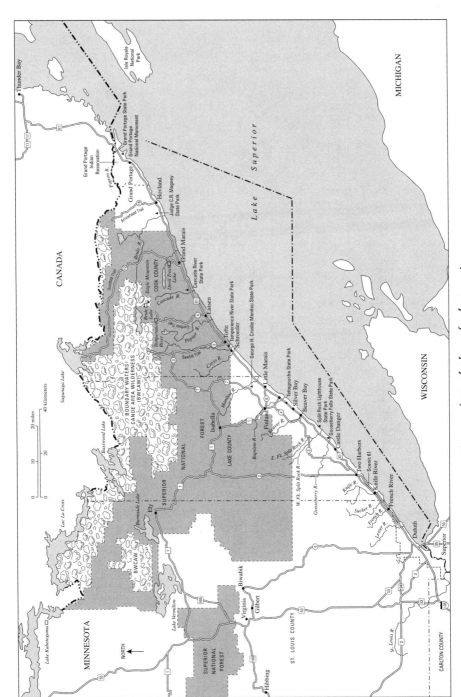

Minnesota's North Shore of Lake Superior

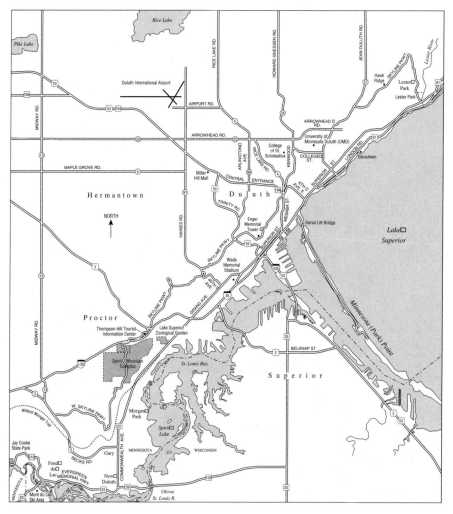

Lake Superior and the general area of Duluth, Minnesota, and Superior, Wisconsin

Preface to the Third Edition

IT'S STILL THE SAME PREHISTORIC NORTH SHORE RIDGELINE rising out of Lake Superior. Highway 61 is still the road that leads to it all; it just has broader shoulders, a smoother surface, and some of the kinks have been worked out, a bittersweet development for me – I think you should have to drive slowly along the Shore. Changes have taken place, big and little, but I wasn't really aware of how many until I went to update this book, which has turned into a rewrite.

Some exciting changes include the near completion of the Lake Superior Water (Kayak) Trail; creation and progress on the paved Gitchi Gami Trail running adjacent to Highway 61; new attractions, accommodations, shops, and restaurants in Duluth and along the Shore. I have added a section dedicated to spas and wellness, another that notes the designated scientific and natural areas, and a list of safe harbors. Almost everybody now has a Web site, and you wouldn't believe the changes in trails: there are lots more mountain biking trails and snowshoe trails and rentals, hiking and cross-country ski trails have been fine-tuned, and a few ski-joring trails are available.

Use this book as a resource for ideas, information, and details, a collection of suggestions about everything North Shore and a guide to where you might go to make your own discoveries. But let common sense prevail. By the time the first book is off the press, changes will have occurred. To be sure about a really important part of your trip, call ahead. Make a reservation. Double check directions. And everyone loves a good guest, so please respect our North Shore.

Come as often as you'd like. For really current information, you can check out my corresponding Web site, NorthShoreVisitor.com.

Thanks for letting me share the North Shore with you. Wishing you big fun on the big lake and in the big woods!

Nina

Key to Symbols
🏃 Attractions suitable for families with children
🐕 Accessible to persons with disabilities

*Nina, Bill, and Max enjoy another adventure
on the North Shore.*

Introduction

I LOVE WHERE I LIVE. I LOVE THE HUGE STEADY CYCLE OF CON-
trasts that occur throughout a year on the North Shore. It leaves me
breathless and energized. Winter's deep, dark onset presses us indoors
before afternoon is complete, motivating us to light loads of candles and
build comfort-giving fires each evening. But snow changes it all. We crawl
out from our twelve-hour stints under blankets to play in the brilliant white
snow. We build complex forts and sledding runs, ski, snowshoe, dig holes in
the ice, then pull fish out of them. We can't help but comment daily on the
sky, the dominant highlight color of the season. *Look at that color. It must be
blue concentrate, the blue every other blue is derived from.* At night, we go
back out, or turn out the lights and press our noses to the windows and look
up again. Stargazing is magnificent on these dry, clear winter nights.

And then we have mud. We mourn the loss of snow until it hits fifty
degrees one day and we all start planning our gardens. We become weather
martyrs, sighing over the fact that southern Minnesota already has grass.
Grass, mind you! And it's not even the opening of fishing. We are not so
secretly boastful of the fact that we still have stubborn snow piles along
forest edges the third week of May. And then we go on chlorophyll overload.
Everything greens up in days, hours, at jungle speed or faster. *Did you see the
hillside? It wasn't green yesterday. It's spring-green today. What's that? It's that
yellow-green of spring that lasts only a week or so.* We don't care anymore that
our lilacs barely bloom in time for the summer solstice.

Our gardens grow, producing really, really good produce. Good because
we have been without for so long, and good because of an unusual sugar-
making reaction that occurs during these long, warm days and cool nights.
Then we have our one day of humidity and almost fall apart. Everyone up
from the Twin Cities is in sheer relief and we grumble about having to buy a
tank top. We go swimming in Lake Superior. Our sleep needs dwindle to
about five hours. We follow the light, cramming in every activity we can

think of. *Do you see what time it is? If it was winter it would have been dark for four hours now!* Then one night it's dark by nine.

And we start seeing a yellow leaf here or there. The tank top gets put away and the ever-present polar fleece gets steady dawn to dusk use. And the chlorophyll says adiós and heads off to some never-changing climate. Finding the coast clear, the latent plant colors give off a secret signal and show their gaudy little selves. The sugar maples are downright ostentatious. We love it, this six-week visit from the hot side of the color chart. And for once we don't talk about it; we just have to be out in it, sponges, absorbing the color. I love this time of year.

But I say that every season on the North Shore. I love where I live.

Make vacation a contrast to your daily life. Slow down. Relax. Look out the window.

READERS TAKE NOTE!

The Gunflint Trail, the paved road leading north out of Grand Marais through the north woods to Lake Saganaga, is being rerouted. The start of the Trail is slated to move east about one mile by late 2004. The new Gunflint Trail (Co. Rd. 12) will start off Highway 61 just past the IGA grocery store. The existing Trail will be renamed 5th Avenue/Co. Rd. 15 and will eventually intersect with the new Gunflint Trail. All directions in the book refer to the existing (soon-to-be "old") Gunflint Trail. The folks at the County Highway Department say everyone will be happier driving on the new Gunflint Trail.

In Days of Old

A BRIEF HISTORY

PEOPLE HAVE BEEN HEADING UP THE SHORE FOR MORE THAN twelve thousand years. When they began writing back home about it, more folks were enticed to come explore. One of the first to make mention of his travels was Etienne Brule, who is reputed to have noted and named Lake Superior during his travels in 1623. He chose the name because the translation of the Ojibwe name for the lake, Kitchigumi, means Great Water, and because the lake is the largest and highest of the five lakes tributary to the St. Lawrence River. Daniel Greysolon, Sieur du Lhut, a French Canadian, explored Lake Superior from 1676 to 1678 with the intention of creating a chain of trading posts. Greysolon worked to form alliances for the French with the Dakota and Assiniboin and spent time in the late summer of 1679 with area tribes at what is now Fond du Lac, west of Duluth, which became his namesake in 1856. Frenchman Jacques de Noyons became the first European to explore the inland woods adjacent to Lake Superior's northern shore in 1688. Noyons was continuing the search for a northwest passage to the Orient and hoped to establish fur trade relations. About the same time, the Ojibwe (Chippewa) tribe moved in from the east to participate in the fur trade, eventually evicting the resident Dakota (Sioux) tribe west to prairie lands. With fur trading came the first European settlement to the North Shore of Lake Superior.

To some extent the pioneers moved on since northeast Minnesota was Indian territory. Evidence of woodland Indian cultures dates back twelve thousand years. The Lake Superior Ojibwe originated from the La Pointe, Wisconsin, tribe on Madeline Island, part of the Apostle Islands on Superior's South Shore. They first traveled across the big lake to Isle Royale, where they mined copper and established fishing and sugar camps. Indians mined copper on Isle Royale from about 2000 B.C. to 1000 B.C. The French claimed the island in 1671, and in 1783 the United States claimed it. Europeans mined copper from the 1840s to 1899. Ojibwe still came to the island to fish off Grace Island and work their sugar camp on Sugar Mountain. The American Fur Trading Company gill-netted whitefish, trout, and siskiwit to feed their men and later as a commercial venture. The Ojibwe continued to reside along the North Shore up to and after the Treaty of 1854 (in which the Chippewa of Lake Superior ceded a great deal of land to the United States) but have congregated on the Grand Portage Indian Reservation.

A variety of immigrants homesteaded this area after 1854. Germans came for a chance to own land and avoid military service and were the largest non-English population in Minnesota in the 1860s. Swedes made up the second largest group and came, with the Cornish and Welsh pioneers, most often to mine. More Scandinavians came to Minnesota than to any other state, and many chose the North Shore as their new home. They established the fishing, boatbuilding, shipping, and lumber trades that prevailed through the mid-1900s. Tourism became an established industry after World War II and has grown as other trades have plateaued or declined. Duluth remains the center of all the industries.

An 1800s missionary center in Fond du Lac was the first Duluth township. Fur was the going trade, but speculation on copper ore in the 1850s brought permanent settlers. The Minnesota Point lighthouse was built in 1858 and is today the oldest remaining architecture in Duluth. The 1870 completion of the Lake Superior & Mississippi railroad from St. Paul to Duluth clinched the town's existence. Their simple frame depot still stands at 13308 West Third Street.

From the late 1880s through the first decade of the 1900s, a multitude of building projects in Duluth reflected growing businesses and affluent owners. Constant improvements were made to the port area, including the building and expansion of the canal and docks and recurrent dredgings of the harbor. In 1889 the Masonic Temple Opera House, a Moorish Romanesque edifice at Second Avenue East and Superior Street, and the Hartley Building, which now houses the Kitchi Gammi Club, at Ninth Avenue East and Superior Street, were constructed.

Residential neighborhoods also expanded. In 1890 the first townhouses in Duluth were built at Chester Terrace, 1210 to 1228 East First Street. Benjamin Wells saw his home completed that year, too. His mammoth frame house is at Forty-Eighth Avenue East and London Road. Identifying features are the two opposing octagonal towers, one topped by a mushroom cap and the other by an octagon cone. A few more notable homes of the era are the often photographed Arthur P. Cook stone and timber home built into a rock headland at 501 West Skyline Drive, the neo-Greek Corinthian-columned Louis S. Loeb Home at 1123 East Superior Street, and George C. Crosby's home at 2031 East Superior Street. Look for master stonework sculpting in the lion's head gracing the entryway of the Crosby home.

With families came the need for schools, churches, and public services. The 1889 Duluth Police Station and City Jail building can be seen at 126 and 132 East Superior Street, and the 1892 Fire House No. 1 stands at First Avenue East and Third Street. The Lakewood Pumping Station on Congdon Boulevard (at the start of the North Shore Scenic Drive) was erected in 1897. Duluth Central High School, a three-story Lake Superior brownstone at Lake Avenue and Second Street, was built during 1891 and 1892. Note the 210-foot clock tower flanked by lesser turrets. Nearby is the 1891 First Presbyterian Church at 300 East Second Street and the 1892 Sacred Heart Cathedral and Cathedral School at 206 and 211 West Fourth Street.

The Chateauesque French Norman Duluth Union Depot was also erected in 1892. This passenger and freight depot is highlighted by its steep symmetrical roofs with opposing circular towers set off by flared conical tops. A cast-iron portico was added early in the twentieth century, and in 1953 the original slate roof and ornate chimneys were removed. You can visit The Depot at Michigan Street and Fifth Avenue West. The 1899 depot of the Duluth Missabe & Iron Range Railway is now home to the Waterfront Visitors Center at 100 Lake Place on the Lakewalk.

With the increased population and workforce came the need for beer. The A. Fitger Brewhouse was built in 1900 and housed a brewery throughout most of this century.

Looking back toward the canal from Fitger's, you will see Duluth's trademark, the Aerial Lift Bridge, first built in 1905. At that time, a gondola traveled over the canal, suspended by cables attached to two 186-foot towers, one on each pier. The gondola could carry 125,000 pounds and make up to twelve trips per hour. C.P.A. Turner modified the bridge design in 1929, modeling it after a bridge in Rouen, France.

Rapid growth in the grain, coal, iron ore, and eventually lumber trades led to Duluth's expansion across the hillside. The Treaty of 1854 opened much of the North Shore to white settlers, mainly Scandinavian immigrants, who clustered along the natural bays and river mouths. A winter route from Duluth to Grand Marais was cleared in 1899, but no true roads were created for another twenty years.

The original wagon trail leads up today's North Shore Scenic Drive. Fishermen chose Knife River as a natural spot to settle in the 1880s. Fish were plentiful, and the settlers soon began sending shipments to Duluth. A Michigan logging company established headquarters in Knife River and built a railroad northeast to the Cascade River. By 1909, a dock was required to allow for shipping the eight trainloads of wood per day. Within a decade, however, the company folded, the railroad was removed, and the community returned to fishing.

The first North Shore post office was located at Buchanan, five miles northeast of Knife River. Settlers in 1856 named their site after the new president-elect. They intended to mine copper, but failed and abandoned the town, which was later destroyed by fire.

Larsmont, just up the road on the Scenic Drive, received its name in 1914 from an early settler who was originally from Larsmo, Finland. Initially a major logging operations hub in the 1880s and 1890s, Larsmont stabilized as settlers became established in railroading and fishing.

Ojibwe often hunted and fished in the two protected bays known today as Agate Bay and Burlington Bay. European settlement came in 1856, and the Duluth & Iron Range Railroad extended their railway line to these "Two Harbors." The railway bought the 3 Spot locomotive in 1883 and towed it up the lake on a scow. The 3 Spot and a Mallet engine are displayed in the Two Harbors waterfront district. That year, 1883, Dock #1, Lake Superior's first ore dock and the largest in the world, was built. Within a year, Two Harbors became Minnesota's first iron ore port.

The Two Harbors Light Station was completed in 1892 and was instrumental to the harbor at a time when it surpassed Duluth in importance as a port. Today, the Lake County Historical Society runs the Lighthouse Point and Harbor Museum, which features commercial fishing and shipping displays, the pilothouse from an iron ore freighter, and a renovated commercial fishing boat. The light keeper's quarters are a bed and breakfast with the lighthouse open for tours. The 1890s brought construction of the railway's twenty-five-bed Budd Hospital. Dr. J. D. Budd was one of the first directors of Minnesota Mining & Manufacturing (3M), which had set up headquarters in Two Harbors. John Dwan, a Two Harbors lawyer, was the first corporate secretary of 3M. His home can be seen at 508 Second Avenue, next door to the home of Thomas Owen, the first locomotive engineer for the Duluth & Iron Range Railroad.

After the turn of the century, the Duluth & Iron Range Railroad, which later became the Duluth Missabe & Iron Range Railroad, began passenger service to Two Harbors and constructed a depot on the waterfront. In use through 1961, the depot now houses the Lake County Historical Society, which exhibits local shipping, logging, and mining artifacts. Nearby you can visit the tugboat *Edna G.* Named after Edna Greatsinger, the daughter of one of the early Duluth & Iron Range Railroad presidents, the *Edna G.* was one of the first and was the last steam tug in operation on the Great Lakes. She was placed on the National Register of Historic Places in 1975 and was retired in 1981 and remains the trademark of Two Harbors.

In the 1890s the Nestor Logging Company began operations at the mouth of the Gooseberry River. A railway system carried pine down to the lake, where it was rafted to a sawmill. By the 1920s, Nestor closed due to fire and lack of pine.

Up the road just west of Gooseberry Falls is the tiny burg Castle Danger, where large-scale logging operations took place before the turn of the century. The site was settled by three Norwegian fishermen who focused the community on commercial fishing before and after the logging era. This village may have received its odd name after a boat, the *Castle,* that ran aground nearby.

The neighboring villages of Beaver Bay and Silver Bay are the oldest and youngest settlements, respectively, along the Shore. On June 24, 1856, the sidewheel steamer *Illinois* arrived at the mouth of the Beaver River with twenty-five passengers, including the Wieland brothers, German immigrants who arrived with hopes to farm. Upon landing, they reviewed the area, built homes along the Beaver River, and opened a sawmill. The Wielands were the family that took in the survivors of the 1879 crash of the tug *Amethyst.* During the Panic of 1857, when several North Shore settlements were abandoned, Beaver Bay persisted. In the 1890s Scandinavian fishing families moved in, and commercial fishing established its hold until the 1960s, when fishing regulations were tightened and the fish populations were depleted by sea lampreys.

Fishermen fished the Silver Bay in the early 1900s, and the *America* began stopping there in 1903, but the city of Silver Bay wasn't developed until the early 1950s, when Reserve Mining opened a large-scale taconite processing plant. With the decline of the steel industry in the 1980s, Silver Bay felt the economic pinch. Cyprus Mining reopened the plant in 1989 and the town has stabilized. North Shore Mining now runs the plant.

Illgen City is a classic blink-and-you'll-miss-it place. Like Silver Bay, Illgen's roots have nothing to do with fur, fish, or timber. In 1902, corundum, an aluminum oxide occurring as a very hard crystallized mineral, was found here. With the finding, 3M was incorporated and mined the rock for use as an abrasive. Unfortunately, the corundum turned out to be a much softer rock, beanorthosite, and stock in the company took a dive. Don't worry, they landed on their feet. The Rudolph Illgen family took advantage of 3M's conundrum, purchased 40 acres in 1924, and opened a sawmill, store, and cabins.

Logging, fishing, and fur were also the draw in Cook County. In the early 1900s the John Schroeder Lumber Company employed around a thousand men in the recently established village of Schroeder. By damming the headwaters of the Cross River until spring, they could shoot logs downriver to Lake Superior, where they were bound into rafts and floated over to Ashland and Superior, Wisconsin.

Fishing appealed to Norwegian immigrants Andrew and John Tofte, and Torger and Hans Engelsen. Arriving in 1893, they founded Tofte and began fishing. Their original fish house was destroyed in the storm of 1905, so they built a bigger and better double fish house. The twin fish houses were painted "Scandinavian red" with white trim and were protected by a breakwater extending about 150 feet into Bluefin Bay. To commemorate local commercial fishing, the North Shore Commercial Fishing Museum opened in 1995 in Tofte, on the east side of Bluefin Bay. The museum is a replicate of the original twin fish houses and displays many relics, artifacts, and pictures kept by the descendants of the Engelsens, Tofteys, and Toftes. Edward Toftey

had arrived in 1899 and opened up a sawmill, where he employed up to 25 men. The mill and most of the original town were burned in a 1910 forest fire.

Swedish homesteader Charles Axel Nelson was eighteen years old in 1881 when he left Norrköping, Sweden, destined for the North Shore. He joined other settlers in naming their new home Lutsen to commemorate the town where Swedish King Gustavus Adolphus fell in 1632. Nelson homesteaded at the mouth of the Poplar River. As new immigrants arrived, he provided lodging and meals. A post office, school, general store, and town hall cropped up to serve the local loggers and fishermen. Lutsen Village was also an important timber shipping point in the 1890s. Nelson's son Charles opened the first ski resort in Minnesota and continued the tradition of providing hospitable lodging and meals to visitors. Charles's granddaughter Cindy helped put the local ski hill on the map when she competed in the 1984 winter Olympics.

Grand Marais evolved into the focal village on the Shore. When explorer Pierre d'Esprit, commonly known as Sieur de Radisson, traveled Superior's shores to Canada in 1657–58, Grand Marais was a thriving Indian fishing camp. In 1823, John Jacob Astor's American Fur Company employed nearly a thousand men at the company's trading post at the site of Grand Marais, and in 1832 the company added a fishing station. After the Treaty of 1854, a Frenchman by the name of Richard B. Godfrey took over the post and fish house. In 1856 he became the first postmaster and established a monthly route to Canada.

It wasn't until 1871 that Henry Mayhew and Sam Howenstine founded the Village of Grand Marais, referred to as "double bay" by the Ojibwe. Minnesota's governor alloted Mayhew the east bay and Howenstine the west bay. Three years later, the Minnesota legislature created Cook County. Today's Drury Lane Books used to be known as the Pioneer House, home to George Mayhew, the first child of immigrants to be born in Grand Marais. The 1880s brought breakwaters, a lighthouse, and later, the lighthouse keeper's home, now the Cook County Historical Society. In 1891, A. DeLacy Wood started the *Grand Marais Pioneer,* forerunner to the *Cook County News Herald.*

Grand Marais was incorporated in 1903, about the time the Lake Side Hotel was built on the east bay. Mrs. Sterling ran the restaurant and eventually bought the hotel, changing the name to the Sterling Hotel. In 1945 the Dalbecs and Blackwells purchased it and changed the name to Hotel East Bay. It was managed by Jim and Lena Pederson. Their son Jim and his wife Lois purchased it and ran it until 1994, when their children took over operations.

Just east of Grand Marais is an old Native American settlement known as

Chippewa City. Look for St. Francis Xavier Catholic Church, which was erected in 1895 to serve the Ojibwe.

Heading north out of Grand Marais, the Gunflint Trail was cut in 1893 in order to transport iron ore from a mine at Gunflint Lake. The lake and trail were named for the abundance of flint rock, which pioneers and Ojibwe used in their firearms. The trail eventually led to Saganaga Lake. The woods of the Superior National Forest became a national forest in 1909, and in 1978 the Boundary Waters Canoe Area Wilderness was designated within the forest.

East of Grand Marais on the shores of the Brule River and Lake Superior sits Naniboujou Lodge. Named after a prankster American Indian storm god, this 1920s resort incorporates Cree Indian art. The twenty-five-foot-high arched ceiling of the great room represents the bottom of a canoe. Paintings tell of American Indian travels and depict storm gods at work. At its inception, Naniboujou had over thirty-three hundred acres and planned to add on eight thousand more. The proposal included golf, tennis, a marina, hunting, horseback riding, and fishing. The main lodge was dedicated in 1929, just before the stock market crashed. In 1934 the state built a camp for men who were displaced by the Depression. The men worked on public service projects, logged, and fought the big fire of '35 that burned more than ten thousand acres. After the fire, they set up a sawmill and salvaged the fire-damaged wood. Further development at the resort ceased and adjacent lands were sold to the state, which established Bois Brule State Park in 1957. In 1963 the park name was changed to Judge C. R. Magney State Park to honor this advocate of state parks and waysides, especially on the shores of Gitche Gumee.

Before European arrival, generations of Native Americans used Wauswaugoning Bay as a summer camp, where they harvested and prepared fish, nuts, and berries for winter. The eight-and-a-half-mile Grand Portage, "the great carrying place," was a link from the big lake to their winter camp inland. Late-1600s explorers and, eventually, fur traders were introduced to the route by Native American guides. The Grand Portage became an important link in the three-thousand-mile route to the Canadian Northwest. The network reached as far north as Great Slave Lake (Northwest Territories) and as far west as Lake Athabaska (Saskatchewan and Alberta).

In 1784 Scotsman Simon McTavish and his partners established the inland headquarters of their North West Company at Wauswaugoning Bay. They ran the most profitable fur trading company on the Great Lakes. Each year in July, the company sponsored a rendezvous. Paddling up the Ottawa

River and through the Great Lakes came the "pork-eaters," French voyageurs from Montreal, at the headwaters of fur trading. Some of the voyageurs were "winterers," who traded at remote northern posts during the winter. The "northmen" traded pelts – "soft gold" – for supplies from the Montreal men. Ojibwe traders continued to provide pelts and essential equipment to the voyageurs.

About August, the headquarters would empty out as everyone headed for their winter destination before freeze-up. Only a skeleton crew stayed behind to maintain the post. Winter survival could not have been possible without food supplies traded by the Ojibwe, who in return received wool blankets, woven cloth, beads, tin, iron, and copperware.

The winter of 1801 was the last winter the North West Company spent at Grand Portage. McTavish relocated to Fort William, Ontario (now Thunder Bay), to avoid citizenship complications: he was a Highland Scottish Brit doing business on American soil. The French had ceded Canada to Britain after the 1763 French and Indian War, so Fort William was part of the king's land.

The portage and trading post became overgrown in the 1820s while sitting idle. In the 1950s, Grand Portage was designated a national monument, and extensive archaeological excavations revealed enough information to accurately replicate the historic post. Today the stockade and four of the original sixteen buildings have been reconstructed. For additional information, see the National Parks and Monuments chapter.

Adjacent to the monument, the Grand Portage Band of Ojibwe and the U.S. Park Service are cooperatively re-creating an Ojibwe village to commemorate and share the fascinating heritage of the Band. The two also join forces on the second weekend of August each year to host and celebrate Rendezvous Days, a reenactment of the old North West Company's annual event. Highlights include the Ojibwe village; a voyageur encampment; Native American arts, crafts, and foods; and the powwow. Held on traditional grounds, the powwow brings Ojibwe singers and dancers from throughout the United States and Canada to celebrate their cultural heritage.

Part of the celebration is the hiking of the Grand Portage. During peak use, voyageurs carried two ninety-pound packs over this portage in about two and a half hours. The less adventurous today may opt for a hike up Mount Rose or Mount Josephine.

A visit to the sacred Little Spirit Cedar Tree, or "Witch Tree," on Hat Point requires a guide from the Band. American Indians believed this three-hundred-year-old gnarled cedar was possessed by evil spirits that caused many Indians to lose their canoes on the nearby treacherous rock point. To appease the spirits, gifts were left at the base of the tree. Inquire at the Grand Portage Lodge and Casino for guided tour times. A classic book, *The Grand Portage Story* by Carolyn Gilman, describes in great detail the history of Grand Portage.

In 1917 the Outlaw Bridge was constructed over the Pigeon River. Completion of the bridge established international trade with Canada and a circle route around Lake Superior. Improved road conditions led to increased tourism, which began in the 1910s and grew significantly after the Second World War. Tourism continues to be a leading industry in Duluth and along the North Shore today.

Shipwrecks of the North Shore

I T WAS A DARK AND STORMY NIGHT. WAVES CRASHED. THE WIND
howled. All over the Great Lakes, wooden schooners were colliding,
breaking away, and sinking. Others were destroyed by fire. Actually, it
wasn't usually the dark, stormy night but an inexperienced crew that caused
most of the shipping accidents in the late 1800s.

Shipping on Lake Superior began in the mid-1800s. The original brick
lighthouse on Minnesota Point marking the Superior entry was built in 1858.
In 1861 the first dredging of the Duluth harbor took place, and plans were
under way for rail transportation to St. Paul. The original port facilities were
built on an outer harbor protected by a breakwater. The next few decades
brought extensive changes. The Duluth Ship Canal was excavated in 1871.
New shipping docks were built within the confines of the safer inner harbor.
In a series of dredgings, the natural harbor depth of six feet was deepened to
sixteen feet. Cargo tonnage increased a hundredfold and surpassed ten million tons in 1900.

Initially, grain, iron ore, and coal were the primary trade goods. With the
introduction of wood products from northeast Minnesota and northern
Wisconsin, lumber quickly became the major cargo and remained so until
the 1920s, when the world turned to the Pacific Coast for its lumber supply.
The aerial transfer bridge erected in 1905 was updated in 1929 to a lift
bridge. The canal and adjacent harbor were deepened and expanded, providing access to the massive lakers and oceangoing ships that now primarily carry taconite and grain.

Changes in the shipbuilding and navigation industries brought corresponding changes in the shipping business. Wooden boats were built until the
introduction of modern steel vessels in the early 1890s. Ship size increased in
hundred-foot lengths from two hundred to five hundred feet by the turn of
the century. Advances in navigational equipment came at a slower rate, but
qualifications for ship officers became more stringent.

Horrific shipwrecks and terrific rescues occurred throughout the shipping season across Lake Superior. Wrecks were most numerous off the Keweenaw Peninsula in Upper Michigan, at ports, and in the waters surrounding Isle Royale. Much of the shipping traffic along the North Shore included passengers as well as cargo, since no roadways existed northeast out of Duluth.

The Lake Superior Maritime Center in Duluth, Split Rock Historical Center, and North Shore Commercial Fishing Museum in Tofte offer displays, exhibits, and videos on Lake Superior's shipping activity. The quintessential shipwreck reference is Dr. Julius Wolff's *The Shipwrecks of Lake Superior.*

Major shipwrecks and numerous fires, collisions, and sinkings took place in the vicinity of the Duluth harbor. One of the two worst wrecks in Duluth history happened on June 7, 1902. The morning was calm and clear as the 288-foot wooden ship *George G. Hadley* steamed inbound toward the Duluth Ship Canal. Meanwhile, the 308-foot steel whaleback *Thomas Wilson* steamed out of the harbor into the canal. (Remember, only the canal existed; no bridge had been erected yet.) A half mile off the piers, the *Hadley* was directed by the tug *Annie L. Smith* to enter the Superior harbor. The *Hadley* captain changed course to the left without blowing the required whistle signals or noticing the *Wilson* coming down the canal. The *Wilson* captain attempted a starboard (right) turn, since a port turn would have stranded the ship. Neither captain was able to turn sharply enough. The *Hadley*'s wooden prow drove hard into the whaleback's steel side. Within three minutes, the *Wilson* rolled, tipped bow (front) down, and dove to Superior's bottom, taking nine men with her. The *Hadley* rescued the remaining *Wilson* crew before staggering off to the sandy beach south of the canal, where she sank. The *Hadley* crew and *Wilson* survivors made it to shore safely. Any remnants of the *Hadley* and *Wilson* remain today on the lake bottom.

Throughout the violently stormy afternoon of November 28, 1905, three ships attempted entry into the Duluth Ship Canal: one vessel beached, two sank, and nine more lives were lost. Shortly after noon, the year-old steel steamer *R. W. England* advanced through rough seas toward the canal. Realizing he couldn't navigate through the piers, the *England*'s captain turned back into the open lake. Gale winds caught the 363-foot steamer and threw her aground two and a half miles south of the piers on Minnesota Point. That afternoon, rescue workers fought the waves to bring the crew ashore. Three days later, tugs freed the *England.*

A half hour after the *England*'s approach, the 478-foot *Isaac L. Ellwood* reached the canal entry. The *Ellwood* had departed from the Duluth port earlier that day and was en route to Two Harbors to pick up the barge *Bryn Mawr* when turbulent winds took over. Unable to make the Two Harbors entry, the captain opted to return to the safety of the Duluth harbor. Loaded with iron ore, the *Ellwood* had passed the pierheads when the big lake slammed her into the north pier. She careened into the south pier and was carried under the aerial transfer bridge. Nearby tugs promptly dragged her down to the Duluth Boat Club, where she sank in twenty-two feet of water. Only her deckhouses remained above water, but that was enough for crew to be saved.

The crew of the steamer *Mataafa* wasn't as lucky. The 430-foot *Mataafa* had left Duluth midafternoon the day before, November 27, with the 366-foot barge *James Nasmyth* in tow. Troubles began that evening. The *Mataafa* used her 1,400-horsepower engine to fight the seas, but had made no headway after ten hours. She, too, chose to return to Duluth. Turning into nasty waters with zero visibility, the *Mataafa* crept back to Duluth, where she ordered the *Nasmyth* to drop anchor a half mile off the canal. Luckily, the *Nasmyth* lines held, and she rode out the storm. The captain of the *Mataafa* went full steam ahead to approach the canal. A gargantuan wave rose and hit the ship, propelling her bow to the bottom and tossing her into the northern pier. Another massive wave hit. The *Mataafa* was flipped perpendicular to the pier. Her engines were dead. The seas turned her half circle and tossed her six hundred feet off the shoreline north of the piers. Wave after wave struck the ship, and she broke in two with twelve crew members in each section. Lifesavers were aiding the *England,* tugs couldn't approach in the seas, and launching lifeboats would have been fatal. Ten thousand Duluthians gathered onshore praying for the safety of the crew. A stunning rescue was made the next day as lifesavers thrust their boats through mammoth waves and hauled ashore the surviving fifteen crew members in two trips. Four men died, frozen to the deck, and five bodies were never found. Unbelievably, six months later the *Mataafa* was hauled away and rebuilt.

Knife Island, off Knife River, was the site of a mysterious ship disappearance on April 28, 1914. Savage spring gales surpassing sixty-four miles per hour shaped mountainous waves that doused the light on Duluth's south pier and put the foghorn out of operation. The 239-foot steel steamer *Benjamin Noble* struggled out on the lake. She was last spotted by another ship near Knife Island. They saw her lights disappear, but assumed the rain had obscured them. The next day, debris from the *Noble* washed ashore from south of Knife Island to Lester River and on Minnesota Point. The location of the *Noble* remains unknown. All twenty of her crew were lost.

The port of Two Harbors has had its share of beachings and accidents, too. The most famous incident took place October 30, 1896. A Duluth cargo freighter, the *Hesper,* was towing a converted three-masted schooner, the *Samuel P. Ely,* to Two Harbors. Both vessels withstood the roaring squall and entered the harbor. The towline either broke or was cast off too soon, and the 200-foot *Ely* was rammed first into a docked scow, then the western break-wall. As the tug *Ella G. Stone* approached, the *Ely* began breaking up. The tug was able to retrieve the crew and two men from the scow. The *Ely* settled to the harbor bottom and eventually became part of the new western break-water. In 1962 divers found the *Ely* in about thirty feet of water. Since she was well preserved, they started a diving service that took folks to the wreck and allowed divers to keep one set of dishes. A skeptical journalist made the dive, collected his set of dishes, and exposed the service for planting dishes from Goodwill onboard the *Ely.* The diving service quickly folded, but the *Ely* remains one of the most-visited wrecks, safe within the harbor refuge.

The *Hesper*'s luck held for the next eight and a half years. Then the 250-foot wooden steamer was driven off course during a spring nor'easter on May 3, 1905. Waves from the sixty-mile-an-hour winds hurled the *Hesper* onto a reef southwest of present-day Silver Bay. Another wave hoisted the steamer over the reef, dropped her, and smashed her to bits in forty-two feet of water. The crew were able to save themselves on lifeboats.

A late-fall nor'easter wreaked havoc on the fishing tug *Siskiwit,* out of Grand Marais. She was on a routine supply run in early December of 1879, returning from Duluth, when she hit a reef near Good Harbor Bay. The *Siski-wit* limped into Grand Marais with a severely damaged propeller. The 45-foot tug *Amethyst* was preparing for a homebound voyage to Duluth and offered to tow the *Siskiwit.* During the return trip, a wild snowstorm broke loose, snapping the towline. The *Siskiwit* took on water and began to go down off the mouth of the Manitou River. In a courageous attempt to save the *Siskiwit* crew, the *Amethyst* pulled alongside the sinking tug and brought all men aboard. A few miles farther into the storm, the captain of the *Amethyst* knew he couldn't continue taking on water and drove the ship aground at Belmore Bay. All made it ashore except a fisherman who was hit by the tug's falling smokestack. The ten survivors bore the brunt of the storm in spruce bough lean-tos. The horrid night was followed by a fifty-two-hour, thirteen-and-a-half-mile trek through drifting snow to Beaver Bay, where a pioneer family, the Wielands, took them in. All survived and ultimately reached Duluth aboard a small boat.

One blizzard cost the Pittsburgh Steamship Company two men and four ships. On November 28, 1905, the 478-foot iron ore carrier *William Edenborn* was towing the 436-foot barge *Madeira* in the early-morning hours of the storm. About 3:00 A.M. the towline parted. The unpowered *Madeira* floundered and crashed into the craggy rock shores of Gold Rock Point, near modern-day Split Rock Lighthouse. As the barge broke in two, nine of the ten crew members made it safely to shore. One man died. At about the same time, the *Edenborn* was whipped into the mouth of the Split Rock River. With her bow driven into the wooded shoreline, her stern in the lake, and the waves pounding, the *Edenborn* split in two. One crew member perished. The *Edna G.* provided lifesaving services to both crews.

Twenty miles to the southwest, two sister ships were experiencing similar fates. The steel steamer *Lafayette* was towing the 436-foot barge *Manila*. Darkness and ceaseless sheets of snow combined for zero visibility. The captain had no idea where they were until he heard breakers hitting shore on the starboard side. A few moments after this realization, waves smashed the 454-foot *Lafayette* into massive rocks fifty feet offshore. With no time to react, the *Manila* drove into the *Lafayette*'s stern, busting her in two in minutes. Both crews made it safely to shore. The cliff the ships rammed into has been

named Lafayette Bluff (the site of the northeastern tunnel on Highway 61). The casualties and wrecks of this storm precipitated the building of the lighthouse at Split Rock.

The reefs, rock outcrops, and islands of Isle Royale have proved to be fatal obstacles for a great number of ships and their crews. One of the earliest recorded North Shore wrecks transpired July 23, 1877, at Rock of Ages, Isle Royale. En route to Duluth, the 204-foot sidewheeler *Cumberland* of the Canadian Northern Railroad fleet stranded herself. The crew and passengers were rescued by local fishermen, but late-summer storms destroyed the vessel.

Isle Royale is the site of two unexplained disappearances. During the great storm of 1913 the steel freighter *Leafield* vanished, taking eighteen men with her. The 250-foot ship, loaded with steel rails and track fastenings, was on a routine run to Fort William, Ontario. The passenger steamer *Harmonic* last saw her riding a mammoth wave during a raging snowstorm off Angus Island. Her hull has never been found.

Late in 1927, the radioless 250-foot freighter *Kamloops* was somehow disabled, vanishing with her crew of twenty. A stranded steamer, the *Martian,* later reported seeing the ship east of Isle Royale on December 7, 1927. In the spring of 1928, fishermen came upon two bodies wearing *Kamloops* preservers and a five-hundred-foot stretch of wreckage in a secluded bay between Green and Hawk Islands. Forty-nine years after the disappearance of the *Kamloops,* her hull was discovered by divers off Twelve O'Clock Point.

A few months later, one of the most famous Isle Royale wrecks took place. The 183-foot steel coastal steamer *America* had unloaded at Washington harbor and was making an early-morning departure. Following the route through the North Gap (between the main island and Thompson Island), the mate made a navigational error and sideswiped a shoal. It appeared no harm was done, and the *America* made for the open waters. However, word came from the engine room that the pumps couldn't handle the increased water in the bilge. The mate reentered the North Gap with plans to beach in a shallow bay. Instead he made a direct hit into the same shoal and rode the bow up the bank. After listing heavily to each side, the *America* sat back and sank at a 45-degree angle on the shoal's sloping edge. All aboard safely escaped. Her bow still sits just a few feet below the water, making her the most diveable wreck of the ten in Isle Royale National Park. Renowned Isle Royale artist Howard Sivertson has painted watercolors of the *America,* which can be seen at Sivertson's Gallery in Grand Marais.

Since 1930, only seventeen major ships have been lost. The loss of the iron ore carrier *Emperor* at dawn on June 4, 1947, was a shock. Rounding the northwest end of Isle Royale in near-zero visibility, the 525-foot, 4,641-ton steamer smashed into Canoe Rocks with such terrific impact that she split at hatch no. 4. A Coast Guard cutter four miles away responded to the first SOS, saving twenty-one sailors. Twelve men drowned, and the *Emperor* sank to depths of 140 to 180 feet.

Seventeen more lives were lost when the 427-foot *Henry Steinbrenner* went down May 11, 1953. The iron ore carrier had left Duluth on Saturday, May 9, under sunny, 78°F skies. Sunday temps rose to 65°F, but by evening, incredible gales gusting up to seventy-two miles per hour created nineteen-foot-high waves. During the night, temperatures dropped, blinding snow swirled, and gale winds ripped off three sternward hatch covers. At 6:30 A.M., she foundered. Distress signals brought in other ships, which rescued fourteen crew members aboard three life vessels.

The *Steinbrenner* was the last of the North Shore wrecks. On November 10, 1975, the world was astonished by the loss of the "*Fitz*." Seventeen miles from Whitefish Point, Michigan, on the South Shore, the 729-foot *Edmund Fitzgerald* vanished at sea amidst hurricane winds and a malevolent storm. All twenty-nine crew members and the eight-million-dollar ship were lost. Superior's latest claim was the U.S. Coast Guard cutter *Mesquite* on December 4, 1989, off Keweenaw Point, Michigan. Shipwrecks are not a thing of the past.

Lake Superior Facts

AREA: *31,820 square miles – the largest freshwater lake in the world*

DEPTH: *1,333 feet – deepest of the Great Lakes*

DISTANCE: *383 miles east-west; 160 miles north-south*

VOLUME: *Three quadrillion gallons of water, 10% of the world's fresh water*

AVERAGE WATER TEMP: *+40°F*

LAST FROZE: *Winter of 2003; before that, nearly 100% winter of 1996; 96% winter of 1994; and 95% winter of 1972*

WAVE HEIGHT: *Can exceed 30 feet*

TIDE: *No, but a seiche occurs. A seiche is the oscillations in the lake due to natural disturbances, such as a change in wind or air pressure, landslide, or earthquake.*

A Few of My Favorite Things

NOTHING BEATS FUN FOR HAVING A GOOD TIME.

The Fabulous Minnesota Barking Ducks

Featured sites in Duluth

1 Aerial Lift Bridge and Canal
2 Lake Superior Maritime Visitors Center
3 DeWitt-Seitz Marketplace
4 Lake Place
5 William A. Irvin
6 OMNIMAX
7 Vista Fleet Harbor Cruises
8 Duluth Entertainment and Convention Center (DECC)
9 Bayfront Park
10 The Depot
11 North Shore Scenic Railroad
12 Duluth Public Library
13 Fond Du Luth Gaming Casino
14 Fitger's Brewery Complex
15 Duluth Convention and Visitors Bureau
16 Holiday Center
17 Radisson Hotel
18 Best Western Downtown Motel
19 Comfort Suites of Duluth
20 Inn at Lake Superior
21 Hampton Inn
22 Canal Park Inn
23 Hawthorn Suites and Suites at Waterfront Plaza
24 Voyageur Lakewalk Inn
25 Playfront Park
26 Minnesota Slip Drawbridge
27 South Pier Inn

Good Times in Duluth

THE PORT CITY'S ATTRACTIONS

ULUTH FLAUNTS THE BEST THAT IT HAS THROUGH DISTINC-
tive parks and attractions. With the harbor as its hub, the Port City
evolved up the hill, along the lake, and down the river. Attractions
focus on these natural highlights.

Winding its way along the ridgeline, Skyline Parkway showcases impressive views of waterfalls, forest preserves, the meandering stretch of the city,
and, of course, Lake Superior. It is the greatness of this lake that draws hundreds of thousands of people each year to Duluth. Concentrated around the
famed Duluth Ship Canal and Aerial Lift Bridge, Canal Park hosts an abundance of attractions.

The following attractions are located in Canal Park and throughout
Duluth. For specifics on shopping, dining, lodging, walking paths, and such,
please review the related chapters in this book.

Many of the attractions are closed on major holidays, so call ahead or stop
at nearby tourist information centers at Endion Station, off the Lakewalk in
Canal Park (open Monday through Friday year-round), and the Waterfront
Center at the Vista dock on Harbor Drive (open May through October).

Now, I don't want to hear any whining about there being nothing to do.

AERIAL LIFT BRIDGE
This is the center of it all! Watch the gargantuan counterweights slowly drop,
raising the 900-ton span nearly 140 feet in the air to allow 1,000-foot ore
boats to pass into the harbor. Then drive over and watch from the other side!
The Aerial Lift Bridge, Ship Canal, and lighthouses are all on the National
Register of Historic Places.

The Duluth Ship Canal was excavated in 1871 and is a deceptive 300 feet
wide and 1,650 feet long. Spurred by the shipping of iron ore from the Mesabi
Range, an aerial transfer bridge was erected in 1905 across the canal. It allowed

vessels to enter and depart the Duluth side of the harbor more quickly. In 1929 the bridge was modernized to the more efficient lift bridge it is today, rising the entire height in just 55 seconds. Subsequent work in 1985–87 added strength and stability. Duluth-Superior harbor is the busiest bulk cargo port on the Great Lakes, so you'll have plenty of opportunities to watch ships from around the world pass through the canal and under the Aerial Lift Bridge.

duluthshippingnews.com/aerialliftbridge.htm

BOAT WATCHER'S HOT LINE

Get up-to-the-minute information on shipping traffic! The hot line gives the names, home ports, and arrival and departure times of lakers and salties (ocean-bound ships) for the Duluth harbor, Two Harbors, North Shore Mining, and Taconite Harbor. Some shipping traffic information is also available at the Maritime Center in Canal Park.

(218) 722-6489

duluthshippingnews.com

THE OTHER BRIDGES

The Blatnik Interstate Bridge, locally known as the High Bridge, rises above the Seaway Port Terminal to connect Duluth and Superior. The Richard I. Bong Bridge spans the St. Louis River and connects I-35 with U.S. 2 and Wisconsin 35. The 1.5-mile Bong Bridge has a pedestrian walkway on the west side. The Minnesota Slip Drawbridge is the blue drawbridge that connects Canal Park to the harbor waterfront by crossing the Minnesota Slip, home of the *William A. Irvin* ore boat and *Lake Superior* tugboat.

LAKE SUPERIOR MARINE MUSEUM AND MARITIME VISITORS CENTER

To learn more about the history of Lake Superior shipping, visit the Maritime Center (formerly the Marine Museum). Operated by the U.S. Army Corps of Engineers, the museum houses actual-size replicas of a ship cabin, pilothouse, and massive steam engine. Exhibits and displays include several scale ship models, a working radar, and video presentations. Kids, try to move the ship through the model Soo Locks. Excellent!

In Canal Park at the piers

Open daily 10 A.M. to 9 P.M. from late May to late October, 10 A.M. to 4:30 P.M. Friday through Sunday in winter, with slightly expanded hours from late March to late May

Free admission

(218) 727-2497

lssmma.com

CARRIAGE RIDES

Ride in style through Canal Park, downtown, and the waterfront (May through October). Carriages can be rented in the parking area near the canal, spring to fall only. Reservations are accepted. Carriages are also available for special events, winter outings, and sleigh rides.

River's Bend Carriage Service: (218) 729-5873

PORT TOWN TROLLEY

Motor to your next destination aboard an old-fashioned trolley. Catch the trolley at one of 13 stops along the half-hour loop from Canal Park to Fitger's Brewery Complex to the harbor front area.

Runs from 11 A.M. to 7 P.M. from Memorial Day through Labor Day and
on weekends in September
Fare: 25 cents (under 3 free)
(218) 722-SAVE
duluthtransit.com

DEWITT-SEITZ MARKETPLACE

The big brick building two blocks north of the Aerial Lift Bridge houses 14 wonderful, locally owned specialty shops and restaurants, including the Art Dock gallery, a bakery, and Hepzibah's, a divine candy shop. I especially like the Blue Heron Trading Co. for kitchen gadgets, gourmet delicacies, and funky food gifts. J. Skylark has all the cool toys you won't find at the big national toy stores.

Buchanan Street and Lake Avenue
dewitt-seitz.com

BANANAZ AND VERTICAL ENDEAVORS

Big arcade fun and all kinds of climbing walls. For all ages and skills – they'll introduce you to rock climbing or challenge you on their 43-foot wall.

329 South Lake Avenue in Canal Park
Open Monday through Friday noon to 9 P.M., Saturday 11 A.M. to 9 P.M.
and Sunday noon to 6 P.M.

LAKEWALK

This is the best walk in town! The side-by-side boardwalk and paved path begin at the ship canal and wind seaside past Fitger's Complex to Leif Erikson Park and the Rose Garden and down to 26th Avenue East. Stroll, amble, bike, run, roll, skip, or hop – this is a must-do in Duluth.

LAKE PLACE

This plaza area sits atop a freeway tunnel system just above the Lakewalk. While traffic rushes by below, slow down to appreciate the exquisite lake view, gardens, and sculpture.

WILLIAM A. IRVIN GREAT LAKES SHIP AND
THE LAKE SUPERIOR TUG

Be amazed at the sheer size of this ship! And at 610 feet, it's a little one compared to the 1,000-footers you'll see pass under the Aerial Lift Bridge. The *William A. Irvin* sailed for more than 40 years and was the flagship of U.S. Steel's Great Lakes fleet. Tours take you from bow to stern exploring the massive cargo holds, crew quarters, pilothouse, and formal dining room. Canvassing the *Irvin* gives a whole new meaning to boat watching.

Docked next to the *Irvin* is the tugboat *Lake Superior*. Originally a World War II tug, it towed ammunition across the English Channel and was sunk near the end of the war. It was raised and recommissioned for work on the St. Lawrence Seaway, Lake Superior, and Duluth harbor. You can take a self-guided tour of just the tug, but it is included, at no extra cost, when you tour the *Irvin*.

301 Harbor Drive at the Minnesota slip

Open late April through October; tours (one hour) depart every 20 minutes.

Package tours (*Irvin* and *Lake Superior* tug) cost $6.75 for adults, $5.75 for students and seniors, $4.50 for kids 3 to 12; admission for *Lake Superior* tug only is $3 for adults and $2 for kids 3 to 12; a package including admission for the *Irvin* and the *Lake Superior* tug and a pass to the Duluth OMNIMAX is $11.00 for adults, $10.00 for students and seniors, and $8.00 for children 3 to 12.

(218) 722-7876 in season; (218) 722-5573 out of season

williamairvin.com

OMNIMAX

In the OMNIMAX theater, images are projected with a 180-degree lens onto a giant domed screen. The specially designed theater's steeply pitched seating and stereo sound create a feeling of being in the picture instead of just watching.

Harbor Drive

Call or check the newspaper for show schedules

Adults $6.75, students and seniors $5.75, children (12 and under) $4.50;

Sunday is Family Day, $4.00 per person; a package including admission to the *William A. Irvin* and *Lake Superior* tugboat plus a pass to the OMNIMAX is $11.00 for adults, $10.00 for students and seniors, and $8.00 for children 3 to 12.

(218) 727-0022 or (888) OMNIMAX

duluthomnimax.com

VISTA FLEET HARBOR CRUISES

Take advantage of this opportunity to get out on the big lake. Cruising on board one of the Vista Fleet boats will give you a fresh perspective of the hillside, harbor, and lake. Narrated sight-seeing cruises head out under the Aerial Lift Bridge and into Lake Superior. After a short lake loop, you return under the bridge and tour the largest international harbor on the Great Lakes. You will be treated to up-close encounters with foreign ships, lakers, and massive grain elevators. The *Vista Star,* the biggest and fanciest of the fleet, offers buffet luncheon, dinner, and moonlight pizza cruises.

Harbor Drive across from the Duluth Entertainment and Convention
Center

Sight-seeing cruises (1 hour and 15 to 45 minutes) run daily from mid-
May through mid-October; moonlight pizza cruises (1 hour and 45
minutes) run Saturdays from late June to September and Mondays
from late June to August; lunch cruises (90 minutes) run daily from
mid-June to early September and Saturday only through mid-
October; dinner cruises (2 hours) run Tuesday through Saturday
from June to September.

Sight-seeing cruises cost $10 for adults, $5 for children; moonlight pizza
cruises are $13.50 for adults, $6 for children; lunch cruises are $14.95
for adults, $6 for children; dinner cruise prices vary with the menu
from $15 to $35 for adults, $6 to $15 for children.

(218) 722-6218

vistafleet.com

SCENIC SEAPLANE RIDES

Circle over Park Point, the Aerial Lift Bridge, the piers, and Canal Park. A great ride and friendly pilots!

End of Park Point at Sky Harbor Airport
20-minute ride, $30 per person, 2 person minimum
(218) 733-0078

LUTH ENTERTAINMENT AND CONVENTION CENTER (CC) ♿

meeting and convention center stages a variety of entertainment events in the 8,000-seat arena and 2,400-seat auditorium.

Harbor Drive

Business office: (218) 722-5573; ticket information: (218) 727-4344

decc.org

GRANDMA'S MARATHON

Each year thousands of runners, from amateurs to Olympic hopefuls, gather on Scenic 61 to begin the winding 26.2-mile course to Canal Park. The marathon has grown to include the Garry Bjorklund Half Marathon and the William A. Irvin 5K plus great entertainment, food, and speakers. The marathon is typically held the third Saturday in June.

P.O. Box 16234, Duluth, MN 55816

(218) 727-0947

grandmasmarathon.com

INTERNATIONAL FOLK FESTIVAL

Held the first Saturday in August from 10 A.M. to 5:30 P.M. at Leif Erikson Park, the folk festival showcases dancers, musicians, and entertainers reflecting the region's diverse ethnic backgrounds. Vendors sell an incredible assortment of international products and especially tasty food items.

ymcaduluth.org/event_folk.html

LAKE SUPERIOR DRAGON BOAT FESTIVAL

You and two dozen of your good friends row a long, multicolored boat 500 meters. For fun. For charity. Don't miss it. Third weekend in August.

Spectators get in free

lakesuperiordragons.com

BAYFRONT BLUES FESTIVAL

Darn good music all weekend long! More than 20 national performers play on two concert stages, plus blues bands perform at 25 local nightclubs. The Bayfront Blues Festival is one of the largest blues festivals in the Midwest and is held the middle weekend in August at Bayfront Park.

bayfrontblues.com

HAWK RIDGE

Observe the amazing migration of birds as they funnel past Hawk Ridge each autumn. Noted for birds of prey, including hawks, eagles, and falcons.

From I-35N, take 21st Avenue East, exit north to Woodland Avenue,
north on Woodland to Snively Boulevard, east on Snively to
Glenwood, south on Glenwood to sign on left.
hawkridge.org

NORTH SHORE IN-LINE MARATHON

Duluth's newest marathon follows the same beautiful course as Grandma's
Marathon. Mid-September each year, thousands of skaters race for cash and
prizes totaling over $20,000. But you don't need to be a professional to
compete – the race is designed for everyone 13 years of age or older.

P.O. Box 22, Duluth, MN 55801
(218) 723-1503
northshoreinline.com

DULUTH AIR AND AVIATION EXPO

Minnesota's largest airshow features daring feats, military aircraft displays,
and hands-on exhibits. Third weekend in September.

Duluth International Airport
Adults $15, children $10 (6 and under free); Family Pass $40 (2 adults,
2 kids)
(218) 628-9996
duluthairshow.com

DULUTH WINTER FESTIVAL AND
BEARGREASE SLED DOG MARATHON

The Beargrease Marathon runs from Duluth 330 miles along the North
Shore ridgeline and backwoods to the Grand Portage Indian Reservation at
the border of Minnesota and Canada. Spectators can watch the start, then
follow the race by stopping at the checkpoints. You can volunteer to be a
timekeeper or assist as mushers bring in their teams.

Definitely a one-of-a-kind sport, the Beargrease heads a list of fantastic
winter activities held during the two-week Winter Festival. Other events
include broomball, hockey, skiing, snow sculpting, and a horse-drawn sleigh
and cutter parade.

(800) 438-5884 or (218) 722-4011 (Duluth Convention and Visitors
Bureau)
beargrease.com

SNOCROSS

A really, really, really, really long snowmobile race held each Thanksgiving weekend at Spirit Mountain.

(218) 722-4011

visitduluth.com/snocross

PLAYFRONT PARK

Now this is a playground! Teeter-totters, whirlamagigs, slides, swings, and lots of room to run. A great place to let the kids expend a little energy.

5th Avenue West and Harbor Drive

THE DEPOT

Fusing heritage and history with world culture and art, The Depot is a splendid combination of museums and performing arts. Built in 1892, the original railroad station served as many as 55 trains per day. Railway decline led to its closing in the 1960s. A 1977 renovation updated the station to house the St. Louis County Heritage and Arts Center, or as the locals say, The Depot. Within its grand confines are the St. Louis County Historical Society, Duluth Children's Museum, Lake Superior Museum of Transportation, Depot Square, Duluth Art Institute, Minnesota Ballet, Duluth Playhouse, Duluth-Superior Symphony Orchestra, Matinee Musicale, and Arrowhead Chorale. See the Museum chapter for more information.

5th Avenue West and Michigan Street

Open 9:30 A.M. to 6 P.M. daily Memorial Day to Labor Day, 10 A.M. to
    5 P.M. Monday through Saturday and 1 P.M. to 5 P.M. Sunday the
    remainder of the year

Adults $8.50, children (6 to 11) $5.25, family (2 adults and 2 children
    under 13) $23.50

(218) 727-8025; recorded hotline, (888) 733-5833

duluthdepot.org

NORTH SHORE SCENIC RAILROAD

Ride the rails! Take advantage of an opportunity to go on an old-fashioned train ride. Board at The Depot and tour Duluth and Lake Superior's shores or ride all the way to Two Harbors. The very popular Pizza Train includes pizza and soda and you travel as far as the Sucker River, where you cross a darn big trestle before switching directions and heading back. Ask about special events including Saturday night Dinner Trains and Sunday afternoon Tea Trains.

Departs from The Depot in Duluth

Open late May through mid-October; the Lester River Run (90 minutes) leaves daily late May through Labor Day at 12:30 P.M. and 3 P.M. and at 10 A.M. on Fridays and Saturdays, Labor Day to mid-October at 12:30 P.M. and 3 P.M. Friday through Sunday; the Two Harbors Run (6 hours) leaves at 10:30 A.M. on Fridays and Saturdays only (includes 2 hours in Two Harbors); the Pizza Train (2.5 hours) leaves at 6:30 P.M. Wednesday through Saturday late May through August and at 5:30 P.M. Friday and Saturday September 1 through mid-October

Lester River Run costs $10 for adults, $5 for children (3 to 13), under 3 free; the Two Harbors Run costs $18 for adults, $8 for children (3 to 13), under 3 free; the Pizza Train costs $16 for adults, $11 for children (3 to 13), under 3 free, and includes half a 14-inch Domino's pizza and one can of soda

(218) 722-1273 or (800) 423-1273

lsrm.org

DULUTH PUBLIC LIBRARY
All the amenities and then some.

Main branch is across from The Depot at 520 West Superior Street

Open Monday through Thursday 10 A.M. to 8:30 P.M., Friday 10 A.M. to 5:30 P.M., and Saturday 10 A.M. to 4 P.M.

(218) 723-3800

duluth.lib.mn.us

FOND-DU-LUTH GAMING CASINO
Bingo, 16 gaming tables, and more than 510 slots with jackpots up to $20,000. You must be at least 18 years of age to enter and at least 21 to participate. Full lounge. Eight blackjack tables, $3 to $1,000.

129 East Superior Street

Open 10 A.M. to 2 A.M. daily and 24 hours Friday and Saturday

(218) 722-0280 or (800) 873-0280

fondduluthcasino.com

DULUTH HUSKIES BASEBALL
Duluth-Superior's Northwoods League team plays 32+ home games, June through August at Wade Stadium. The 10-team league is made up of college players from Minnesota, Wisconsin, and Iowa. Good family fun at an affordable price.

Wade Stadium is at the corner of Stadium Road and West 2nd Street;

from I-35, take the 40th Avenue West exit to Grand Avenue to 34th Avenue West.

(218) 310-5272

northwoodsleague.com

STORA ENSO DULUTH PAPER MILL

Free 1-hour tours are offered Monday, Wednesday, and Friday at 9 A.M., 10:30 A.M., 1 P.M., and 3 P.M. throughout the summer by reservation only. Tickets are available at the waterfront tourist information center on Harbor Drive.

Free admission, but you must be 10 years of age or older; no high heels or open-toed shoes.

(218) 722-6024 Duluth Visitor Center

(218) 628-5312 for group tours on Tuesdays by appointment

LAKE SUPERIOR ZOOLOGICAL GARDENS

Polar bears and penguins, a kookaburra and kodiaks, otters and owls, wallabies and wild turkeys – you'll find them all at the zoo in exhibits such as Polar Shores, Australian Outback, Northern Territory, the Nocturnal Exhibit, and the hands-on Children's Zoo. An extensive renovation project upgrading animal habitats is making the Lake Superior Zoo a prime attraction. The adjacent Fairmount Park has a playground, picnic tables, grills, summer restrooms, and a hiking trail that overlooks the zoo. Inside are the Tiger Shop and Safari Cafe snack bar.

Grand Avenue and 72nd Avenue West

Open daily 9 A.M. to 6 P.M. from April 1 through October 31 and 10 A.M. to 4 P.M. from November 1 through March 31

Admission is $6 for ages 12 and over, $2.50 for kids 4 to 11, 3 and under free.

(218) 733-3337

lszoo.org

LAKE SUPERIOR & MISSISSIPPI RAILROAD COMPANY

Hop aboard and cruise the shores of the St. Louis River in a vintage train featuring an open Safari Car. Enjoy a great ride at a reasonable price! This nonprofit is run by volunteers dedicated to the preservation of railroad history and the restoration of railroad artifacts.

Freemont Street and Grand Avenue (across from the Zoo behind the Little Store)

Saturdays and Sundays from mid-June through early October; tours (90 minutes) depart at 10:30 A.M. and 1:30 P.M.

Adults $8, children (under 12) $6
(218) 624-7549
lsmrr.org

VIEW FROM THOMPSON HILL VISITORS CENTER
Before cresting the hill on the I-35 approach to Duluth, take exit 249 and follow the signs to the visitors center. Savor the stunning panorama of the St. Louis River bay, Duluth-Superior harbor, and Lake Superior stretching eastward.

8525 West Skyline Drive
(218) 723-4938

KARPELES MANUSCRIPT MUSEUM
Karpeles is dedicated to the preservation of original, handwritten letters and documents of the women and men who have shaped and changed history. This amazing museum houses changing displays that have included the original manuscripts of the Bill of Rights, the Emancipation Proclamation, Handel's *Messiah,* and others.

902 East 1st Street
Open daily from noon to 4 P.M., except closed on Mondays from Labor
    Day through Memorial Day
Free admission
(218) 728-0630
rain.org/~karpeles.dul.htm

GLENSHEEN
Built at the turn of the century by Chester Congdon, this magnificent estate is situated on 7.6 acres on Lake Superior's shoreline in East Duluth. The 39-room Congdon mansion has been preserved in its original state and sits at the center of beautiful formal gardens and manicured grounds. See the Museum chapter for more information. Tours available every ½ hour and last for 1¼ hour.

3300 London Road
Open daily from 9:30 A.M. to 4 P.M. in May through October, Friday
    through Sunday from 11 A.M. to 2 P.M. in November through April
Adults $9.50, juniors (12 to 15) and seniors $7.50, children (6 to 11) $4.50
(218) 726-8910 (888) 454-GLEN
d.umn.edu/glen

GREAT LAKES AQUARIUM

The aquarium has a major tank, the 120,000-gallon Isle Royale tank, several smaller tanks, and interactive exhibits that allow visitors to explore and learn about the aquatic life of Lake Superior and the inland lakes of the region. Exhibits focus on the formation and changing nature of the lakes, native vegetation, and efforts needed to maintain and improve the condition of the lakes. The Aquarium is owned by Ripley's Believe It or Not, and there are plans to expand exhibits and programs beginning the summer of 2004. Call ahead or go online for updated information.

353 Harbor Drive

Adults $10.95, seniors (age 62+) $8.95, children (ages 4 to 17) $5.95

(218) 740-3474

glaquarium.org

North Shore Attractions

I enjoy Duluth as a city. I grew up there and I often visit. But I choose to live on a hillside overlooking Lake Superior on Minnesota's North Shore. This is where I can live my life on vacation. This is where I retired at the age of 24.

The outdoor recreation opportunities on the Shore are truly limitless. A bit later I describe some of them. But here are a few of my favorite things to do as you travel up the Shore. I heartily recommend a walking tour of all the burgs and villages along the Shore. You get a better sense of what the community is all about, of who lives here and why. Talk to the shopkeepers and clerks. Drive some back roads. Make your own discoveries about the land that borders the big lake.

FRENCH RIVER FISH HATCHERY

The Minnesota Department of Natural Resources incubates herring, suckers, walleye, rainbow trout, steelhead, and chinook salmon at this cold-water fish hatchery. If you are traveling in September and October, stop to see the heavy fall spawn run. In the spring, spawn often occurs in late morning.

Scenic 61 at French River

Self-guided tours are available weekdays from 8 A.M. to 4 P.M.

(218) 525-0867

TOM'S LOGGING CAMP

Families love this authentic re-creation of a 1900s logging camp and North West Company fur trading post. A nature trail, Hell's Creek, and eight museum buildings are spread under the shade of a thick conifer forest. Buildings include the Old North West Company Trading Post, museum, harness shop, shoe shop and horseshoeing stall, horse barn and blacksmith shop, bunkhouse and cook's shanty, and a Finnish sauna. Tom also has llamas, a rainbow trout pond, bunnies, and pygmy goats.

Scenic 61 about 13 miles northeast of Duluth

Open seasonally

Adults $3, children (6 to 15) $2, 5 and under free
(218) 525-4120
tomsloggingcamp.com

STONY POINT DRIVE
Locals love to wave-watch in stormy weather, picnic on calm days, and shoreline-fish here.

> A loop off Scenic 61 along Lake Superior, about 15 miles northeast of Duluth

SMOKED FISH
Sample the local specialty at Russ Kendall's (my favorite), Smokey Kendall's, or Mel's along Scenic 61, Lou's on Highway 61 in Two Harbors, Big Dollar or Gene's IGA in Grand Marais, or seasonally at the Dockside Fish Market on the harbor in Grand Marais.

SILVER CLIFF
Silver Cliff is the highest bluff rising directly out of Lake Superior. In 1923 builders carved Highway 61 out of the cliffside 125 feet above the lake. The 1400-foot tunnel provides a safer thoroughfare and features a pull-off area, allowing visitors to take in the cliffside views.

> Highway 61 northeast of Two Harbors

VIRGIN PINE AND CEDAR AT ENCAMPMENT FOREST
As you come to the close of the first passing lane east of Two Harbors, observe the virgin (uncut) pine and cedar stretching to the Lafayette Bluff tunnel. The forest is located entirely on private land, so admire the view from your car.

> Highway 61 northeast of Two Harbors

LAFAYETTE BLUFF TUNNEL
On your return trip down the Shore (heading southwest), admire the particularly nice vista that opens up as the bend of the tunnel straightens out to the west.

> Highway 61 southwest of Gooseberry Falls

LAKE SUPERIOR EXCURSIONS ABOARD the *GRANDPA WOO III*
Board the 40-passenger *Grandpa Woo III* at the public launch in East Beaver Bay and tour Superior's coastline. Highlights on this two-hour cruise include

the craggy shoreline, river mouths, Silver Cliff, Encampment Island, Split Rock Lighthouse, and Palisade Head.

Tickets and boarding dock on Highway 61 in East Beaver Bay

Contact Lake Superior Excursions for information on schedules, special dinner tours, 2- and 3-day Thunder Bay tours departing from Grand Portage, and prices.

(218) 226-4100

grampawoo.com

BAYSIDE PARK AND SILVER BAY MARINA

This park has an overlook, lovely picnic sites, a short trail system, 68 slips, and a full-service marina. It is also a great spot to watch ships load at the North Shore Mining dock.

Highway 61 just northeast of Beaver Bay and southwest of Silver Bay

(218) 226-3121 in season; (218) 226-4088 off season

silverbay.com/marina.htm

ST. MARY'S CATHOLIC CHURCH

A 5,000-pound block of polished taconite was used to create the altar and baptismal font.

Horn Boulevard and Edison; from Highway 61 in Silver Bay, go north on Outer Drive, then east on Edison to 57 Horn Boulevard

(218) 226-3691

PALISADE HEAD

Follow the paved road to the top for incredible views of Lake Superior and Shovel Point and over the 320-foot cliffs.

Watch for signs from Highway 61 about four miles northeast of Silver Bay.

Open seasonally; part of Tettegouche State Park

(218) 226-6365

ROCK CLIMBING

Rock climbing aficionados will be pleased by the challenge and scenery presented at Palisade Head, Shovel Point, and Section 13. See the hiking section ("Out Walkin'") for location and specifics. Call or stop by Superior North Outdoor Center in Grand Marais or the UMD Outdoor Program in Duluth (218) 726-8743 or online at umdoutdoorprogram.org.

WOLF RIDGE ENVIRONMENTAL LEARNING CENTER

Focusing on outdoor programs, this internationally recognized residential school offers workshops for school groups, families, and the general public. Visitors are welcome, but preregistration is required for programs.

From Highway 61 in Little Marais, go about 3.5 miles north on Co. Rd. 6 to driveway that is 2.5 miles long.

(218) 353-7414

wolf-ridge.org

FINLAND, MINNESOTA

The community of Finland best represents what a number of the small shoreline villages were like 25 years ago. Tourism has an impact, but it is not the end-all. Finland is set in the picturesque valley behind the Sawtooth Range. The residential area spreads to either side of the main street. The very hospitable folks at the Four Seasons restaurant, the West Branch, Our Place, and the Trestle Inn serve up tasty fare. Plan a stop on your way to nearby Crosby Manitou State Park or Isabella.

Off the beaten track at the intersection of Minnesota 1 and Co. Rds. 6 and 7, about seven miles north of Highway 61

finlandmnus.com

CROSS RIVER HERITAGE CENTER

Exhibits, artifacts, and events to celebrate the history of Schroeder.

Winter hours: 9 A.M. to 4 P.M. Monday, Thursday, and Friday; 11 A.M. to 4 P.M. Sunday

Summer hours: 9 A.M. to 5 P.M. Monday through Friday, 9 A.M. to 4 P.M. Saturday, 11 A.M. to 4 P.M. Sunday

Highway 61 in Schroeder

(218) 663-7706

NORTH SHORE COMMERCIAL FISHING MUSEUM

Built across the bay from the original site of the twin fish houses, the museum is a replica of the Tofte brothers' and Hans Engelsen's 1905 fish house. Displayed within the museum are many relics, photos, and artifacts that were passed down by the Tofte, Toftey, and Engelsen families. This great little museum tells the story of commercial fishing along the Shore and at Isle Royale. Watch for special events. The Lutsen Tofte Visitors Center is also located here.

Highway 61 in Tofte

(218) 663-7804

commercialfishingmuseum.org

FOURTH OF JULY CELEBRATION IN TOFTE

Tofte offers up a classic small-town Fourth of July with a cannon shoot, Tofte Trek foot race, parade, music, brats on the grill, and fireworks at dusk. Tofte Park has a playground, boat access, pavilion, and outhouses.

Centered around the fire hall and Tofte Park Road, south off Highway 61

HOMESTEAD STABLES

Guided 1-hour trail rides four times a day (includes a lesson), 2-hour lunch ride spring and fall, and a 3-hour dinner ride in the summer. Open early May through late October.

From Highway 61 in Lutsen, go north on Ski Hill Road.

(218) 663-7281 ext 505

lutsen.com

LUTSEN MOUNTAINS ALPINE SLIDE, GONDOLA RIDE, AND MOUNTAIN BIKE PARK

Summer fun at the Midwest's largest and highest alpine ski center. Take the chairlift to the summit of Eagle Mountain and return on the exhilarating half-mile ride through dips and turns, or bring your bike and ride the rugged backcountry trails. Additional biking and hiking trails start at the top of Moose Mountain. Ride the gondola! Board at the main chalet, cross the Poplar River Valley at treetop level, and make the final 800-foot ascent to the peak of Moose Mountain, where a picnic area, deli restaurant, and trails await you. The gondola ride is spectacular in the fall, as you rise above the maples awash in red, orange, burgundy, and gold. Open daily late May through mid-October.

From Highway 61 in Lutsen, go north on Ski Hill Road.

Alpine rides can be purchased singly or in a book of five or eight; gondola ride fees are per person; an unlimited-ride day pass is available for all ages and is valid for both the gondola and alpine slide.

(218) 663-7281

lutsen.com

LUTSEN REC

Paintball and mini-golf! Grab the whole gang for an exciting game of paint-ball tag in the woods. Concessions and souvenirs, too.

From Highway 61 in Lutsen, go north on the Ski Hill Road.

(218) 663-7863

lutsenrec.com

DOWNTOWN LUTSEN

Get what you need at the Clearview boardwalk. If they don't have it, you don't need it. Or you could cross Highway 61 to Lockport Market and Deli, the rest of downtown.

Highway 61

GOOD HARBOR BAY PANORAMA

Just past Thomsonite Beach, Highway 61 curves left, revealing picturesque Good Harbor Bay, Seagull Rock, and Grand Marais in the distance. Vehicle pull-overs are on the lake side of the road, or stop at the Cut Face Creek wayside rest on the eastern edge of the bay.

GRAND MARAIS-GUNFLINT RANGER STATION

More than a place to get a permit, the ranger station has a number of animal and bird mounts; information on hiking, camping, and recreation in the Superior National Forest; and a few gifts and books. And it is the place to get current information on the Boundary Waters Canoe Area Wilderness.

Highway 61 just west of Grand Marais

(218) 387-1750

COOK COUNTY COMMUNITY RADIO

The North Shore's only radio station was established in 1998. Tune in to WTIP at 90.7 FM!

GRAND MARAIS RECREATION AREA

Fun, fun, and more fun on Grand Marais's harbor. The pool building houses an Olympic-size pool, kids' pool, whirlpool, and sauna. The campground has over 300 sites. Recreate at the playground, ballfield, picnic pavilion, public boat launch, cobblestone beach, hiking trail, and winter sledding hill.

Off Highway 61 on 8th Avenue West

The pool building is open daily.

(218) 387-1712 or (800) 998-0959; pool complex: (218) 387-1275

boreal.org/cityhall/recharbor.html

NORTH HOUSE FOLK SCHOOL

An amazing group of people had an idea to build a place where people could come together to promote and preserve the knowledge, skills, crafts, and stories of the past and present and to use these elements as a way of helping people develop their creative natures. And they built this amazing place, the North House Folk School. Half-day, full-day, and multi-day classes offered include boat building (from Inuit kayaks to Gloucester dories to 18-foot,

8-inch Mackinaw boats), felting, making boiled wool clothing, maple sugar-ing, wild ricing, basic timber framing, building with rock, rock climbing, toolmaking, basket weaving, spinning, woodworking, and lots more!

The North House is also home of the *Hjordis,* a 50-foot vintage, gaff-rigged schooner. The Lake Superior Education Program takes place on board the *Hjordis.* Half-day, full-day, and multi-day sails cover everything from an introduction to the vessel to the geology and biology of the lake, navigational instruction, scientific studies, and basic seamanship skills. This is a great way to get out on Lake Superior and learn something, too.

North House is a nonprofit organization that offers memberships.
Highway 61 in Grand Marais on the harbor
(218) 387-9762 or (888) 387-9762
northhouse.org

GEORGE MORRISON'S TOTEM
Admire the beauty and artisanry of George Morrison's glorious totem.
In the lobby of the Grand Marais Clinic and Hospital; from Highway 61, go north on the Gunflint Trail (Co. Rd. 12) to the junction with Co. Rd. 7; the entrance is off Co. Rd. 12.

COOK COUNTY COMMUNITY CENTER AND CURLING CLUB
You never know what will be going on at the Community Center, so just stop by. In winter, this is the site of the Curling Club, outdoor pleasure rink, and youth hockey program. Summertime brings the county fair in mid-August and families enjoying the playground, pavilion, and basketball court. Adja-cent to the center are the Cook County schools and tennis courts. We have a very active tennis club here. Stop by and pick up a game!
From Highway 61 in Grand Marais, go north on the Gunflint Trail (Co. Rd. 12), then east on Co. Rd. 7 for one block.
(218) 387-3015

ARROWHEAD CENTER FOR THE ARTS
This is the performing arts center in Grand Marais and home to the North Shore Music Association, WTIP radio, and the Grand Marais Playhouse. See the Arts and Culture chapter for more information. The Grand Marais Play-house stages a number of shows throughout the year, including plays, read-ings, and musical events.
From Highway 61 in Grand Marais, go north on the Gunflint Trail (Co. Rd. 12), then east on Co. Rd. 7 for two blocks; the center is located in the school campus.

(218) 387-1284
northshorearts.org

GRAND MARAIS PUBLIC LIBRARY

This is one of my favorite places to go in town. Our library has a great layout with sun streaming in from the south-facing windows and groupings of comfortable chairs. The library has a helpful staff, an impressive selection of books, tapes, and videos, and offers computer use and Internet access. Check it out!

Highway 61 at 2nd Avenue West
(218) 387-1140
grandmaraislibrary.org

COOK COUNTY FARM AND CRAFT MARKET

A wide variety of crafts and fresh produce Saturdays, 9 A.M. to 1 P.M., mid-May through the end of September.

Senior Center parking lot; from Highway 61 in Grand Marais, go south 1½ blocks from the stoplight.

JOHNSON HERITAGE POST ART GALLERY

The works of painter Anna Carolina Johnson, who settled on the North Shore in 1907 with her trader husband, are permanently displayed in the west wing. The great room and east wing display rotating exhibits of area and regional artists. See the Arts and Culture chapter for more information.

115 West Wisconsin Street; from Highway 61 in Grand Marais, take the main street downtown.
(218) 387-2314

SUPERIOR COASTAL SPORTS

Guided half-day, full-day, and multi-day kayak tours, lessons, and no experience is required. Complete kayak outfitting and rentals are available. New 3-story retail shop with plans for an indoor climbing wall.

In Grand Marais, one block south of the stoplight on Highway 61 and a half-block east of Broadway Avenue
(218) 387-2360 or (800) 720-2809
superiorcoastal.com

GRAND MARAIS VISITORS CENTER

From Highway 61 in Grand Marais at the stoplight, go south a block and a half.

(218) 387-2524 or (800) 622-4014

GUNFLINT TRAIL VISITOR CENTER
At the junction of Highway 61 and main street in downtown Grand Marais, adjacent to the Java Moose.

gunflint-trail.com

SUPERIOR NORTH OUTDOOR CENTER
It's the bike shop! These folks will direct you to the best trails, fix your bike, rent you a bike, and outfit you with whatever you need. They are the resident rock climbing experts, too.

In the raspberry-colored building adjacent to the parking for the Grand Marais Visitors Center; from Highway 61 at the stoplight, go south a block and a half, and enter the visitors center parking area.

(218) 387-2186

GRAND MARAIS HARBOR, ARTIST POINT, THE BREAKWALLS, AND GRAND MARAIS LIGHTHOUSE
Well-known landmarks all.

From Highway 61 at the stoplight, go south three blocks to parking.

KADUNCE RIVER STATE WAYSIDE
Refer to the parks, hiking, and snowshoeing sections for more information. I like it so much I just had to mention it again.

Highway 61 about eight miles northeast of Grand Marais

GRAND PORTAGE CASINO AND HIGH-STAKES BINGO
Bingo, video slot machines, and live blackjack. Adjacent to the casino is the 100-room Grand Portage Lodge with restaurant, lounge, firelit lobby, and nearby tennis, hiking, and marina.

Highway 61 about 30 miles northeast of Grand Marais

Open daily

(218) 475-2401 or (800) 232-1384; from Canada only: (800) 543-1384

grandportagemn.com

ISLE ROYALE SCENIC TOURS
A great day trip to Isle Royale; highlights include being out on Lake Superior, the "Witch Tree," passing over the sunken steamship *America,* and time to explore a little bit of Isle Royale National Park.

Departs from Grand Portage daily mid-June through mid-September at 9:30 A.M., returning at 5:30 P.M.

Adults $40 plus $4 national park fee; children (4 to 11) $20

(888) 746-2305
grand-isle-royale.com

THE INTERNATIONAL BORDER BETWEEN THE UNITED STATES AND CANADA

To continue your travels, cross the border and refer to the chapter on Canada.

Highway 61 about 36 miles northeast of Grand Marais

UP THE GUNFLINT TRAIL

Plan a drive up the trail. Yep, all 56 miles are paved. Fish, hike, shop, dine, paddle, and explore!

SEE A MOOSE

Check out the moose viewing area 24 miles north of Highway 61 on the Gunflint Trail. Walk ⅓ mile in to the viewing platform. Best chance to see a moose is dawn or dusk ... and shhh, they can hear you.

TWO GREAT EVENTS TO SUPPORT THE GUNFLINT FIRE DEPARTMENT

4th of July Fest
   At Voyageurs Canoe Outfitters at the end of the trail
   (218) 388-2224
   canoeit.com
Gunflint Canoe Races
   Mid-July at Gunflint Lodge
   (218) 388-2294

DAY TRIPS

Canoe, kayak, bike, or hike. You can even stay overnight in a bunkhouse! Check out the outfitters chapter for more information.

Family Fun

Wondering where to take the kids? Try the following places, which are especially suitable for families with kids from ages 3 to 12.

IN DULUTH

AERIAL LIFT BRIDGE AND CANAL PARK
LAKE SUPERIOR MARITIME VISITORS CENTER
Excellent hands-on exhibits and info about ships – and it's free.
   In Canal Park

WILLIAM A. IRVIN
Tour an ore boat.
   In the Minnesota Slip adjacent to Canal Park

PLAYFRONT PARK
Centrally located playground when the kids just need to run.
   5th Avenue West and Harbor Drive

THE DEPOT
Especially the kids' museum and train museum.
   5th Avenue West and Michigan Street

NORTH SHORE SCENIC RAILROAD
The Pizza Train is a family favorite.
   Departs from The Depot

LAKE SUPERIOR ZOOLOGICAL GARDENS
A darn nice zoo.
   Grand Avenue and 72nd Avenue West

PARK POINT REC AREA
Six miles of sand beach.
> 45th Street and Minnesota Avenue

SCENIC SEA PLANE RIDE
At the end of Park Point at Sky Harbor Airport.

BRIGHTON BEACH
The first cobblestone beach on the North Shore.
> London Road, a quarter mile east of Lester River

AGATE HUNTING
Search them out at Brighton Beach, Burlington Bay, Flood Bay state wayside, Cut Face Creek state wayside, Grand Marais harbor, the Kadunce and Brule river mouths, and the coast of Horseshoe Bay.

ALONG THE SHORE

FRENCH RIVER FISH HATCHERY
So this is where little fish come from.
> Scenic 61 at French River

TOM'S LOGGING CAMP
Vintage tourist stop.
> Scenic 61 between the French and Knife Rivers

TWO HARBORS WATERFRONT
Tugs, trains, ships, and lighthouses.
> Waterfront Drive off Highway 61

GOOSEBERRY FALLS STATE PARK VISITORS CENTER
Exhibits, programs, hikes, restrooms, and gifts.
> Highway 61 about 12 miles northeast of Two Harbors

CROSS-COUNTRY SKIING
Try the trails at Spirit Mountain, Gooseberry Falls, Sugarbush, and Pincushion and the George Washington Memorial Pines Trail. See the cross-country section ("Skinny Skiers Rejoice!") for more details.

SPLIT ROCK LIGHTHOUSE HISTORICAL CENTER
The lighthouse, signal building, and great exhibits.
Off Highway 61 about 20 miles northeast of Two Harbors

BAYSIDE PARK AND SILVER BAY MARINA
Beach, picnic area, overlook, and observation area to watch ships being loaded at nearby North Shore Mining.
Highway 61 in Silver Bay

ALPINE SLIDE AND GONDOLA RIDE
Ride, baby, ride.
From Highway 61 in Lutsen, go north on Ski Hill Road.

LUTSEN MOUNTAINS ALPINE SKIING
Best skiing for hundreds of miles.
From Highway 61 in Lutsen, go north on Ski Hill Road.

GRAND MARAIS HARBOR, ARTIST POINT, AND LIGHTHOUSE
The place to throw rocks in the lake and walk to the lighthouse.
From Highway 61, go south from the stoplight 3 blocks.

INLAND LAKE FISHING
Especially at the fishing piers on Crescent, Sawbill, Whitepine, Mink, and Trestle Pine Lakes. See the fishing section ("What's Biting?") for more details.

KADUNCE RIVER STATE WAYSIDE
Quiet cobblestone beach, easy river hike, and picnic tables.
Highway 61 about eight miles northeast of Grand Marais

GRAND PORTAGE NATIONAL MONUMENT
Enjoy this leisurely step back in time.
Off Highway 61

HIGH FALLS OF THE PIGEON RIVER
An easy walk for everyone to magnificent falls, the highest in the state.
Off Highway 61 at the Canadian border in Grand Portage State Park

RYDEN'S BORDER STORE
Geegaws, souvenirs, and a black bear at the bar.
Highway 61 at the border

Aaah ... Spas and Wellness

VACATIONS, GETAWAYS, WEEKENDS AWAY ARE SUPPOSED TO BE relaxing, a contrast to our daily harried lives. Some of us do a great job of flipping the switch from Work/Life to Vacation. For a lot of us, that transition is harder. All of us can reap the benefits of wellness therapies, be it relaxation massage or healing touch or learning to train our brain through neurofeedback.

For years, my friends and I have had Jerry, a massage therapist, join us on our getaways. We started out receiving relaxation massages, but over the years Jerry has introduced us to a variety of helpful therapies that he individually incorporates into our massage sessions. There are loads of great therapists, and many are willing to travel to your resort or hotel.

In Duluth, I would ask for a recommendation at the front desk and skim through the yellow pages. I have listed five spas/therapy centers in Duluth and noted two b&bs that specifically offer massage services. Along the Shore, I would definitely ask the front desk. I have listed the resorts and individuals (including Jerry) who provide services, including the new Northwoods Wellness Practitioners Group, a group of complementary and alternative health care professionals practicing in Cook County, Minnesota. The Practitioners Group works together and can provide a variety of services to you during your stay. Watch for special events and monthly meetings hosted by the group; it's a great way to learn more about wellness therapies and services.

Call these people. You're supposed to feel better after vacation!

IN DULUTH

EAGLE'S NEST MASSAGE THERAPY

Over 14 therapists with many specialties. Open daily by appointment (Monday through Friday 8:30 A.M. to 8:30 P.M., Saturday 9 A.M. to 5 P.M., Sunday noon to 6 P.M.).

Downtown at 324 West Superior Street in the Medical Arts Building,
Suite 509
(218) 722-2918
Miller Hill at 1417 Sunby Road, next to Schneiderman's
(218) 625-2353
eaglesnestmassage.com

CHRISTAL CENTER
Wellness therapies, natural products, holistic healing, and sauna. Open daily
by appointment (Monday though Friday 9 A.M. to 9 P.M., Saturday 10 A.M. to
6 P.M., Sunday 11 A.M. to 5 P.M.).
DeWitt-Seitz Marketplace in Canal Park
(218) 722-2411
christalcenter.com

ELYSIUM SALON AND DAY SPA
Full- and half-day packages including 30-, 60-, and 90-minute massages,
aromatherapy, hydrotherapy, and body wraps.
2230 London Road
(218) 724-7232

COMFORT ZONE THERAPEUTIC MASSAGE
Fifteen therapists, by appointment, Monday through Saturday, offering various modalities, massage, yoga classes, and Saturday retreats.
Downtown at 31 West Superior Street, Suites 302 and 303
(218) 720-4444
comfortzonetherapeuticmassage.com

DULUTH AREA FAMILY YMCA
Three therapists available by appointment. Need to be a member; daily
memberships available.
Downtown at 302 West First Street
(218) 722-4745
duluthymca.org/health.htm

YOGA NORTH
Open, registration, and private classes in kundalini, hatha, and power yoga.
Daily classes.
East Duluth in St. Michael's School at 47th Avenue East and Pitt Street
(218) 733-1375
yoganorthduluth.com

MASSAGE AT A. G. THOMSON HOUSE
Therapists from the Center for Personal Fitness at SMDC.
> For guests of the B&B located at 2617 East Third Street
> (218) 724-3464 or (877) 807-8077
> thomsonhouse.com/specials/

WOODLAND SPA AT FIRELIGHT INN
Massage therapy Monday through Saturday by appointment, including hot stone therapy.
> For guests of the B&B located at 2211 East Third Street
> (218) 724-0272 or (888) 724-0273
> firelightinn.com/massage.html

ALONG THE SHORE

GRAND SUPERIOR LODGE
By appointment for guests and non-guests.
> On Highway 61 near Gooseberry Falls
> (218) 834-9565 or (800) 627-9565
> grandsuperior.com/massage.htm

BLUEFIN BAY ON LAKE SUPERIOR
By appointment for guests and non-guests. Guests receive 25% discount.
> On Highway 61 in Tofte
> (218) 663-7296 or (800) BLUEFIN
> bluefinbay.com/massage.htm

CARIBOU HIGHLANDS LODGE
By appointment and stop-in for guests and non-guests, including hot stone therapy.
> On the Ski Hill Road at Lutsen Mountains
> (218) 663-7241 or (800) 642-6036
> caribouhighlands.com

NORTH SHORE HEALTH THERAPIES
By appointment at two locations, Guest Services at Bluefin Bay in Tofte and the third floor of the East Bay Hotel in Grand Marais.
> (218) 370-0699
> nsmassagetherapy.com

JERRY LAWSON
(Yes, that Jerry.) By appointment in the Fireweed Building in downtown Grand Marais.

(218) 387-1004

BEARSKIN LODGE
By appointment for guests at this Gunflint Trail resort.

(218) 388-2292 or (800) 338-4170

bearskin.com

GUNFLINT LODGE
By appointment for guests at this Gunflint Trail resort.

(218) 388-2294 or (800) 328-3325

gunflint.com

NORTHWOODS WELLNESS PRACTITIONERS GROUP – CENTERS

SWEETGRASS COVE GUESTHOUSE AND BODYWORK STUDIO
Rick Anderson provides a wood-fired Finnish sauna, sea salt body scrub, wild herbal body wrap, relaxing and therapeutic massage and myofascial release, and an outdoor hot tub as an overnight guest or as a day spa guest.

6880 East Highway 61 near Grand Portage

(218) 475-2421 or (866) 475-2421

sweetgrasscove.com

SUPERIOR FITNESS II
Chris McClure, a certified personal trainer, provides fitness evaluations/ interviews, one-on-one training, and a fitness studio, plus she is a fit-ball instructor.

320 First Avenue East

(218) 387-9654

THERAPY BY THE LAKE
Christal Kelahan specializes in myofascial release, therapeutic and relaxation massage, pregnancy, labor, and postnatal massage, and LaStone Therapy.

Lower level of the Sawtooth Mountain Clinic in Grand Marais and at
Caribou Highlands Lodge at Lutsen Mountains

(218) 663-0076

NORTH SHORE NEUROFEEDBACK
Karl Hansen and Lee Stewart can teach you to adjust your brain to improve its performance, which can help with a variety of disorders, pain syndromes, and depression and improve creativity, memory, well-being, and athletic performance.

702 West Second Street in Grand Marais

(218) 387-2983

northshoreneurofeedback.com

NORTHWOODS WELLNESS PRACTITIONERS GROUP – SERVICES

ANAHATA HEALING TOUCH AND GUNFLINT HERBAL SALVES
Debi Westby provides healing touch sessions and natural healing products, some of which can be found at Birchbark Books and Gifts in Grand Marais.

(218) 387-2799

BARBARA KOUGH, REIKI PRACTITIONER
Barbara offers Reiki, energy activation, and energy interference patterning treatments.

(218) 663-0035

CAMERON NORMAN BODY BALANCE
Cameron teaches meditation, relaxation, tai chi, and offers Reiki, herbal tinctures, and colloidal silver.

(218) 387-9067

HEALING TOUCH
Jeanette Lindgren provides a healing touch for those who need emotional, spiritual, and/or physical balancing.

(218) 387-3113

HERBAL AND ENERGY HEALING
Wendy Michelle Olson offers individual consultations, classes, and workshops and personally prepared herbal formulas.

(218) 663-7009

RAVENWOOD MASSAGE
Lukas Bollinger travels from Beaver Bay to Lutsen to your accommodations to provide 1- to 1½-hour massages, specializing in kripalu bodywork.

  (218) 220-9198 to leave a message

SECOND NATURE – HEALING BODYWORK MASSAGE
Margy Nelson specializes in craniosacral therapy, energy balancing, bodywork dialoging and relaxation massage.

  (218) 387-2597 (summers in Grand Marais); (218) 525-2371 (winters in
    Duluth); (218) 343-7770 (cell)

TRUE NORTH COACHING
Debra Joy Mueller is a personal coach for people and businesses looking for a change in their life and for folks in transition.

  (218) 475-0047 and (612) 789-2255
  hometown.aol.com/truenorthc

Rainy Days

WHERE I LIVE, IT'S 70°, SUNNY, AND THE FISH ARE BITING every day from Memorial Day to Labor Day. If you happen to be up when I'm out of town and it's raining, consider the following options.

IN DULUTH

DULUTH PUBLIC LIBRARY
Books, magazines, multimedia items, and a children's section.
  Between Superior and Michigan Streets on 5th Avenue West

LAKE SUPERIOR ZOOLOGICAL GARDENS
Indoor displays, petting zoo, cafe, and gift shop.
  Grand Avenue and 72nd Avenue West; from I-35, follow the zoo signs.

SKYWALK SYSTEM
Take a walk in inclement weather; kids love it, too.
  Enter from a variety of locations on Superior Street in downtown or at
    the Duluth Entertainment and Convention Center or OMNIMAX.

THE DEPOT
Three museums, the Duluth Art Institute, Duluth Playhouse, the Symphony Orchestra, and regional performing arts center.
  Michigan Street and 5th Avenue West

DEWITT-SEITZ AND CANAL PARK
Shop!
  Canal Park

BARNES & NOBLE
A zillion books, coffee cafe, kids' area, and special events.
    Miller Trunk Highway

MARSHALL W. ALWORTH PLANETARIUM
Look into the night skies all day long. Also enjoy a walk through the university complex and take in the Tweed Museum of Art.
    At the University of Minnesota, Duluth
    (218) 726-7129

OMNIMAX THEATER
Watch something on the big screen.
    Harbor Drive

Buy postcards and send them.

Take your film to a one-hour photo and have it developed.

Go antiquing.

ALONG THE SHORE

STOP AT RUSS KENDALL'S FOR SMOKED FISH
Sample local smoked fish and browse Russ's assortment of antiques.
    Scenic 61, just west of Knife River on the north side of the road

TWO HARBORS LIGHT STATION AND HARBOR MUSEUM
Oldest operating lighthouse on the North Shore.
    On the harbor; take Waterfront to South Avenue, then go west and
        follow signs.

TWO HARBORS PUBLIC LIBRARY
An original Carnegie library.
    6th Street and 4th Avenue

Shop, shop, shop from Duluth to the Canadian border.

GOOSEBERRY FALLS STATE PARK VISITORS CENTER
Beautiful building houses interactive exhibits, displays, a gift shop, naturalist programs, and a stone fireplace.
    Highway 61 about 12 miles northeast of Two Harbors

SPLIT ROCK LIGHTHOUSE HISTORICAL CENTER
Interesting displays and exhibits about the lighthouse, local history, and fishing, plus an informative video about the creation and evolution of the lighthouse.

Off Highway 61 about 20 miles northeast of Two Harbors at Split Rock Lighthouse State Park

SILVER BAY PUBLIC LIBRARY
Off Highway 61 in Silver Bay at 9 Davis Drive

Go out for lattes, cocoa, and biscotti.

NORTH SHORE COMMERCIAL FISHING MUSEUM
The red fish house on the side of the road is a museum filled with local families' personal archives, including photos, nets, floats, boats, and more.

Highway 61 in Tofte

TOFTE AND GUNFLINT RANGER STATIONS
Check out the animal mounts and learn something new about the Superior National Forest.

Highway 61 in Tofte and Grand Marais, respectively

SWIM AT YOUR LODGE'S INDOOR POOL OR AT THE GRAND MARAIS REC AREA
Includes an Olympic-size pool, kids' pool, whirlpool, and sauna.

Off Highway 61 on 8th Avenue West in Grand Marais

GRAND MARAIS PUBLIC LIBRARY
One of my favorite spots in town.

Highway 61 at 2nd Avenue West

Buy a rain jacket and get outside!

Get a deck of cards and play.

Take a Look Around

THERE IS JUST AS MUCH BEAUTY
VISIBLE TO US IN THE LANDSCAPE
AS WE ARE PREPARED TO APPRECIATE –
NOT A GRAIN MORE.

Henry David Thoreau, from his essay "On Seeing"

Of Rocks and Ridges

A GEOLOGY LESSON

WHEN NATURE HAS WORK TO BE DONE,
SHE CREATES A GENIUS TO DO IT.

Ralph Waldo Emerson, *Method of Nature*

G LACIAL GROOVES SCRATCHED INTO WHALEBACKS, PENETRAT-
ing river gorges, stubborn basalt outcrops – this is the genius of the
North Shore. The beauty of the land is striking. Our semirugged
topography climbs to Minnesota's highest peak, Eagle Mountain at 2,301
feet, and plunges to the cold depths 1,333 feet below Lake Superior. This work
in progress began 4,500 million years ago during the early Precambrian age.

You don't need a geology degree to appreciate the view. But as I learn
about this land (with a little help from my husband, who does have a geology degree), it becomes vastly more intriguing. While you drive the shoreline, take a fresh look out the window. It's more than just rocks and ridges.

This area of northeast Minnesota was shaped by differential erosion of
bedrock, which means this territory was generally beneath glacial ice that
was eroding rather than glaciers that were moving and depositing. The pressure caused weak spots in the bedrock to become depressions, many of
which are today's lakes. *Bedrock* is the solid rock underlying superficial
deposits.

Igneous rock is formed by the cooling and recrystallization of molten
magma and either occurs beneath the earth's surface or is extruded as lava.
Basalt and granite are igneous rock. Magma that cools rapidly and is fine-
grained is called *basalt* (found on the North Shore). The coarse-grained
equivalent of basalt is *gabbro* (native to Duluth). *Granite* is magma that

cooled slowly beneath the earth's surface with the attribute of large crystals. Also, granite-forming magma has a very different mineral composition than basalt-forming magma. *Rhyolite* is granitic magma that surfaced as lava and then cooled (as at Palisade Head, Shovel Point, and Grand Marais). But that's enough science – let's look at rocks.

We'll start with the smallest rocks – sand. Minnesota Point (Park Point) evolved about five thousand years ago from drifting sand from the North and South Shores and the mouth of the St. Louis River. One of the largest sandbars in the world, Park Point was key in the formation of the Duluth harbor as a safe inland port. Farther up the Shore, beaches turn to *cobblestone,* which are glacial deposits worn smooth by wind and waves.

You can skip some cobblestones at Lester River. The river formation at Lester and up the Shore was primarily a pervasive erosion in lava flows. View glacial quarrying, widespread erosion, and abrasion-sculpted, blunt-nosed hills called *whalebacks* at Lester River. Whalebacks are ideal for napping in the afternoon sun.

Before we continue up the shoreline, note the Point of Rock, an interesting rock formation on Duluth's hillside. Duluth is essentially basalt flows, which extend northeast up the lakeshore, and gabbroic rocks, which spread southwest. On Mesabi Avenue from Sixth Avenue West to Eighth Avenue West is the Point of Rock, the separation line between the gabbroic rock and basalt flows.

Basalt flows make up the majority of the landscape from Duluth to the Canadian border. However, plate activity and other factors contributed to the more rugged reliefs up north. Specifically, the Sawtooth Mountains were created as the earth's crust was stretched and thinned, causing the midsection to sink (now under Lake Superior). Adjacent portions tilted to the southeast, causing the sawtooth appearance. As the crust thinned, basalt and granitic magma (rhyolite) were extruded over the old flows.

Silver Creek Cliff, the tunnel site a few miles northeast of Two Harbors, is a black, coarse-grained mafic sill. As this sill cooled, joints were formed perpendicular to the cooling surface. Thus, at the wayside rest, adjacent to the old roadbed, you can see the steep, nearly vertical columns. The lava flows under the sill are still visible and appear red, suggesting that the flows were baked by the heat of the magma. Weathering erodes the columns into a tan-colored soil. No need to take a close look at the rocks decorating the tunnel entries – they are fake.

Up the road at Gooseberry, the erosion of three different lava flows formed the various waterfalls and cascades, which drop a total of one hundred feet. At the base of the main falls is a broad rock ledge or bench. An abundance of *amygdules* – gas cavity fillings – some containing agates, dot this particular ledge. Note that a number of amygdules have already weathered out, leaving small cavities. Large-scale erosion is evident on the Shore as well.

In Search of the Agate

Water circulating through gas cavities (amygdules) in rock deposits mineral residues, which build up on each other until the cavities are full. If the main residue left is silica, the finished product is an agate. Agates in situ, or in rock, tend to be white, while those in gravel tend to be the brick orange of the Lake Superior agate. Colorization occurs when trace amounts of iron are oxidized as weather and erosion remove the rock.

Cobblestone beaches are great hunting grounds for agates. I've collected my share of agates at Brighton Beach. You may want to expand your search to Burlington Bay Beach in Two Harbors; Flood Bay State Park; the mouth of Two Island River; Cut Face Creek wayside rest; all along the Grand Marais shoreline; the mouths of Devil's Track, Kadunce, and Brule Rivers; Paradise Beach; and the cobblestone coast of Horseshoe Bay.

In 1998, an agate vein was discovered just north of Thunder Bay. It is one of only three agate mines in the world and houses the largest agate in North and South America. To find out more about the new agate mine, see the chapter on Canada ("Beyond the Border").

Wave action is the major erosion agent at Split Rock, where the lighthouse sits on a 130-foot-high cliff. Peer over the cliff to catch a glimpse of the massive portion of rock that waves have brought down into Lake Superior.

Along Highway 61, development and construction have exposed unique formations to the elements. As the highway has been shaped and reshaped, the Minnesota Department of Transportation has built around and through the intractable rock. Near Silver Bay, a tall road cut stands across from North Shore Mining, the world's first taconite plant (built in the 1950s). The road-cut rock is part of the Beaver Bay Complex, a unique black diabase rock that is between basalt and gabbro in the size of its grain.

Up the road at the intersection of Highway 61 and Minnesota 1, the road cut was made through a rhyolite body. A 270-foot-thick granitic magma flow surfaced and spread over six miles. Rhyolite, the cooled magma, is visible at the road cut and as it reaches into the lake as Shovel Point. From Shovel Point, look back southwest to the 320-foot Palisade Head, highlighted by 216-foot cliffs, part of the same rhyolite flow. Note Palisade's column structure, which is similar to that of Silver Creek Cliff.

In addition to cliffs, the North Shore has its share of extensive gorges. Three nearby rivers notable for their river paths are the Baptism, Manitou, and Temperance. Because the lower Manitou is surrounded by private land, your best options for exploring are at Tettegouche (Baptism River) and Temperance River State Parks. Several hiking trails line the Baptism and Temperance, providing superb views of gouged-out rock, swirling potholes, and terrific gorges. To survey the Manitou River Valley, pull off the highway and look up the river. From this great vantage point you can see how the upper falls cut away at the weak flow top and the underflow occasionally collapsed, forming this ravine. The quarter-mile portion of the Temperance River just north of the highway has the most impressive river gorge on the Shore.

In the Tofte area, you will be driving over the topmost lava flow of the North Shore Volcanic Group. This is the youngest rock around. Inland a short way is Carlton Peak, where 3M quarried anorthosite for use in producing their sandpaper products. A unique feature is the small steam vent, which releases hot vapors from below the earth's surface, located on the hillside of Carlton Peak.

Southwest of Grand Marais, the highway rounds a magnificent corner onto Good Harbor Bay. The road cuts through a 150-foot-thick basalt flow that spreads into Lake Superior. Embedded in this flow is a 120-foot-thick section of black basalt carrying the concentrically banded green, white, and pink stone *thomsonite*. Thomsonite is formed in amygdules and is freed by Lake Superior's wave action. For a close-up view of thomsonite, visit the Thomsonite Beach Museum and Gift Shop. Some shops in Grand Marais also carry the semiprecious stone, which is found only two other places in the world, Scotland and Australia.

Grand Marais's waterfront was etched out as softer flows eroded behind an impervious basalt flow. Shoring up the east side of the harbor is a *tombolo,* a gravel bar connecting the mainland to the island known as Artist Point. Capture a bird's-eye view of the village and harbor by heading a few miles up the Gunflint Trail to the scenic overlook.

The Gunflint Trail holds its own geological wonders and is a worthy side trip. Be sure to travel the complete trail, since the topography changes in the last fifteen miles. You can overlook the Laurentian Divide, where the watershed separates north to Hudson Bay and east out the St. Lawrence Seaway. An aside: the earliest reference to iron ore in Minnesota was by J. G. Norwood referring to the rocks near Flint (Gunflint) Lake, which was named by early explorers for the flint obtained from the rocks of its beaches.

East of Grand Marais, Highway 61 fronts the lake more often. Highlights include Five Mile Rock, the Devil's Kettle about a mile up the Brule River, Horseshoe Bay just outside Hovland, Grand Portage Bay, the sisters – Mount Maud, Mount Josephine, and Mount Rose – Wauswaugoning Bay, and Pigeon River.

Your reward for finishing the drive is a truly spectacular landscape – the invigorating panoramas of Isle Royale and the Susie Islands from Mount Jo. You may even see the tip of Pigeon Point, the easternmost point of Minnesota. Underlying this area are unyielding dikes and sills, which remain as high points, and softer slates, which have eroded and are the lower sections and river paths. The High Falls on the Pigeon River are Minnesota's highest waterfalls and can be accessed at Grand Portage State Park and Middle Falls Provincial Park (across the border).

Well, we're at the end of the road. I hope I've roused a bit of curiosity about the rocks and ridges that are a backdrop for this land and a route for our incredible rivers and waterfalls.

Rivers and Waterfalls

A MASS OF WATER HAS THE ABILITY TO MESMERIZE. A GLINT of water grabs your eye, then slowly ensnares your full attention, leaving you rapt and absorbed. Waves refract sunlight. Rivers pound over basalt ledges. Ponds lay calm in the quiet afternoon.

This territory is inundated with rivers that make fabulous leaps off fir-lined ridges. By virtue of motion, rivers change every moment and every season. Bordered by the slower moving, warm-water St. Louis River to the south and the Pigeon River to the north, the North Shore boasts over two dozen streams and rivers with various degrees of downward slope.

In the 1930 Shipstead-Nolan Act, Congress prohibited the construction of dams or other water-fluctuation structures in St. Louis, Lake, and Cook Counties, thus ensuring that these rivers remain in their natural state. In general, the main stems of these waterways are twenty miles long, with headwaters reaching up to one hundred miles. The average gradient is fifty to one hundred feet per mile, with waterfalls and rapids sections dropping up to three hundred feet per mile.

Along the southwest half of the North Shore, streams tend to be showy. With no headwaters, the rivers swell and pound during spring runoff and heavy rains and run low during dry times. Rivers without headwaters can discharge up to four times as much water as those with headwaters. From the Manitou River northeast, the rivers have headwaters and, thus, a more stable flow. But it's a close call to the best performance during runoff.

Described below are some waterways to explore.

In Duluth, the quiet, warm waters of the **St. Louis River** are conducive to canoeing and fishing for walleye and northern pike. Moving east, you can go tadpole hunting in Chester Park along the shores of **Chester Creek**. The entrance at Skyline Parkway is the mark of the upper beach of Glacial Lake Duluth.

Amity Creek is a feeder stream into **Lester River** and is worth noting for the seven stone bridges that cross it. To see the bridges, built in the 1930s by the Works Progress Administration (W PA), drive up Occidental Avenue on the western side of Lester River or take the Hawk Ridge cutoff from Skyline Parkway. Lester River's original Ojibwe name was *busa-bika-zibi,* meaning "river where water flows through a worn place in the rocks." Lester received her white man name from an original homesteader.

Spanning Lester

In 1893 the first vehicular bridge was built over the Lester River. John Busha, a Civil War veteran of Ojibwe and French parentage, replaced the old bridge in 1898 with a new bridge of Ojibwe design. Built over the rapids, it featured an open well (surrounded by railings) for viewing the gushing water below. The bridge was a popular tourist destination at the turn of the century, but for safety reasons the upper deck was removed in 1916 and the lower deck in 1931. In 1925 the Works Progress Administration (W PA) built the bridge that now spans the river at Superior Street and Sixtieth Avenue East.

Consider taking Scenic 61 rather than Highway 61 to view more streams, their flows into Lake Superior, and some fishing action. The Lester, **French, Sucker,** and **Stewart** (past Two Harbors) **Rivers** all have spring steelhead runs. The Sucker River also has an abundant spring sucker run.

On the northeast side of the Lafayette Bluff tunnel, you will cross **Crow Creek.** See if it is running. It was originally named Prohibition Creek, because it usually ran dry.

Get out of the car at **Gooseberry River.** Two waterfalls are visible from the bridge, and three more are within a short hike. The three lower falls drop more than one hundred feet, and the river path is beautiful. To see Gooseberry in all her glory, visit during spring runoff in April and early May. Gooseberry was named for the French fur trader and explorer Medard Chouart, Sieur des Groseilliers. The English found it too difficult to pronounce his name and called him "Mister Gooseberry."

Up the highway a few miles you will cross the **Split Rock River.** You can access the river at the trailhead in the parking lot on the west side of the river or at an old road turnoff about a quarter-mile east of the river on the lake side. Three miles upstream, the west and east branches of the Split Rock join, beginning a four-hundred-foot tumble over cascades and rapids terminating in a high falls about one mile from the mouth. Named for this split rock canyon, the river spreads into a wide, flat valley before discharging into Lake Superior.

You should also get out of the car at the **Beaver River** at Beaver Bay. Named *ga-gi-ji-ken-si-keg,* or "place of little cedars," by the Ojibwe, the stream and bay are beautiful. The river drops three hundred feet in a series of cascades and falls above the bridge and enters the sedate bay. Highway 61 leads to East Beaver Bay, providing additional panoramas.

The **Baptism River** has the highest falls entirely within Minnesota and can be seen at Tettegouche State Park. From the campground, it is a one-mile hike in to the falls. This superb trout stream descends more than seven hundred feet, including the seventy-foot Baptism Falls and the fifty-foot Illgen Falls farther upstream. To explore the lower reaches and river mouth, stop at the wayside rest, where map platforms describe access points. For more discoveries, you can enter the state park and head upstream.

Palisade Creek pales in comparison to the big rivers, but it originates in a stunning valley in the rocky ridges above Silver Bay. Check the hiking chapter for details on how to get there, and bring a rod and reel – the brook trout can be thick.

From this point north, the rivers have headwaters, typically lakes, streams, and swamps. In addition, the **Caribou** and **Manitou Rivers** have plentiful springwater sources, which, when coupled with relatively stable flows, means excellent trout habitat. You will encounter the Caribou River at the junction of Lake and Cook Counties. This border river begins in the swamps and then cascades and falls to Lake Superior. On the immediate eastern side of the river, there is a small parking area on the northern side of the road. From there you can get to the river and a path that leads about a half-mile up the river to the falls.

The Manitou, Ojibwe for "great magical spirit," features eight major waterfalls; the last one drops almost directly into Lake Superior. Access is limited, but tour or charter boats provide excellent views of the last falls.

Two Island River near Taconite Harbor is named for the two islands, Gull and Bear, opposite the mouth of the river. With lake and swamp headwaters, Two Island descends the last miles into rapids and cascades.

Cross River in Schroeder is a sight to behold. The bridge spans the river almost midfalls, providing an awesome water display, especially in the spring. You'll find ample room to pull over on both sides of the river, which features five major falls in the lower six miles. The Ojibwe called this Tchibaiatigo zibi, "wood of the spirit river," after the wooden cross placed at the river mouth in 1845 by Father Baraga.

In my book, the easiest access to the best river presentation is at **Temperance River**. A mere quarter-mile upstream, the river makes a spectacular last drop into a gorge so narrow you can't always see the bottom. Upstream a few yards more are roaring cascades. Just below Highway 61 is a footbridge showcasing the river's mouth, for which the river was named: Temperance was credited as the only river along the North Shore without a sand "bar" at its mouth (although in some years it actually does have a bar). The headwaters of the Temperance include Brule Lake, which is also a headwater for **Brule River**. Rarely does the same lake serve as a source for two different river systems.

Gamanazadika zibi, "place of poplars," known today as the **Poplar River**, provides water for Superior National at Lutsen and snowmaking at Lutsen Mountains and is restful in the last mile of descent. A few miles inland, however, is a roaring falls followed by canyons and cascades.

You haven't seen cascades until you've seen the **Cascade River**. Ten miles above the mouth the river abruptly falls into the descent to Lake Superior. Dropping nine hundred feet in the lower three miles, the river takes a steep final run in the last quarter-mile as it plunges 120 feet through a deep, churning gorge. Hike both sides of the Cascade River by parking at the river mouth and following the trail signs.

Swamp River enters Devil Track Lake (eight miles northwest of Grand Marais) and at the outlet of the lake becomes **Devil Track River**. The river is slow moving with beaver ponds in its upper stretches, but then enters a barely visible gorge by thunderously leaping over a sheer vertical wall of red rhyolite. Composed almost entirely of shards of rhyolite, the riverbed winds a last mile down to Lake Superior.

The **Kadunce River** in Colvill is a wonderful river hike. The lower reaches have red rhyolite gorges and waterfalls. You can follow the path on the east side of the river or hike right up the river. Wear a pair of rubber-soled shoes and be prepared to get a little wet. At the mouth of the river are a few picnic tables and a great cobblestone beach.

The **Brule River** at Judge Magney State Park and Naniboujou Lodge is the third largest after the St. Louis and Pigeon Rivers. The Brule's most famous feature is the Devil's Kettle. A mile inland are the Lower Falls, then the Upper Falls and the Devil's Kettle, where the river course splits. About half of the river's water flows over the Upper Falls, while the other half enters a cauldron, the Devil's Kettle, and disappears. It is presumed that some of the water goes into an underground waterway and some reappears in a pool in the lower river reaches, but the point of reentry remains unknown.

Reservation River is unique in that it has no waterfalls near the mouth, so lake-run rainbow trout can ascend and spawn almost the entire length of the stream.

Pigeon River was named for the large flocks of now-extinct passenger pigeons that once called the river home. A continental divide between North and South Lakes divides the watershed of Lake Superior and Hudson Bay. From the divide, the Pigeon drops 950 feet; the fifty-foot Partridge Falls are a precursor of the lower twenty miles of cascades and falls that end with the 120-foot drop at Pigeon Falls (High Falls). This lower reach is particularly rugged until a short distance after the falls, where the river widens. An easy half-mile trail in Grand Portage State Park leads to the High Falls. The trail end has two great viewing decks where you can feel the spray of the falls!

As the international boundary, the Pigeon River also had a part in American history. In 1783 the Treaty of Paris between Canada and the United States set up an international boundary along the usual waterway line. But that line varied with time and was still debated after the War of 1812 when the Treaty of Ghent included provisions for a further look at the border. In the 1820s a British and American survey party set to the task and came up with three options: the St. Louis River (the British choice), the Kaministikwia (the American choice), and the Pigeon River as an alternative. The Pigeon River was settled on as a compromise in 1842 when the British determined that the wilderness area between the St. Louis and Pigeon Rivers was of little value.

Getting to Know Flora

PLANTS AND BERRIES

I WILL MAKE A PALACE
FIT FOR YOU AND ME
OF GREEN DAYS IN FORESTS
AND BLUE DAYS AT SEA.

Robert Louis Stevenson, in a poem to S. R. Crockett

DOUBTLESS GOD COULD HAVE MADE
A BETTER BERRY, BUT DOUBTLESS
GOD NEVER DID.

Izaak Walton, *The Compleat Angler,* referring
to a wild strawberry

I KNOW IT IS A BIT TRITE, BUT YOU REALLY SHOULD TAKE TIME TO smell the flowers, or at least look at them. When you're out hiking on the Shore, often your eyes are drawn to the magnificent views of river gorges, waterfalls, and Lake Superior. Next time you're out, look down. The shaded habitat of wooded river edges favors wonderful little flowers like trillium, columbine, and dewberry plants.

Heck, if you don't want to hike, just look out the window as you drive up Highway 61. Marsh marigolds fill spring ditches with masses of yellow heads, while lovely bluebells sway in the growing grass along ditch edges. Throughout summer, contrasting daisies and black-eyed Susans; orange and black paintbrushes; tall, willowy, hot pink fireweed; and lavender lupine are everywhere.

Unique or infrequently seen wildflowers grow in mini-tundra ecosystems found in places along the North Shore. One such area is the Butterwort Cliffs along Lake Superior a few miles northeast of, but within, Cascade River State Park. A variety of colorful lichen and rare arctic-alpine plants grow here, including Hudson Bay eyebright and butterwort. Butterwort is a small, carnivorous plant typically found closer to Hudson Bay and north. It grows in fragile mats with sticky yellow-green leaves. Another carnivorous flower is the northern pitcher plant, found in swampy areas and where shallow creeks join lakes. The pitcher plant looks a bit like a muted red lady's slipper. The lady's slipper itself, Minnesota's state flower, can sometimes be seen in openings in wooded areas, where you may also spot wild lilies and orchids.

The absolute best way to familiarize yourself with northland flora is to borrow or buy a guide to North American trees and plants. I recommend either *The Audubon Society Field Guide to North American Wildflowers, Eastern Region,* or *A Field Guide to Wildflowers of Northeastern and North-Central America* by Roger Tory Peterson and Margaret McKenny. Both books categorize plants by color and provide either color photos or drawings of the plant along with the descriptions.

The guides will also confirm fruit and berry types. The most common

edible berries in the north woods are blueberries, raspberries, strawberries, and highbush cranberries. Blueberries grow in swamps and rocky upland forests. They flower in May or June and produce fruit from late June through August. Wild strawberry habitats are at dry edges of woods and in open fields. Runners full of small, white flowers produce the most succulent, tiny berries from June into July. Thickets of raspberries grow wild in cutover areas. These thorny bushes produce juicy red fruit from late June through August. If, when raspberry picking, you come across what appears to be a mammoth, softer raspberry with less distinct lobes, you've discovered thimbleberries, which are edible, just not as tasty. Highbush cranberries grow in clusters on bushes overhanging lakeshores and in bogs and swamps. A bit acidic, the cranberries are often picked from late August into September. Check at the U.S. Forest Service to find out which berries are ripe and where to look for them.

The Forest Service manages all federal lands along the North Shore, and the rangers have information on wooded areas they are planning to harvest, second-growth areas, and uses for timber. The Stora Enso Duluth Paper Mill offers free tours on Monday, Wednesday, and Friday throughout the summer; admission is free, but you must be more than ten years old. Reservations are required and can be obtained by calling (218) 722-6024. Hedstrom's Mill on the Gunflint Trail also gives fascinating tours of their sawmill operations all summer long. Call for tour times at (218) 387-2995.

Most of the logging along the Shore is boreal, or northern, woodland trees. They include spruce, a variety of pine, cedar, quaking aspen or poplar, and paper birch trees. The hardwood forests to the south include sugar maple, elm, northern red oak, and yellow birch. Over thousands of years the hardwoods have spread north, regenerating burned and cutover areas. Someday the North Shore will primarily be hardwoods. The new habitat will mean a change in where the wild things are.

Where the Wild Things Are

ANIMALS AND BIRDS

... AND HE SAILED OFF THROUGH NIGHT
AND DAY AND IN AND OUT OF WEEKS
AND ALMOST OVER A YEAR TO WHERE
THE WILD THINGS ARE.

Maurice Sendak, *Where the Wild Things Are*

... AWKWARD LOOKING ANIMALS,
WITH LONG LEGS AND SHORT BODIES,
MAKING A LUDICROUS FIGURE WHEN IN
FULL RUN, BUT MAKING GREAT HEADWAY
NEVERTHELESS.

Henry David Thoreau, *Ktaadn*, referring to moose

OUR NORTH WOODS ARE ONE OF THE LAST TIMBER WOLF habitats in the lower forty-eight states. Moose, river otters, pine martens, boreal chickadees, goshawks, and ruffed grouse call our backyard home. Scattered with lakes, the forest is hardwood to the south, boreal to the north, and transition where the two meet.

Lots of folks hope to chance upon a critter, but you can increase your opportunity for sightings by considering a few points. First, look in the right place at the right time, keeping the season in mind. For instance, look for white-tailed deer yarded up midday in clearings during winter when snows are deep. Second, become aware of signs and learn to read them. Winter is an ideal time to learn animal tracking. Third, be patient and bring field glasses. The thick foliage and bounty of summer make wildlife sightings tougher. Consider spring and fall, when migration, courtship rituals, and feasting mean high activity levels.

If you have questions or need additional information, stop by a Forest Service ranger station. Wildlife is their business. At the Tofte ranger station, you can study mounts of a timber wolf, bald eagle, osprey, goshawk, peregrine falcon, merlin, and six owls – the great horned, saw-whet, boreal, snowy, long-eared, and great gray. Up the road at the Gunflint station are mounts of a white-tailed deer, ermine, fisher, timber wolf, Canadian lynx, porcupine, pine marten, weasel, blue heron, bald eagle, loon, peregrine falcon, ruffed grouse, and great horned, great gray, boreal, snowy, and barred owls. Several resorts also have mounts on display. I believe Buck's Hardware Hank and Conoco station in Grand Marais has the finest bull moose mount around. Buck also has a beaver and moose calf on display. The mounts at the U.S. Forest Service and Buck's are from animals taken illegally, and the unborn moose calf was taken from a cow moose killed by a car.

A few final suggestions: wear a blaze orange cap or jacket in the woods from September 1 through the end of the year, since several hunting seasons are open at this time. Stay at least fifty feet from wild animals. They are wild.

Hundreds of species of animals, birds, amphibians, and reptiles are found along the North Shore; here I comment on those folks most want to see or those considered unique to the area.

MAMMALS
Moose (*Alces alces*) thrive in regrowth forests that have been devastated by pest infestation, fire, beavers, or logging. These areas provide some of the fifty-plus pounds of browse moose eat per day. Moose feed mainly on broadleaf shoots of quaking aspen, paper birch, sugar maple, and mountain ash at dawn and dusk, although they will feed all day. To fulfill their sodium requirement, they seek aquatic plants in the summer and lick the salt off roads in the winter.

Drive backcountry roads at dawn and dusk in spring through fall. In summer, look carefully in swamps or lake inlets and outlets where water is shallow. Moose escape to water to avoid bugs, cool down, and feed. You will be amazed at how quickly a moose can swim! Seek out second-growth areas that have been cleared for pulpwood. These animals are not aggressive except during the fall rut or if you come between a cow and her calf or calves (twins are prevalent).

Adult bulls average eight to nine hundred pounds, with horns coming in each spring. Only after the third year do the horns become palmated. They reach full size in the fifth year and begin to decrease in size after the tenth year. Moose lose their horns in December to January. All mature moose have a shoulder hump and a bell, or dewlap, hanging from their throat. All immature moose slouch and wear baggy trousers.

The **white-tailed deer** (*Odocoileus virginianus*) habitat is similar to moose habitat in that both animals need access to young, leaf-bearing saplings typically associated with second-growth or regrowth areas. Whitetails eat six to eight pounds of leaves, bark, twigs, roots, and grasses per day. To avoid deep snow, deer yard up in clearings near lakes surrounded by young aspen and shrubs or white cedar swamps. They stamp out openings and trails to food supplies. In the spring, whitetails move to south-facing hillsides that quickly lose their snow and supply the first green food of the season. Summer through autumn, deer move back into the woods where food is plentiful and dangers are fewer. Male deer drop their antlers from December through March. To go antler hunting, look in winter yards and related trails as soon as the snow melts. Calcium-rich deer antlers and moose horns are terrific food sources for small rodents.

In Minnesota, the **black bear** (*Ursus americanus*) is found almost exclusively in the Arrowhead region, where it is quite prevalent. These omnivores feed primarily on a vegetarian diet of berries, nuts, and aspen catkins and buds, but are notorious for rummaging through garbage. Black bears will also eat insects, larvae, and carrion. Females fiercely defend their territory, about four square miles, whereas males roam over a ten-square-mile area and don't mind sharing their domain with other males. Bears den up in hollows in trees, rocks, brush piles, and hillsides, and in the nook between a fallen tree and its upturned roots.

Prime bear habitat is midsize to large forest clearings that allow enough sun penetration for berry thickets to grow. Like deer, bears establish trails from their dens to food and water sources. Hibernation commences in October and can last for seven months. Females give birth in January to cubs that are subsequently nursed in between massive naps. The sow often gives birth without coming out of hibernation (and they say we are at the top of the evolution heap). In the spring, bears start the task of regaining lost weight and feed most actively at dusk. As summer food supplies peak, bears eat throughout the day, and in the final fall gorge, they eat day and night. If bears are in human territory, they avoid conflict by eating from dusk to dawn.

The dog family is well represented in the north woods by the red fox (*Vulpes vulpes*), gray fox (*Urocyon cinereoargenteus*), coyote or brush wolf (*Canis latrans*), and timber wolf (*Canis lupus*). The **gray fox** is slightly smaller than the **red fox** and is the only member of the dog family that will climb trees. Foxes have many color phases, making it difficult to distinguish between the two. Both live in a mixed habitat of field and forest and feed on rodents, small birds, amphibians, and some vegetation. They are often sighted at the edges of woods. Listen for their howling after dark. Foxes and wolves alike are crepuscular; that is, active at twilight and dawn.

A **coyote** looks like a small, sinewy German shepherd with gray-brown, coarse fur and an excessive bushy tail that it holds low when traveling. Habitat is the same as for foxes, but with larger ranges. Coyotes are scavengers. Feeding habits vary with availability. They prefer deer kill, snowshoe hares, and rodents but will eat anything to survive. Coyotes avoid wolf territory.

Timber wolves den under low rock ledges and brush piles and in holes dug into the ground. Traveling in packs of five to eight, wolves can cover several hundred square miles, depending on the availability of prey. Pack control is established by a dominant pair and established caste system. Wolves communicate via unparalleled howling. Listen for wolves howling at night throughout summer and during January and February mating. Wolves choose easy travel routes, similar to humans. In the winter, they avoid deep snow and move along packed edges of woods and lakeshores. One of my most memorable observations was watching three timber wolves travel along Lake Superior's frozen edge under a near-full moon. Look for wolves along roadsides, trails, and ridgetops. Many sightings are at night. Isle Royale wolf populations range from twelve to fifty.

Beavers (*Castor canadensis*) are also primarily nocturnal and are quite precise in their twilight departure to feed. Look in ponds and streams surrounded by dense birch and aspen forests. Beavers feed almost exclusively on the twigs, bark, and leaves of birch and aspen. Throughout autumn, they are busy as beavers transporting aspen branches to a winter cache near their lodge. Beavers remain active in their lodges during winter. It is a fallacy that beavers fell trees in a specific direction. Rather, they usually choose easy-access shoreline trees that lean naturally or have more branches on the lake side and thus fall into the lake. Beavers are infrequently killed when they drop trees on themselves.

What do they do with the felled trees? They build beaver dams – which back up a water supply and create a pond – and lodges, or homes. Both structures are multiple layers of sticks and mud. Lodges are built to size atop islets or banks. As many as nine beavers live together communally as a colony. Dam building and size are random. Dams range from two to ten feet high and have measured up to two thousand feet long. Beavers are persistent critters.

The **river otter** (*Lutra canadensis*) is intriguing to observe. Otter habitat is in and along rivers and lake edges where crayfish, frogs, turtles, fish, and insects are abundant. Streamlined bodies, webbed feet, and high-capacity lungs enhance their swimming abilities. For sheer speed, a river otter undulates its body, using its tail as a rudder. Watch for belly sliding on shore and a small, dark brown head and nose creating a V-shaped ripple across the water. These social animals play and feed from daybreak to midmorning and in the evening.

The **woodland caribou** (*Rangifer tarandus*) has a bit of mystique to it in this neck of the woods. Caribou are almost never spotted today, although they were once native to northeastern Minnesota, and a caribou hunting season was in effect as late as 1906. It is said a few still live in the woods and meadows behind Hovland. Caribou have been sighted in outlying areas around Thunder Bay, and a herd lives near Armstrong, Ontario, north of Thunder Bay. Caribou are arctic deer, and they look like large mule deer or small elk. Their trademark antlers swoop down to a pair of small palmated antlers over their eyes and muzzle. Both sexes can grow antlers. Caribou are often on the move in search of lichen, their major food source, and to avoid blackflies. Reindeer are domesticated caribou. Eurasian cultures do not even use the word "caribou," but identify them as either wild or tame reindeer.

BIRDS

Birds, on the other hand, are easy to spot, but can be hard to identify. More than two hundred native species reside from Duluth up the North Shore. Some rare and unusual birds can be seen on the highly traveled Lake Superior migration route. Several bird watching groups choose the North Shore as a field trip destination for this reason and for the opportunity to observe birds of the boreal forests. I recommend bringing field glasses and a guidebook (consider the National Audubon Society's *Field Guide to North American Birds,* the Roger Tory Peterson *Field Guide to the Birds of Eastern and Central North America,* and the National Geographic Society's *Field Guide to the Birds of North America*).

Minnesota's state bird, the **common loon**, can be observed nesting on inland lakes, while nonbreeders linger along Superior's shores. Listen for their distinctive yodeling cry. A less common sighting is the **double-crested cormorant** with its matching white tufts curving back above and behind its eyes. These large, dark waterbirds have set-back legs, long necks, and hooked orange bills. They are found on rocky beaches and inland lakes. The long-legged, long-necked **great blue heron** flies with a slow, methodical wing beat. Look for this wading bird nesting in summer in marshes, ponds, and lakes and migrating in spring and fall along the big lake.

Canada geese and **snow geese** also migrate in spring and fall along Superior, and many Canada geese have marked Grand Marais as their summer breeding destination. Listen for the honk and watch for the uneven V typical of geese traveling across the sky. Did you ever wonder why one side of the V was longer? It's because there are more birds on that side.

A variety of ducks pass over this area during migration. The most uncommon are the stocky, short-necked diving sea ducks. **Black, white-winged,** and **surf scoters** can be seen in October. **Old squaws** can be observed during winter months in the Grand Marais harbor and at the Duluth Port Terminal.

Familiar puddle ducks, those that feed by tipping tail-up and that spring into flight, are the **mallard** and **black duck**, which spend summers and winters on Lake Superior. **American widgeons** and **northern pintails** can also be seen winters on Superior.

Those not familiar with **wood ducks** will be pleased by the sight of the male's colorful plumage. Look for this perching duck in tree cavities or nest boxes.

Ring-necked ducks nest on inland lakes in the summer. As is typical for pochards, their legs are set far back and wide apart, which makes for good diving, but tough walking. Watch ringnecks take their running start across the water before takeoff.

Mergansers fly fast and low in single file over the water. Their narrow, serrated bills are adept at catching fish. Male **hooded mergansers** are distinguished by their slicked-back, white-streaked, black crowns. Hooded and **common mergansers** nest inland, but migrate along the Shore. **Red-breasted mergansers** have a less prominent crown and can be seen during the smelt run along Superior's stream mouths.

Shorebirds are occasionally sighted in spring on Park Point in Duluth, and the July to August migration turns up flocks of **semipalmated, black-bellied,** and **golden plovers** and **Baird's sandpiper**. Great and **lesser yellowlegs** and **whimbrels** migrate through, too.

Herring gulls are permanent residents, but **glaucous, ring-billed,** and

Bonaparte's gulls migrate through in winter. Look for **Caspian terns** among gulls in May along Park Point in Duluth. The term "seagulls" is a misnomer.

An impressive group of large birds nest in summer near inland lakes. At two feet tall with a six-foot wingspan, the **turkey vulture** is second in size to the bald eagle and resembles it in flight. The vulture is characterized in flight by its red, featherless, low-held head and dihedral (slight V) wing formation. With weak talons, this scavenger feeds on carrion, refuse, and small animals.

A true bird of prey, the stunning **bald eagle** uses its hooked bill and powerful talons to snatch and devour its prey. Bald eagles stand up to three feet tall, with wingspans of more than seven feet. Immature bald eagles are often mistaken for **golden eagles**, which are the size of turkey vultures and have an amber head and neck. Eagles build massive nests in very tall pines. Watch for them soaring on thermals, in autumn at Hawk Ridge, and before the snow and ice melt in spring. We have seen an eagle on Christmas Day for several years.

Lake Superior and northwest winds funnel migrating hawks past Hawk Ridge every fall. In mid-September, thousands of **broad-winged, red-tailed,** and **rough-legged hawks** ride the thermals over this popular viewing bluff. **Sharp-shinned hawks, Cooper's hawks,** and **goshawks** pass through in mid-October. Each fall, **merlins** and **American kestrels** follow a route that parallels Park Point. Both these birds are spring nesters on balsam or spruce crowns. The largest of all hawks, the **osprey,** builds large nests along inland lakeshores. This fish hawk has wings that bend back like those of a herring gull and makes terrific headfirst dives for fish, switching to feetfirst just before reaching the water surface. Ospreys stand two feet tall and have a five- to six-foot wingspan.

Somewhere between mid-September and October, viewers can expect a rare **peregrine falcon** to pass over Hawk Ridge. **Gyrfalcons** prey on pigeons from December through February at the Duluth Port Terminal. Female gyrfalcons are the hunters; they are larger than the males, with tremendously powerful wings.

Six different owls can be observed in our area. The small **boreal** and **saw-whet owls** migrate from mid-April into May and nest in summer and winter along Lake Superior. In the late fall, **great gray, long-eared,** and **snowy owls** migrate down the shore, and many overwinter at the Duluth Port Terminal. **Barred owls** are permanent residents in the upland woods. Listen for their rhythmic hoot, "Who cooks for you?"

Ruffed and **spruce grouse** are native to boreal forests and sought after by birders from other areas. Watch for them along logging roads and pine thickets in early spring and from July to November. See the hunting chapter for additional comments.

The largest populations of pigeons and doves are found in the Duluth area; dense clusters live at the Duluth Port Terminal. Millie Croft and I spotted a rare **band-tailed pigeon** April 29, 1994, east of Grand Marais at Millie's home. The last recorded sighting was in the fall of 1982 along Hawk Ridge.

The loopy flying pattern of woodpeckers is accentuated by the size of the prehistoric-looking, red-capped **pileated woodpecker**. Pileated, **downy,** and **hairy woodpeckers** are permanent residents. The most common is the downy woodpecker, seen summers and winters pecking at birch and poplar trees. The **black-backed three-toed** and **rare northern three-toed woodpeckers** can be seen in conifer forests and along Superior in the fall.

The **olive-sided flycatcher** is a summer nester in boreal habitats. Visiting birders seek this bird with its "quick three beers" song.

Gray and **blue jays** are especially popular with touring birders. These permanent residents are joined by the **common crow** and the **common raven.** Ravens are the larger of the two and have a higher, angled, Neanderthal-looking forehead. In flight, crows display their squared-off tail and ravens their wedge-shaped tail.

The best way to view some migrant birds is to find a local bird feeder. Visiting and winter migrant birds include the **Bohemian** and **cedar waxwing, Lapland larkspur, snow bunting, pine siskin, pine grosbeak, common redpoll, purple finch, horned lark, water pipet,** and **Harris, white-crowned, fox,** and **chipping sparrows.**

Summer nesters that live off feeders and an ample food supply include **thrushes, robins, vireos, warblers, blackbirds, orioles** and **tanagers, rose-breasted** and **evening grosbeaks, goldfinches, flycatchers, swallows** and **purple martins, whippoorwills, ruby-throated hummingbirds, belted kingfishers, snipes, woodcocks** and **nighthawks, sapsuckers,** and **juncos. Jaegers** can be sighted in the late summer into fall along Superior. The first time I heard the repetitive call of the whippoorwill, I started looking for an irritating electric alarm clock. Familiar and sought-after permanent songbirds include **black-capped** and **boreal chickadees** and **nuthatches.**

Oh, Heavens!

CELESTIAL PHENOMENA

THE COLDEST WINTER I EVER SPENT
WAS A SUMMER IN DULUTH.

Mark Twain

WHO BUT GOD CAN CONCEIVE
SUCH INFINITE SCENES OF GLORY?
WHO BUT GOD COULD EXECUTE THEM,
PAINTING THE HEAVENS IN SUCH
GORGEOUS DISPLAY?

Polar explorer and author Charles F. Hall,
referring to the aurora borealis

WEATHER IS A GREAT TOPIC OF DISCUSSION ON THE SHORE. People often ask if you have heard the forecast. But forecasts are only given for Duluth and Thunder Bay. So if you are farther up the Shore, you start making your own weather predictions based on whether you think the front will get this far east; whether you are going to be near the lake, within a few miles of the lake, or over the ridge; and what your personal plans are for the day. Then you make a wild guess. And after a while you totally quit watching the weather forecast and just look out the window. When you look, you begin to see the ever changing skies manifest some awesome celestial phenomena.

83

The atmosphere is a composite of gases, mostly nitrogen and oxygen with a very small amount of trace gases. Interaction of these gases with foreign particles (dust and debris) creates weather conditions.

In 1803 Luke Howard, an English pharmacist and amateur naturalist, named eight types of clouds and grouped them into three categories. Using Latin, he classified cumulus, meaning "heap" or "pile"; cirrus, or "curl"; and stratus, "stretched-out" clouds.

The nature of precipitation released from these clouds is determined by ground and air temperatures. If both are above freezing, we get rain, and as the temps drop, wet snow. When both are below freezing, clouds produce freezing rain, and as it turns colder, sleet, and finally dry snow. Snowfalls are heaviest when temperatures are just below freezing, since colder air holds less moisture.

The North Shore area receives more snow than anywhere else in Minnesota because of lake-effect snow. Lake-effect snow occurs as clouds collect the moisture that is continually evaporating from the lake. When the clouds move over the colder ground, they release massive amounts of snow. The North Shore receives on average one hundred inches of snow each winter.

Another lake effect is the varying temperatures on the shoreline, up the hillside, and over the ridge. In winter, the lake, which rarely freezes in its entirety, acts as a big warm-water bottle emitting balmy air in the mid-40° range. These above-freezing air temps warm the shoreline and the area edged in by the ridgeline. The opposite occurs the rest of the year. Then we get the effect of standing near an open refrigerator. The nice thing is you can always cool off by going closer to the lake or enjoy the heat of summer by driving away from the lake over the hilltops. After dark, drive away from the lake and the lights of the cities and towns. Spread out a blanket, lie down, and really look at the night sky.

One of the biggest pleasures you can receive is a showing of the northern lights. Shafts of luminescent green light dance across the sky. Fans of pink glow for hours. Vibrant, pulsating white wands illuminate the night heavens. This is the aurora borealis (auroras seen in the Southern Hemisphere are known as aurora australis).

Scientifically, auroras are created as gases on the sun's surface release protons and electrons into space. Disturbances ranging from mild eruptions to violent storms emit masses of these atomic particles. In their approach to earth, they become ensnared in the earth's magnetic field and are attracted to the north and south magnetic poles. The interaction of molecules and the release of different gases in the upper atmosphere generate the different

colors of the lights. For instance, the release of oxygen creates a green light. Auroras cannot be forecast, but they are known to arise when sunspot activity peaks.

Scientists offer no explanation for the swishing, hissing, howling, and crackling sounds so many aurora observers report hearing. Eskimo legend tells that the sounds are from the spirits of the aurora. Some believe the noises are the spirits of children who died at birth, now dancing in their celestial home. I like the legend that says auroras are the souls of the dead heading to heaven. Other groups are divided between those who claim the northern lights are spirits of the dead playing ball with a walrus head, and those who say they are walrus spirits playing with a human skull. Hmmm …

A more consistent evening display is the Milky Way. Our entire solar system sits minutely amid the Milky Way Galaxy. This massive spiraling star formation has a dense nucleus and thin surrounding disk. When we see the hazy band of light bending across the night sky, we are looking out at the Milky Way, the most compact part of our galaxy. The Milky Way arches across the sky throughout the year but is brightest in the summer and is most easily seen on moonless nights away from obstructing lights. Locate the misty band in the southeast summer sky. Use binoculars to focus in on the stunning mass of shimmering stars.

In the southeast sky, you can also spot the large Summer Triangle. The brightest star, Vega, is directly overhead from July through September. Vega is at the intersection of a 90-degree angle. Directly below Vega is Altair, and to the east of Vega is the third corner star, Deneb. Deneb also acts as the uppermost star in the Northern Cross, or Cygnus, constellation. Made up of five stars, it looks like a Christian cross lying on its left side at a slight upward angle.

The highly recognizable Big Dipper isn't a true constellation, but a modern name for the seven brightest stars of Ursa Major, the Great Bear constellation. Visible in the northern sky, the Big Dipper has a three-star handle attached to a four-star cup. It rotates around the North Star, Polaris, each year. From July through September, the Dipper hangs from its handle, facing east, in the northwestern sky. In autumn, it sits low in the sky in a horizontal position, with the handle to the west and the cup facing north. The Dipper begins a winter ascent into the northeast sky, facing west with the cup above and handle underneath. In April through June it sits high in the sky in an upside-down horizontal position.

Autumn skies are highlighted by the Cassiopeia constellation, a five-star grouping that looks like a W. Locate the third star down the handle of the Big Dipper. With your eyes, draw a line through Polaris and continue eastward to the bright middle star of the W. The three stars making up the right V are brighter.

Orion, the hunter, is an indicator to the winter sky. Look into the southern sky for a vertical rectangle. A star marks each corner, the upper two being the hunter's shoulders and the lower two, his knees. Three close-set, smaller bright stars form the hunter's belt in an upward westerly diagonal. Orion's east shoulder is the reddish-hued star Betelgeuse. Leading directly upward from the middle star in Orion's belt is the magnificent glittering star Capella. Placed just below the belt is the Orion Nebula, a blurry cloud of gas and dust that is partially collapsing within itself to form new stars. By using binoculars, you may be able to gaze upon one of the Nebula's newest creations in a galaxy that is billions and billions of years old.

Fall Colors and Suggested Tours

A UTUMN ON THE NORTH SHORE COMES EARLY, STAYS LATE, and leaves lasting impressions. Colors start with a leaf, a streak of red, or an occasional tree, isolated and orange. This is the season of the maple in the valleys behind the headlands rising out of Superior. From the ridgelines, colors wash down the hillsides, surrounding deep green-black stands of pine. The colors peak between the first week in September and mid-October.

As the maples fade and Lake Superior begins to cool, autumn comes to the lakeshore. A second fall color season occurs from the last week of September through late October. Lake Superior's cooling effect retards the metabolic rate of the coastal trees. Yellow stains the treetops, creating a canopy over the birch and aspen, and the tamaracks shed golden needles amid the leaf litter. Flaming underbrush makes guest appearances in the company of brown grasses.

As the colors subside, Superior rages, smashing steel blue waves against craggy basalt shorelines. Hugging the coast, 1,000-foot oreboats take heed of waves that can exceed 20 feet. November is the best month to watch the big lake.

Why Leaves Change Color

Leaves change color because of a change in the amount of chlorophyll present. In spring and summer, trees manufacture chlorophyll in such abundance that the ever present red, yellow, and blue pigments are concealed. With cooler temperatures and fewer hours of sunlight, trees quit producing chlorophyll, and the other pigments become conspicuous. Each tree species has a specific blend of pigments, thus the different leaf colors.

Venture out by foot, by car, by mountain bike, or by boat. The choice is yours, and the rewards are spectacular. Remember that the maple colors cannot typically be seen from the lakeshore; they require the warmer, inland temperatures of valleys and south-facing secondary hillsides. For better photos, travel west in the morning and east in the afternoon. Plan on layering clothes, since morning temps may dip into the upper 30s or 40s, with afternoon highs reaching the 60s. Traditionally, this is a dry season, but bring a raincoat and don't let a few sprinkles stop your plans. Some of the most breathtaking autumn days are those with a light mist.

Since most of Duluth is spread across the hillside and atop the ridge, the city's walks and drives showcase the slightly more subdued second season of colors. The situation is similar along the North Shore, except for the vast network of county and Forest Service roads that cover the unpopulated valleys behind the Sawtooth Ridge. Thus, the best area to view the maple colors is inland along the North Shore. Autumn is an exceptional time for being out of doors, with warm late-summer days, crisp nights, and bugs that have disappeared for the season. Listed below are suggested fall color tours. Refer to the hiking chapter ("Out Walkin'") for more information on suggested walking trails.

FALL COLOR TOURS IN DULUTH

SKYLINE PARKWAY
Duluth's signature boulevard, Skyline Parkway, crests a ridge 600 feet above Superior's shore from Spirit Mountain to Hawk Ridge. A scenic drive any time of the year, this boulevard affords views of urban fall colors. Follow the signs past Enger Tower, the College of St. Scholastica, and the University of Minnesota to Seven Bridges Road at Hawk Ridge for the final descent to the mouth of the Lester River.

From I-35, take exit 249 and head east.

MISSION CREEK TRAIL
This West Duluth hiking and walking trail features stands of hardwood, especially on the eastern side of the creek.

From I-35, take Grand Avenue west to 131st Avenue West to Fond du Lac park on the right.

PARK POINT BEACH

Walk the deserted beaches toward the city for all-encompassing views of the Duluth hillside. Best during the late fall season.

> From I-35, go south on Lake Avenue, cross the Aerial Lift Bridge, and drive to either 12th Street or 45th Street to parking areas.

CHESTER BOWL

Drive to the back of the park and hike the cross-country ski trails that circle a portion of the bowl. The park is a lovely picnic spot, too.

> From I-35, go north on Mesaba Avenue, then east on Skyline Parkway to the park entrance.

CONGDON TRAIL

This easy walking trail lets you explore autumn under the forested canopy along Tischer Creek. Best during the late fall season.

> From I-35, take the 21st Avenue East exit north to Superior Street, then head east past Hawthorne Road to the park road on the creek's west side.

FALL COLOR TOURS ALONG THE NORTH SHORE

TWO HARBORS TO BEAVER BAY DRIVE

Climbing up away from the lake, the road explores the backcountry, crossing more than a dozen rivers. Northern hardwood forests of oak, maple, and basswood give way to boreal forests of pine, spruce, and cedar and regrowth areas of aspen, birch, and spruce. The drive is 30 miles, plus 24 miles to return to Two Harbors along Highway 61.

> From Highway 61 northwest of Two Harbors, head north on Co. Rd. 3 for 28 miles to the Lax Lake Road (Co. Rd. 4), then go south on Co. Rd. 4 for 2 miles to Beaver Bay; this triangular route uses Highway 61 as the third, returning leg; to continue on, see the listing below for the Beaver Bay to Illgen City drive.

SCENIC FOREST HIGHWAY 11

Grab a picnic and go for a fall drive!

> From Highway 61 in Two Harbors, drive north on Co. Rd. 2 about 25 miles to Forest Highway 11, drive southeast on Forest Highway 11

about 25 miles to Silver Bay, and return on Highway 61 to Two Harbors (about 27 miles).

SUPERIOR HIKING TRAIL FROM CASTLE DANGER TO GOOSEBERRY FALLS

A great "two-car" hike. Leave one car at Gooseberry Falls for this stunning 8.5-mile hike, and take one to the trailhead. Highlights include overlooks at Wolf Rock, Crow Creek Valley, and Mike's Rock. The upper reach area of the Gooseberry River is particularly gorgeous. The round-trip hike to the Crow Creek Overlook and back is 2.5 miles.

From Highway 61 just past mile marker 36, go north on Co. Rd. 106 (near the Rustic Inn), which turns into Silver Creek 617, to parking on the right.

GOOSEBERRY FIFTH FALLS TRAIL

Winding up the east bank of the Gooseberry River, this 1.5-mile loop passes the Lower and Upper Falls as it leads to the Fifth Falls. Not as spectacular as farther inland, but an enjoyable autumn stroll with great vistas. Best during the late fall season.

From Highway 61, head south into the state park visitors center.

BEAVER BAY TO ILLGEN CITY DRIVE OR LITTLE MARAIS

Backcountry terrain similar to that seen on the route from Two Harbors to Beaver Bay. Watch for deer and moose on this narrow, winding road. A good picnic spot is along Lax Lake, about seven miles into the tour. As an option, head north on Minnesota 1 to Isabella or Ely. The drive is 16 miles, plus 7 miles to return to Beaver Bay along Highway 61.

From Highway 61, drive north on the Lax Lake Road (Co. Rd. 4) to Minnesota 1, then south on Minnesota 1 back to Highway 61. Or, at Minnesota 1, go north to Finland and return to Highway 61 on Co. Rd. 6 to Little Marais.

SPLIT ROCK RIVER LOOP

The upstream portion of this superb trail sits 50 feet above the river along a rocky ledge. On the downstream, eastern leg, you will be treated to overlooks of the river valley, and as you head inland, you can look out to Lake Superior. Best during the late fall season.

Highway 61 about 15 miles northeast of Two Harbors; watch for parking on the west side of the river.

SECTION 13

Hike through boreal forests before climbing maple ridges that showcase magnificent fall colors and imposing sheer rock outcrops. The trail is 4.5 miles round-trip.

From Highway 61 at Little Marais, drive north on Co. Rd. 6 for two miles to the Superior Hiking Trail sign and parking.

HEARTBREAK RIDGE

Make this fall color tour number one on your list. It is breathtaking. The short drive is one of the prettiest maple-canopied drives along Minnesota's North Shore. A roadside plaque explains how Heartbreak Ridge was named. Best during the early fall season.

From Highway 61, head north on the Temperance River Road (Forest Rd. 343), then east on Forest Rd. 166 and south on the Sawbill Trail (Co. Rd. 2); Heartbreak Ridge is on Forest Rd. 166.

CARLTON PEAK

Massive blocks of resistant gray anorthosite form Carlton Peak. This heady peak gives bird's-eye views of the maple forests you crossed to reach the summit. A nearby overlook has panoramas of Lake Superior, Tofte, and the Temperance River Valley.

From Highway 61, drive north on the Sawbill Trail (Co. Rd. 2) about 2.25 miles to the parking area on the east.

BRITTON PEAK

A steep half-mile grade leads to Britton Peak and views of Superior, adjacent hardwood forests, and Carlton Peak to the west.

From Highway 61, drive north on the Sawbill Trail (Co. Rd. 2) about 2.5 miles to the parking area on the east.

THE RAILROAD GRADE (FOREST RD. 170)

This drive is pretty any time of the year. As you travel through conifers and hardwoods and past eight lakes, keep an eye out for moose. Fifteen miles of road between the Sawbill and Caribou Trails.

From Highway 61, drive north on the Sawbill Trail (Co. Rd. 2) to Forest Rd. 170; travel east on Forest Rd. 165 to the Caribou Trail (Co. Rd. 4); return by going south on Co. Rd. 4 to Highway 61.

LUTSEN MOUNTAIN GONDOLA RIDE

Treat yourself to a beautiful gondola ride over the Poplar River Valley and up Moose Mountain. Opt for the gondola ride back or return on the moderately difficult 3.6-mile trail through maples back to the main chalet or Caribou Highlands Lodge. Very nice!

From Highway 61, drive north on the Ski Hill Road to the main chalet.

WHITE SKY ROCK

A steep half-mile trek leads to the overlook of Caribou Lake and the surrounding maple forests. Best during the early fall season.

From Highway 61, drive north on the Caribou Trail (Co. Rd. 4)
about four miles to the brown and yellow trailhead sign.

OBERG MOUNTAIN

Oberg is *the* trail to hike during the peak maple colors of early autumn. This maple hillside will surpass all expectations. The hike includes seven overlooks, so don't forget your camera!

From Highway 61 about five miles northeast of Tofte, drive north on the
Onion River Road for two miles to parking.

PIKE LAKE LOOP

The entire drive showcases maple stands and aspen and birch intermingled with conifers. Especially beautiful is the rock outcrop hillside rising to the east of the Cascade Palisades. Decked out in sugar maples, it is one of the prettiest spots in the county.

From Highway 61, drive northeast on Co. Rd. 7 to Co. Rd. 44; head north
on Co. Rd. 44 to the Pike Lake Road; drive west on the Pike Lake
Road, then north on the Cascade River Road, following as the road
curves east and becomes Forest Rd. 157 to the Bally Creek Road; go
south on the Bally Creek Road to Co. Rd. 48, south on Co. Rd. 48 to
Co. Rd. 7, and either east to Grand Marais or west to Lutsen.

PINCUSHION MOUNTAIN OVERLOOK

The Gunflint Trail climbs 1,000 feet in the first few miles to a maple ridgeline. The Pincushion Mountain and Devil Track River trails lead through these maples to overlooks of Lake Superior, the maple forests, and falls and gorges of the Devil Track River.

From Highway 61 in Grand Marais, head north on the Gunflint Trail
(Co. Rd. 12) for two miles to Co. Rd. 53, then go east on Co. Rd. 53 to
parking.

MAPLE HILL

The picturesque Maple Hill Church sits center stage surrounded by maples –
this great drive is best during the early fall season.

From Highway 61 in Grand Marais, drive north on the Gunflint Trail
(Co. Rd. 12) for four miles to the gravel road just past Co. Rd. 8, and
head northwest on the gravel road.

MAPLE CANOPY DRIVE

A lovely drive when time is short but you want to see great maple colors.

From Highway 61 in Grand Marais, drive north on the Gunflint Trail,
then east on Co. Rd. 60, and either go north on Co. Rd. 14, looping to
Highway 61, or directly south on Co. Rd. 14 to Highway 61.

LIMA MOUNTAIN

From the top of this peak where a fire lookout tower once stood, full-circle
panoramas show the golden autumn tones of the backcountry. The one-mile
hike is best during the late fall season.

From Highway 61 in Grand Marais, drive north on the Gunflint Trail
(Co. Rd. 12) for about 20 miles to Lima Mountain Road; drive west
on Forest Rd. 152 for 2 miles to Forest Rd. 315, then north on Forest
Rd. 315 to parking off the road's edge.

HONEYMOON BLUFF

A more difficult half-mile climb up Honeymoon Bluff showcases the fall colors of the trees circling Hungry Jack Lake. Best during the late fall season.

From Highway 61 in Grand Marais, drive north on the Gunflint Trail (Co. Rd. 12) for 27 miles to Clearwater Road, head east on Clearwater Road to Flour Lake campground and the trailhead.

HOVLAND LOOKOUT TOWER

The tower overlooks sugar maples, quaking aspen, and conifers. This is a good wildlife viewing spot.

From Highway 61 in Hovland, go north on the Arrowhead Trail (Co. Rd. 16) 2.5 miles to the Tower Road, then go 1.5 miles north on the Tower Road.

ARROWHEAD LOOP

A real backcountry drive through the woods.

From Highway 61 in Hovland, drive north on the Arrowhead Trail about 5 miles, then east and north on the Jackson Lake Road and west on the Otter Lake Road. Either return south on the Arrowhead Trail or cross the Arrowhead Trail to the Esther Lake Road, go south and stay on the road as it turns into the Tom Lake Road, take it to the Arrowhead Trail, and return south to Highway 61.

MOUNT JOSEPHINE

The spectacular views of Superior's shores, Pigeon Point, Susie Islands, and islands from Mount Jo's summit are enhanced by fall colors.

From Highway 61, drive northeast on Co. Rd. 17; take the Upper Road to the parking area.

Green Spaces, Large and Small

ALL NATURE WEARS ONE UNIVERSAL GRIN.

Henry Fielding, *Tom Thumb the Great*

Duluth's Parks

INTERSPERSED ALONG THE 26-MILE STRETCH OF DULUTH ARE more than 129 parks, playgrounds, and public areas. Described here are the major city parks. More details on parks can be found in other relevant chapters. I first describe two central parks, Park Point and Enger Tower, then three west Duluth parks and five east Duluth parks. Additional information can be obtained from the City of Duluth, Department of Parks and Recreation, 12 East 4th Street, (218) 723-3337 or (218) 733-3612.

PARK POINT RECREATION AREA
Cross the Aerial Lift Bridge to Duluth's favorite summer getaway. At the end of the six-mile sandbar, you will find a beach house with an accessible restroom, a pavilion, 10 permanent docks at the pier, two ballfields, four miles of hiking trails, a playground that incorporates a laker passing under a mini-lift bridge, two swimming beaches with lifeguards, and a picnic area with 25 tables and six grills. Get a little sand in your shoes this summer!

From I-35, take the Canal Park exit, then cross the Aerial Lift Bridge to 45th Street.

ENGER TOWER PARK
If you stand on Park Point and look up the hillside to the west, you will see a stone tower breaking the horizon. Amidst Japanese gardens, Enger Tower rises five stories to a crowning perch with a commanding vista across Lake Superior. At the base of the octagonal tower are the Peace Bell, a pavilion with a fireplace, summer-use washrooms, and a picnic area with 20 tables and four grills. Enger is a nice little woodland park.

From I-35, take exit 249E to 17th Avenue West.

LINCOLN PARK
A quiet neighborhood park, Lincoln Park features a pavilion with tables and accessible restrooms, a playground, 1.5 miles of hiking trails, a ballfield, a fireplace, and 15 additional tables with six grills.

From I-35, take 21st Avenue West north to Superior Street, then go west
to 25th Avenue West and north to 3rd Street.

FAIRMOUNT PARK
Adjacent to the Zoo, Fairmount was once an amusement park with a four-
car ferris wheel, humongous slide, and miniature train offering rides around
the park. A bit more sedate and picturesque today, Fairmount is an ideal spot
for feeding your animals. The picnic area includes 40 tables, summer restrooms, a playground, seven grills, a pavilion with a fireplace and 10 tables,
and 1.3 miles of hiking trails. And, of course, it's next to the Zoo!

From I-35, follow the signs for the Zoo.

CHAMBERS GROVE PARK
A kingdaddy of a park, Chambers Grove is big enough to bring all your
friends and relations and still get along. At your disposal are a pavilion with
accessible restrooms, fireplaces, three grills and 50 tables, a ballfield, and a
playground.

From I-35, take Grand Avenue west to 137th Avenue West.

CHESTER BOWL
As we head east, let me introduce you to my alma mater. This is where I
learned to ski, saw a fox, caught minnows, climbed Big Chester, and crashed
the toboggan on the Snake Path. Chester holds dominion over three ski
jumps, three kilometers of cross-country ski trails, three alpine runs, a portion of Chester Creek, a chalet with accessible restrooms, a ballfield, a playground, 2.5 miles of hiking trails, a picnic area, 33 tables, three fire pits, and
two grills. If you can't grow up here, I recommend a visit.

From I-35, go north on Mesaba, then east on Skyline Parkway to park
entrance.

LEIF ERIKSON PARK AND THE DULUTH ROSE GARDEN
Running along the rocky shores where Leif and his Norwegian cohorts
made their legendary landing, the park incorporates more than 3,000 rose
bushes, beautiful landscaping, and a handsome stone pavilion and band-
stand at the center of a mammoth lawn. The garden is dotted with park
benches, making it a perfect resting place along the Lakewalk.

From I-35, exit at Lake Avenue; go north to Superior Street, east to
London Road, then east to 11th Avenue East.

HAWK RIDGE

Curving along the ridgeline, the road gives way to grand views of adjacent hills, the Lakeside residential area, and out to the big lake. Hawk Ridge is internationally famous as a key spot to view fall (August through December) bird migration. Among the countless birds that fly over are hawks and other birds of prey. Cross the Lester River as you continue down Seven Bridges Road to Lester Park.

From I-35, take exit 249E to the area between Glenwood Street and Lester Park.

LESTER PARK

Set aside as parkland in 1890, Lester Park has been a favorite tourist stop since the early 1900s. Turn-of-the-century picture postcards featured local boys swimming in the Deeps. Rumor has it they had to paint swimsuits on the boys before going to print. The park encompasses a triangular 47 acres edged by the west and east branches of the river. A several-mile-long hiking trail leads through the park, which also has a nice playground, pavilion, 26 tables, and six grills. Swimming is at your own risk.

From I-35, continue on London Road, then go north on 61st Avenue East, which turns into Lester River Road.

BRIGHTON BEACH (KITCHI-GAMI PARK)

The park road veers off just east of the Lester River tourist information center and farther up the road connects to Scenic 61. The cobblestone beach running the length of the park is perfect for skipping stones, agate hunting, ship watching, and the sheer pleasure of sitting in the sun listening to the lake. Swimming is at your own risk. Brighton has a pavilion with a fireplace, summer-use restrooms, 18 picnic tables, and seven grills.

From I-35, continue on London Road to the park entrance.

HARTLEY FIELD AND NATURE CENTER

660 acres of forests, fields, ponds, wetlands, rock outcrops, and views of Lake Superior. The Nature Center offers educational and public programming throughout the year.

From I-35, take 21st Avenue East north to Woodland Avenue, follow northeast to park entrance.

State Parks and Waysides

ROM GOOSEBERRY TO GRAND PORTAGE, THE EIGHT STATE parks are quintessential North Shore. The parks encompass some of the most striking natural features of the area: the incredible falls of the Temperance, Baptism, and Pigeon Rivers; the Devil's Kettle; Superior's coast; Mic Mac Lake; and the stony cliff base of Split Rock Lighthouse. Stop at as many state parks as you can. It is the most delightful, and easiest, way to explore the Shore.

Another beauty of the parks is their accessibility; all but George H. Crosby Manitou State Park are adjacent to Highway 61. Within a quarter-mile of parking, every park offers spectacular views. Well-maintained trails crisscross the parks, leading to vistas and picnic sites. Visitors centers offer exhibits, naturalist programs, displays, information, and gifts. All state parks are open year-round, but visitors centers may be closed in winter. Check with each park.

Interested in more than a picnic? Consider camping. Campsites vary from secluded backpack sites to kayak, tent, and RV sites. Cascade River and Gooseberry Falls State Parks have rustic group camps available that offer tables, fire rings, toilets, and a water source. Tettegouche, Cascade, and Gooseberry Parks maintain heated shower and restroom facilities for winter campers, and Tettegouche also has cabin rentals. To ensure a campsite, make a reservation by calling (866) 85PARKS or TDD (866) 290-2267. A nonrefundable reservation fee of $8.50 is charged. Reservations are accepted from 3 to 90 days in advance for camping and up to 1 year for lodging. Camping rates are generally $15 per night, plus $3 for electricity. Backpack and kayak sites are $7. Carts are provided at campgrounds with cart-in sites. Gathering firewood on parkland is prohibited, but many parks sell firewood. The walk-in/ski-in cabins at Tettegouche are $60 to $110 per night, and the Illgen Cabin is $120 to $150 per night. Seniors can camp Sunday through Thursday for half-price.

To enter any of the state parks, a vehicle permit is required. Permits are currently $25 per year or $7 per day and are available for purchase at each park. Annual permits give everyone in the vehicle unlimited access to all Minnesota state parks.

Activities within the parks are generally free of charge. Fishing requires a license and any applicable stamps. Cross-country skiing requires a Minnesota Ski Pass for skiers 16 years of age and older. For hiking or cross-country ski trail maps, ask at the visitors center or office. All trailheads have "You Are Here" signs and boxes with maps.

Pets, except for trained guide dogs, are not allowed in any buildings or cross-country trails. All pets must be personally attended and on a leash no more than six feet long. In maintained areas, owners should clean up after their pets.

For additional information on Minnesota's state parks, contact the Minnesota Department of Natural Resources (DNR): call them at (888) MINN-DNR or (651) 296-6157, look them up at dnr.state.mn.us, or write to them at DNR Information, 500 Lafayette Road, St. Paul, MN 55155. You can contact Jay Cooke State Park, south of Duluth, by calling them directly at (218) 384-4610. Information on Canadian parks between the border and Thunder Bay is included in the chapter about Canada ("Beyond the Border"). More information on particular activities and features is included in other chapters in this book. For example, if you want to find out more about ski trails at Gooseberry, read the cross-country skiing chapter ("Skinny Skiers Rejoice!").

As you drive up Highway 61, you will encounter the following state parks: Gooseberry Falls, Split Rock Lighthouse, Tettegouche, George H. Crosby Manitou, Temperance River, Cascade River, Judge C. R. Magney, and Grand Portage. Also included in this chapter is information about state waysides and pull-offs along the route.

STATE PARKS

GOOSEBERRY FALLS STATE PARK

Gooseberry in the summer is a veritable hive of video camera-wielding vacationers. For many this is the first stop along the way. A must-see look over the bridge rewards sightseers with waterfalls on both sides. A short walk either up or down the river reveals additional falls. Inside the beautiful visitors center are naturalist programs, interactive exhibits, restrooms, and a gift shop. The center is the main trailhead in the park. But Gooseberry is hardly a one-season stop. Spring runoff and fall colors are grand, but the true splendor of the park comes through along the wintery cross-country ski trails. Trust me on this one.

Highway 61, 40 miles northeast of Duluth and 12 miles northeast of Two Harbors

(218) 834-3855

VISITORS CENTER: Open 9 A.M. to 4 P.M. year-round with extended summer hours; offers naturalist and interpretive programs, exhibits, a theater, touch-screen kiosks, and a gift shop

RESTROOMS: In the ♿ visitors center and some outhouses

HISTORIC SITE: The buildings and bridge were built by the Civilian Conservation Corps and are on the National Register of Historic Places.

PICNIC FACILITIES: Tables at several areas (mouth of the river, Lake Superior shore, and Agate Bay) and an enclosed shelter near Lake Superior that is available to rent

WATERFALLS: Five falls extending from Lake Superior up the river

HIKING: 18 miles; part of the Superior Hiking Trail; includes several small spur trails to different falls, to overlooks, up the river, and down to Lake Superior; 1-mile accessible trail; 4 miles of winter hiking

MOUNTAIN BIKING: 8 miles of hard-packed dirt trails north of the highway plus connects to the Gitchi Gami Trail

FISHING: Lake and stream

CAMPING: 70 nonelectric drive-in sites with 3 pull-through, 40-foot RV length limit; 2 accessible sites, 1 kayak site, group camp with 3 sites; ♿ flush toilets and showers; seasonal dumping station; public phones; firewood and ice for sale

CROSS-COUNTRY SKIING: 20K, all groomed for diagonal stride, most are moderately difficult; a warming house in the visitors center with fireplace, restrooms, and vending

SNOWMOBILING: 2 miles of groomed trails, then 6-mile access trail to State Corridor Trail

SNOWSHOEING: Anywhere except groomed trails

SPLIT ROCK LIGHTHOUSE STATE PARK   ♿

The horrific shipwrecks of November 1905 fueled the demand for a lighthouse along Superior's North Shore. The amazing construction process was completed in 1910, and the light at Split Rock shone until 1968. The history center's superb displays, exhibits, and video presentation showcase the evolution of the lighthouse. For a glimpse of this remote lifestyle, include a visit to the lighthouse keeper's home and outbuildings. (Did they really sleep in those little beds?) The path leading southwest down to Lake Superior presents a distinctive view of the lighthouse and remnants of the lift that was used to haul supplies up from the lake. Climb the short, steep circular stairs to the top of the lighthouse. Spend some time at this historic treasure!

Off Highway 61, 48 miles northeast of Duluth and 20 miles northeast of
    Two Harbors

(218) 226-6377 (general)

(218) 226-6372 (lighthouse)

VISITORS CENTER: Lighthouse open 9 A.M. to 6 P.M. May to October, admission is charged; history center open year-round (12 P.M. to 4 P.M. Friday to Sunday from mid-October through mid-May) with exhibits and films; fee charged to visit the lighthouse; state park open 9 A.M. to 9 P.M. Memorial Day to Labor Day with decreased hours the remainder of the year

RESTROOMS: In ♿ history center and picnic pavilion

HISTORIC SITE: The lighthouse and surrounding buildings are on the National Register of Historic Places.

PICNIC FACILITIES: Tables with fire rings; 2 shelters, 1 open and 1 enclosed shelter with restrooms, patio, and wood stove

HIKING: 12 miles; part of the Superior Hiking Trail; trails to Lake Superior just below and west of the lighthouse, up the river, to Split Rock Point, Corundum Point, and through adjacent woods; ¼-mile accessible trail along the shore

MOUNTAIN BIKING: 6 miles of trails from picnic area along hiking trails; connects to Gitchi Gami Trail

FISHING: Lake, stream, and river

CAMPING: 20 walk-in sites including 2 accessible sites, 4 backpack sites (2 are backpack/kayak sites), 1 kayak site; ♿ flush toilets and showers; carts available for campers to tote gear; public phones; firewood and ice for sale

CROSS-COUNTRY SKIING: 13K, all groomed for diagonal stride, most are moderately difficult; warming house at the enclosed picnic shelter with restrooms and a wood stove

SNOWSHOEING: Anywhere except groomed trails

TETTEGOUCHE STATE PARK ♿

Spread over 9,300 acres, Tettegouche is a handful of overlapping parks, which earned it the distinction of being classified as a North Shore Biocultural Region. The park features a mile of Lake Superior coast, including the Baptism River mouth; the river's cascades and falls; four inland lakes; rugged, semimountainous reliefs; and an undisturbed northern hardwood forest.

Tettegouche is Algonquin for "retreat." The park received its name from the 1910 Tettegouche Camp on Mic Mac Lake, where the park now rents out the original cabins. The Tettegouche Club, a group of businessmen from Duluth, purchased the camp, and it remained with a member until 1971. Tettegouche became a state park in 1979.

Highway 61, 60 miles northeast of Duluth and 5 miles northeast of
    Silver Bay

(218) 226-6365

VISITORS CENTER: Open year-round

RESTROOMS: In the ♿ visitors center (nicest on the Shore!)

HISTORIC SITE: Tettegouche Camp is on the National Register of
    Historic Places; the cabins of the old hunting camp are now rented as
    walk-, bike-, or ski-in lodging.

PICNIC FACILITIES: Four areas with tables and fire rings and an enclosed
    shelter at Tettegouche Lodge

WATERFALLS: Three falls, including the highest waterfall contained entirely in Minnesota

HIKING: 23 miles; part of the Superior Hiking Trail; includes moderate trails to Lake Superior, to Shovel Point, up the river, to all three falls, throughout the park, to overlooks, and around interior lakes

MOUNTAIN BIKING: 1.5 miles on service road into Tettegouche Camp and on multiseason trails

FISHING: Lake and stream

ROCK CLIMBING: At Palisade Head

ATV RIDING: 6.5 miles in the park that connect to more outside the park

LAKES: Mic Mac, Nipisquit, Nicado, and Tettegouche (no motors allowed)

CAMPING: 28 nonelectric drive-in sites, 60-foot RV length limit, 13 cart-in sites, 5 backpack sites on the Superior Hiking Trail (first-come, first-served), 6 walk-in sites of which 5 are kayak sites; ♿ flush toilets and showers; dumping station near park; public phones; firewood and ice for sale

TETTEGOUCHE CABINS: Four log cabins, three sleep 6 and one sleeps 2, with kitchenettes and woodstove heat on Mic Mac Lake for walk-, bike-, or ski-in lodging, plus shower/toilet building and common lodge with fireplace, lounge chairs, and dining tables

ILLGEN CABIN: An accessible cabin overlooking Illgen Falls on the Baptism River; loft bedroom, main bedroom, full kitchen, bath, living room with gas fireplace, gas grill, picnic table, and campfire ring

CROSS-COUNTRY SKIING: 25K, all groomed for diagonal stride, most moderate to difficult, and a 6.4K skating loop with a warming house

SNOWSHOEING: Anywhere except groomed trails

SNOWMOBILING: 12 groomed miles, including access to the State Corridor Trail

GEORGE H. CROSBY MANITOU STATE PARK

Crosby Manitou is the quiet park. Off the beaten path of Highway 61, Manitou is more primitive, offering fewer amenities but more-secluded sites. From its inception in 1955, Manitou was designated as a park with limited development, and the camping areas remain backpack-only. Several trails approach the river, offering campers a choice of sites. An easy walk-in picnic area is available for day-hikers, too. Wildlife sightings are frequent. Parklands encompass the area around the river down near the shores of Superior, but do not include access to the mouth of the river.

From Highway 61 at Illgen City, go north on Minnesota 1 about
seven miles to Co. Rd. 7, then northeast another seven miles.

(218) 226-6365 (Tettegouche State Park takes calls and correspondence
for both parks.)

RESTROOMS: Outhouses

PICNIC FACILITIES: Tables in a quiet, secluded area near Lake Benson

WATERFALLS: Several cascades along the Manitou River

HIKING: 24 miles; includes eight loops, one to a walk-in picnic area,
an extensive trail along the Manitou River, and trails through the
forested area (5 miles are part of Superior Hiking Trail)

FISHING: Lake and stream

LAKES: Benson, with carry-in boat access; only electric motors allowed

CAMPING: 21 backpack sites with water in day-use areas; ½ to 4 miles
from parking, many on Manitou River

SNOWSHOEING: Anywhere in park

TEMPERANCE RIVER STATE PARK

Temperance was said to be the only river along the North Shore without a
sand "bar" at its mouth; hence the name. However, it is hardly a moderate
river. A few hundred feet upstream, a thunderous water force continues to
carve out a deeper path in the amazing gorge. Just a few steps away is an
equally splendid falls. Farther upriver, the waters calm, and many locals
swim in the pools.

Highway 61 in Schroeder, 77 miles northeast of Duluth

(218) 663-7476

RESTROOMS: In campground

HISTORIC SITE: Several stone overlooks were built in the 1930s by the
Civilian Conservation Corps.

PICNIC FACILITIES: Tables, an open shelter, and fire rings near the
lakeshore

WATERFALLS: Two falls cut gorges just north of Highway 61.

HIKING: 22 miles; part of the Superior Hiking Trail; includes several
short, easy spurs down either side of the river to Lake Superior, a
catwalk bridge, and trails up both sides of the river and through the
adjacent woodlands; 2 miles of winter hiking

FISHING: Lake and stream

CAMPING: 55 drive-in sites with 2 pull-through and 18 electric, 50-foot
RV length limit, 3 cart-in sites, 1 kayak site; flush toilets and
showers; public phones; firewood and ice for sale

CROSS-COUNTRY SKIING: 13K, all groomed for diagonal stride
SNOWMOBILING: 8 groomed miles, including access to the State
    Corridor Trail
SNOWSHOEING: Anywhere except groomed trails

CASCADE RIVER STATE PARK   ♿

Cascade follows the park tradition of bringing you to the river. Parking is at the mouth of the Cascade and Superior's expanse. A quick jaunt up well-maintained trails brings you to overlooks and walking bridges spanning the cascades. Picnic spots are a quarter-mile farther northeast along Highway 61. Like Gooseberry, Cascade touts its fishing and fall colors, but outdoes itself on its cross-country ski trails. If you want to ski over the river and through the woods, strap on your skinny skis at Cascade.

Highway 61, 100 miles northeast of Duluth and 8 miles northeast of
    Lutsen

(218) 387-3053

RESTROOMS: Outhouse and ♿ in campground
PICNIC FACILITIES: Tables and an enclosed shelter with a fireplace
WATERFALLS: Stair-step cascades up the river
HIKING: 18 miles; part of the Superior Hiking Trail; includes a short
    spur up the river to a bridge; trails to Lake Superior, Lookout
    Mountain, up both sides of the river, and throughout the park
FISHING: Lake and river; a favorite spot in the spring and fall for the
    steelhead and salmon runs, respectively
CAMPING: 40 nonelectric drive-in sites with 3 pull-through, 35-foot RV
    length limit, 5 winter sites, 5 backpack sites, 2 group sites; ♿ flush
    toilets and showers; dumping station; public phones; firewood and
    ice for sale
CROSS-COUNTRY SKIING: 27K, all groomed for diagonal stride, and a
    warming house with a fireplace
SNOWMOBILING: 2 groomed miles; part of the North Shore State Trail
SNOWSHOEING: Anywhere except groomed trails

JUDGE C. R. MAGNEY STATE PARK

Magney reflects Manitou's essence, but is more accommodating to tent and trailer campers. While many boast of the Brule's fishing, the park's real claim to fame is the Devil's Kettle. Rumored to have no bottom, this watery cauldron perpetually churns and froths. The hike up treats you to excellent vantage points of the lower and upper falls and Devil's Kettle. The park name honors Judge Magney, an advocate of state parks, who helped establish 11 state parks and waysides on the Shore. Take a moment and tip your hat to this visionary.

Highway 61, 124 miles northeast of Duluth and 14 miles northeast of Grand Marais

(218) 387-3039

RESTROOMS: Outhouses in campground

HISTORIC SITE: The remains of a 1930s WPA camp are still evident throughout the campground.

PICNIC FACILITIES: Two areas, one near day-use parking and one on the Brule River, both with tables and fire rings

WATERFALLS: Dramatic upper and lower falls of the Brule River

HIKING: 9 miles, including 2.25-mile round-trip trail to Devil's Kettle

FISHING: Lake and river

CAMPING: 27 drive-in sites, 45-foot RV length limit; ♿ toilets and showers; public phones; firewood and ice for sale

CROSS-COUNTRY SKIING: 8K, all groomed for diagonal stride

SNOWSHOEING: Anywhere in park

GRAND PORTAGE STATE PARK

The Grand Portage Band of Ojibwe share their land at Minnesota's newest state park. The desire for a safe approach to the 120-foot High Falls of the Pigeon River brought about this unique cooperative effort between the state and the Band. This is the only park in the nation that is managed in partnership with a local American Indian band. The result is access for everyone to one of the area's most impressive natural features.

Off Highway 61, 146 miles northeast of Duluth and 5 miles northeast of Grand Portage at the international border

(218) 475-2360

VISITORS CENTER: Open year-round, with exhibits, programs, a naturalist, and gift shop

RESTROOMS: Outhouses

PICNIC FACILITIES: Tables, grills, and an open shelter overlooking the river

WATERFALLS: Middle and High Falls of the Pigeon River

HIKING: 3.5 miles, including 1-mile accessible round-trip trail to the High Falls

FISHING: On the Pigeon River; follow border water regulations

SNOWSHOEING: Anywhere in park; rentals for half and full days

WAYSIDES

A number of wayside rests along Highway 61 and Scenic 61 offer a place to stretch your legs, have a picnic, and take pleasure in your surroundings. Many of the following waysides and pull-off areas also offer access to Lake Superior.

LESTER RIVER
Lake Superior, at London Road and 61st Avenue East just east of the river

BRIGHTON BEACH
Features summer restroom facilities, picnic areas, and swimming (no lifeguards).
Lake Superior, at London Road a quarter-mile east of the Lester River

FRENCH RIVER
Lake Superior, on Scenic 61 just east of the fish hatchery

BLUEBIRD LANDING
Lake Superior, on Scenic 61 between the French and Sucker Rivers

STONY POINT
Lake Superior; take the road directly across from Tom's Logging Camp on Scenic 61 about 13 miles northeast of Duluth; this loop reconnects with Scenic 61 about a mile northeast.

KNIFE RIVER
The frontage road has summer-use restroom facilities.
Scenic 61 just west of the river; take the road across from Emily's 1929 Eatery, Deli, and Inn to the frontage road and take a left.

BUCHANAN WAYSIDE
Scenic 61, about five miles north of Knife River

FLOOD BAY STATE WAYSIDE
Lake Superior, on Highway 61 just east of Superior Shores in Two Harbors

GOOSEBERRY FALLS
At the state park visitors center

PALISADE HEAD WAYSIDE
Take the summer-access road to the 320-foot cliff at the top; very dramatic and usually not too busy.
Lake Superior, on Highway 61 about three miles northeast of Silver Bay

TETTEGOUCHE
At the state park visitors center

CARIBOU RIVER WAYSIDE
Offers a half-mile hiking trail along the river to falls.
> Highway 61, about 5.5 miles northeast of Little Marais on the north side
> of the road

CROSS RIVER STATE WAYSIDE
An excellent stop for taking pictures of the falls.
> Highway 61 just before the river

RAY BERGLUND MEMORIAL WAYSIDE
An unmaintained half-mile trail leads inland adjacent to the Onion River.
> Highway 61, about 3.5 miles northeast of Tofte

GOOD HARBOR BAY AND CUT FACE CREEK WAYSIDE
Great panoramas of the lake open up as you round the corner onto Good
Harbor Bay. Cut Face Creek Wayside is about a quarter-mile farther and is a
nice spot for a picnic and skipping stones.
> Highway 61, about 12 miles northeast of Lutsen

KADUNCE RIVER STATE WAYSIDE
I really like this quiet picnic spot with its beach and river trail.
> Lake Superior, on Highway 61 about eight miles northeast of
> Grand Marais

MOUNT JOSEPHINE AREA
This rugged area features Mount Josephine, Mount Rose, and Mount Maud
and views of the Susie Islands, Isle Royale, and Hat Point. Three pull-offs are
situated on the lake side of the road, and there is a lookout at the tourist
information center (open May to October) located a short distance up the
road on the north side. Bathrooms are available at one of the pull-offs and at
the visitors center.
> Highway 61, about 32 miles northeast of Grand Marais

GUNFLINT TRAIL
Moose viewing area 22.5 miles from Highway 61; Swamper Lake area 23.5
miles from Highway 61; Laurentian Divide overlook 33 miles from Highway
61; Gunflint Lake scenic overlook 44 miles from Highway 61.

Scientific and Natural Areas

A LONG THE NORTH SHORE AND THROUGHOUT THE STATE ARE natural resources that are rare or of exceptional scientific and educational value. The Minnesota Department of Natural resources preserves these living museums through designation as a Scientific and Natural Area (SNA). The seven SNAs along the Shore are open primarily for public observation and education and are not typically recreational areas. As such, the SNAs usually do not have any facilities, trails, or restrooms, and pets are not allowed.

If the naturalist in you is intrigued, choose a drive-to, hike-to, or canoe-to area from just east of Duluth as far north as Hovland. No permits are required. Additional information can be obtained online at dnr.state.mn.us/snas/index.html.

MOOSE MOUNTAIN SNA

A 177-acre old-growth northern hardwood forest that features the forest succession one hundred years after wildfire. Excellent viewing of the old-growth area is at the top of the hill, south of the power line, while the "newer" growth is to the north. Visit during the spring wildflower season to view the rare white baneberry and moschatel (muskroot) plants. Moschatel is especially uncommon and is the only species in its family that grows in North America. An autumn visit will highlight the colors of the sugar maples, basswood, and yellow birch.

From Highway 61 in Duluth, drive north on the Lester River Road (just east of the river) about 3 miles to a signed area. Park on the road and walk a half-mile in to the south and east.

SAND LAKE PEATLAND SNA

It may take a bit of work to reach Minnesota's only large peatland complex, but it's a solitary treat. At almost 5,000 acres, Sand Lake Peatland is unusual in that it is situated on an outwash plain versus the typical lake plain, is spreading outward versus stabilizing, and shows how a spreading peatland creates internal water tracks. It's a great bog ecosystem, too!

From Highway 61 in Two Harbors, drive north on Co. Rd. 2 37 miles to the Sand Lake public access, park and canoe/snowshoe/ski to the north shore at the far west end of the lake. Walk upland to the bog.

IONA'S BEACH SNA

Drive right up to this huge North Shore beach! Few beaches of this size are found along the southern portion of the North Shore. This one is book-ended by cliffs, rhyolite, and bedrock to the north and basalt to the south. Nor'easters work away at the northern cliff, breaking off shards of rhyolite and transferring them downshore to the base of the southern cliff. Once home to Twin Points Resort, now named after its longtime owner Iona Lind, the area is also a safe harbor.

On Highway 61, 3 miles northeast of Gooseberry Falls State Park.

SUGARLOAF POINT SNA

Home to the Sugarloaf Interpretive Center, this area was used as a pulpwood landing from the 1940s through 1971. All winter wood was brought in by truck and stacked, waiting for spring when it was sent by chute to Lake Superior. The wood was rafted, boomed, and towed to Ashland, Wisconsin, for processing. About 1.1 billion years earlier, volcanoes were erupting all over the North Shore. The unique thing at Sugarloaf is that the lava never deformed or changed so that today you can see (and touch!) the thin basalt lava flows from the Precambrian Age. Ice sheets and subsequent waves have deposited a variety of smoothed cobblestone, pebbles, and boulders. The Sugarloaf Interpretive Center Association is working to preserve and protect this unique geological resource and to restore the native vegetation to the area. Take time to walk the trail and watch for more kiosks and a center in the future.

On Highway 61 about 6.5 miles northeast of Little Marais and 6 miles southwest of Schroeder at the signs.

LUTSEN SNA

At 720 acres, this is one of the largest undisturbed old-growth hardwood forests on the North Shore. Massive trees are estimated to be up to 300 years old. The area includes great vistas of nearby ridgelines, cliffs, and adjoining valleys and, like the Moose Mountain SNA, is home to white baneberry and moschatel (muskroot) making it a good spring wildflower visit. Autumn is extraordinary as the predominant sugar maples blaze in color.

From Highway 61 in Lutsen, drive north on the Ski Hill Road to the snowmobile or ski trail and hike in to the east.

SPRING BEAUTY NORTHERN HARDWOODS SNA

Rare Chilean sweet cicely, blunt-fruited sweet cicely, and Carolina spring beauties are all protected plant species found in this rare old-growth northern hardwood forest. Old-growth sugar maples form a canopy over smaller maples making it another wonderful autumn visit.

From Highway 61 in Hovland, drive north on the Arrowhead Trail to the Tower Road, then west to parking near the Hovland Fire Tower.

HOVLAND WOODS SNA

At just over 2,800 acres, this is the largest SNA with virgin and mature forests, which can be contrasted to a 10-acre section undergoing regrowth after a 1998 wildfire. The Swamp River watershed is a unique micro-environment that plays host to a variety of diverse plant life as well.

From Highway 61 in Hovland, drive north on the Arrowhead Trail to the Tower Road, then west to the junction with Tom Lake Road and north to a washed-out hill. Hike ¾ mile to the SNA. Or, from Highway 61 in Hovland, drive 7 miles north on the Arrowhead Trail to the Irish Creek Road, then drive west 1¼ miles to the bridge and park. Hike ¾ mile south on the Boyd Trail to the SNA.

National Parks and Monuments

ISLE ROYALE NATIONAL PARK

In 1931 Congress made Isle Royale a national park. As part of the 1976 National Wilderness Preservation System, more than 90 percent of Isle Royale was appropriated as wilderness. In 1981 the United Nations designated Isle Royale as an International Biosphere Reserve. The island is accessible only by boat or floatplane, and land transportation is over 165 miles of foot trails. Nonmotorized vessels can paddle the inland streams and lakes.

Running the length of this stunning island is the multimillion-year-old Greenstone Ridge. Formed at the rift of an ancient glacial plate, Isle Royale came into being a mere 10,000 years ago as lake levels dropped. Six peaks, 1,100 to 1,400 feet high, stand lookout over the primitive archipelago.

Animal life on Isle Royale is in a state of flux. At the turn of the century, caribou and lynx populated the island. Coyotes and white-tailed deer attempted residency, but disappeared. In the early 1900s moose swam over from the mainland. At first they enjoyed a plentiful food supply, and their numbers grew until the 1930s, when they had ravaged their food sources. Moose began dying off and were nearly devastated when a 1936 fire burned a fourth of the island and their remaining browse. Ironically, the fire established a second-growth forest, which is ideal moose habitat. The cycle was played out again, with populations soaring and crashing.

The introduction of the eastern timber wolf during the winter of 1948-49 has helped to stabilize moose numbers. A small pack of wolves crossed the ice bridge formed between Canada and the island. Current numbers of wolves fluctuate from 12 to 50. As on all island habitats, the interplay of flora and fauna establishes a constantly changing balance.

Isle Royale National Park, 800 East Lakeshore Drive, Houghton,
    MI 49931
Open mid-April through October
User fee: $4 per person per day, 11 and under are free; an individual
    season pass is available for $50.

(906) 482-0984

nps.gov/isro

VISITORS CENTERS: Rock Harbor and Windigo; open mid-June to
early September

RANGER STATIONS: Rock Harbor, Windigo, Amygdaloid, and
Malone Bay

OTHER: No pets (not even on boats); alcohol ban in campgrounds and
on docks

Transportation

The Grand Portage Isle Royale Transportation Line (GPIR) services Isle
Royale from Grand Portage. Other companies provide service from the
Upper Peninsula area of Michigan. The GPIR line makes daily passenger
runs to Windigo from mid-June through Labor Day. The steel-hulled, twin-
engined *Wenonah* carries 149 passengers and leaves the Grand Portage
National Monument at 9:30 A.M., arriving on Isle Royale about 12:30 P.M.
Return trips depart at 3 P.M. and arrive on the mainland at 6 P.M. Onboard
sight-seeing includes views of the Little Spirit Cedar Tree, Susie Islands,
Sleeping Giant, sunken steamer *America,* and Rock of Ages lighthouse. Rates
are $40 for adults and $20 for children (ages 4 to 11).

The GPIR also runs the *Voyageur II* out of Grand Portage on Mondays,
Wednesdays, and Saturdays. This combination mail and passenger service
circumnavigates the island clockwise, spending the night at Rock Harbor.
The *Voyageur* will stop at any other of the specified docks if reservations are
made in advance. Tickets can be purchased at the Grand Portage dock
between 9 A.M. and 3 P.M.

Grand Portage Isle Royal Transportation Line, 1507 North 1st Street,
Superior, WI 54880-1146

(715) 392-2100

Minimum Impact Camping

Thirty-six camping areas are spread over the shores and bays of inland lakes
and streams and Lake Superior. Each area typically has two or three sites and
includes a combination of tent sites and three-sided wooden structures with
screened-in fronts. Some sites include group areas. All camping is on a first-
come, first-serve basis. Tent and shelter sites are limited to 6 people, and
group site maximum capacity is 10 people. Permits are required and can be
picked up upon arrival on the island at Rock Harbor or Windigo. Keep in
mind that sites have limits on the maximum number of consecutive nights
campers can stay, averaging three nights.

To help perpetuate the fragile island environment, low-impact camping is highly encouraged. Minimize erosion by walking only on marked trails. Do not dig trenches or alter the soil. Make campfires only where allowed. Bring a backpack stove for cooking. Drinking water is available at Rock Harbor and Windigo. Assume all island water is contaminated with the eggs of the hydatid tapeworm. Chemical purification will *not* kill the eggs. All water needs to be filtered or boiled rapidly for two minutes. Pack out everything you pack in. No pets are allowed in the park (even on boats). Bring a complete first aid kit. There are no medical facilities on the island.

Accommodations at Rock Harbor Lodge

Rock Harbor Lodge rents 60 American-plan rooms in four lodges and 20 furnished cabins, each with one double bed and two bunk beds. Amenities include a dining room, snack bar, grocery and marina store, laundry facilities, boat and motor rental, guided fishing, sight-seeing tours, and 450 feet of dock space taking boats up to 65 feet. The Windigo store has grocery and sundry items; vending machines; boat, canoe, and motor rentals; marine fuel; and laundry and shower facilities.

National Park Concessions, Inc., P.O. Box 405, Houghton,
MI 49931-0405 (May to September); Mammoth Cave, KY 42259-0027
(October through April)
Open from June to mid-September
(906) 337-4993 (May through September);
(270) 773-2191 (October through April)
isleroyaleresort.com

Fishing

Fishing on Lake Superior waters of Isle Royale National Park requires a Michigan fishing license, which can be purchased at Windigo, Rock Harbor, Amygdaloid, and Malone Bay Ranger Stations. Inland lake and stream fishing does not require a license, but Michigan fishing regulations apply. Artificial bait and lures only. To dispose of fish remains properly, use the cleaning station at Rock Harbor or bag and trash the remains at Windigo. In other areas, cut the remains into pieces four inches square or smaller, puncture the fish's swim bladder, and submerge the pieces in Lake Superior at depths of 50 or more feet. Inland, prepared remains can be placed on shore above wave and vegetation lines and at least 100 feet away from any development.

Boating

Boat owners must obtain permits upon arriving on the island and can purchase daily or seasonal user passes. Limited docking is provided, and anchoring is encouraged. Fuel is sold mid-May through September at Windigo (no diesel) and Rock Harbor. There is restricted use of generators and electronic and motorized devices. All vessels entering from Canada must clear customs at one of the four ranger stations. Canoers and kayakers can travel over on the passenger ferry to Rock Harbor and take a water taxi to the northeast half of the island, where most routes are located, or do a day trip from Rock Island.

Maps and Lake Charts
Isle Royale Natural History Association, Isle Royale National Park, 800 East Lakeshore Drive, Houghton, MI 49931
  (800) 678-6925
  irnha.org; nps.gov/isro/maps.htm

GRAND PORTAGE NATIONAL MONUMENT

Kitchi Onigaming, "the great carrying place," is the Grand Portage that, along with the stockade, is the monument. The 8.5-mile portage was the principal route for traders and trappers heading to Fort Charlotte on their way to the Northwest. Summer headquarters for the North West Company were located here until 1802, when they moved to Fort William, Ontario (now Thunder Bay). Ongoing exhibits and demonstrations take place in the reconstructed historic buildings, including the Great Hall, a kitchen, warehouse, lookout tower, fur press, and Ojibwe village. Ask about the Junior Ranger program, the interpretive programs, and the short video presentations.

The pinnacle of summer is Rendezvous Days, held in conjunction with the Grand Portage Band of Ojibwe's annual powwow. Rendezvous Days, typically the second weekend of August, are a reenactment of the old North West Company's annual event. Highlights are the Ojibwe village; a voyageur encampment; Native American arts, crafts, and foods; and the powwow. Held on traditional grounds, the powwow brings Ojibwe singers and dancers from throughout the United States and Canada to celebrate their cultural heritage.

The entrance is 1 mile south of Highway 61, about 36 miles northeast of Grand Marais, 1 mile northeast of Grand Portage.

An entrance fee of $3 per person or $6 per family is charged.

(218) 387-2788 voice or TDD

nps.gov/grpo/

VISITORS CENTER: Open mid-May through mid-October from 9 A.M. to 5 P.M. daily; (218) 475-2202

HISTORIC SITE: The 8.5-mile portage

PICNIC FACILITIES: Tables adjacent to the park

HIKING: The 8.5-mile (one-way) Grand Portage and half-mile (one way) Mount Rose trail

CROSS-COUNTRY SKIING: Ungroomed, along the Grand Portage

SNOWSHOEING: Along the Grand Portage and throughout the park

CAMPING: At Fort Charlotte, 2 primitive sites that can hold up to 10 people; picnic table, fire ring, and pit toilet; no fee, but you need a permit that you can get at the monument, or self-register at three locations along the trail

Our Backyard

THE SUPERIOR NATIONAL FOREST
AND THE BOUNDARY WATERS
CANOE AREA WILDERNESS

COME ON OVER AND PLAY, WE HAVE A BIG BACKYARD – ABOUT 3 million acres. Of course, 445,000 acres of that is lakes and ponds, and then there are the 2,250 miles of streams and rivers. But all in all, it's pretty big and pretty nice.

It is the Superior National Forest, established in 1909 by a proclamation by Teddy Roosevelt. The million-acre Boundary Waters Canoe Area Wilderness (BWCAW) within the Superior National Forest was established in 1978 under the Wilderness Act of 1964, which sought to "secure for the American People of present and future generations the benefit of an enduring resource of Wilderness."

The BWCAW is managed by the U.S. Forest Service. It is the most heavily used designated wilderness in the United States. Permits are required year-round, and quotas apply to permits from May 1 through the end of September for day-use or overnight parties. Self-issued permits are required for day or overnight use between October 1 and April 30 and for nonmotorized day use during the summer season. The permit allows the party to enter at a specific site on a specific date. Heaviest use occurs from late July through August and on holidays and weekends. The most popular entry sites are Sawbill, Seagull, and Saganaga Lakes (all in Cook County). To be assured of entry, consider starting your trip midweek and make a reservation.

Your permit is not granted until your money is received, so I suggest calling and providing a Visa, MasterCard, or Discover credit card number. You may also stop at the Tofte or Gunflint Ranger Station to try to obtain last-minute permits. Rangers can only issue permits within 24 hours of their intended use. If you are planning your trip through an outfitter (see "Getting

Outfitted" for a list of outfitters), they may be able to obtain the permit for you. When requesting a permit, have an alternate date and/or entry point in mind. You will also need to designate a party leader and alternate and state your method of travel and party size, which is limited to 10.

Campsites in the BWCAW have a fire ring or grate and a primitive latrine. Few have room for more than two tents. Cans and bottles are not allowed, and no drinking water is provided. You must pack out what you bring in.

If you are planning to cross into Canada or enter Quetico Provincial Park, first check Canadian regulations by contacting the Ministry of Natural Resources, Atikokan, Ontario POT 1CO; (807) 597-2735. Remote Area Border Crossing permits are required and can be obtained by contacting Canadian Immigration at (807) 964-2093.

BWCAW Reservation Service, P.O. Box 462, Ballston Spa, NY 12020; reservations are taken by mail beginning mid-January.

The fee is $10 per adult per trip and $5 per youth (to age 17), Golden Access Passport holder, or Golden Age cardholder per trip. There is a nonrefundable reservation fee of $12. A seasonal fee card can be obtained by mail after November 15, by phone after February 2, or in person after May 1 at a Superior National Forest District Office. Seasonal fees are $40 per adult and $20 per youth, Golden Passport holder, or Golden Age cardholder. The

Golden Age card fulfills the fee requirement, but you still need to obtain the appropriate permits.

(877) 550-6777; reservations are taken by phone starting in February.

(877) TDD-NRRS (TDD)

bwcaw.org

BWCAW ENTRY POINTS (AND NUMBERS) IN THE TOFTE AND GUNFLINT DISTRICTS

Tofte District (218) 663-7280

36 Hog Creek/Perent Lake: 15-rod portage to Hog Creek, then paddle to Perent Lake

37 Kawishiwi Lake: canoe landing

38 Sawbill Lake: boat landing

39 Baker Lake: boat landing with 10-rod portage to Peterson Lake and first campsite

40 Homer Lake: boat landing

41 Brule Lake: boat landing; large lake with many campsites

86 Pow Wow Trail: 25-mile hiking trail

Gunflint District (218) 387-1750

43 Bower Trout Lake: 72-rod portage from parking into Bower Trout Lake

44 Ram Lake: 90-rod portage from parking into Ram Lake

45 Morgan Lake: 320-rod portage to Morgan Lake, which has no campsites; need to do short portage to other lakes

47 Lizz and Swamp Lake: 320-rod portage from Poplar Lake

48 Meed Lake: 320-rod portage from Poplar Lake

49 Skipper and Portage Lakes: access from Poplar Lake (320-rod portage) or Iron Lake (230-rod portage)

50 Cross Bay Lake (from Ham Lake): via Cross River with 50-rod and 40-rod portages to Ham Lake, and 24-rod portage to Cross Bay Lake

51 Missing Link Lake (from Round Lake): canoe landing at Round Lake with 142-rod portage to Missing Link Lake

52 Brant Lake (from Round Lake): canoe landing at Round Lake with 85-rod and 35-rod portages to Brant Lake

54 Seagull Lake: boat landing (paddle or 10 hp motor to Three Mile Island)

54A Seagull Lake only

55	Saganaga Lake: boat landing; access to Canada; paddle or 25 hp motor to American Point
55A	Saganaga Lake only
56	Kekekabic Trail (from the east): 36-mile remote hiking trail
57	Magnetic Lake (from Gunflint Lake): paddle to Granite River and Magnetic Lake from Gunflint Trail
58	South Lake (from Gunflint Lake): 10-mile paddle and two short portages to South Lake
59	Partridge and South Lake Trail: hiking only
60	Duncan Lake (from West Bearskin Lake): 75-rod portage to Duncan Lake and Stairway Portage
61	Daniels Lake (from West Bearskin Lake): 60-rod portage to Daniels Lake and 460-rod portage to Rose Lake
62	Clearwater Lake: boat landing; paddle or 10 hp motor
64	East Bearskin Lake (to Alder Lake): boat landing; paddle or 25 hp motor to Alder or Canoe Lake
66	Crocodile River: no options, must spend all nights on Crocodile River
68	Pine Lake (from McFarland Lake): canoe landing
69	John Lake: canoe landing; must paddle from Little John Lake
70	North Fowl Lake (to Moose Lake): access from Little John Lake with 78-rod and 160-rod portages to North Fowl Lake
71	Canada (if your trip starts in Canada)
78	Brule Lake Trail: hiking only, 9-mile trail
79	Eagle Mountain Hiking Trail: hiking only; 7 miles round trip
80	Larch Creek: canoe landing
81–83	Border Route Trail: hiking only (81 west, 82 central, 83 east)

Day Use Motor

J	Saganaga Lake: 25 hp motor to American Point
K	Seagull Lake: 10 hp motor to Three Mile Island
L	Clearwater Lake: 10 hp motor
M	Bearskin Lake: 25 hp motor

Sunny, 70°, and the Fish Are Biting

SUMMERTIME FUN

GIVE ME THE SPLENDID SILENT SUN WITH
ALL HIS BEAMS FULL-DAZZLING.

Walt Whitman

The back of your neck may feel hot and gritty in the city, but here it's sunny, 70°, and the fish are biting from Memorial Day through Labor Day. The hiking trails are being brushed and cleared. The outfitters are preparing the canoes. The shop owners are adding new inventory weekly. The restaurateurs are receiving fresh food daily. The bike shop is spinning tires. The kayak shop is floating boats. The crews are mowing the golf courses. The ships are sailing under the bridge. The road construction crews are blasting and hauling and grading and surfacing. Yep, it's summer on the Shore.

And what do you do in the summer? Why, you play, of course. Up on the Shore, we mostly play outside. In Duluth, you can play outside, but you have some indoor options, too. This section is the variety pack of summer activities: a sampler of hiking trails, a fine mix of biking trails, an assortment of fishing locales, the Lake Superior Water Trail, all the local golf courses, and some tips on hunting and on finding a canoe outfitter. For more ideas, see the sections on Duluth and North Shore attractions, suggestions for family fun, museums and historic sites, what to do on a rainy day, and such. The state and national parks chapters describe some additional amenities and activities. Remember to relax – it's summertime.

What about swimming? Good question. Swimming in Lake Superior is a personal issue. Some folks look at it as a death wish, while others see it as an incredibly invigorating experience. Park Point is *the* place to swim on the big lake. The sand beaches rank with any tropical isle, and the water level is knee-high for a good fifty yards out. Not only is that great for kids, but the sun actually warms up the water. Of course, you can swim at any public beach along Superior.

Other places to swim include the pool at your lodging, river pools, and inland lakes. Lodges on inland lakes usually have beaches for their guests. All swimming is at your own risk. Be careful of river swimming in the spring or after a big rain, when the water will be moving very fast. (Note: don't wear loose or strapless suits in fast-moving rivers.) Swimming spots to try are Lester River in the park, Burlington Bay beach in Two Harbors, Gooseberry River pools, Split Rock River pools, Lax Lake north of Beaver Bay, Temperance River pools, the upper reaches of the Cascade River, Devil Track Lake north of Grand Marais, and the Kadunce River.

Out Walkin'

HIKING AND WALKING TRAILS

I GO OUT WALKIN' AFTER MIDNIGHT,
OUT IN THE MOONLIGHT,
JUST LIKE WE USED TO DO.

Patsy Cline, "Walkin' after Midnight"

PUT ONE FOOT IN FRONT OF THE OTHER,
AND SOON YOU'LL BE WALKING
OUT THE DOOR.

Frosty the Snowman

THERE IS NO BETTER WAY TO KNOW THIS LAND THAN TO WALK it. Walking brings into perspective all the wonderful details that make the whole picture. When out walking, you see, you hear, you touch, you taste, and you smell. Do not deprive yourself of this pleasure.

The walks and hikes included here are a partial list of what is available. Some are quick leg-stretchers, like the half-mile loop to Cascade Falls. Others – the four-mile Park Point loop, for instance – require a few hours. Or you may choose to take two weeks and hike the Superior Hiking Trail. Plenty of trail choices await you.

When walking or hiking, consider the following:
- Obtain a map and familiarize yourself with the walk or trail.
- Allow an hour for each 1½ to 3 miles of trail.

- Let someone (perhaps the front desk at your lodging) know your trail route and expected return time.
- Always carry water, high-energy snacks, sunscreen, bug repellent, a flashlight, and rain gear.
- Binoculars and cameras come in handy on the trail.
- Consider bringing a wildflower guide or bird book.
- Always pack out what you bring in – dispose of trash responsibly.
- Wear sturdy shoes or hiking boots on trails.
- If you bring pets, clean up after them.
- Spring hiking can be treacherous – avoid washed-out areas and slippery, steep grades.
- Fall hiking is especially enjoyable with the cool air and no bugs!
- Wear blaze orange during hunting seasons (September 1 through December 31).
- No fees are charged for using state trails, but state park rules apply.
- Trails cross private, county, state, and federal lands – please respect this.
- Use common sense.

IN DULUTH

WESTERN WATERFRONT TRAIL
A multiseason trail that offers walking, hiking, biking, snowshoeing, and cross-country skiing along the St. Louis River; pack a picnic lunch; a great spot to take kids; nice birding spot. Access to the 70-mile paved Willard Munger Trail; first 15 miles are very scenic.

From I-35, take Grand Avenue/Highway 23, west to 71st Avenue West; parking is on the south.

LENGTH: 5 miles to Jay Cooke State Park

TRAILHEAD: From parking lot

LEVEL OF DIFFICULTY: Easy (paved)

AMENITIES: Picnic areas and boat access; additional services at Jay Cooke State Park

MISSION CREEK TRAIL
The trail heads north through a climax forest of hardwoods (maple, oak, and basswood). After following a short portion of the Willard Munger multiple-use trail, the path spans the creek at four places on footbridges, climbs, and finally descends a steep grade to cross the river and return to the trailhead.

The old Ojibwe Lodge was moved from Fairmount Park in the late 1930s to serve as a warming house for the skating rink and sleigh rides.

> From I-35, take Grand Avenue/Highway 23 west to 131st Avenue West; go right at Fond du Lac Park to parking.

LENGTH: 3.75-mile loop

TRAILHEAD: At DNR holding dam

MAPS: Call Duluth Parks and Rec at (218) 723-3337 or stop at 12 East 4th Street.

LEVEL OF DIFFICULTY: Difficult (muddy and slippery, with steep grades)

AMENITIES: Outhouses and water

KINGSBURY CREEK TRAIL

From a white pine area, you enter the creek floodplain, then cross the creek on a snowmobile bridge; after a climb into paper birch and aspen woods, you head back down, recross the river, and take the old Thompson Hill Road past a crumbling foundation (made of bluestone) to the final leg. The dense bluestone rocks, 1.7-million-year-old Duluth gabbro, were used for their strength in local buildings before World War II.

> From I-35, take Grand Avenue/Highway 23 west to Fremont; go north to the picnic grounds adjacent to the Zoo (follow the Zoo signs).

LENGTH: 1.3 miles over three attached loops

TRAILHEAD: Under the old Duluth Winnipeg & Pacific railroad bridge

MAPS: Call Duluth Parks and Rec at (218) 723-3337 or stop at 12 East 4th Street.

LEVEL OF DIFFICULTY: Moderate

AMENITIES: Restrooms, water, and phone at the Zoo

LINCOLN PARK TRAIL

Walk north through white pine, white cedar, and birch to a glacial whaleback named the Elephant Rock. Use caution when walking the portion of the trail along the park road. Numbered trail markers correspond to the map brochure. One of Duluth's oldest parks.

> From I-35, go north on 21st Avenue West to Superior Street, west on Superior Street to 25th Avenue West, and north on 25th Avenue West to 3rd Street; the park is between 25th and 26th Avenues West and extends north to Skyline Parkway.

LENGTH: 1.5 miles total

TRAILHEAD: At the pavilion, about a block up from 3rd Street

MAPS: Call Duluth Parks and Rec at (218) 723-3337 or stop at 12 East
4th Street.
LEVEL OF DIFFICULTY: Easy

LAKEWALK
Stroll along this old-fashioned boardwalk at the water's edge or bike,
rollerblade, or jog on the adjacent paved path; features benches, informa-
tional markers, the Vietnam Veterans Memorial, Lake Place, and Image Wall.
Along Lake Superior's shore from Bayfront Park to 26th Avenue East
LENGTH: 3 miles each way
TRAILHEAD: Anywhere along the Lakewalk including 5th Avenue West
and Harbor Drive, Canal Park, 26th Avenue East and London Road
LEVEL OF DIFFICULTY: Easy

PARK POINT TRAIL
The trail parallels the airport runway on the Duluth harbor side to pumping
stations, where you take the right fork and enter a virgin pine forest. After
passing a lone private cabin, you walk past an abandoned boathouse to the
ruins of the Minnesota Lighthouse, continue to the Superior Entry and Wisconsin Point opposite the canal, and return either along the beach (Lake
Superior) or on the original path. If you go along the lakeshore, cross the
dunes and return to the airport when you are parallel to the airport signal
tower. Caution: poison ivy is abundant in the Park Point area.
From I-35, go south on Lake Avenue, cross the Aerial Lift Bridge, and
continue to 45th through the park to parking near the airport.
LENGTH: 4-mile loop
TRAILHEAD: At airport parking on the harbor side
MAPS: Call Duluth Parks and Rec at (218) 723-3337 or stop at 12 East
4th Street.
LEVEL OF DIFFICULTY: Moderate (you have the option of walking
in sand)
AMENITIES: Available seasonally at the Park Point beach house

CHESTER PARK TRAIL
The path heads downstream past falls and bedrock boulders that reveal
layers of lava flows, lots of flora, and old-growth white pines. Walk 1.25 miles
down to the 4th Street Bridge (across 4th Street you can get a snack at the
Whole Foods Co-op), where you cross and return upstream past a silver
maple stand. You can also walk the 3K cross-country ski trails that traverse
the park.

From I-35, go north on Mesaba Avenue to Skyline Parkway, then east on Skyline Parkway to the park entrance.

LENGTH: 2.5 miles total

TRAILHEAD: Walk over the bridge on Skyline Parkway and descend to the river on the southwest side of the bridge, or start at 14th Avenue East and 4th Street.

MAPS: Call Duluth Parks and Rec at (218) 723-3337 or stop at 12 East 4th Street.

LEVEL OF DIFFICULTY: Moderate; some steep sections and some wet areas

AMENITIES: Restrooms, water, and phone in the park chalet

CONGDON PARK TRAIL

A footbridge allows access to the east bank of Tischer Creek, but the trail is on the west and leads upstream. Woodlands of white and Norway pine, waterfalls, red feldspar rock, and creatures from chipmunks to foxes.

From I-35, take the 21st Avenue East exit, go north to Superior Street, then east past Hawthorne Road to the park road on the west side of the creek.

LENGTH: 1.5 miles total

TRAILHEAD: East of the parking at the bottom of a stone stairway

MAPS: Call Duluth Parks and Rec at (218) 723-3337 or stop at 12 East 4th Street.

LEVEL OF DIFFICULTY: Easy

HAWK RIDGE NATURE RESERVE TRAILS

Short walks through all conditions, from low and wet to high, bare rock outcrops. Trails offer superb vantage points from which to view the fall hawk migration and the city of Duluth laid out along Superior's shore.

From I-35, take exit 249 and follow Skyline Parkway through Duluth; or from I-35, follow London Road north to 60th Avenue East, drive north to Glenwood, then west-northwest to the gravel road on the east.

LENGTH: Several spur trails each under a mile

TRAILHEAD: Off the gravel road near parking and overlook

LEVEL OF DIFFICULTY: Easy to moderate

LESTER PARK TRAIL

Cross the bridge over the river (note the DNR dam put in place to raise water levels to aid spawning fish in moving upstream), cross another bridge, and walk adjacent to the west branch of the Lester River past a century-old cedar stand to the waterfall. Below the next footbridge is "the Deeps," a popular local swimming hole. The trail leads under the power line through a newer forest of aspen, birch, balsam fir, and white spruce; when you leave the power line, look for signs of deer, rabbits, and moose in this popular feeding area. The final approach leads to a footbridge over the east branch of the Lester River and back to the trailhead.

> From I-35, continue on London Road to 61st Avenue East, which turns into Lester River Road and leads to parking.
>
> LENGTH: 9-mile loop with optional spur trails
>
> TRAILHEAD: South end of parking
>
> MAPS: Call Duluth Parks and Rec at (218) 723-3337 or stop at 12 East 4th Street.
>
> LEVEL OF DIFFICULTY: Easy
>
> AMENITIES: Restrooms, water, and an excellent playground

ALONG THE NORTH SHORE

THE SUPERIOR HIKING TRAIL

The Superior Hiking Trail (SHT) is the finest hiking trail in the Midwest and among the top ten trails in the nation. Originating in Duluth, this long-distance trail clings to the scenic ridgeline above Lake Superior to its final destination: Canada. Almost the entire 240 miles are finished. The termination point of the SHT will intersect with the Border Lake Route, which ends near the Kekekabic Trail to Ely, Minnesota. Thus, within a few years more than 400 miles of trail will explore Minnesota's North Shore, border country wilderness, and the Boundary Waters Canoe Area Wilderness.

Hikers access the SHT at points along the county and forest roads and in the state parks that the trail links together. The SHT is closed to all motorized vehicles, bikes, and horses. It is suitable for snowshoeing, but not cross-country skiing. Trails are created and maintained by the volunteers of the Superior Hiking Trail Association, which offers memberships and a catalog of merchandise. They are the source for maps, hike schedules, trail detail sheets, and a guidebook, which I strongly recommend, titled *Guide to the Superior Hiking Trail*. Contact the Association at 731 7th Avenue (Highway 61), P.O. Box 4, Two Harbors, MN 55616-0004, call them at (218) 834-2700, or check their website at shta.org.

The Superior Shuttle service picks up and drops off hikers at about two dozen trailheads. The service runs Fridays, Saturdays, and Sundays from mid-May to mid-October. The shuttle makes its first stop at Castle Danger at 8:20 A.M., makes specified stops up to Pincushion Mountain at 11:30 A.M., and makes stops with a confirmed reservation at Judge C. R. Magney State Park. The shuttle returns to Castle Danger at 3:40 P.M., stopping back at each trailhead. Cost is based on the number of stops ($10 to $50), and you should call (218) 834-5511 first. Web site is at superiorhikingshuttle.com.

Campsites typically are found every five to eight miles along the SHT and are available first-come, first-served. Campsites have latrines, campfire rings, and tent pads. If campsites are occupied, campers may camp elsewhere along the trail. Follow wilderness camping etiquette; do not camp within 100 feet of the trail or a water source, and bury all human waste products.

SONJU TRAIL

Two Harbors' waterfront trail! Stroll from the waterfront near the *Edna G.* along the shoreline, on Lighthouse Point, and to Burlington Bay near the campground.

> From Highway 61 in Two Harbors, turn at the stoplight and follow waterfront signs or park at Burlington Bay campground area.

SILVER CREEK TO CASTLE DANGER (SHT)

Choose this as a day hike and follow the trail through valleys, up along ridgelines, over the quiet Encampment River, past several scenic vista stops to Castle Danger.

> From Highway 61 past Flood Bay, drive north on Co. Rd. 3, then northeast on Forest Rd. 301 to parking area.
> LENGTH: 6.3 miles one way to Silver Creek Road 617
> TRAILHEAD: At Forest Rd. 301
> MAPS: *SHT Guide,* maps at visitors centers, call SHTA at (218) 834-2700, or shta.org
> LEVEL OF DIFFICULTY: Moderate

CASTLE DANGER (SHT)

A great 2.5-mile option is to walk in a half-mile to Wolf Rock for spectacular full-circle views at 1,200 feet, then continue another half-mile to the spur trail (quarter-mile) to the Crow Creek valley overlook, and return by the same route. Or continue on high ground to Mike's Rock for views of Gooseberry River valley and Superior, then descend to lower ground to and along the Gooseberry River and into the state park. This inland area is gorgeous during fall color, and the gravel bar along the river is a good spot to hunt for agates. The final descent leads past the stunning Fifth Falls.

From Highway 61 just past marker 36, go north on Co. Rd. 106 (which turns into Silver Creek 617) to parking on the right.

LENGTH: 8.6 miles one-way to Gooseberry Falls State Park

TRAILHEAD: Right side of parking lot

MAPS: SHT *Guide*, maps at visitor centers, call SHTA at (218) 834-2700, or shta.org

LEVEL OF DIFFICULTY: Moderate

AMENITIES: Services available at Gooseberry Falls State Park visitors center; 3 regular and 1 multigroup campsite on the trail

GOOSEBERRY FALLS STATE PARK

Gitchi Gummi Trail is one mile; this trail slowly climbs the east side of the river through an aspen forest and along a ridge overlooking Superior before cutting back along Nelson's Creek and returning to the lower falls. Voyageur Trail is also one mile; this loop heads past the upper falls adjacent to the river, then cuts through upland forests and drops back to the visitors center. Fifth Falls Trail winds up the east bank past the upper falls; this 1.5-mile hike peaks at the Fifth Falls (a spur trail leads to a nearby overlook), then descends the west side of the Gooseberry River. The Upper and Lower Rim Trails are about 2.5 miles; the Lower Rim Trail leads past the lower falls on the west bank, where it picks up an old logging grade and leads to the mouth of the river and Superior's shoreline, at which point the trail becomes the Upper Rim Trail and leads around the point and slowly back inland to the falls. A half-mile accessible trail departs the visitors center, leads past the Lower Falls, under the Highway 61 bridge, and to an overlook of the Upper Falls.

Highway 61, 12 miles northeast of Two Harbors, with parking at the visitors center

(218) 834-3855

LENGTH: 18 miles

TRAILHEAD: From the visitors center

MAPS: At the state park, and trails are marked; call the DNR at (888) MINN-DNR or (651) 296-6157, or northshorevisitor.com

LEVEL OF DIFFICULTY: The five main trails are easy to moderate, with increased difficulty on inland trails.

AMENITIES: Restrooms, water, and picnic sites at the visitors center

SPLIT ROCK RIVER LOOP (SHT)

A first-choice hike! Head upstream on the west side of the river, at 50 feet above the river, past rock cliffs and vertical drops to a footbridge. The eastern, downstream portion initially showcases the river valley, then heads inland for an overlook of Superior before the final spur to Highway 61, about a third of a mile east of the parking area.

> Highway 61, about 15 miles northeast of Two Harbors, with parking on the west side of the river
>
> LENGTH: 5 miles
>
> TRAILHEAD: East side of the parking area
>
> MAPS: SHT *Guide,* pick up maps at visitors centers, or call SHTA at (218) 834-2700, or shta.org
>
> LEVEL OF DIFFICULTY: Moderate to more difficult (some washouts and steep grades)
>
> AMENITIES: Available at nearby Split Rock Lighthouse State Park; 3 regular and 1 multigroup campsite along the trail

SPLIT ROCK LIGHTHOUSE STATE PARK

Lots of trails! Walk 1.5 miles around the lighthouse and history center complex down to the old dock and pump house on Superior's shore. A favorite of mine is the Little Two Harbors Trail (half-mile each way), which leads from the lighthouse to the one-mile Day Hill loop to the two-mile Corundum Mine Trail, which explores Split Rock Point (hike all 3 trails!), while the three-mile Merrill Logging Trail meanders up Split Rock Creek, west through the backwoods to an overlook, and across Highway 61 before heading back to the Day Hill Trail. The trails around the main complex and picnic area are especially good for children.

> Off Highway 61 about 20 miles northeast of Two Harbors, with parking in the state park and at the lighthouse
>
> General information: (218) 226-6377
>
> LENGTH: 12 miles of trails including the SHT
>
> TRAILHEAD: At the lighthouse and history center parking area, or farther into the park at the picnic area
>
> MAPS: Available at the state park, and trails are marked, or call the DNR at (888) MINN-DNR or (651) 296-6157, or northshorevisitor.com
>
> LEVEL OF DIFFICULTY: Easy to more difficult (stairs, length, and grade)
>
> AMENITIES: Bathrooms, some paved trails, and picnic area

BEAVER BAY TO SILVER BAY (SHT)

The 2.25-mile trip to the falls and back follows the snowmobile trail across the Beaver River, where the SHT curves through cedar and pine along the east bank as this gentle river flows into roaring rapids and a waterfall (return by the same route). Or continue across the railroad tracks to Sulheim's Overlook, a rock outcrop with nearly full-circle views. The SHT continues over roads, the snowmobile trail, and a pipeline into a birch forest to a ridge overlooking Silver Bay. The final walk to Penn Boulevard leads past an active beaver pond.

From Highway 61 in Beaver Bay, drive north on Lax Lake Road
(Co. Rd. 4) for 0.8 miles to the parking area.

LENGTH: 4.5 miles to Penn Boulevard north of Silver Bay

TRAILHEAD: On the east side of the road at the snowmobile trail

MAPS: SHT *Guide,* pick up maps at a visitors center, call SHTA at (218)
834-2700, or shta.org

LEVEL OF DIFFICULTY: Moderate

AMENITIES: Outhouse at trailhead on Beaver River; 1 campsite on
the trail

BACKPACKER'S FAVORITE WITH A DAY TRIP OPTION

Hike over 11 miles from Silver Bay through Tettegouche State Park to Minnesota Highway 1. The length and rises and falls make this one of the more challenging sections of the SHT. Consider a day hike from Silver Bay; come in past Bean and Bear Lakes and return to Penn Boulevard. Maple forests make this a first-choice fall hike!

From Highway 61 in Silver Bay, drive north into town on Penn
Boulevard to the parking area.

LENGTH: 11.1 miles plus spurs

TRAILHEAD: Parking on Penn Boulevard

MAPS: SHT *Guide,* pick up maps at visitors centers, call SHTA at
(218) 834-2700, or shta.org

LEVEL OF DIFFICULTY: Moderate to most difficult

AMENITIES: In Silver Bay; 4 regular and 1 multigroup campsites on trail

PALISADE CREEK VALLEY IN TETTEGOUCHE STATE PARK

Walk in on the service road 1.5 miles to Tettegouche Camp, then head south to the Palisade Valley overlook. About half a mile in on the service road, you can pick up a two-mile trail system that showcases overlooks of Tettegouche, Lax, and Cedar Lakes plus Floating Bog Bay; from here it is just a third of a mile to the Palisade Valley overlook.

From Highway 61 in Beaver Bay, go north on Lax Lake Road (Co. Rd. 4) to the service road for Tettegouche State Park personnel only; park on the blacktop.

LENGTH: 4 miles total, plus optional spurs

TRAILHEAD: Walk in on the service road.

MAPS: Use a Tettegouche State Park map.

LEVEL OF DIFFICULTY: Easy to moderate

TETTEGOUCHE STATE PARK

The rest area has a short walk (less than a mile) along the ridge above Superior that features six overlooks, and a one-mile (total) spur trail to Shovel Point that has three overlooks. From the campground, you can also walk the two-mile (total) trail to the high falls. From the inland trailhead, you have the option of larger loops leading to Nipisquit, Mic Mac, and Tettegouche Lakes, with overlooks of these lakes, Lake Superior, Papasay Ridge, Raven Rock, the Conservancy Pines, Mount Baldy, and Floating Bog Bay.

Highway 61, five miles northeast of Silver Bay

(218) 226-6365

LENGTH: 23 miles of trails

TRAILHEAD: At parking lots in wayside (note podium maps throughout the trail system), or follow the road through the park to interior trails.

MAPS: Trails are marked, maps are available at the state park, call the DNR at (888) MINN-DNR or (651) 296-6157, or northshorevisitor.com

LEVEL OF DIFFICULTY: Easy to more difficult

AMENITIES: Restrooms and picnic area

SECTION 13 (SHT)

Enter birch and spruce woods and climb to maple ridges; one mile in, the trail ascends a steep outcrop, giving a first highland glimpse of the surrounding area. Moving on, you approach Section 13, a ridge popular with rock climbers that affords fabulous vistas.

From Highway 61 in Little Marais, go north on Co. Rd. 6 for two miles to the SHT sign and parking lot in gravel pit.

LENGTH: 2.25 miles total

TRAILHEAD: 0.1 mile west on Co. Rd. 6

MAPS: SHT *Guide,* maps at visitors centers, call SHTA at (218) 834-2700, or shta.org

LEVEL OF DIFFICULTY: More difficult (steep grades)

AMENITIES: 1 regular and 1 multigroup campsite on trail

GEORGE CROSBY MANITOU STATE PARK

Seven loops crisscross this less-frequented state park; paths lead through dense forest to the rushing rapids of the upper Manitou River and into the gorges of the river valley; open views of Lake Superior to the south. To explore the park completely, consider staying overnight at one of 21 backpack campsites.

> From Highway 61 at Illgen City, go north on Minnesota 1 for seven miles to Co. Rd. 7, then east on Co. Rd. 7 another seven miles.

> (218) 226-6365 (Tettegouche State Park also takes calls for Crosby Manitou Park.)

> LENGTH: 24 miles of trails

> TRAILHEAD: Three trails leave from the parking area, including the short Benson Lake trail to picnicking.

> MAPS: Trails are marked, call the DNR at (888) MINN-DNR or (651) 296-6157, or northshorevisitor.com

> LEVEL OF DIFFICULTY: Moderate to most difficult

> AMENITIES: Picnic area, outhouses, and water

MANITOU RIVER TRAIL (SHT)

As you follow the Middle Trail, consider the short (70-yard) spur leading downhill to view the river and Superior. About a mile in, the trail heads downstream, then over bluffs and into a descent to the river and a bridge. Across on the east bank, an 1,800-foot section of path climbs steeply 300 feet into the woods, where you are rewarded with four overlooks of the rugged Manitou, its valley, and Lake Superior. Return by the same route.

> From Highway 61 at Illgen City, go north on Minnesota 1 for seven miles to Co. Rd. 7, then east on Co. Rd. 7 another seven miles.

> LENGTH: 3.2 miles total

> TRAILHEAD: State Park parking lot; enter on the middle trail.

> MAPS: SHT *Guide,* maps at visitors centers; call SHTA at (218) 834-2700, or shta.org

> LEVEL OF DIFFICULTY: More to most difficult (steep grades)

> AMENITIES: Picnic area, outhouses, and water

CARIBOU STATE WAYSIDE

This well-traveled trail heads north alongside the river about half a mile to a waterfall; a steep grade leads to the top of the falls; watch for loose soil; what appears to be a trail continuing north comes to an end. You may enjoy the return trip along the upper river trail, or return by the same route.

Highway 61, about 5.5 miles northeast of Little Marais, with parking on
the north side
LENGTH: 1 mile total
TRAILHEAD: At north end of parking
LEVEL OF DIFFICULTY: Moderate (not maintained)
AMENITIES: Outhouses

CROSS RIVER STATE WAYSIDE
Follow this short, gradual incline for spectacular glimpses of the river gorges,
and be sure to view the falls from both sides of the Highway 61 bridge.
Highway 61 in Schroeder, with parking on both sides
LENGTH: 0.5 mile total
TRAILHEAD: At parking on northwest side of river, or one block north
on gravel road to parking area.
LEVEL OF DIFFICULTY: Easy (not maintained)

TEMPERANCE RIVER STATE PARK
Trails below the highway bridge lead to a catwalk bridge over the river and to
the river mouth, adjacent Superior shoreline, and campground; the path-
ways above the highway bridge bring you right to the edge of spectacular
gorges, with several stone overlooks on the east side of the river. Hike farther
upstream to encounter additional pools and cascades; you can also step
away from the river's turmoil onto paths leading through birch forests in this
glacial river valley, and 4.8 miles to Carlton's Peak and the Sawbill Trail.
Highway 61 in Schroeder, with parking on both sides
(218) 663-7476
LENGTH: 22 miles of trails
TRAILHEAD: On all four corners of the Highway 61 bridge
MAPS: Trails are marked; maps available at the state park, call the DNR
at (888) MINN-DNR or (651) 296-6157, northshorevisitor.com, use the
SHT *Guide,* maps at visitors centers, call SHTA at (218) 834-2700, or
shta.org
LEVEL OF DIFFICULTY: Easy to more difficult; use caution, especially
with young children, at the sheer drop-offs.
AMENITIES: Restrooms in the park campground

CARLTON PEAK (SHT)
Follow the snowmobile trail across an open expanse of grassland into a
maple forest. The path slowly ascends through the maples past massive
boulders to two spurs to the summit; follow the left path to the main peak,

the right path to a secondary peak. A half-mile past these spurs in the birch woods and beyond an old access road is a sign leading to an overlook with wide-open views of Lake Superior, Tofte, the Temperance River Valley, and west past Taconite Harbor.

From Highway 61 in Tofte, go north on the Sawbill Trail (Co. Rd. 2) for two miles to parking area on right.

LENGTH: 3.4 miles round-trip to the peak or 5.2 miles round-trip to the overlook

TRAILHEAD: Cross the Sawbill Trail and follow the snowmobile trail.

MAPS: SHT *Guide*, maps at visitors centers, call SHTA at (218) 834-2700, or shta.org

LEVEL OF DIFFICULTY: Easy to moderate (final ascent to peak)

AMENITIES: Outhouse

BRITTON PEAK

A short, steep, rocky trail takes you to the peak and a memorial to W. L. Britton of the U.S. Army, plus panoramas of Lake Superior, Carlton Peak, and Temperance River Valley.

From Highway 61 in Tofte, go north on the Sawbill Trail (Co. Rd. 2) for 2.5 miles to parking area on right.

LENGTH: 0.5 mile total

TRAILHEAD: North end of parking; *not* the Sugarbush cross-country ski trail.

LEVEL OF DIFFICULTY: More difficult (steep grades)

AMENITIES: Outhouse

RAY BERGLUND MEMORIAL WAYSIDE

This trail has developed from people walking up the Onion River from the wayside. Go half a mile up the river's edge, then return on the same path past cascades, rapids, and old white pines.

Highway 61, about four miles northeast of Tofte, with parking on north side

LENGTH: 1 mile total

TRAILHEAD: Just right of memorial plaque

LEVEL OF DIFFICULTY: More difficult (not maintained and a few steep drop-offs)

OBERG AND LEVEAUX MOUNTAINS

Oberg is a premier North Shore trail, with a switchback climb to an easy circular loop showcasing nine overlooks; especially beautiful during fall colors,

Oberg offers views of Lake Superior, the Sawtooth Mountain Range, scenic Oberg Lake, and the surrounding maple-covered hillsides. The less frequented LeVeaux trail has fewer overlooks but is quite appealing as it directs you to Oberg's sister peak (both peaks are about 1,000 feet). The first leg of the LeVeaux trail is a good spot to watch for deer and moose feeding at dawn and dusk.

From Highway 61 about five miles northeast of Tofte, go north on Onion River Road (Forest Rd. 336) for two miles to parking.

LENGTH: Oberg is 2.25 miles and LeVeaux is 3.5 miles round-trip

TRAILHEAD: On the east side of Forest Rd. 336 for the Oberg trail; the LeVeaux trail leaves the parking area and heads west.

MAPS: Trails are marked.

LEVEL OF DIFFICULTY: Oberg trail has a moderate ascent to an easy loop; LeVeaux trail is moderate.

AMENITIES: Outhouse

WHITE SKY ROCK

A steep uphill climb to a peak overlooking Caribou Lake and surrounding maple forests; named after an area Ojibwe trapper who was an early forest ranger.

From Highway 61 in Lutsen, go north on the Caribou Trail (Co. Rd. 4) about four miles to small pull-over area.

LENGTH: 0.7 mile total

TRAILHEAD: Look for the brown and yellow sign on the west side of the road.

LEVEL OF DIFFICULTY: More to most difficult; steep and not maintained

CASCADE RIVER STATE PARK

An easy half-mile loop leads up the west bank, past the Cascade Falls, and across the river and returns on the east bank. Trails continue up the river on both sides for about 1.5 miles. A 2.25-mile loop skirts the lakeshore for more than a mile before climbing inland and returning to the river through birch and pine forests. The trails have several spurs and options, including the popular hike to Lookout Mountain, 600 feet above Superior. The most direct (and steepest) route is about 2.25 miles total. I recommend you hike up the west side of the river a half-mile, then take the SHT west another one-third mile over Cascade Creek, and then follow the Lookout Mountain trail the remaining two miles to the top; you can take the steeper, more direct SHT route back to the Cascade River mouth.

Highway 61, with parking at the river and in the park

(218) 387-3053

LENGTH: 18 miles of trails

TRAILHEAD: On west side of river at pull-over; at trailhead in park
   campground.

MAPS: Trails are marked; you can also pick up a map at the state park,
   call the DNR at (888) MINN-DNR or (651) 296-6157, or
   northshorevisitor.com

LEVEL OF DIFFICULTY: Easy to more difficult (length and steep
   grades)

AMENITIES: Outhouses (restrooms in park) and picnic area

IN GRAND MARAIS

SWEETHEART'S BLUFF

This picnic walk steeply climbs the Rec Area's western bluff. Treat your
sweetie to picturesque vistas of Lake Superior and the Grand Marais harbor,
and lunch under the picnic shelter.

   Off Highway 61 at the Grand Marais Rec Area

   LENGTH: 1 mile

   TRAILHEAD: Drive through the park and head west till the road ends.

   LEVEL OF DIFFICULTY: More to most difficult

   AMENITIES: Restrooms, water, and phone in Rec Center

ARTIST POINT AND LIGHTHOUSE

Meander south and east to Artist Point to take in the stunning Sawtooth
Mountain backdrop gracing the village, then explore the eastern breakwall
on your walk out to the Grand Marais Lighthouse – and don't forget your
camera.

   Off Highway 61 in Grand Marais; go south at the stoplight three blocks
      to parking.

   LENGTH: Less than 1 mile

   TRAILHEAD: Behind the Coast Guard building

   LEVEL OF DIFFICULTY: Easy

   AMENITIES: Picnic tables

UP THE GUNFLINT TRAIL

PINCUSHION MOUNTAIN AND DEVIL TRACK RIVER TRAILS (SHT)

Head north on the ski/hiking trail to the junction where you can continue to the peak of Pincushion Mountain (from there, you can continue on to the river or return) or head left along the ski trails for 1.5 miles to the SHT, which descends to the river. Hike a half-mile along the canyon floor to a 50-foot, A-shaped bridge, followed by a short climb to Spruce Knob for additional scenic views of the falls and red rhyolite cliffs. Ahead you will find the Barrier Falls overlook, directing your view deep into this hidden gorge. As you continue to the trail's end, you will find short spurs to the water's edge. This is a great two-car hike: leave one car 0.8 mile north of Highway 61 on Co. Rd. 58, and drive the other car back to the trailhead.

From Highway 61 in Grand Marais, go north on the Gunflint Trail (Co. Rd. 12) for about two miles to Co. Rd. 53, then east on Co. Rd. 53 to scenic overlook and trailhead.

LENGTH: 4.8 miles for Pincushion loop or 4.8 miles to Co. Rd. 58

TRAILHEAD: At overlook parking at cross-country ski trailhead

MAPS: SHT *Guide,* maps at visitors centers, call SHTA at (218) 834-2700, or shta.org

LEVEL OF DIFFICULTY: Moderate

AMENITIES: Outhouse

GEORGE WASHINGTON MEMORIAL PINES

A short spur leads to the loop; turn right, entering gorgeous stands of tall pine intermingled with birch as this quiet trail leads to the shores of the Elbow River. The relatively flat walk is highlighted in the last mile by large, lovely, fragrant cedar trees. You'll get your feet wet!

From Highway 61 in Grand Marais, go north on the Gunflint Trail (Co. Rd. 12) about eight miles to the parking area (on west side).

LENGTH: 2.25 miles

TRAILHEAD: At parking area

MAPS: U.S. Forest Service Gunflint Ranger Station on Highway 61 in Grand Marais, or call (218) 387-1750.

LEVEL OF DIFFICULTY: Easy (moderate length)

EAGLE MOUNTAIN TRAIL

Plan a full day or overnight trip (Boundary Waters Canoe Area Wilderness permit required) to Minnesota's highest point (2,301 feet). Initially the rocky course rolls along small, birch-covered hills, dipping into spruce bogs, with planked boardwalks spanning the worst wet areas. About three miles in, the woods change to birch and the path leads to and along Whale Lake to an old logging camp (designated campsite) and the northwest corner of the lake. The trail forks right to Brule Lake (seven more miles) and left to a sharply graded incline to the bluffs; admire your bird's-eye vantage as you take in Crow, Eagle, Shrike, and Zoo Lakes to the west, the Misquah Hills to the north, the Brule Lake lookout tower to the northwest, and on a clear day, Lake Superior to the south. To reach the Eagle Mountain summit, start from the southwest end of the bluffs and follow the cairns (small, formed rock piles); bring lunch, binoculars, and a camera.

> From Highway 61 past Cascade State Park, go northeast on Co. Rd. 7 to Co. Rd. 48, then north on Co. Rd. 48 to the Bally Creek Road, drive west on the Bally Creek Road until it intersects The Grade. Or from Highway 61 in Lutsen, go north on the Caribou Trail 15 miles, then east on The Grade for four miles to parking on north.
>
> LENGTH: 7 miles total
>
> TRAILHEAD: At northeast end of parking
>
> MAPS: U.S. Forest Service Gunflint Ranger Station on Highway 61 in Grand Marais, or call (218) 387-1750, or Gunflint Trail Visitors Center at Highway 61 and main street
>
> LEVEL OF DIFFICULTY: More difficult (steep grades and rocky portions)
>
> AMENITIES: Outhouse

NORTHERN LIGHT LAKE AND BLUEBERRY HILL TRAIL

This half-mile jaunt gives you a quick thrill atop Blueberry Hill, where you'll admire Northern Light Lake and, in season, succulent wild blueberries. Use your energy from the descent to hike a quarter-mile to where the Brule River flows into Northern Light Lake (return by the same route).

> From Highway 61 in Grand Marais, go north on the Gunflint Trail (Co. Rd. 12) for about 13 miles to parking on east side.
>
> LENGTH: 0.5 mile each, or 1 mile combined
>
> TRAILHEAD: At parking, go right to Blueberry Hill or left to Brule River.
>
> MAPS: U.S. Forest Service Gunflint Ranger Station on Highway 61 in Grand Marais, or call (218) 387-1750, or Gunflint Trail Visitors Center at Highway 61 and main street

LEVEL OF DIFFICULTY: Easy to Brule; moderate climb up
Blueberry Hill

LIMA MOUNTAIN TRAIL

A short ascent to westward views of the Misquah Hills and surrounding forest. Lima Mountain was the site of a fire lookout tower from 1935 to 1956; the tower was removed in 1978.

From Highway 61 in Grand Marais, go north on the Gunflint Trail (Co. Rd. 12) about 20 miles, west on Lima Mountain Road for 2 miles, and north on Forest Rd. 315 to parking off the road's edge.

LENGTH: 1 mile total

TRAILHEAD: From road

MAPS: U.S. Forest Service Gunflint Ranger Station on Highway 61 in Grand Marais, or call (218) 387-1750, or at Gunflint Trail Visitors Center at Highway 61 and main street

LEVEL OF DIFFICULTY: Moderate

BORDER ROUTE TRAIL

The 70-mile Border Route Trail spans the border lake country; much of the trail lies within the Boundary Waters Canoe Area Wilderness (permit required). On the western edge, access can be gained at Gunflint Lake and several other points. The route dips below Rose Lake before skirting the northern edge of Clearwater Lake, then heads due east, winding south between John and MacFarland Lakes. The trail continues east to South Fowl Lake, then turns 90 degrees south to Otter Lake and then a final eastern leg to the intersection of Swamp River and the Otter Lake Forest Road (east off the Arrowhead Trail). The trail crosses the Grand Portage Indian Reservation and connects to the Grand Portage for a final hike down to Lake Superior.

Obtain information at a U.S. Forest Service Ranger Station.

HONEYMOON BLUFF TRAIL

Especially colorful in the fall, the short, steep trek to Honeymoon Bluff lets you admire the spacious prospect of Hungry Jack Lake. This west-facing bluff is popular at sunset, but bring a flashlight for the descent.

From Highway 61 in Grand Marais, go 22 miles north on the Gunflint Trail (Co. Rd. 12), then east on Clearwater Road past Flour Lake campground.

LENGTH: .75 mile total

TRAILHEAD: Marked with a sign

MAPS: U.S. Forest Service Gunflint Ranger Station on Highway 61 in
Grand Marais, call (218) 387-1750, or Gunflint Trail Visitors Center at
Highway 61 and main street
LEVEL OF DIFFICULTY: More difficult (steep grade)
AMENITIES: Outhouses and water at campground

CARIBOU ROCK AND SPLIT PINE TRAILS

Take the steep quarter-mile hike to the overlook of Bearskin Lake; continue
on the demanding 3.25-mile trail that intersects with the Border Route Trail
near Rose Lake and the Stairway Portage (between Duncan and Rose Lakes).
Travel through woods with clearings providing views of Moss, Duncan, and
Daniels Lakes. Plan on five hours plus lunch near the waterfalls at Stairway
Portage.

From Highway 61 in Grand Marais, go north on the Gunflint Trail
(Co. Rd. 12) for 28 miles, then east on Hungry Jack Road for 2 miles
until you see the trail sign and parking.
LENGTH: 0.5 mile to 7 miles total
TRAILHEAD: At parking
MAPS: U.S. Forest Service Gunflint Ranger Station on Highway 61 in
Grand Marais, call (218) 387-1750, or Gunflint Trail Visitors Center at
Highway 61 and main street
LEVEL OF DIFFICULTY: Most difficult

GUNFLINT LAKE TRAILS

The resorts on Gunflint Lake will provide maps to local trails showcasing the
lake, adjacent ridges, and forests. Most are moderate in length and level of
difficulty.

MAGNETIC ROCK TRAIL

Test the magnetic attraction of Magnetic Rock at the end of this relatively
easy three-quarter-mile hike; on your return, look for berries and signs of
moose and beaver along Larch Creek and the nearby bog.

From Highway 61 in Grand Marais, go north on the Gunflint Trail
(Co. Rd. 12) 45.5 miles to parking and trailhead on the east.
LENGTH: 1.5 miles total
TRAILHEAD: Marked with a sign on the east side
MAPS: U.S. Forest Service Gunflint Ranger Station on Highway 61 in
Grand Marais, call (218) 387-1750, or Gunflint Trail Visitors Center at
Highway 61 and main street
LEVEL OF DIFFICULTY: Easy

KEKEKABIC TRAIL

From the Gunflint Trail, the Kekekabic winds 40 miles through the Boundary Waters Canoe Area Wilderness (permit required) to Ely, Minnesota. The Friends of the Kekekabic group attempts to clear the trail every few years; however, uncleared windfalls can make the trail impassable. Before attempting this trail, contact the U.S. Forest Service Gunflint Ranger Station for updated information, or call the Kekekabic Trail Club at (800) 818-HIKE, (651) 254-9885, check their Web site at kek.org, or write to them at 309 Cedar Avenue South, Minneapolis, MN 55454.

BLUEBERRY HILL TRAIL

Walk through a spruce forest to a fork in the trail. On the left is the quarter-mile trek to Blueberry Hill, 140 feet above Saganaga Lake, offering a beautiful overlook. The right fork continues through hilly and swampy terrain to a campsite at Maraboeuf Lake.

From Highway 61 in Grand Marais, go north on the Gunflint Trail
(Co. Rd. 12) 56 miles, then east on Co. Rd. 81 for an eighth of a mile
to the gate; do not block the driveway.
LENGTH: 2.5 miles, or 1.5 miles just to Blueberry Hill and return
TRAILHEAD: Near gate
MAPS: U.S. Forest Service Gunflint Ranger Station on Highway 61 in
Grand Marais, call (218) 387-1750, or at Gunflint Trail Visitors Center
at Highway 61 and main street
LEVEL OF DIFFICULTY: Moderate

ON HIGHWAY 61 NORTHEAST OF GRAND MARAIS

WOOD'S, DURFEE, CLIFF, AND KIMBALL CREEKS (SHT)

Follow Wood's Creek for 1.25 miles through birch and dark spruce as the SHT bends eastward through birch stands and cutover areas where Lake Superior, Five-Mile Rock, Pincushion Mountain, and the Sawtooth Range come into view. At the three-mile mark, you reach the Durfee Creek campsite and begin crossing a series of 24 board bridges. It is another mile to Cliff Creek, then one mile to the Red Cliff overlook; continue on along and over the Kimball Creek to a final steep climb to Co. Rd. 14. Note the red rhyolite throughout the trail.

From Highway 61 about 4 miles northeast of Grand Marais, go north
   on Co. Rd. 58 for 0.8 mile to parking.
LENGTH: 9.2 miles to Kadunce River Wayside
TRAILHEAD: East side of Co. Rd. 58 at Wood's Creek
MAPS: SHT *Guide,* maps at visitors centers, call SHTA at
   (218) 834-2700, or shta.org
LEVEL OF DIFFICULTY: Moderate to more difficult (grades and length)

KADUNCE RIVER STATE WAYSIDE

Be adventurous and hike the river upstream! You may get a little wet as you
ascend the small waterfalls, but it's a lot of fun. The adjacent trail brushes the
water's edge, then climbs to ridgelines and overlooks. About a mile upstream
the trail intersects with the SHT. Bring a picnic and spend some time on the
cobblestone beach at the river mouth.

Highway 61, about eight miles northeast of Grand Marais
LENGTH: 2 miles total
TRAILHEAD: At wayside parking on east bank of river
MAPS: SHT *Guide,* maps at visitors centers, call SHTA at
   (218) 834-2700, or shta.org
LEVEL OF DIFFICULTY: Easy to more difficult (if you hike in the river)

DEVIL'S KETTLE TRAIL AND JUDGE C. R. MAGNEY STATE PARK

This mildly hilly trail has a long uphill rise through thick pine forests above
the Brule River, then almost 200 steps lead down to the river and past the
lower falls, followed by a short climb to the upper falls and the Devil's Kettle.
At the upper falls, the river separates, with half of the water flowing into the
legendary bottomless cauldron and half the river running over the upper
falls. The trail offers some pretty dramatic overlooks into the massive river
gorge, and a short spur leads to a large rock outcrop at the base of the lower
falls where you can feel the spray. Additional trails explore the woodlands on
the west side of the Brule above the campground.

Off Highway 61 about 14 miles northeast of Grand Marais
(218) 387-3039
LENGTH: 7 miles of trails; the Devil's Kettle Trail is 2.25 miles total.
TRAILHEAD: On the east side of the Brule River
MAPS: Trails are marked; pick up a map at the state park; call the DNR at
   (888) MINN-DNR or (651) 296-6157, or northshorevisitor.com
LEVEL OF DIFFICULTY: Moderate to most difficult (area with almost
   200 steps)
AMENITIES: Outhouses, water, and picnic area

MOUNT ROSE TRAIL

Climb 300 feet on a paved pathway up Mount Rose. Informational panels detail the history of the fur trade at Grand Portage, while turn-around views lay the grounds of the National Monument Center at your feet.

From Highway 61 about 36 miles northeast of Grand Marais, go south at the signs to Grand Portage National Monument.

(218) 387-2788

LENGTH: 1 mile total

TRAILHEAD: At the national monument

MAPS: Self-guided brochures are available at the monument.

LEVEL OF DIFFICULTY: Moderate (steep with stairs)

AMENITIES: Restrooms, water, and picnic area at the monument

THE GRAND PORTAGE

This long, scenic, and historically significant trail leads 630 feet above Lake Superior to the site of Fort Charlotte on the Pigeon River (where campsites are available). Once used by Ojibwe and voyageurs as the first leg of the trip to the great Northwest, the Grand Portage is an epic trail.

From Highway 61 about 36 miles northeast of Grand Marais, go south at the signs to Grand Portage National Monument.

(218) 387-2788

LENGTH: 17 miles total

TRAILHEAD: At the national monument

MAPS: A detailed brochure is available at the monument.

LEVEL OF DIFFICULTY: Most difficult (length)

AMENITIES: Restrooms, water, visitors center, and picnic area at the monument

MOUNT JOSEPHINE TRAIL

Climb 800 feet on a switchback trail to Mount Jo's summit for an outstanding scene that takes in Pigeon Point, Wauswaugoning Bay, the Susie Islands, and Isle Royale.

From Highway 61 about 36 miles northeast of Grand Marais, go east on Co. Rd. 17 to Upper Road to parking.

LENGTH: 1½ miles including walk to trailhead

TRAILHEAD: A quarter of a mile from parking on Co. Rd. 17

LEVEL OF DIFFICULTY: Most difficult (steep grade)

AMENITIES: At the Grand Portage National Monument

GRAND PORTAGE STATE PARK

The trail follows an old roadbed half a mile to two spectacular overlooks of the High Falls; take some time to meander down side trails to quiet pools. New more difficult Middle Falls Trail winds over scenic ridgetops through the woods, along the river to the falls, and loops back.

Off Highway 61 about five miles northeast of Grand Portage

LENGTH: 4.5 miles total

TRAILHEAD: At parking area (a state park permit is required)

LEVEL OF DIFFICULTY: Easy to High Falls; more to most difficult Middle Falls Trail (terrain)

ISLE ROYALE NATIONAL PARK TRAILS

Hike along rocky shorelines, through dense interior woodlands, and along ridgetops where you may have the opportunity to spot moose, foxes, and deer. Topographic maps are helpful and recommended.

Three-hour boat trip from Grand Portage to Isle Royale National Park

LENGTH: 165 miles of trail tangle themselves on this 45-mile-long island.

TRAILHEADS: Washington Harbor on the west end, Rock Harbor on the east end, and throughout the island

MAPS: Write to Isle Royale National Park, Houghton, MI 49931, or call (906) 482-0984.

LEVEL OF DIFFICULTY: Some trails are easy, but most are moderate to more difficult (grades and wet or slippery).

AMENITIES: Shelters, campsites, picnic areas, outhouses, and water

LODGE-TO-LODGE HIKING

Sister to the ski program, the lodge-to-lodge hiking program offers hikers packages with lodging, transportation, and some meals. Hikers get the full experience of exploring the north woods and Lake Superior while also enjoying all the amenities and comforts of a resort. After a full day of hiking, you will find dinner ready and your luggage waiting. Resorts that participate in this program extend from Silver Bay to north of Grand Marais. Contact Boundary Country Trekking for more information and to make reservations.

Boundary Country Trekking, 173 Little Ollie Road, Grand Marais, MN 55604

(800) 322-8327 or (218) 388-4487

boundarycountry.com

Pedal Pushers

BIKING TRAILS AND PATHS

CYCLING THE NORTH SHORE IS EXHILARATING! OBSERVE spring runoff, ride to a swimming hole, or admire the colors of fall. Duluth trails, typically paved, are perfect for family picnic rides. As you move up the Shore, countless logging, forest, and backcountry roads are available for mountain biking. And the new Gitchi Gami Trail will ultimately allow bikers (and hikers, walkers, and inline skaters) to ride from Two Harbors to Grand Marais. Do not bike on Highway 61 southwest of Grand Marais or on the Gunflint Trail, The Grade road (in Cook County), or other major thoroughfares; there are no bike lanes, and traffic often has limited visibility. Bikes are not allowed on the Superior Hiking Trail. Obtain maps from tourist information centers and U.S. Forest Service Ranger Stations.

When mountain bike riding, consider the following:

- Obtain a map and familiarize yourself with the trail.
- Let someone (perhaps the front desk at your lodging) know your trail route and expected return time.
- Most trails tour isolated areas that offer no immediate services.
- It can get hot – pack and drink plenty of water.
- Pack high-energy snacks and rain gear.
- Be prepared for breakdown, and bring a tool and patch kit.
- Binoculars and cameras come in handy on the trail.
- Consider bringing a wildflower guide or bird book.
- Always pack out what you bring in – dispose of trash responsibly.
- Wear blaze orange during hunting seasons (September 1 through December 31).
- Trails cross private, county, state, and federal lands – please respect this.
- Use common sense.

LAKEWALK
Ride Duluth's most famous waterfront trail.

Along Lake Superior's shore from Bayfront Park to 26th Avenue East
LENGTH: 4 miles
TRAILHEAD: Anywhere along the Lakewalk including 5th Avenue West and Harbor Drive, in Canal Park, and at 26th Avenue East and London Road
TRAIL SURFACE: Easy, paved roadway

WESTERN WATERFRONT TRAIL
A great trail for family riding. Portions of the trail run parallel to the St. Louis River; features picnic sites and boat access.

From I-35S, go west on Grand Avenue/Highway 23 to 71st Avenue West.
LENGTH: 5-mile pathway (10 miles total) with access to the Munger State Trail
TRAILHEAD: At parking area on south side
TRAIL SURFACE: Smooth pathway

WILLARD MUNGER STATE TRAIL
Ideal for children and family rides, this smooth trail covers gentle terrain from West Duluth to Jay Cooke State Park (which offers picnic sites, restrooms, water, and telephone).

From I-35S, go west on Grand Avenue/Highway 23 to 75th Avenue West.
LENGTH: 14-mile pathway (28 miles total) to Jay Cooke State Park; total trail is 70 miles one way
TRAILHEAD: Adjacent to Indian Point Park
TRAIL SURFACE: Smooth pavement

HAWK RIDGE AND SEVEN BRIDGES ROAD
Leave one car on Superior Street and 60th Avenue West and drive another to Hawk Ridge; ride the ridge and descend across seven stone bridges over the Amity Creek to the Lester River.

From I-35, continue on London Road, go north on 60th Avenue East, then west on Glenwood to Hawk Ridge/Skyline Boulevard
LENGTH: Up to 7 miles
TRAILHEAD: At Hawk Ridge
TRAIL SURFACE: Hard-pack gravel and a portion of paved roadway

BRIGHTON BEACH AND SCENIC 61

Watch for traffic on these routes. A one-mile-plus paved road runs through Brighton Beach, which offers summer outhouses, drinking water, and picnic sites. A bike ride along Scenic 61 showcases Lake Superior and allows you to explore the shops along the way, stop for lunch, and pick up smoked fish at Russ Kendall's Smoke House (on the north side of the road).

From I-35, continue on London Road to just east of the Lester River.

LENGTH: Varies

TRAILHEAD: At the entrance to Brighton Beach or anywhere along Scenic 61

TRAIL SURFACE: Paved roadway

SONJU TRAIL

A paved lakeshore path in Two Harbors; ride from the Depot/*Edna G.* in the harbor past the lighthouse to Burlington Bay near the campground.

From Highway 61 in Two Harbors, turn at the stoplight toward the waterfront and park near the *Edna G.*

LENGTH: 2-mile round-trip plus spurs

TRAILHEAD: Two Harbors waterfront or Burlington Bay

TRAIL SURFACE: Paved

GITCHI GAMI TRAIL

This paved trail parallels Highway 61 and will ultimately run from Two Harbors to Grand Marais. Projections are for the trail to be completed in the summer of 2007. Currently the following sections are complete:

1.2 miles from Gooseberry Falls east connecting to

3.5 miles of trail leading to the Split Rock River (scheduled to be done in spring 2004)

3.0 miles from the Split Rock River to Split Rock Lighthouse and State Park

4.8 miles of Chapins Curve, from Split Rock Lighthouse to Beaver Bay

.6 mile in Beaver Bay scheduled to be completed in 2004

4.5 miles from Beaver Bay to Silver Bay to be completed in late 2004

2.5 miles from Tofte to near the Onion River

5.0 miles under construction to Co. Rd. 34/Hall Road

1.2 miles east of Grand Marais into town

For updates, events, and membership information, visit gitchigamitrail.com

GOOSEBERRY FALLS STATE PARK

Ride 8 miles of packed-dirt trails north of Highway 61 and access the paved Gitchi Gami Trail to the northeast

> Off Highway 61, 40 miles northeast of Duluth, and 12 miles northeast of Two Harbors
>
> (218) 834-3855 at Gooseberry
>
> gitchigamitrail.com and northshorevisitor.com

SPLIT ROCK LIGHTHOUSE STATE PARK

Ride 4 miles of packed-dirt trails from the picnic area along hiking trails and access the paved Gitchi Gami Trail to the southwest and northeast.

> Off Highway 61, 48 miles northeast of Duluth, and 20 miles northeast of Two Harbors.
>
> (218) 226-6377 at state park
>
> gitchigamitrail.com and northshorevisitor.com

TETTEGOUCHE STATE PARK

Ride the all-season trails through the park (not the snowmobile-only trails – ask at the visitors center) and the 1½-mile paved service road into Tettegouche Camp.

> On Highway 61, 60 miles northeast of Duluth and 5 miles northeast of Silver Bay.
>
> (218) 226-6365 at state park
>
> northshorevisitor.com

SUGARBUSH LOOP TRAILS

Bike along sugar maple ridgelines, then descend into grassy openings and muddy drainage areas; be prepared to ride through some wet, swampy areas. Trail intersections have "You Are Here" maps, or get the Sugarbush cross-country map at the Lutsen Tofte Visitors Center. These trails intersect with the Superior Hiking Trail, which is closed to mountain bikes.

> From Highway 61 in Tofte, go north on the Sawbill Trail (Co. Rd. 2) about two miles to Britton Peak parking.
>
> LENGTH: Up to 17 miles
>
> TRAILHEAD: At Britton Peak parking on the cross-country ski trails
>
> TRAIL SURFACE: All dirt trail, with wet and muddy areas
>
> sugarbushtrail.org

CARLTON PEAK/TOFTE TRAILS

From the grassy, packed-dirt, 1½-mile snowmobile trail to Carlton Peak – it's a 5-minute walk to the summit. Return on the same route or, near the Sawbill Trail, take the 3-mile Tofte Trail, all downhill to Highway 61; a grassy trail with small creeks.

From Highway 61 in Tofte, go north on the Sawbill Trail about 2.5 miles to parking, cross west over the Sawbill Trail, and head south to trailhead.

LENGTH: 3 to 6 miles

TRAILHEAD: On Sawbill Trail

TRAIL SURFACE: Grassy and hard-packed dirt

PANCORE LAKE LOOP

Ride the narrow, hard-packed forest road through boreal forests past Pancore Lake to the junction with Forest Rd. 339. Just east of this junction is a great picnic site at Clara Lake. Follow Forest Rd. 339 northwest, crossing the Poplar River to Forest Rd. 338, where you turn around for the final leg of the loop.

From Highway 61 in Tofte, go north on the Sawbill Trail (Co. Rd. 2) to Forest Rd. 338.

LENGTH: 25 miles total

TRAILHEAD: At the junction of Co. Rd. 2 and Forest Rd. 338

TRAIL SURFACE: Gravel logging roads

LUTSEN MOUNTAINS BIKE PARK

Lutsen Mountains maintains a variety of mountain biking trails on their cross-country ski system. Most of the 32 miles of trails are more to most difficult. An easy trail choice is on Mystery Mountain. Ride the lift to the top and follow the relatively gentle return. North Road is an easy 3-mile gravel/packed-dirt trail near the Poplar River. More difficult loops are on Ullr and Mystery Mountains. Expert and technical riders will be thrilled with the Moose Mountain loops. Call or stop by for maps and information. Gondola is open daily. Mystery lift is open Friday through Sunday.

From Highway 61 in Lutsen, go north on the Ski Hill Road to the main chalet.

Trail pass $16, with Mystery Lift $23, with Gondola $30

(218) 663-7281

lutsen.com

OLD HIGHWAY 61/CASCADE BEACH

Ride the 4.7-mile paved and gravel road from just west of Cascade River State Park, then cross Highway 61 and ride the 3.2-mile grassy old road bed just north of the highway.

From Highway 61, park at the northeast end of the Cascade Beach Road.

LENGTH: Up to 7.9 miles

TRAILHEAD: Cascade Beach Road or Clearview in Lutsen

TRAIL SURFACE: Paved, gravel, and grassy

WARD LAKE ROAD

An easy road ride with some hills, this out-and-back trail runs 4.7 miles in to Deer Yard Lake. One mile in, the road changes to Forest Rd. 1410, which continues another 2.7 miles to Ward Lake and then another mile to Deer Yard Lake access. You can access the northeast junction with the Pike Lake Loop, or access the Hall Road for a fun, bumpy 3-mile ride south to Highway 61.

From Highway 61 northeast of Lutsen, go north on Co. Rd. 7, north on Co. Rd. 44, west on the Pike Lake Road as it turns into Forest Rd. 332.

LENGTH: 9.4 miles total

TRAILHEAD: At Caribou Trail and Ward Lake Road

TRAIL SURFACE: Gravel road

ONION RIVER ROAD/NORTH SHORE TRAIL/POPLAR RIVER

Drive north to the Oberg/LeVeaux parking area and ride the gravel forest road 3 miles to the 2.5-mile North Shore Trail, which skirts Barker Lake. Continue on to Forest Rd. 337 and return south on the North Road along the Poplar River, 4 miles to the Lutsen Mountains area.

From Highway 61, drive north on the Onion River Road, or from Highway 61, drive north on the Caribou Trail, west on the Honeymoon Trail, and south on Barker Lake.

LENGTH: Up to 10 miles

TRAILHEAD: Oberg/LeVeaux or Barker Lake

TRAIL SURFACE: Gravel and packed dirt

PIKE LAKE LOOP

On this scenic trail, a large loop with a bisecting trail, hardwood forests give way to pines and spruce. Ride east on Forest Rd. 332, with a portion adjacent to Pike Lake, then head north on Forest Rd. 159, where you can choose to return on Forest Rd. 161 or continue north to a rougher road, Forest Rd. 1265. This more difficult riding continues on to Forest Rd. 331 until you reach the Caribou Trail (Co. Rd. 4). Be especially alert for traffic on the Caribou Trail.

From Highway 61 in Lutsen, go north on the Caribou Trail (Co. Rd. 4) to Forest Rd. 332.

LENGTH: Up to 42 miles total

TRAILHEAD: At the junction of Co. Rd. 4 and Forest Rd. 332, or farther north at the junction of Co. Rd. 4 and Forest Rd. 161

TRAIL SURFACE: Gravel county, forest, and logging roads

DEVIL TRACK LAKE LOOP AND BALLY CREEK AREA

Ride west on the Devil Track Road out of the Devil Track Lake campground, then south on Forest Rd. 158 along the pretty shores of the Cascade River; watch for the junction with the lower loop on Forest Rd. 157, go back over Nester Creek and north on a gravel/grass trail past Monker Lake to the eastern end of Devil Track Lake. Return on Co. Rd. 8 and Co. Rd. 57 to the campground. An easy family ride would be along Forest Rd. 158/Bally Creek Road along the Cascade River; great picnic site!

From Highway 61 in Grand Marais, go north on the Gunflint Trail (Co. Rd. 12), then west on Co. Rd. 8, which turns into North Shore Road (Co. Rd. 57), to the Devil Track Lake campground.

LENGTH: 25 miles total

TRAILHEAD: At the campground (has outhouses, water, and lake access)

TRAIL SURFACE: Paved and hard-pack gravel roads and soft- and hard-pack dirt trails

PINCUSHION MOUNTAIN TRAILS

Ride the cross-country ski trail network; intersections are marked, or get a Pincushion ski map. Loops from 1 to 13 kilometers; the most difficult ski trails will be the hilliest. Ride the Pincushion Mountain loop and take the short spur to the peak for beautiful overlooks. These trails intersect with the Superior Hiking Trail, which is closed to mountain biking.

From Highway 61 in Grand Marais, go north on the Gunflint Trail (Co. Rd. 12) for about two miles, then east on Scenic Overlook Road (Co. Rd. 53) to the overlook.

LENGTH: 15 miles of trails

TRAILHEAD: At the overlook parking at the cross-country trailhead

TRAIL SURFACE: Soft-pack dirt trails

MAPLE OR ELIASON TOWER LOOP

From the junction, ride north on Co. Rd. 14, then west on Forest Rd. 304 over Kimball Creek, returning south on a dirt trail to Co. Rd. 60. This ride is especially pretty in the fall. Watch for moose and deer at any time of the year at dawn and dusk.

> From Highway 61 northeast of Grand Marais, go north on Co. Rd. 14 to Co. Rd. 60.
>
> LENGTH: 12 miles total
>
> TRAILHEAD: At the junction of Co. Rd. 14 and Co. Rd. 60
>
> TRAIL SURFACE: Hard-pack gravel roads and soft-pack dirt trails with muddy spots

LIMA MOUNTAIN TRAIL

Ride forest roads that skirt the Boundary Waters Canoe Area Wilderness. From the junction of Forest Rd. 325 and Forest Rd. 152, ride south over the Brule River to East Twin and West Twin Lakes, or ride north to Lima Mountain, where Forest Rd. 152 turns into Forest Rd. 315; continue north to the southeast end of Poplar Lake.

> From Highway 61 in Grand Marais, go north on the Gunflint Trail to Forest Rd. 315 near Poplar Lake, or from the Gunflint Trail access/shortcut by going west on South Brule Road or Lima Mountain.
>
> LENGTH: 10 miles of road (20 miles total)
>
> TRAILHEAD: At the junction of Co. Rd. 12 and Forest Rd. 315, or the junction of Forest Rd. 325 and Forest Rd. 152
>
> TRAIL SURFACE: Hard-pack gravel forest road

OLD GUNFLINT TRAIL

Ride this wide, and at times hilly, road through birch forests and logged-off areas and along Iron Lake. The Iron Lake campground has picnic sites.

> From Highway 61 in Grand Marais, go north on the Gunflint Trail past Poplar Lake to the Old Gunflint Trail on the west.
>
> LENGTH: 5 miles total
>
> TRAILHEAD: At the junction of the old and new Gunflint Trails
>
> TRAIL SURFACE: Hard-pack gravel

KING'S ROAD TRAIL

The wide trail leads over hilly terrain to an overlook at the Cross River bridge. Look for moose in the swampy area. A half-mile spur leads to Ham Lake.

From Highway 61 in Grand Marais, go north on the Gunflint Trail
(Co. Rd. 12) just past South Gunflint Lake Road to a gravel logging
road on the west side.

LENGTH: 2 miles total

TRAILHEAD: At the intersection of Co. Rd. 12 and the logging road

TRAIL SURFACE: Hard-pack gravel

MOUNTAIN BIKE LODGE-TO-LODGE

Enjoy a self-guided or a custom-guided mountain biking trip along the
ridges, inland lakes, and woods near Grand Marais and up the Gunflint Trail.
Customized packages start from two days and two nights and include lodging, shuttle transportation, breakfast, trail lunch, and some dinners. Participating lodges are the Dream Catcher B&B, Pincushion B&B, Poplar Creek
Yurt, Clearwater Lodge, Poplar Creek Guesthouse, and Trail Center. For
more information, contact Boundary Country Trekking.

(218) 388-4487 or (800) 322-8327

boundarycountry.com

GUIDED DAY AND MULTIDAY MOUNTAIN BIKING TOURS

New in the Cook County area are guided mountain bike tours, which take
all the worry and planning out of your expedition. Day tours (priced on a
per-person basis) can be scheduled anytime and are custom-designed for
the group. Custom guided tours can also be arranged for multiday adventures. Boundary Country Trekking typically organizes five to six guided
tours from June to mid-September. Tours last four to five days, and each day
begins in the backwoods and ends with a descent to lodging on Lake Superior's shores. All tours include shuttle service and guide; multiday tours
include luggage transfer, food, and lodging. For more information, contact
Boundary Country Trekking.

(218) 388-4487 or (800) 322-8327

boundarycountry.com

BIKE REPAIRS AND/OR RENTALS

TWIN PORTS CYCLERY (REPAIRS)

2914 West 3rd Street in Duluth

(218) 624-4008

AVALANCHE CYCLE COMPANY (REPAIRS AND RENTALS)
Downtown Two Harbors
  (218) 834-0555

SAWTOOTH OUTFITTERS (RENTALS AND SOME REPAIRS)
Highway 61 in Tofte
  (218) 663-7643
  sawtoothoutfitters.com

SUPERIOR NORTH OUTDOOR CENTER (RENTALS AND REPAIRS)
Downtown Grand Marais; sales and guided tours, too!
  (218) 387-2180

GUNFLINT LODGE (RENTALS)
South Gunflint Lake
  (218) 388-2294
  gunflint.com

GUNFLINT PINES (INQUIRE ABOUT RENTALS)
South Gunflint Lake
  (218) 388-4454
  gunflintpines.com

What's Biting?

FISHING NORTHERN WATERS

OH, SON! I GOT ME A HAWG ON!

Roland Martin, fishing show host

THE GREAT SPORT OF FISHING IS SO PREVALENT IN MINNESOTA, the Department of Natural Resources (DNR) has a Take a Mom Fishing Weekend during opening weekend and a Take a Kid Fishing Weekend in early June each year to encourage the infrequent angler. Opportunities to fish are limitless. Walleye pike, smallmouth bass, northern pike, and trout swim the cool, clear waters of wilderness lakes, while Lake Superior puts forth record lake trout and salmon.

From an afternoon of shorecasting to a two-week trophy trip, an abundance of fishing holes lay waiting. All you need is a rod, reel, and license (and some charter boats supply all three!). If you're over 16 years of age, you need a fishing license. The DNR has reduced rates for husband-and-wife licenses. Nonresident licenses are available for individuals (24-hour, three-day, seven-day, and season), husband-and-wife 14-day, and families (season). Trout stamps are required if you'll be fishing a designated trout stream, designated trout lake, or Lake Superior. Purchase a license at resorts, bait shops, convenience stores, and service stations. To be up-to-date on all relevant laws, get the current fishing regulation brochure when you buy your license. Keep in mind that, in general, anglers may use only one line per person, except on Lake Superior.

Because mercury and polychlorinated biphenyls (PCBS) can be found in some fish from some lakes, I include the DNR recommendation, which states, "Most fish are healthy to eat and fish are an excellent source of low-fat protein. But any fish (store-bought or sport-caught) could contain contaminants … that can harm human health." For more information, obtain a copy of the Minnesota Department of Health's fish consumption advisory booklet by calling (651) 215-0950 or (800) 657-3908, or health.state.mn.us/divs/en/fish/eating/index.html. The advisory booklet covers more than 700 lakes and rivers in Minnesota that have been tested for contamination.

Boats up to 18 feet in length can be launched at most ramp accesses. Lake Superior ramps handle larger boats. To find the location of boat access ramps, call the DNR at (888) MINN-DNR or (651) 296-6157, check regional maps, or ask at local bait shops.

Boats must be licensed by the Minnesota DNR, except those registered in another state (or from another country) and not kept in Minnesota for more than 90 consecutive days, and nonmotorized watercraft nine feet or less in length. Each person aboard must have readily accessible a Coast Guard-approved personal flotation device (PFD), which must be the appropriate size for the intended wearer. Youth under the age of 13 must wear a PFD.

To prevent the introduction or spread of exotic plants and animals, please follow these precautions: remove all plant fragments from boats, trailers, outboard motors and props, anchors, live wells, and depth finder transducers; drain and dry all live wells, bait boxes, bilge areas, and engine intakes; do not transfer water, bait, or other objects between lakes and rivers; and if mooring in infested waters, dry your boat for seven days before relaunching.

The U.S. Forest Service provides 15 accessible fishing piers in the Superior National Forest, 10 of which are in the North Shore area. The Forest Service offers a mixture of different amenities at each site, including campgrounds, picnic sites, drinking water, swimming, and boat and/or canoe access. Be sure to bring a long-handled landing net!

The main game fish prized in our region are walleye, northerns, smallmouth bass, lake and stream trout, and salmon. Some inland lakes near Duluth also have excellent crappie populations. Other fish you may catch include muskellunge, sunfish (bluegills), burbot (eelpouts), suckers, smelt, ciscoes, and whitefish. Details on the most-sought-after fish are given below. Bait and lure suggestions are included, but remember they are just suggestions, and each fisherman has his or her own preference. For information on local waters, ask at a bait and tackle shop.

While fish are a renewable resource, populations can become severely depleted. Please be a generous angler, taking only a few fish and releasing the rest, especially undersize, spawning, and big fish. Your released fish establish future populations.

WALLEYE

Walleye average 1 to 2 pounds but can exceed 10 pounds. Being light-sensitive, they feed in shallow waters (less than 15 feet) at dawn and dusk and seek shadows or deeper water during daylight hours. A "walleye chop" on the water or overcast skies mean more active fish. Try a fluorescent orange or chartreuse spinner-bait combination or a worm harness. Use nightcrawlers, leeches, or minnows for bait. If you're going to bobber-fish, consider a jig-head with bait. In late summer try casting diving Rapalas over reefs in the evening.

SEASON: Mid-May to mid-February (extended for some Canadian border lakes)

LIMIT: Six, with not more than one over 24 inches daily, and on Saganaga Lake (trophy lake), not more than one over 19.5 inches

State Records

The following state record fish were caught in the North Shore vicinity:

ATLANTIC SALMON: *12 pounds, 13 ounces; Baptism River near Silver Bay*

CHINOOK SALMON: *33 pounds, 4 ounces; Poplar River and (same size) Lake Superior northeast of Duluth*

COHO SALMON: *10 pounds, 7 ounces; Lake Superior northeast of Two Harbors*

PINK SALMON: *4 pounds, 8 ounces; Cascade River near Lutsen*

STEELHEAD/RAINBOW: *17 pounds, 6 ounces; Knife River between Duluth and Two Harbors*

LAKE TROUT: *43 pounds, 8 ounces; Lake Superior near Hovland*

BROWN TROUT: *16 pounds, 12 ounces; Lake Superior northeast of Two Harbors*

BROOK TROUT: *6 pounds, 5 ounces; Pigeon River at the U.S.-Canada border*

WALLEYE: *17 pounds, 8 ounces; Seagull River at the end of the Gunflint Trail*

NORTHERN PIKE

The Minnesota state record northern weighing 45 pounds, 12 ounces was taken out of Basswood Lake in northern Lake County. However, a typical catch is in the two- to five-pound range. Small northerns stay in shallow, weedy areas, while larger pike move deeper. Northern fishing ebbs in warm weather, with peak fishing around the opener through June. Try trolling with Rapalas or casting with leeches or other bait. Northerns are territorial and will bite on anything dropped in their area. Steel leaders and spoons are another good option.

SEASON: Mid-May to mid-February (continuous for some Canadian border lakes)

LIMIT: Three, with not more than one over 30 inches daily (six on some Canadian border lakes)

SMALLMOUTH BASS

Ounce for ounce the best fighting fish, smallmouth usually weigh in at a pound. Smallmouth habitat and fishing are similar to those of walleye; smallmouth prefer clear, cool waters with rocky bottoms and irregular shorelines. They tend to feed in the shallows, moving to deeper water as temperatures increase. Try a spinner-bait combination or jigs, and enjoy the challenge.

Speaking of challenge, I was trolling with Rapalas one day when I had a good hit. I hooked the fish, which was a pretty good fighter. I figured I had on a four-pound smallmouth, but as I brought the fish to the boat, I realized I had on two smallmouth, one on each end of the Rapala! One weighed one pound, the other one and a half pounds. My sister Clare has a great smallmouth story, too. She was fishing the same lake with my husband, Bill. They each had a fish on. Bill brought in his walleye, and Clare let her smallmouth swim near the canoe, intending to release it. While she was waiting, a northern approached the smallmouth and started biting at it. Clare let out some line, and the northern kept after the smallmouth. After a bit, she began reeling in, and the northern made a huge lunge at the smallmouth. The smallmouth flipped away, shaking the hook loose from its mouth, and at that split second, the northern bit into the hook. She kept the northern. Really.

SEASON: Mid-May to mid-February (continuous on some Canadian border lakes)

LIMIT: Six; immediately release all fish 11 inches or larger from Flour, Hungry Jack, Pike, and Two Island Lakes.

LAKE TROUT

A good eating-size lake trout is 2 to 3 pounds, but the cool, dark waters of Lake Superior are domain to monsters that tip the scales at over 40 pounds. Peak fishing is early in the season when waters are cooler on inland lakes, but lasts all summer on the big lake. Lure recommendations vary with the type of fishing: for flyfishing, try spawn bags, yarn flies, or tiny spinners; shore-casters might use a dodger-fly or spoon combo; Lake Superior boat fishers usually fish with downriggers or planer boards; and if you're ice fishing, try a smelt or other small bait fish. Remember to have enough weight to get your line down deep.

SEASONS: Inland lakes, mid-May to late September; winter 1, mid-January to mid-March, for lakes outside or partially outside the Boundary Waters Canoe Area Wilderness (BWCAW), except Snowbank, Clearwater, Seagull, Ram, Magnetic, East Bearskin, and Saganaga Lakes; winter 2, early January to late March, for lakes entirely within the BWCAW; Lake Superior, early December to late September

LIMIT: Two, with special rules for Turnip, Thrush, and Boys Lakes; check regulations for details; three on Lake Superior

STREAM TROUT: BROOK, BROWN, SPLAKE, AND RAINBOW

Landing the elusive stream trout requires a bit more patience and a willingness to walk in to small, hard-to-fish tributaries. Flyfishers are most at home on these shaded streams, but you can land stream trout on a rod and reel if you gently drop your line in either just above or below the pool. Average stream brookies are one-half to one pound. Stream rainbow rarely exceed three pounds. Try small spinners, nightcrawlers, or flies.

You will pull larger fish out of inland lakes than you will out of streams. Again, try spinners or nightcrawlers, and for ice fishing try jigging with minnows (in designated trout lakes, you must use preserved dead minnows; no live minnows are allowed, and only one line per person is allowed).

Browns may enter barrier-free Lake Superior streams and swim to the headwaters to spawn in mid-October. Brown trout are rarely caught along the Shore but are reported once in a while. You could try using steelhead techniques. Kamloop rainbow peak from December through March. Try casting with artificial lures, jigging with spawn bags, or using the effective steelhead techniques.

Splake are a very tasty hybrid cross of lake and brook trout.

Note that parts of the Devil Track, Kadunce, Knife, Little Knife, Gauthier, and St. Louis Rivers are posted fish sanctuaries; check regulations for specifics.

STREAM SEASON: Mid-April to late September (includes Lake Superior watershed *above* posted boundaries)

STREAM LIMIT: Five combined, with not more than 1 over 16 inches; above posted boundaries, the limit is 10 combined, but not more than 5 can be brown trout with not more than 1 over 16 inches; also, the minimum rainbow size is 16 inches.

INLAND LAKE SEASON: Mid-May to mid-October; winter 1, mid-January to mid-March for lakes outside or partially outside the BWCAW; winter 2, early January to late March for lakes entirely within the BWCAW

INLAND LAKE LIMIT: Five combined, with not more than three over 16 inches

LAKE SUPERIOR SEASON: Continuous (includes tributaries *below* the posted boundaries)

LAKE SUPERIOR LIMIT: Five combined, with not more than three over 16 inches and a minimum size of 10 inches (see specific limitations for steelhead, below)

STEELHEAD – MIGRATORY RAINBOW TROUT

Steelhead enter streams that are swollen with meltwater in the spring (late April when the water exceeds 41°F) to spawn. They reenter streams in the fall, around the first week in October, and remain until mid-November. Steelhead vary in size, averaging 24 to 28 inches and 3 to 8 pounds. Be aware of limitations for keepers. Stream fishermen have luck with yarn flies or spawn bags (remember – *no* treble hooks, only single hooks), while lake trollers typically use flashy spoons on a planer board system.

LAKE SUPERIOR SEASON: Continuous (includes tributaries *below* posted boundaries; for areas above boundaries, see stream trout seasons)

LIMIT: Three, only one of which can have an unclipped adipose fin; minimum size is 28 inches for an unclipped steelhead and 16 inches for a clipped steelhead.

CHINOOK, COHO, PINK, AND ATLANTIC SALMON

Size varies with the type of salmon. Smaller pinks typically run in odd-numbered years and are caught on yarn flies, small spoons, or tiny spinners in September. Named for the color on their sides and backs during spawning, pinks swim in the upper 60 feet of Lake Superior. Larger coho, chinook, and Atlantic prefer cool water (53 to 57°F) and are easily spooked. By mid-June coho are being taken out of Lake Superior with spoons or dodger-fly combos on a planer board system. Coho fishing is good into September. The chinook run peaks in mid-September, especially on stocked streams. Try yarn flies and spawn bags. Atlantic salmon fishing is similar to the fall run of steelhead, beginning around the first of October; these salmon are taken on yarn flies or spawn bags.

LAKE SUPERIOR SEASON: Continuous (includes tributaries *below* posted boundaries)

LIMIT: 10 combined, only 1 of which can be an Atlantic; minimum size on all is 10 inches.

CRAPPIES

These panfish are caught in weedy bays of inland lakes and slow-moving rivers when they feed at dusk. Several lakes just north of Duluth have superb crappie populations. As you move northeast into the colder, clear waters of wilderness lakes, you will find fewer crappie lakes. Bobber-fish from shore with minnows, leeches, or nightcrawlers, or troll bay areas with the same bait.

SEASON: Continuous

LIMIT: 15 (30 on some Canadian border lakes)

ACCESSIBLE FISHING PIERS IN DULUTH

These piers are perfect fishing spots if you don't have a boat. The DNR provides four accessible fishing piers on the St. Louis River in Duluth. Parking is generally located within 300 feet of the fishing facility, and a hard-surface path from the parking area is provided.

ST. LOUIS RIVER AT BOY SCOUT LANDING

From I-35, go south on Highway 23/Grand Avenue one-half block past McCuen Street.

ST. LOUIS RIVER AT CLYDE AVENUE

From I-35, go south on Highway 23/Grand Avenue; southeast of the junction with U.S. Highway 2, go east on Clyde Avenue; the pier is on the west shore.

ST. LOUIS RIVER AT THE INTERSTATE BRIDGE

From I-35, go south on 5th Avenue West, then west on Garfield Avenue to the east end of Rice's Point; the pier is directly beneath the I-35 bridge.

ST. LOUIS RIVER AT PERCH LAKE

From I-35, go south on Highway 23/Grand Avenue, cross the St. Louis River Bridge, then go east half a mile to Perch Lake.

ACCESSIBLE FISHING PIERS
NORTH OF DULUTH

WHITEFACE RESERVOIR I AND II
The two piers both have 12- by 24-foot decks and nearby accessible toilets. A 250-foot paved path leads to Pier I, a 200-foot packed gravel path to Pier II. Fish for walleye and northern.

> From I-35, go north on 21st Avenue East, northeast on Woodland Avenue, west on Arrowhead Road, north on Rice Lake Road (Co. Rd. 4) to Co. Rd. 16, and east seven miles to the campground sign.

CADOTTE LAKE
A 150-foot paved path leads to a 12- by 16-foot deck with nearby accessible toilet.

> From I-35, go north on 21st Avenue East, northeast on Woodland Avenue, west on Arrowhead Road, north on Rice Lake Road (Co. Rd. 4) to Co. Rd. 16, then 18 miles east on Co. Rd. 16 to the campground sign.

ACCESSIBLE FISHING PIERS
NORTHEAST OF DULUTH

DUMBBELL LAKE
Fish for smallmouth bass, walleye, and northerns off the 12- by 16-foot deck. A 20-foot packed gravel trail leads to the pier, nearby accessible toilets, and a picnic area.

> From Highway 61 at Illgen City, go north on Minnesota 1, then east on Forest Rd. 172 about four miles.

HOGBACK LAKE
A 75-foot paved path leads to a 12- by 16-foot deck with nearby accessible toilets. Rainbow trout are the main game fish in Hogback.

> From Highway 61 at Illgen City, go north on Minnesota 1, then east on Forest Rd. 172 about 12 miles.

CRESCENT LAKE
Fish for walleye and an occasional muskie off the 12- by 16-foot pier. The pier and accessible toilets are 150 feet from the parking area on a paved pathway. An accessible campsite and picnic area are adjacent to the pier.

From Highway 61 in Tofte, go north on the Sawbill Trail (Co. Rd. 2)
about 20 miles, then eight miles east on Forest Rd. 170.

SAWBILL LAKE

A 100-foot paved path leads to the 12- by 16-foot deck where you can fish for
northern, smallmouth bass, and walleye. An accessible toilet, campsite, and
picnic area are nearby.

From Highway 61 in Tofte, go north on the Sawbill Trail (Co. Rd. 2)
about 24 miles.

WHITE PINE LAKE

A 40-foot packed gravel path leads to a 12- by 16-foot pier where you can fish
for walleye, northerns, and panfish. An accessible toilet, campsite, and picnic
area are nearby.

From Highway 61 in Lutsen, go north on the Caribou Trail (Co. Rd. 4)
about seven miles, then west on Forest Rd. 164 about three miles.

MINK LAKE

Fish for splake and rainbow trout from the 12- by 24-foot pier. Follow the
230-foot paved path to the pier and accessible toilet.

From Highway 61 in Grand Marais, go north on the Gunflint Trail
(Co. Rd. 12) about nine miles, then west on Forest Rd. 140 about
two miles.

(TRESTLE) PINE LAKE

A short 20-foot packed gravel trail leads to a 12- by 16-foot pier and accessible toilet. Like Mink Lake, Trestle Pine Lake has rainbow and splake populations. Note the old railroad trestle crossing the lake.

From Highway 61 in Grand Marais, go north on the Gunflint Trail
(Co. Rd. 12) about three miles, then west on Co. Rd. 8, northwest
on North Shore Road (Co. Rd. 27), and east on Forest Rd. 1365 about
two miles.

CHARTER FISHING

You can fish the big lake aboard a chartered fishing boat. A variety of vessels
ranging from 25 to 42 feet in length feature state-of-the art safety, navigational, and fishing equipment; a heated and air-conditioned cabin; private

head; and food and beverage service upon request. Fishing on Lake Superior runs from early May through September, and most boats will take one to six people. Ask whether your captain will supply a fishing license, or purchase your own before departure. You will also need to bring appropriate clothing, soft-soled shoes, food and beverages, cameras, and coolers for your catch. For four people, full-day (9 to 10 hours) rates vary from $340 to $395, and half-day (5 to 6 hours) rates run $235 to $260. Each additional person is about $25. Isle Royale day trips run $500 to $700 for up to six people. If you are interested in charter fishing, contact one of the charters listed below.

DULUTH

Adventure Sportfishing: Captain Jon Dahl, (218) 624-2553 or (218) 393-1051

All Out Charters: Captain Don Szczech, (651) 653-0001 or (651) 653-3631

Bag Limit Fishing Charters: Captain Don Kuznin, (218) 525-7621; baglimit.com

Barry's White Water Charters: Captain Barry LeBlanc, (218) 624-0865 or (218) 349-2368; whitewatercharter.com

Bill's Great Lakes Charters: Captain Bill Judnick, (218) 741-0747; duluthfishing.com/sh_home

Capt. Gary's Charters: Captain Gary Hanson, (218) 624-2828 or (800) 457-9402; captaingaryscharter.com

Cats Paw Charters: Captain Gerry Downes, (218) 727-2360 or (800) 519-2360

Dr. Juice Charters: (218) 525-3418

Duluth Charter Fishing: Captains Adam and Dick Bohlmann, (218) 348-BOAT and (218) 722-3649; duluthcharterfishing.com

E. Fish N. Sea Charters: Captain David Wait, (218) 720-6148 or (800) 980-4814; efishnsea.net

End of the Line Charter Fishing: Captain Joel Kilichowski, (218) 879-6237 or (888) 846-6536; fishontheline.com

FinnTastic Charters: Captain John Raisanen, (651) 459-8872; finntasticcharters.com

First Mate Charters: Captain Dexter Nelson, (715) 392-3177 or (800) 824-6466; fishduluth.com/firstmate

Goddess III Charters: Captain Tom Wentz, (218) 729-6632 or (888) 846-3337; fishduluth.com/goddess

Hang Loose: Captain Chet Kwiatkowski, (218) 390-8640 or (888) 691-3133; hanglooseduluth.com

Happy Hooker Charters: Captain Peter Dahl, (218) 624-2674 or
(218) 940-9400; fishduluth.com/happyhooker
KDK Charter Service: (218) 724-1264 or (888) 724-1264; kdkcharters.com
Lake & River Charters: Captain Don Nelson, (218) 624-9284 or
(800) 932-9787; fishduluth.com/lakeandriver
Lake Superior Fishing: Captain Steve Johnson, (218) 724-4214,
(218) 724-9104, or (800) 531-FISH; lakesuperiorfishing.com
Lucky Star Charters: Captain Randol Lamere, (218) 727-3439 or
(800) 777-8568; fishduluth.com/luckystar
Multi-Species Fishing Adventures: Captain Steve Butchart, (218) 525-3252;
duluthfishingguide.com
Rusty Duck Charters: Captain Dave West, (877) 726-7775; rustyduck.net
Time Out Charters: (218) 525-4598 or (800) 355-9505
Work Knot Charters: Captain Wayne Compton, (218) 525-9466;
workknot.com
Yankee Marine: Captain Dennis Goman, (218) 722-5215 or (218) 786-9695

KNIFE RIVER TO GRAND PORTAGE
Osprey Charters: Captain Bernie Hall, Knife River, (218) 384-9282
Rainbows End: Captain James Latvala, Knife River, (218) 834-4270 or
(218) 830-1050
Fugitive Charters: Silver Bay, (218) 226-3628
Sunrise Charters: Silver Bay, (218) 226-4117
Captain Kelly: Captain Kelly Schliep, Taconite Harbor, (218) 370-8050 or
(218) 387-9180; northshorevisitor.com
North Coast Charters and Tours: Captain Tom Muntean, Tofte,
(218) 663-7384; northshorevisitor.com
Tofte Charters: Captain Darren Peck, Bluefin Bay in Tofte, (218) 663-9932 or
(800) 258-3346; toftecharters.com
Far Superior Charters: Captain Clint Helmerson, Grand Marais,
(218) 387-2248

GUIDES
Many resorts offer or can recommend guide services for fishing. Refer to the
outfitters chapter ("Getting Outfitted"), go online to northshorevisitor.com,
or inquire when making a reservation.

SAFE HARBORS

Safe access points to/from Lake Superior listed southwest to northeast.

MCQUADE ROAD ACCESS
In progress, this protected access will be within a 3-acre safe harbor.

KNIFE RIVER HARBOR AND MARINA
A full-service, 100-slip marina and safe harbor.

TWO HARBORS
Safe access is within the commercial harbor with plans for a new safe
   harbor within the marina.

TWIN POINTS
A scenic protected access northeast of Gooseberry Falls.

SILVER BAY HARBOR AND MARINA
A 7-acre safe harbor; full-service, 68-slip marina; and adjacent park.

TACONITE HARBOR
A 2-acre safe harbor.

TOFTE
Protected access off the Tofte Beach Road.

GRAND MARAIS
Safe harbor within the commercial harbor; limited marine facilities and
   mooring for traveling boats.

HORSESHOE BAY
Protected access midway between Grand Marais and Grand Portage.

GRAND PORTAGE
Private marina with protected access within Grand Portage Bay.

Sea Kayaking

THE LAKE SUPERIOR WATER TRAIL

FROM THE EARLIEST DAYS OF EXPLORATION IN THIS AREA, MOST travel was by boat. Voyageurs built immense canoes and traveled the St. Lawrence Seaway. Schooners, tugs, steamers, cargo boats, and barges hugged the shores of Lake Superior. Communities were built in bays and along the rivers that empty into the lake. As time passed, a road was carved between the shoreline and the ridgeline, connecting the villages of the North Shore. Cargo ships continued to haul lumber, iron ore, and fish, but noncommercial travel increasingly relied on the new network of roads.

The immensity of Lake Superior and the apparent dangers of sailing on the lake have kept the majority of visitors on shore. The desire remains, however, to be out on the big lake. In part, this desire is what lies behind the creation of the Lake Superior Water Trail. The trail is being developed primarily for sea kayakers and will eventually enable them to paddle Superior's coast from the St. Louis Bay in Duluth to the Pigeon River on the Canadian border. Portions of the trail have been completed from Two Harbors to Grand Marais.

The Water Trail is intended for experienced kayakers. Safety concerns include rapid weather changes, fog, hypothermia, and overestimation by kayakers of the distance that can be covered in a given time period. A limited number of campsites are available and are listed below. Most sites do not have drinking water, so be prepared to purify all water from lakes and rivers. Always respect the private property along the shoreline. For further information, contact the Department of Natural Resources (DNR) at (888) MINN-DNR or DNR Trails and Waterways at (218) 327-4408, or visit the Lake Superior Water Trail Association's Web site at lswta.org.

ACCESS POINTS AND AREAS OF INTEREST

TWO HARBORS
AGATE BAY: Ramp access, parking, and a picnic area
BURLINGTON BAY: Ramp access and a full-service campground

SUPERIOR SHORES RESORT
Picnic site

FLOOD BAY
Carry-down access, parking, rest area

STEWART RIVER
Carry-down access, parking, rest area

SILVER CLIFF RESORT
Emergency landing only

HALCYON HARBOR CABINS
Rest area

No public landing from Halcyon Harbor Cabins to Castle Danger (4½ miles as the crow flies).

GRAND SUPERIOR LODGE
Rest area

GOOSEBERRY FALLS STATE PARK
Carry-in access, parking, picnic area, campground, and a first-come, first-served kayak campsite. Features include the river mouth and small beach cliffs.

THOMPSON BEACH
Four first-come, first-served kayak campsites, a rest area, and two pit toilets.

TWIN POINTS
Rest area only; camping is prohibited.

SPLIT ROCK CABINS
Emergency landing only.

SPLIT ROCK RIVER
Carry-down access, parking, and a rest area.

CRAZY BAY
In state park. Two campsites, one first-come, first-served, and one backpack/kayak site with reservations recommended. Features Split Rock Point cliffs.

SPLIT ROCK CREEK
In state park. One backpack/kayak campsite, with reservations recommended. Features Corundum Point cliffs.

LITTLE TWO HARBORS
In state park. Carry-down access; nearby picnic area, campground, and trails.

GOLD ROCK POINT
No access here (next access is 3.4 miles away). Features site of the *Madeira* shipwreck, which is visible in certain areas; rest area.

NADINE BLACKLOCK LAKESHORE
Near Gull Rock; rest area and campsite.

COVE POINT LODGE
Rest area.

BEAVER BAY
Rest area; services are available in town.

BAYSIDE PARK AND SILVER BAY MARINA
Ramp access at boat landing and carry-down access at beach; parking and a picnic area.

PALISADE HEAD
In state park. Features 300-foot cliffs and sea caves. Use caution – this area can have hazardous conditions.

PALISADE HEAD CAMPSITE
In state park. Four first-come, first-served kayak campsites, a pit toilet, and rest area. No fires.

BAPTISM RIVER
In state park. Carry-down access, parking, trails, and picnic area with campground 1.5 miles inland.

SHOVEL POINT
In state park. Features rock arch and cliffs.

CRYSTAL BAY
In state park. Rest area; features one of the largest sea caves on the North Shore.

MILE 59.7 REST AREA
Just that, a rest area northeast of Kennedy Creek

No public landing until Sugarloaf Cove (10.8 miles as the crow flies). Emergency landing at Stone Hearth Inn and Fenstad's in Little Marais. Scenic spot ... waterfall and arch at Manitou River mouth.

SUGARLOAF COVE
Rest area; interpretive trail; Scientific and Natural Area.

LAST CREEK
Kayak campsites and rest area.

TACONITE HARBOR OF REFUGE
Ramp access, parking, and rest area at the safe harbor.

LAMB'S RESORT
Full-service campground with carry-down access for guests.

SCHROEDER PUBLIC ACCESS
Ramp access and parking near historical Father Baraga's cross.

TEMPERANCE RIVER STATE PARK
Carry-down access, campground, picnic and rest area, parking, and beach.

TOFTE TOWN PARK
Ramp access, parking, and picnic area.

BLUEFIN BAY RESORT
Rest area with access to lakewalk.

LEVEAUX CREEK
Scenic spot ... cliffs and small caves.

ONION RIVER
Rest area, scenic spot ... cliffs and small caves.

LUTSEN KAYAK CAMP
Kayak campsites and rest area.

LUTSEN RESORT
Rest area.

No public landing from Poplar River (Lutsen Resort) to Cascade River.

CASCADE RIVER
In state park. Carry-down access, rest area; nearby parking; picnic area further northeast along shoreline.

CUT FACE CREEK
Carry-down access, rest and picnic area, and parking.

FALL RIVER
Campsite and rest area; scenic spot ... waterfall.

GRAND MARAIS

Campground has ramp access and full-service campground; scenic spot . . . lighthouse.

ARTIST POINT: Ramp access, rest area, and parking.

EAST BAY: Carry-down access, rest area, and parking.

If this sounds enticing, but you are a little worried about your skills or don't own a kayak, contact Superior Coastal Sports in Grand Marais at (218) 387-2360 or (800) 720-2809, or visit their Web site at superiorcoastal.com. They offer guided half-day, full-day, and multiday tours, kayak rentals, and lessons. Experienced kayakers can also pick up supplies here and discuss other favorite North Shore kayak destinations. Superior Coastal Sports is located in Grand Marais, one block south of the stoplights on Highway 61 on the east side of Broadway.

Rentals are available at the following businesses:

DULUTH

Ski Hut (sales and rental), 1032 East 4th Street: (218) 724-8525 or
    theskihut.com

Western Lake Superior Kayaks (sales, rental, and guided tours) at
    Twin Points Cyclery, 2914 West 3rd Street: (218) 720-3577 or
    duluthkayaks.com

Park Point Paddling Center, daily in summer, off Minnesota Avenue on
    16th Street.

TOFTE

Sawtooth Outfitters (rentals), Highway 61 in Tofte: (218) 663-7643 or
    sawtoothoutfitters.com

GRAND MARAIS

Bear Track Outfitting (rentals), Highway 61 in Grand Marais: (218) 387-1162
    or bear-track.com

Superior Coastal Sports, (218) 387-2360 or (800) 720-2809
    superiorcoastal.com

Wilderness Waters Outfitting, Hwy 61 in Grand Marais: (218) 387-2525 or
    wilderness-waters.com

ALONG THE GUNFLINT TRAIL

Clearwater Lodge and Outfitters, on Clearwater Lake: (218) 388-2254 or
    clearwateroutfitters.com

Hungry Jack Outfitters, on Hungry Jack Lake: (218) 388-2275 or hjo.com
Gunflint Lodge, on Gunflint Lake: (218) 388-2294 or gunflint.com
Gunflint Pines Campground & Resort, on Gunflint Lake: (218) 388-4454 or
  gunflintpines.com
Superior North Canoe Outfitters, on Saganaga Lake: (218) 388-4416 or
  superiornorthoutfitters.com
Voyageur Canoe Outfitters, on Seagull River: (218) 388-2224 or
  canoeit.com
Way of the Wilderness Canoe Outfitters, on Seagull River: (218) 388-2212 or
  wayofthewilderness.com

And a great kayak event . . .

TWO HARBORS KAYAK FESTIVAL
Fun festival first weekend in August! Guided tour, demos, 18-mile marathon, fun paddle race, kids kayak race, clinics, seminars, and gear swap.
  (218) 343-2526
  kayakfestival.org

Superior Golfing

IT IS A TEST OF TEMPER, A TRIAL
OF HONOR, A REVEALER OF CHARACTER.
IT MEANS GOING INTO GOD'S
OUT-OF-DOORS, GETTING CLOSE TO
NATURE, FRESH AIR AND EXERCISE, A
SWEEPING OF MENTAL COBWEBS AND A
GENUINE RELAXATION OF TIRED TISSUES.

David Forgan

THE WOODS ARE FULL OF LONG HITTERS.

Anonymous

L ONG HITTERS WILL BE CHALLENGED BY THE FOREST-LINED
six public courses on the North Shore. Each course incorporates and
highlights the native landscape. All six showcase vistas of Lake Superior, feature forest-lined fairways, and are designed to challenge each golfer.

While it is important to call in advance for a tee time, you will be pleased by the quiet, uncrowded atmosphere and the reasonable rates. Courses open in mid- to late May and offer golfing through the spectacular fall color season of October. For specific dates and current fees, contact the individual courses. Out of season, you can contact the Duluth Department of Parks and Recreation at (218) 723-3337 for Enger and Lester; Two Harbors and Silver Bay City Halls at (218) 834-5631 and (218) 226-4408, respectively; Gunflint Hills Golf Course at (218) 387-9988; and the Lutsen-Tofte Tourism

Association at (218) 663-7804 or area resorts for Superior National at Lutsen. Many resorts in the Lutsen-Tofte area also offer golf and lodging packages; refer to the accommodations listings.

All of the courses have a clubhouse, food service, pro shop, rentals, and a driving range. The Silver Bay course also has a practice putting green, and Enger Park and Lester Park offer club repair and individual, group, and video golf lessons. Superior National at Lutsen, Enger Park, and Lester Park have a golf pro on staff.

IN DULUTH

ENGER PARK GOLF COURSE

A 27-hole, par 72/36 over 6,200 yards, Enger Park is not a run-of-the-mill public golf course. While allowing the novice some room for error, the holes require skilled shots. When the designers integrated the new nine holes, they added challenges by way of 11 new ponds, 30 bunkers, and reshaped greens. The beauty of this course is underscored by nearby Enger Tower, the appearance of Lake Superior, and the tremendous view of the St. Louis Bay from the driving range. Reservations up to one week in advance; walk-ins welcome. Full grill and snack menu including breakfast and beverages.

From I-35, take the 21st Avenue West exit west, then go north on
    Piedmont Avenue and east on Skyline Parkway to the clubhouse.
A 9-hole round is $15, an 18-hole round is $25; senior, junior, and fall
    specials.
(218) 723-3451
golfinduluth.com

LESTER PARK GOLF COURSE

At the eastern edge of Duluth amid deciduous forests overlooking Lake Superior is the Lester Park Golf Course. The 27 holes (par 72/36) stretch over 6,300 yards interwoven with pine, maple, birch, and aspen. The trees do not hinder the wide fairways or the picturesque views of Lake Superior. Although not as challenging as Enger, Lester demands more than target shots.

From I-35, follow London Road to the northeast, then go north on
    Lester River Road (at 61st Avenue East) to the clubhouse.
A 9-hole round is $15; an 18-hole round is $25; dawn and twilight
    specials.
(218) 525-0828
golfinduluth.com

NORTHLAND COUNTRY CLUB

An 18-hole, par-72 private course over 6,498 yards, with a clubhouse, dining, pro shop, rentals, driving range, and golf pro.

> 3901 East Superior Street
> (218) 525-1941
> northlandcountryclub.com

RIDGEVIEW COUNTRY CLUB

An 18-hole, par-70 private course over 6,197 yards, with a clubhouse, dining, pro shop, rentals, driving range, and golf pro.

> West Redwing Street
> (218) 728-5128

FAR PAR GOLF

Perfect for beginners and families. Far Par has a 9-hole, par-30 course, driving range, and miniature golf. Group and junior lessons and clinics are offered.

> From London Road/Highway 61, drive north on 60th Avenue East, west and north on Glenwood Avenue, east on Jean Duluth Road, west on Normanna Road, and south on Arnold Road.
> A 9-hole round is $7.50 for adults and $6.00 for kids and seniors.
> (218) 724-0909

ALONG THE NORTH SHORE

LAKEVIEW NATIONAL GOLF COURSE

This 18-hole, par-72 course at Two Harbors is perfect for spur-of-the-moment rounds of play. Spanning 6,429 yards, the course offers lake views and wildlife sightings.

> Enter off Highway 61, just east of Co. Rd. 2 in Two Harbors.
> A 9-hole round is $15; an 18-hole round is $22; reduced rates for seniors; discounted rates available before mid-June and after mid-September.
> (218) 834-2664
> lakecnty.com/twogolf/

SILVER BAY MUNICIPAL GOLF COURSE

Silver Bay is a mature course in great condition, with well-tended greens and fully grown-in fairways. Striking old pines lay claim to the 9-hole, par-36 course, which can also be played as 18 holes. The Beaver River acts as a natural water hazard as it roams through the course.

Go north off Highway 61 and travel about two miles to the golf course
    sign, following the gravel road.
A 9-hole round is $14; an 18-hole round is $22.
(218) 226-3111
silverbay.com/golf.htm

SUPERIOR NATIONAL AT LUTSEN
Bring a camera to Superior National at Lutsen. The 300-acre, 27-hole course
fans its 6,323 yards across the Poplar River Valley. With its lower reaches
approaching Lake Superior and the back nine edging the base of Moose
Mountain, Superior National is every adjective you've heard about the North
Shore: stunning, dramatic, spectacular, breathtaking, wild, isolated, rugged,
and beautiful. Designed to be exceptional, each hole provides challenges and
panoramas. The dramatic par-3 second hole requires a drive across the cas-
cading waters of the Poplar River. Even more stunning is the signature par-3
17th hole. Atop a wildflower-emblazoned bank, golfers tee up and drop their
Titleists 135 feet down to the green, which is partially encircled by the flowing
Poplar River. Forgiving fairways are lined by vengeful woods, so bring extra
balls! Whatever your skill level, you must golf Superior National. Soft spikes
required.
    Enter off Highway 61, just west of Lutsen Resort.
    A 9-hole round is $23 to $28; an 18-hole round is $60 to $75; midweek,
        stay and play, junior, senior, and twilight specials.
    (218) 663-7195
    superiornational.com

GUNFLINT HILLS GOLF COURSE
Set on the scenic Gunflint Trail, this pretty little 9-hole par-35 is a challenge.
Hilly terrain combined with narrow fairways and small greens test the
golfer's skills. Enjoy laid-back play where a golfer is rarely pushed through
and the chance to see a bear, deer, fox, or beaver.
    From Highway 61, go north on the Gunflint Trail (Co. Rd. 12) about
        four miles; course is on the right.
    A 9-hole round is $14 to $16; 18 holes are $24 to $25.
    (218) 387-9988
    boreal.org/cityhall/golfcourse.html

Nature's Balance

HUNTING IN THE NORTH WOODS

OUTDOOR RECREATIONS ARE
ESSENTIALLY PRIMITIVE, ATAVISTIC;
THEIR VALUE IS A CONTRAST-VALUE.

Aldo Leopold, *A Sand County Almanac*

PICKING UP A FIREARM AND HEADING INTO THE WOODS ISN'T hunting. Hunting is the preparation and the search. It is understanding animal behavior and habitat and learning to meld with the forest and marsh environment. It is the divergence from our daily civilized, mechanized world. It is a good walk in the woods.

People hunt a variety of game for a variety of reasons. As with all outdoor recreations, hunting is a matter of ethics. The Minnesota Department of Natural Resources (DNR) has established laws and regulations that intend to provide satisfying outdoor experiences while protecting natural resources and ensuring their continued existence and accessibility. Ethics are a personal matter.

On the North Shore, hunters typically seek out grouse, deer, moose, bear, and waterfowl. Small-game, sportsman, and archery and firearm deer licenses are available from the DNR or at convenience stores, service stations, and some resorts. Complete regulations are available where you purchase a license or from the DNR License Bureau; call (651) 296-4506 or write to 500 Lafayette Road, St. Paul, MN 55155-4040. For general hunting information from the DNR, call (888) MINN-DNR, (651) 296-6157, or TDD (800) 657-3929 or (651) 296-5484, or go online at dnr.state.mn.us/hunting.

GROUSE

To hunt grouse, residents and nonresidents over 16 years of age must have a valid small-game license in their possession; residents may also have a sportsman's license instead. Open season for ruffed and spruce grouse is mid-September through February, with shooting hours from a half-hour before sunrise until sunset. The daily bag limit is 5 combined, with a possession limit of 10 combined. Party hunting is allowed for grouse as long as the total number of birds taken does not exceed the total daily limit for the party members. Grouse you intend to transport must have their feet and a fully feathered head attached.

Ruffed grouse most often feed on aspen twigs and catkins (male flowering buds). Aspen are found in regrowth areas and young upland forests. Since grouse will eat numerous other buds, twigs, and berries, look for them in thickets of alder and willow or scratching on old logging roads. You can't miss the frenzied escape of a grouse that has been flushed out of hiding. As they shoot up out of the brush, they will lead you on a chase into even denser thickets.

DEER

Deer are the most commonly taken big game along the North Shore. Fall seasons vary depending on the weapon used. Archery deer season opens in mid-September and runs through late November. Resident and nonresident archery hunters must have a bow-and-arrow deer license in their possession. They may take a deer of either sex except during the regular deer firearm season, when archery hunters can only take bucks. Hunters may not take deer by bow and arrow if they are in possession of a firearm. Firearm season runs two weeks in early November. Antlerless deer are those without an antler at least three inches long. To take an antlerless deer by firearm, you must apply for and obtain an antlerless deer permit. All deer taken must be tagged on site and registered at a Big Game Registration area.

White-tailed deer feed at dawn and dusk on the twigs, buds, leaves, and bark of leaf-bearing saplings. In the daylight hours, they bed down in dense forests. Deer trails lead from bedding spots to feeding areas and watering holes. Tracks, rubs, and scrapes are all key indicators for sighting deer. Each year in the late summer, bucks' antlers harden up, and they slough off their velvet horn covering. To speed up the shedding process, deer rub their antlers on tree trunks, leaving bloody pieces of velvet. Soon the buck's antlers harden, and he prepares to mate. Bucks communicate that they are in rut by pawing up bare spots of earth and urinating on them. These scrapes are often located below trees with rubs.

MOOSE

Bull moose also go into rut in early autumn, shedding velvet on their hardening horns and confronting other bulls for territorial rights and females. Look for moose in cleared-over areas, where they feed at dawn and dusk on leaf shoots from quaking aspen, paper birch, sugar maple, and mountain ash. Males tend to be alone, while calves travel with cows.

Moose hunts occur provided the population is adequate to support a hunt. Hunts may be added or eliminated to maintain moose numbers. Licenses are difficult to obtain and are given to parties of two to four (Minnesota residents only) via a random drawing. Once you receive a moose license, you are ineligible for all future drawings. Everyone in the hunting party must attend an orientation.

BEAR

Preference drawings are used to award licenses for bear permit areas. Residents and nonresidents may apply individually or as a party of up to four members. Applications are taken from mid-March through April. Preference is given to hunters who have not received licenses in the past. Bear season opens on Labor Day and lasts about six weeks. About 1,200 permits are given in the district encompassing the North Shore inland, and another 300 are given for the Boundary Waters Canoe Area Wilderness district. Shooting hours are a half-hour before sunrise to sunset. Bears must be tagged at the kill site and registered at a Big Game Registration area.

In autumn black bears are active from morning through night in their endeavor to add a thick layer of winter fat. Bears traditionally feed on nuts, berries, and insects but are drawn to human food and garbage. Look for medium to large forest openings that support berry plants and thickets. Like deer, bear establish and follow regular trails.

WATERFOWL

Lake Superior's shoreline and inland lakes mark the migration trail of waterfowl. Mallards and sea ducks gather in sheltered coves and river mouths along the shoreline in the autumn. Diving ducks, such as ringnecks and goldeneyes, use inland lakes as refueling stops on their southbound migration.

Duck hunters must have a small-game license and signed state and federal duck stamps in their possession. Seasons are typically staggered throughout October, closing some midweeks to extend the season. Limits and seasons for waterfowl aren't set until midsummer. Check with the DNR for specifics.

Getting Outfitted

FINDING A CANOE OUTFITTER

TWO ROADS DIVERGED IN A WOOD, AND I –
I TOOK THE ONE LESS TRAVELED BY,
AND THAT HAS MADE ALL THE
DIFFERENCE.

Robert Frost, "The Road Not Taken"

HUNDREDS OF THOUSANDS OF ACRES OF WILDERNESS FORESTS, lakes, and streams spread out from the shores of Lake Superior. To explore the Superior National Forest, the Boundary Waters Canoe Area Wilderness (BWCAW), or the adjacent Canadian Quetico Provincial Park, you don't need to own the equipment. Outfitters provide anything and everything you need (or forgot) from canoes to packs to tents to food and valuable information on the area. They can recommend routes, fishing areas, and camping spots. Many offer a variety of accommodation choices and amenities. Ask about day trips!

Outfitters are based on lakes along the Gunflint Trail, at the end of the Sawbill Trail, and along Highway 61 in Cook County. Most operate from early May through late September. Because of changes in BWCAW legislation, it is imperative to ask whether your outfitter can reserve a BWCAW permit for you or whether you should obtain the permit. Your outfitter will inform you of any relevant Quetico Park camping fees. It is necessary to make reservations with a partial deposit for the BWCAW. For brochures or to make reservations, contact one of the following outfitters. For additional information, news, tips, and outfitter listings, check out northshorevisitor.com. For BWCAW permit info and updates, call (877) 550-6777 or online at bwcaw.org.

What Do You Mean By …

COMPLETE OUTFITTING: Absolutely everything except clothes and personal items, including canoes, paddles, life vests, maps, all camping gear, food, and permits.

PARTIAL OUTFITTING: Canoes or *any* item by the day (perfect for day trips, when you're short an item or forgot something).

TOW SERVICE: A motorized boat carries you, all your gear, and canoes to an access point. This is especially helpful on big lakes like Saganaga.

GUIDES: Someone to keep you on course and help with camp chores (think northwoods concierge/cabana boy).

SAWTOOTH OUTFITTERS
Complete or partial outfitting. Ultralight equipment, canoes, permits and licenses; day-trip rentals on kayaks, mountain bikes, and winter equipment, too.

Highway 61 in Tofte
(218) 663-7643
sawtoothoutfitters.com

SAWBILL CANOE OUTFITTERS
Complete or partial outfitting. Ultralight equipment, canoes, permits and licenses, tackle or bait, day-trip rentals, camping, showers, and toilets.

Sawbill Trail on Sawbill Lake
(218) 387-7150
sawbill.com

BEAR TRACK OUTFITTING CO.
Complete or partial outfitting. Ultralight equipment, canoes, and sea kayaks, permits and licenses, tackle, day trips, lodging, tow service, toilets. Pro fly shop in store. Bally Creek Cabins and group lodging.

Highway 61 in Grand Marais
(218) 387-1162 or (800) 795-8068
bear-track.com

WILDERNESS WATERS OUTFITTERS

Complete or partial outfitting. Ultralight equipment, canoes, permits and licenses, and winter snowshoe and cross-country ski rental.

Highway 61 in Grand Marais
(218) 387-2525 or (800) 325-5842
wilderness-waters.com

CLEARWATER CANOE OUTFITTERS AND LODGE

Complete or partial outfitting. Ultralight equipment, canoes, boats and motors, permits and licenses, tackle or bait, day trips, guides, tow service, and a choice of lodging: B&B rooms, suites, bunkhouses, and 3 screenhouses.

Off the Gunflint Trail on Clearwater Lake
(218) 388-2254 or (800) 527-0554
clearwateroutfitters.com

ADVENTUROUS CHRISTIANS

Providing outfitting to groups interested in ministry in a wilderness environment; guides, sauna, rental cabins, and main lodge. Open year-round.

Off Gunflint Trail on the Bow Lake Road
(218) 388-2286 or (800) 392-1501
adventurouschristians.org

BOUNDARY COUNTRY TREKKING

Lodge-to-lodge hiking and cross-country skiing; BWCAW canoe trips, canoe/bike trips, yurt-to-yurt skiing, inn-to-inn canoeing, guides, day trips, dog sledding, and cabins. Yurts and a guesthouse.

Off the Gunflint Trail on Little Ollie Lake
(218) 388-4487 or (800) 322-8327
boundarycountry.com

HUNGRY JACK CANOE OUTFITTERS AND CABINS

Complete or partial outfitting. Ultralight equipment, canoes, permits and licenses, tackle or bait, day trips, bunkhouses and cabins, guides, and tow service.

Off the Gunflint Trail on Hungry Jack Lake
(218) 388-2275 or (800) 648-2922
hjo.com

NOR'WESTER OUTFITTERS
Complete or partial outfitting. Ultralight equipment, canoes, boats and motors, permits and licenses, tackle or bait, day trips, camping, cabins, bunkhouses and townhome, and guides.

7778 Gunflint Trail on Poplar Lake
(218) 388-2252 or (800) 992-4FUN
norwesterlodge.com

WINDIGO LODGE
Partial outfitting. Canoes, boats and motors, permits and licenses, tackle or bait, day trips, camping and lodging, dining and guides.

7890 Gunflint Trail on Poplar Lake
(218) 388-2222 or (800) 535-4320
windigolodge.com

ROCKWOOD LODGE AND OUTFITTERS
Complete or partial outfitting. Ultralight equipment, canoes, boats and motors, permits and licenses, tackle or bait, day trips, bunkhouses and cabins, guides and tow service.

Off the Gunflint Trail on Poplar Lake
(218) 388-2242 or (800) 942-2922
rockwoodbwca.com

GUNFLINT NORTHWOODS OUTFITTERS
Complete or partial outfitting. Ultralight equipment, canoes, boats and motors, permits and licenses, tackle or bait, day trips, lodging, dining, guides, group facilities, bunkhouses, and Trading Post!

Off the Gunflint Trail on Gunflint Lake
(218) 388-2296 or (800) 328-3325
gunflintoutfitters.com

TUSCARORA LODGE AND OUTFITTERS
Complete or partial outfitting. Ultralight equipment, canoes, permits and licenses, tackle or bait, day trips, camping or lodging, tow service, and boat and motor rentals.

Off the Gunflint Trail on Round Lake
(218) 388-2221 or (800) 544-3843
tuscaroracanoe.com

SEAGULL CREEK FISHING CAMP
Partial outfitting. Canoes, boats and motors, permits and licenses, tackle or bait, day trips, lodging, guides, tow service, showers and toilets.

12056 Gunflint Trail at Seagull Creek

(218) 388-9929 or (800) 531-5510

seagullcreekfishingcamp.com

SEAGULL OUTFITTERS
Complete or partial outfitting. Ultralight equipment, canoes, boats and motors, permits and licenses, tackle or bait, day trips, lodging, guides, tow service, showers and toilets.

12208 Gunflint Trail on Seagull Lake

(218) 388-2216 or (800) 346-2205

seagulloutfitters.com

SUPERIOR NORTH CANOE OUTFITTERS
Complete or partial outfitting. Ultralight equipment, Kevlar packages, canoes, boats and motors, permits and licenses, tackle or bait, day trips, bunkhouse and Sag Lake Store with snacks, convenience and camping items, and beer and ice.

Off the Gunflint Trail on Saganaga Lake

(218) 388-4416 or (800) 852-2008

superiornorthoutfitters.com

VOYAGEUR CANOE OUTFITTERS
Complete or partial outfitting. Ultralight equipment, canoes, boats and motors, permits and licenses, tackle or bait, guides, tow service, bunkhouses, cabins, lodge loft condos, packages, trading post, fly-in trips, and an amazing searchable canoe route feature on their Web site!

Off the Gunflint Trail on Seagull River

(218) 388-2224 or (888) CANOEIT

canoeit.com

WAY OF THE WILDERNESS CANOE OUTFITTERS
Complete or partial outfitting. Ultralight equipment, canoes, permits and licenses, tackle or bait, day trips, bunkhouses, camping, dining, tow service, trading post, and Trails End Cafe serving breakfast, lunch, dinner, pizza, and beer.

On the Gunflint Trail on Seagull River

(218) 388-2212 or (800) 346-6625; in winter: (218) 722-8469

wayofthewilderness.com

Wonderful White Winter

THE [BIRCHES] SEEMED DREAMLIKE ON
ACCOUNT OF THAT FROSTING.

James Taylor, "Sweet Baby James"

WUNNERFUL ... WUNNERFUL
... WUNNERFUL

Lawrence Welk

Up north, we have winter like nobody else has winter. We warm up with a Halloween snow squall and conclude with an Easter ski date. We like winter. It is a season of stunning coastal ice formations, piercing blue skies on blinding sunlit days, shimmering star-strewn heavens on subzero nights, and piles and piles of downy white snow.

We have found every conceivable way to play in that snow. We pile it high and carve it. We glide over it, race down it, ride over it, make tracks through it, and roll around in it. Sometimes we even drill holes and catch fish through it. Mostly, we live in it and love it.

So, as you kick your dead, salt-covered car, try to remember the last time you made a snow angel. This winter, build a crackling fire and make plans to river ski, snowshoe, dogsled, and have a snow angel competition.

Although many may mutter under their breath about subzero cold snaps, they are conducive to setting river ice. North Shore streams are ideal for skiing, as they freeze quite solidly. River skiing, as the name implies, involves ascending the frozen waterway and returning downstream on cross-country skis.

River Skiing, Ice Fishing, Curling, Dogsledding, Ski Joring, Sleigh Rides, Sledding

T

O GIVE RIVER SKIING A TRY, CONSIDER THE LOWER PORTIONS OF THE Knife, Gooseberry, and Baptism Rivers. A bit more difficult skiing can be found on the Lester, Amity, Schmidt, French, and Sucker Rivers and on the upper Cascade River. Accomplished river skiers will be challenged by the terrain of the Beaver, Manitou, Two Island, Onion, Devil Track, and Brule Rivers. Be aware of deep pools beneath falls, and ski with a friend, or contact the University of Minnesota Outdoor Program at (218) 726-6533 or outdoorprogram.org for a group ski.

If skiing rivers isn't your style, consider skiing inland lakes. Once you're there, jig for a fresh brook trout dinner. While some would equate ice fishing with hell, it can be a placid and delicious way to spend an afternoon. Many lodges rent heated icehouses with predrilled holes and offer tips on what's biting. The thicker skinned can ski in to Boundary Waters Canoe Area Wilderness lakes for solitary fishing. In Duluth, and on more popular lakes, ice fishing is a spectator sport. As ice forms along Superior's shore, icehouses crop up in small clusters. A weekend drive along Scenic 61 will reveal varied ice fishing techniques. Some folks jig, some bobber-fish, some lay quietly on the ice and peer into the murky waters waiting for the big one. Information on seasons, limits, and regulations is available at most sporting good stores, or call the Department of Natural Resources at (888) MINN-DNR or dnr.state.mn.us. Pick yourself up some Swedish Pimples and 'Looper bugs and hit the ice!

You can literally hit the ice with a 40-pound stone – a curling stone, that is. The sport of curling is based on sliding stones down an ice lane toward a target circle. Points are awarded to the team with the stones closest to the target center. Teams from the Twin Ports area have traveled as far as the Olympics and brought home medals. To catch a game, visit the Duluth Curling Club (duluthcurlingclub.org) in the Duluth Entertainment and Convention Center, the Two Harbors Curling Club, or the Cook County Community Club. Weekend bonspiels (tournaments) take place from December through March.

Another esoteric northern sport is dogsledding or, as some locals say, sled dogging. Harking back to the days when the only reliable winter transportation was a pack of dogs and a wooden runnered sled, dogsledding is kept alive today through a relatively small group of mushers. Some folks have a half-dozen dogs and sled for their own enjoyment. Others maintain a kennel and compete in such races as the Grand Portage Passage (grandportagemn .com/passage) and John Beargrease (beargrease.com) contests held each winter. A few mushers offer rides to the general public. Contact Silver Creek Sled Dogs in Two Harbors at (218) 834-6592; Arleigh Jorgenson Sled Dog Teams in Grand Marais at (218) 387-2498, (800) 884-5463, or dogmushing .com; or Boundary Country Trekking on the Gunflint Trail at (218) 388-4487, (800) 322-8327, or boundarycountry.com. Gunflint Lodge at (218) 388-2294, (800) 328-3325, or gunflint.com also has mushers and dogsleds available.

So now you're thinking of hooking up the family pet to the toboggan. In true Scandinavian style, you can secure Rover's leash to you via a harness, strap on your skinny skis, and go ski joring. Ah, all the glories of cross-country skiing, and none of the work! To catch ski joring in action, check the Duluth Winter Festival calendar of events, or try trails at Snowflake Nordic (skiduluth.com), to Carlton Peak in Tofte/Schroeder, in Lutsen near Isak Hansen's, and on Gunflint Lake.

Rivers Bend Carriage Service (218-729-5873) and LC's Sleigh Rides (218-721-4603) both offer sleigh rides through the woods outside of Duluth. Up the Shore toward Grand Marais, everyone loves sleighs pulled by Cap and Dan, the 2,000-pound Belgians that pull sleighs for Okontoe (218-388-9423 or okontoe.com). Take a ride on a crisp, bright wintry day or snuggle in for a lantern-lit trail ride beneath a bedazzling starlit sky.

And now, my favorite winter pastime – sledding! Don't you just love flyin' down those hills, bouncing off your sled face-first into powder? Or the classic toboggan ride powered by all that weight, steamrolling down, shaking off end passengers one by one? In Duluth, Mont du Lac ski area (218-636-3797 or skimontdulac.com) has four lanes of tubing lit for nighttime use while Chester and Lester Parks (see parks chapter) offer good old sledding hills. Along the Shore, you can pull out your sled at Lakeview (Two Harbors), Silver Bay, Superior National (Lutsen), and Gunflint Hills (Grand Marais) golf courses. The best sliding hill on the Shore is at the Grand Marais Campground and Rec Park. See you there – I'll be the one wiping out in a flurry of snow.

Get outside this winter. The snow is on us.

Snowshoeing

S NOWSHOEING IS WINTER HIKING. LASH ON A PAIR OF THESE woven frames, and you've commandeered the great outdoors. Venture out for an afternoon wildlife expedition. Track hares, shrews, wolves, deer, and ermine. Step soundlessly through the north woods, stopping to guess the width of a virgin pine, to listen to the chickadees, or just to savor the moment.

Lots of folks like to snowshoe the Superior Hiking Trail, but you can snowshoe anywhere. If the trail is also a groomed ski trail, walk on the sides, not on the tracked trail. Listed below are some suggested routes; see the hiking section ("Out Walkin'") for additional information and resorts and shops that rent showshoes.

IN DULUTH

PARK POINT REC AREA
Snowshoe throughout the park area and south of the airport.
From I-35, go south on Lake Avenue and cross the Aerial Lift Bridge to
45th Street.

KINGSBURY CREEK TRAIL AND LAKE SUPERIOR ZOOLOGICAL GARDENS
Tramp through the Fairmount Park area, up the trail, and through the Zoo.
From I-35s, go west on Grand Avenue and follow the Zoo signs.

LESTER PARK
Snowshoe through the park and adjacent golf course, avoiding tracked ski trails.
From I-35, continue on London Road, then go north on 61st Avenue
East, which turns into Lester River Road.

UMD OUTDOOR PROGRAM
Rents snowshoes and leads a few guided showshoe hikes.

121 Sport and Health Center, UMD campus

(218) 726-8743

umdoutdoorprogram.org

SPIRIT MOUNTAIN (RENTALS, TOO)
Snowshoe through the adjacent woodlands or rent 'shoes and try one of the trails above. Rentals are $12 per day.

From I-35, take exit 249 and follow the sign.

(218) 628-2891 or (800) 642-6377

spiritmt.com

MONT DU LAC
Snowshoe the forested area around the slopes; rentals and a great little chalet.

From I-35, exit west at Highway 23 and follow signs.

(218) 636-3797

skimontdulac.com

ALONG THE SHORE

WOLF ROCK
Make the big climb to Wolf Rock, then return or continue on as far as Gooseberry Falls State Park.
> From Highway 61 in Castle Danger, go north on Co. Rd. 106, which
> turns into Silver Creek Road 617, to the parking area.

STATE PARKS
Snowshoe any of the state parks, but avoid groomed ski and snowmobile trails. Enjoy the amenities.

SAWTOOTH OUTFITTERS (RENTALS)
Highway 61 in Tofte
> (218) 663-7643
> sawtoothoutfitters.com

CARLTON PEAK
Follow the hiking trail to the summit; gorgeous vistas.
> From Highway 61 in Tofte, go north on the Sawbill Trail about 2.25 miles
> to sign.

CARIBOU STATE WAYSIDE
Make tracks up the river and into the woods to Sugarloaf Road.
> Highway 61, about 5.5 miles northeast of Little Marais

OBERG AND LEVEAUX MOUNTAINS
Snowshoe the LeVeaux trail system, the Oberg loop, or plan a longer winter hike to Moose Mountain at Lutsen Mountains, where you can either take the gondola down or hike the last few miles.
> From Highway 61 in Lutsen, go north on the Onion River Road
> (Forest Rd. 336) about two miles to parking.

LUTSEN MOUNTAINS
Rentals available; ask for a trail map, tramp through the woods, or include a gondola ride to Moose Mountain and 'shoe the big loop!
> From Highway 61 in Lutsen, go north on the Ski Hill Road.
> (218) 663-7281
> lutsen.com

LUTSEN REC, INC. (RENTALS ONLY)
From Highway 61 in Lutsen, midway up the Ski Hill Road.
> (218) 663-7863
> lutsenrec.com

SUPERIOR NATIONAL AT LUTSEN
Try out snowshoes on the rolling fairways and through the Poplar River Valley woodlands.
> Off Highway 61 in Lutsen

DEER YARD AND BALLY CREEK
Through the woods, over creeks and beaver ponds you'll go! You can 'shoe alongside ski trails as well.
> From Highway 61, go northeast on Co. Rd. 7. For Deer Yard, go north on Co. Rd. 44, west on the Pike Lake Road to intersection with Forest Road; go west on Forest Road to parking. For Bally Creek, go north on Co. Rd. 48, then north on the Bally Creek Road about 2 miles.

KADUNCE RIVER STATE WAYSIDE
Hike the trail, the shoreline, and, if the river is set, up the river.
> Highway 61, about eight miles northeast of Grand Marais

HIGH FALLS AT GRAND PORTAGE STATE PARK (RENTALS, TOO)
An easy winter hike to the High Falls that leaves plenty of time to explore the lower trails; rentals at park office.
> Highway 61 just southwest of the international border, in Grand Portage State Park

UP THE GUNFLINT TRAIL

PINCUSHION B&B (RENTALS, TOO)
Try loops near the B&B or venture off on your own.
> From Highway 61 in Grand Marais, north 2 miles on Gunflint Trail, east on B&B Road
> (218) 387-1276 or (800) 542-1226
> pincushionbb.com

GOLDEN EAGLE LODGE (RENTALS, TOO)
Try the Big Foot Trail from the lodge on to Flour Lake, around Wolf Point, and back through the woods.

25 miles up the Gunflint Trail, and 2.5 miles east on the Clearwater Road
(218) 388-2203 or (800) 346-2203
golden-eagle.com

BEARSKIN LODGE (RENTALS, TOO)
'Shoe through the woods, on trails, or over East Bearskin Lake.
27 miles up the Gunflint Trail and 1 mile east on East Bearskin Road
(218) 388-2292 or (800) 338-4170
bearskin.com

BOUNDARY COUNTRY TREKKING/BANADAD TRAILS (RENTALS, TOO)
Choose from three loops, each about 2 miles. The Creek Trail follows the Poplar Creek and returns along a low ridge; cross Swamp Lake in the BWCAW on the Swamp Lake Trail, or take the Knopp Trail west and return alongside the Banadad Trail.
32 miles up the Gunflint Trail and 2 miles east on Lima Grade to 1-mile
drive on Little Ollie Road
(218) 388-4487 or (800) 322-8327
boundarycountry.com

TRAIL CENTER LODGE (RENTALS)
Midway up the Gunflint Trail on Poplar Lake
(218) 388-2214
trailcenterlodge.com

OLD NORTHWOODS LODGE (RENTALS)
32 miles up the Gunflint Trail and a quarter-mile in, on Poplar Lake
(218) 388-9464 or (800) 682-8264
oldnorthwoods.com

GUNFLINT LODGE, GUNFLINT PINES, AND HESTON'S LODGE (RENTALS, TOO)
Showshoe on a variety of loops and trails connecting the south shore
Gunflint Lake resorts.
45 miles up the Gunflint Trail and ¾ to 3 miles east on South Gunflint
Lake
GUNFLINT LODGE: (218) 388-2296 or (800) 328-3325, or gunflint.com
GUNFLINT PINES: (218) 388-4454 or (800) 533-5814, or
gunflintpines.com
HESTON'S LODGE: (218) 388-2243 or (800) 338-7230, or hestons.com

Skinny Skiers Rejoice!

CROSS-COUNTRY SKIING

THE NORTH SHORE IS A CROSS-COUNTRY SKIER'S NIRVANA. With great objectivity and a wee bit of personal bias, I am telling you it doesn't get any better than this. Hundreds of kilometers of trails traverse hillsides, lakeshores, river valley ridges, pine plantations, deciduous forests, and alongside beaver dams. Options are unlimited. You can choose trails based on their length, the type of terrain they cover, your level of ability, and whether you want classic (parallel tracks) or skating stride. (The term "skinny skier" refers to the width of the ski, not the skier.)

All the trails discussed here are groomed and trackset at least once a week from December through March. Additional ungroomed or irregularly maintained trails can be found. Those listed here are marked with maps and signs through a cooperative effort by local private enterprises, ski organizations, and the Minnesota Department of Natural Resources (DNR) Grant-in-Aid program.

A Minnesota Ski Pass is required on all trails unless otherwise noted. Daily, annual, and three-year passes are offered. An annual pass currently costs $10 and a three-year pass is $25. People under 16 or over 65 years of age ski free. You can purchase passes at trail centers and businesses or by sending your full name, date of birth, driver license number and state, height, weight, eye color, and a lock of hair (just kidding) along with a check (made payable to MN DNR) to Minnesota DNR License Bureau, 500 Lafayette Road, St. Paul, MN 55155-4026.

The level of difficulty is indicated for each trail. "Easy" trails are relatively level, with few hills, and relatively short. "More difficult" trails have rolling hills throughout and can be quite lengthy. "Most difficult" trails incorporate sharp turns and steep grades as well as extended lengths. Consider these safety precautions: do not ski alone; always let someone know your route and expected return time; carry a map of the system; and know your limitations. People tend to overdo it when skiing, so you may wish to try several short loops rather than one "most difficult" trail.

Locations given below designate the primary parking for trailheads. All trails are open from dawn to dusk, in season, unless otherwise noted. Rentals are available at several businesses and resorts; inquire ahead of time. If you're skiing with children, consider Spirit Mountain, Gooseberry Falls State Park, Sugarbush (Tofte), and Pincushion trails for their short, level loops.

DULUTH TRAIL SYSTEMS

SPIRIT MOUNTAIN NORDIC SYSTEM

22K double-tracked, with skating lane. Four separate, concentric loops: an easy 1K, intermediate 3K and 5K, and most difficult 11K; plus an easy 2K campground loop, which is lit. This system is groomed to perfection and has consistent conditions throughout the season. It is great for groups with skiers of varying skill levels. Trails range from mild and level to lots of hills, curves, and climbs.

From I-35, take exit 249 and follow signs.

No Minnesota Ski Pass required

Open 9 A.M. to dusk daily

$7 full day, $50 season passes available

(218) 628-2891 or (800) 642-6377

spiritmt.com

MAPS: At trail center

LEVEL OF DIFFICULTY: Easy, more difficult, and most difficult

AMENITIES: Warming house with restrooms and refreshments; nearby parking; access to alpine center's main chalet

SNOWFLAKE NORDIC

15K+ double-tracked, with skating lane. A very easy 1K loop, challenging 5K intermediate loop, and very curvy 7.5K advanced trail with a 1.5K cutoff; 6K is lit; biathlon range and 400M speed skating oval.

From I-35, go north on 21st Avenue East, northeast on Woodland Avenue, west on Arrowhead Road, and north on Rice Lake Road (Co. Rd. 4) to 4348 Rice Lake Road.

No Minnesota Ski Pass required

Open daily 9 A.M. to 8 P.M. and 9 A.M. to 5 P.M. weekends

$7 adults, $3 after 6 P.M., $3 kids; season passes available

(218) 726-1550
skiduluth.com
MAPS: At trail center
LEVEL OF DIFFICULTY: Easy, more difficult, and most difficult
AMENITIES: Chalet with restrooms, snacks, fireplace, wax room,
and sauna

MAGNEY-SNIVELY

14K tracked and skating lane. Long uphill climbs and descents through hard-wood forest. From the trailhead, a 0.5K access route takes you to a 7.5K clockwise loop to Ely Peak, with a 5.5K cutoff. The 3.1K Bardons Peak loop, which is 10K in on the trail to Ely Peak, has a scenic overlook of the St. Louis River Valley, Duluth, and Superior.

> From I-35, go west on exit 249 about 2.5 miles past Spirit Mountain; parking is a quarter-mile past the old stone bridge.

Minnesota Ski Pass required

(218) 723-3678, Duluth Cross Country Ski Trail Hotline

MAPS: Map sign at trailheads, call Duluth Parks and Rec at
(218) 723-3337, or northshorevisitor.com

LEVEL OF DIFFICULTY: More and most difficult

PIEDMONT

5K double-tracked. The trail winds through a hardwood forest, has an excellent scenic overlook of the St. Louis River Valley, and offers two cutoff trails. Admire the handmade ski signs!

> From I-35, go north on 21st Avenue West, north on Piedmont Avenue, and west on Hutchinson to the junction with Adirondack and the parking area.

Minnesota Ski Pass required

(218) 723-3678, Duluth Cross Country Ski Trail Hotline

MAPS: Map sign at trailheads, call Duluth Parks and Rec at
(218) 723-3337, or northshorevisitor.com

LEVEL OF DIFFICULTY: Easy to more difficult

CHESTER BOWL

3K tracked and skating lane over very hilly terrain that loops up and down the ridgeline with fabulous Lake Superior views. Park also has downhill skiing, ski jumping, sledding, and speed skating.

> From I-35, go north on Mesaba Avenue, then east on Skyline Parkway.

Minnesota Ski Pass required

(218) 724-9832, and (218) 723-3678 for the Duluth Cross Country Ski
Trail Hotline

MAPS: Map sign at trailheads, or call Duluth Parks and Rec at
(218) 723-3337, or northshorevisitor.com

LEVEL OF DIFFICULTY: Most difficult

AMENITIES: ♿ Restrooms; a warming chalet sells refreshments
afternoons, weekends, and holidays.

HARTLEY

5K single-tracked. Two main loops; more experienced skiers will enjoy the
hilly outer loops, and novices and families can ski the easy 3K inner loop
meandering through Hartley Field and adjacent woodlands. First-time
skiers can avoid the short uphill by accessing the trailhead off Hartley Road.

From I-35, go north on 21st Avenue East, northeast on Woodland
Avenue, and east on Fairmont to trailhead; very beginning skiers will
want to take Arrowhead Road west off Woodland Avenue, then head
north on Hartley Road.

Minnesota Ski Pass required

(218) 723-3678, Duluth Cross Country Ski Trail Hotline

MAPS: Map sign at trailheads, call Duluth Parks and Rec at
(218) 723-3337, or northshorevisitor.com

LEVEL OF DIFFICULTY: Easy to more difficult

LESTER-AMITY

15K tracked and skating lane. The easiest skiing is a 3K loop through adjacent
Lester Park Golf Course (park farther up the Lester River Road at the clubhouse). A 1.4K access trail is a bit difficult because of the climb and descent;
it leads to an easy 3.4K inner loop; plans are in process to light this trail. To
access the more challenging 4.4K to 9K upper loop, head north on Occidental Boulevard (one block east of 61st) to the Lakeside Chalet, where this
rolling hills loop begins. The main loop is 4.4K; to increase the length, add
any or all of the six 0.5K side loops or the 1.2K intermediate loop.

From I-35, continue on London Road, then go north on 61st Avenue
East, which turns into Lester River Road.

Minnesota Ski Pass required

(218) 723-3678, Duluth Cross Country Ski Trail Hotline

MAPS: Map sign at trailheads, call Duluth Parks and Rec at
(218) 723-3337, or northshorevisitor.com

LEVEL OF DIFFICULTY: Easy, more difficult, and most difficult

JAY COOKE STATE PARK

51.5K of cross-country ski trails.

South of Duluth at 500 East Highway 210, Carlton, MN 55718

(218) 384-4610

ALONG THE SHORE FROM TWO HARBORS TO SCHROEDER

TWO HARBORS SKI TRAIL

10.5K tracked and 5K skating lane. A 4.5K easy to more difficult outside loop with 1K of expert loops and a 2.6K intermediate inside loop. Trails run through the rolling hills of the golf course and a forest of paper birch, aspen, spruce, fir, and cedar. A portion of the trail is lit.

From Highway 61, go north on Co. Rd. 2 for 0.75 mile to trailhead

(218) 834-4024 or (800) 554-2116

MAPS: In parking area

LEVEL OF DIFFICULTY: Easy to most difficult

GOOSEBERRY FALLS STATE PARK

24K double-tracked. A 3.3K easy trail winds through the campground area, giving pleasant views of Lake Superior (a great trail for taking kids). The rest of the trails depart from the visitors center and head north under Highway 61 and are more difficult, with most difficult portions. Trails parallel the Gooseberry River past five amazing waterfalls, skirt white pine ridges, and allow exploration of the park's backcountry. Ski 0.7K to the 3.4K intermediate Birch Loop up the west side of the river with a long downhill return through the woods. A 1K access trail also leads up the east side of the river to a more difficult 4.4K loop, with optional additional 2.1K and 5.8K (most difficult) loops. A superb system with trail diversity and scenic beauty.

Highway 61, about 12 miles northeast of Two Harbors, with parking at the visitors center

Minnesota Ski Pass required. If you park in the state park, a park permit is required. Both are sold at the office, open 8:30 A.M. to 4 P.M. daily.

(218) 834-5350

MAPS: At office, trailheads, and at northshorevisitor.com

LEVEL OF DIFFICULTY: Easy, more difficult, and most difficult

AMENITIES: Restrooms; shelter building with a fireplace and winter camping

SPLIT ROCK LIGHTHOUSE STATE PARK

13K double-tracked; 4K of intermediate trails run from the lighthouse along Superior's shores and around Day Hill. From the Day Hill trail you can ski the 3.4K Merrill Logging loop on the north side of the highway or the 5.1K Corundum Mine loop on the lake side of the road; conditions and length can make these trails most difficult.

Off Highway 61 about 20 miles northeast of Two Harbors, with parking in the state park and at the lighthouse

Minnesota Ski Pass required. If you park in the state park, a park permit is required. Both are sold at the office, open 10 A.M. to 4 P.M. on weekends and sporadically during the week.

(218) 226-6377

MAPS: At office, trailheads, and at northshorevisitor.com

LEVEL OF DIFFICULTY: More difficult and most difficult

AMENITIES: Trail center (open 8 A.M. to 10 P.M. daily) with restrooms and a fireplace; Split Rock Lighthouse center is open to the public throughout the winter.

NORTHWOODS SKI TRAIL

35.4K single-tracked. Interconnecting loops provide several route options. Maple Corner is an easy 2.1K or 2.8K loop. Big Pine is easy to intermediate at 4.7K and leads to the 6K connecting trail (very nice) to Tettegouche Camp on Mic Mac Lake. Ski the Birch-Poplar-Spruce loop and Bean Lake spur for the views of this little lake with high rock walls. The trails are mostly easy, roaming through the woods and along the East Branch of the Beaver River and the Cedar Creek.

From Highway 61 in Silver Bay, go 3.2 miles north on Outer Drive, which turns into Penn Boulevard (Co. Rd. 5).

Minnesota Ski Pass required

(218) 226-4105 (snow conditions)

MAPS: At trailhead, with signs along trail

LEVEL OF DIFFICULTY: Easy to more difficult

TETTEGOUCHE STATE PARK

25K single-tracked, with skating lane on 7.5K lower loop, which slowly climbs up from the lake to a great picnic spot at Nipisquit Lake and a downhill return. The Lakes and Hills Trail skirts Papasay Ridge past Nipisquit and Mic Mac Lakes to the 6K connector to Northwoods Trails or on out to the Lax Lake Road (Co. Rd. 4); it includes a 2.6K expert run to Mount Baldy.

Highway 61, about five miles northeast of Silver Bay

Minnesota Ski Pass required. If you park in the state park, a park permit is required. Both are sold at the office, open 10 A.M. to 4 P.M. on weekends and sporadically during the week.

(218) 226-6365

MAPS: At office, trailheads, and northshorevisitor.com

LEVEL OF DIFFICULTY: More to most difficult

AMENITIES: Visitors center has ♿ restrooms open 24 hours a day; winter camping and cabins are available.

SUOMI/FINLAND NORDIC SKI TRAIL

16K single-tracked. A figure-eight system climbs to the halfway point, providing a downhill return trail. The trail features a ski across the northern portion of the Baptism River and has the advantage of being less frequented.

From Highway 61 in Illgen City, go north on Minnesota 1 to Finland, then west on Co. Rd. 7 for one mile to the parking area (shared with snowmobilers).

Minnesota Ski Pass required

(218) 353-7726

MAPS: At trailhead, with signs along trail

LEVEL OF DIFFICULTY: More to most difficult

GEORGE H. CROSBY MANITOU STATE PARK

17.7K of ungroomed, ski-at-your-own-risk trails.

Minnesota Ski Pass required

(218) 226-6365 (Tettegouche State Park takes calls for this park).

FLATHORN-GEGOKA SKI TOURING AREA

37.6K of diagonal-tracked trails.

On Minnesota 1, 29.5 miles north of Highway 61

Minnesota Ski Pass required

(218) 323-7676, National Forest Lodge

ALONG THE SHORE FROM SCHROEDER TO GRAND MARAIS

NORTH SHORE MOUNTAINS TRAIL SYSTEM

196K of interconnected trails originating at Cross River and extending northeast to Bally Creek. Maps and information for the next ten listings are available from local businesses and the Lutsen-Tofte Tourism Association, housed in the twin red fish houses on Highway 61 in Tofte, or call (218) 663-7804 or (888) 61-NORTH.

TEMPERANCE RIVER STATE PARK

12.6K single-tracked; easy to more difficult 1K access to 5.8K intermediate Temperance River loop, which connects to the 5.8K Cross River loop. The Cross River loop is laid out so that a number of variations can be skied, each about 3K; it is mostly easy, with one steep hill.

Highway 61, on the west side of Temperance River in Schroeder;
or east of Cross River, go north on the gravel Skou Road for a quarter of a mile.

Minnesota Ski Pass required. If you park in the state park, a park permit is required. Both are sold at the office, open 8 A.M. to 4:30 P.M. daily.
(218) 663-7476

LEVEL OF DIFFICULTY: Easy to more difficult

AMENITIES: Restrooms in state park and shelters along trail

SUGARBUSH

Features 2.9K of easy inner loops (great for kids) and intermediate loops through rolling, maple-covered hills and hogback ridges. The intermediate 3.1K Hogback trail is a slow climb up and long descent back. The 1.7K Bridge Run is a less challenging intermediate trail that leads to the 7.3K Homestead loop (actually a 12K total ski from Sawbill trailhead). Sugarbush includes part of the 25K Picnic loop for the advanced skier and a 4K connecting trail to the LeVeaux Trail System.

From Highway 61 in Tofte, go north on the Sawbill Trail (Co. Rd. 2)
for two miles.

Minnesota Ski Pass required

LEVEL OF DIFFICULTY: Easy, more difficult, and most difficult

CARLTON PEAK

West of Sugarbush, an intermediate 2.2K takes you to the summit of Carlton Peak, then either loop back to the trailhead or at the intersection ski the intermediate 3K downhill run to Bluefin Bay. The Bluefin Bay trail can be accessed north of Highway 61 across from Bluefin Bay Resort.

From Highway 61 in Tofte, go north on the Sawbill Trail (Co. Rd. 2)
for two miles.

Minnesota Ski Pass required

LEVEL OF DIFFICULTY: Easy and more difficult

MOOSE FENCE

A 1K trail leads to two easy loops, the Upland (2.4K) and the Maple (3.4K), and a 3.1K advanced trail connects to the Picnic loop (see Sugarbush description above). Researchers planted pines that are genetically resistant to white pine blister rust and enclosed the area to protect the tasty young trees from moose – hence the trail designation, "Moose Fence."

From Highway 61 in Tofte, go north on the Sawbill Trail (Co. Rd. 2) for 7.5 miles to the White Pine Blister Rust Research sign.

Minnesota Ski Pass required

LEVEL OF DIFFICULTY: Easy, more difficult, and most difficult

LEVEAUX AND OBERG

Tracked and skating lanes. The more difficult 8K Oberg trail is quite pretty; it starts with a climb and has hills throughout. An easy 3.8K skating trail is the continuation of Forest Rd. 336 north of the parking area. About 2K into the Oberg trail, you can connect to a 2.6K ski to Lutsen Resort's Sea Villas or a 7K trail to the Superior National golf course. The LeVeaux trail connects west to Sugarbush and Moose Fence, and the Oberg trail connects east to Lutsen-Poplar.

From Highway 61 in Lutsen, shortly after mile marker 88, go north on Onion River Road (Forest Rd. 336) two miles to parking.

Minnesota Ski Pass required

LEVEL OF DIFFICULTY: Easy, more difficult, and most difficult

LUTSEN-POPLAR

The golf course offers an easy though windblown 2K ski loop that hooks onto the 5K Homestead trail, which crosses the Poplar River and the Lutsen Scientific and Natural Area of beautiful old-growth trees before terminating on the Caribou Trail (Co. Rd. 4). The trail system connects west to LeVeaux and east to Massie-Hall loops (described in the Solbakken Cascade Area listing next).

Highway 61 at Superior National at Lutsen golf course

Minnesota Ski Pass required

LEVEL OF DIFFICULTY: Easy and more difficult

SOLBAKKEN CASCADE AREA

25K tracked and skating lane. From the Caribou Trail, ski all downhill for 1.8K and pick up the easy 2.6K Isak Flats loop or ski the short way to Solbakken Resort. North of the resort, two easy loops totaling 2.1K connect to the two intermediate loops; the 6.2K Massie trail and the 5.2K Hall loop, which in turn intersects with a 5.8K connector to the Cascade trails. The trail system connects west to Lutsen-Poplar and east to Cascade trails.

The Hall loop is named after Hans K. P. Hall, a boatbuilder who homesteaded this area in 1901. Hans's grandson Jim and his family currently reside nearby and allow the trail to cross their property. Many of the trails included here traverse private land, so please exercise the utmost respect. You're skiing through their backyard.

From Highway 61 in Lutsen, go north about one mile on the Caribou Trail (Co. Rd. 4) to the trailhead, or start at Solbakken Resort, or continue north on the Hall Road (Co. Rd. 41) just east of Solbakken to a third trailhead.

LEVEL OF DIFFICULTY: Easy to more difficult

CASCADE RIVER TRAILS

26.5K tracked trails. There are lots of easy and intermediate loops near the lodge and in the park near Lake Superior. However, I suggest you make it a two-car ski by leaving one car on Highway 61 and driving to Deer Yard (see the next listing for the Deer Yard Trails), where you can ski the more difficult 8K-plus Babineau Run. Ski to the first junction and head toward the beaver pond, then ski the eastern leg of the Pioneer Trail and the River Trails back down to Highway 61. Note that the only skating is on an easy loop just west of the lodge. In the park, ski the easy to intermediate 6.4K Cedar Woods loop, which is uphill the first third, downhill the middle third, and level the last third, if you ski it clockwise. The trail system connects west to Hall loop (described in the Solbakken Cascade Area listing above) and northeast to Deer Yard.

Cascade Lodge trails (on the river's east side) begin at Cascade Lodge on Highway 61 (a parking fee is charged); Cascade River State Park trails (on the river's west side) begin at Highway 61 parking, or take the park road in to parking.

Minnesota Ski Pass required. If you park in the state park, a park permit is required. Both are sold at the office, open 10 A.M. to 4 P.M. on weekends.

LEVEL OF DIFFICULTY: Easy, more difficult, and most difficult

AMENITIES: Restrooms in state park

DEER YARD TRAILS

24.5K tracked-only trails. Ski in on the easy 3K trail to the first junction and return to the trailhead, or plan to ski the more to most difficult Deer Yard loop; this is a great picnic loop that covers a variety of hills, from short, steep, and curvy to medium-length uphill climbs. See the Cascade River description for details on skiing from Deer Yard down to Highway 61 at the Cascade River. Connects southwest to Cascade River and north to Bally Creek.

From Highway 61, go north on Co. Rd. 7, north on Co. Rd. 44, west on Pike Lake Road (Co. Rd. 45), to the intersection with forest road, continue west to parking (known locally as Babineau Corner).

Minnesota Ski Pass required. If you park in the state park, a park permit is required. Both are sold at the office, open 10 A.M. to 4 P.M. on weekends.

LEVEL OF DIFFICULTY: Easy, more difficult, and most difficult

BALLY CREEK TRAILS

30K, with ski joring on 8K of unplowed road (Forest Rd. 158 beyond parking area). Lots of short loops for skiers of all skill levels; ski through deep forest, across ponds, and over the Sundling and Bally Creeks. The 10.4K Moose Trail, a downhill connector to the Cascade State Park system, is more difficult. Connects south to the Deer Yard and Cascade trail systems.

From Highway 61, go northeast on Co. Rd. 7 to Co. Rd. 48, north to Forest Rd. 158 (Bally Creek Road), and take Forest Rd. 158 in about two miles.

LEVEL OF DIFFICULTY: Easy to more difficult

LUTSEN MOUNTAINS NORDIC CENTER

27K tracked and skating lane. Accessible by chairlifts, the trails wind around downhill slopes, into the Poplar River Valley, and along ridgelines offering panoramas of Lake Superior, the Sawtooth Mountains, and Superior National Forest.

From Highway 61 in Lutsen, go north on Ski Hill Road.

A daily fee is charged.

(218) 663-7281

lutsen.com

MAPS: Available at ticket office

LEVEL OF DIFFICULTY: Easy, more difficult, and most difficult

AMENITIES: Rentals, maps, restrooms, and food

ALONG THE SHORE FROM GRAND MARAIS TO GRAND PORTAGE

PINCUSHION MOUNTAIN TRAILS

25K single-tracked, with skating lane; excellent trail design and variety, with Piston-Bully grooming capabilities. Two easy 1K and 1.3K loops leave from the scenic overlook trailhead; there are plans to light these trails and add a 2K easy loop and a 2K more difficult loop. Ski 1K access to the more difficult and very popular 6.8K Pincushion Mountain loop, which has moderate hills and turns. The 7K expert trails include loops from 1K to 4.1K. The entire system is set in a birch forest featuring Devil Track River Valley and hilly terrain.

From Highway 61 in Grand Marais, go north on the Gunflint Trail
  (Co. Rd. 12) about two miles, then east on Co. Rd. 53
  (Pincushion Drive) to scenic overlook.

Minnesota Ski Pass required

(800) 542-1226 or (218) 387-1276 (Pincushion Mountain Bed and
  Breakfast)

pincushiontrails.org

LEVEL OF DIFFICULTY: Easy, more difficult, and most difficult

AMENITIES: Public warming house at overlook trailhead

JUDGE C. R. MAGNEY STATE PARK

8K single-tracked. The 6K Long Loop climbs the bluffs along the Brule River, with a spur trail to an overlook, shelter, and outhouse; great downhill return trip. The Short Loop has a solid climb to overlooks of Superior and the Brule River.

Highway 61, about 14 miles northeast of Grand Marais

Minnesota Ski Pass required. If you park in the state park, a park permit is also required.

(218) 387-3039

MAPS: Along trail and at northshorevisitor.com

LEVEL OF DIFFICULTY: More difficult

GRAND PORTAGE INDIAN RESERVATION TRAILS

24K single- or double-tracked, with skating lanes, plus 26K ungroomed. Two easy 4K trails meander through maple forests adjacent to the trail center; three intermediate loops cover the hilly terrain west of the trailhead. Highlights include scenic overlooks at both ends of Loon Lake, an overlook of North Lake, and the advanced 1.6K round-trip trail to Mount Sophie, 1,200 feet above Lake Superior.

From Highway 61, go northwest on Co. Rd. 17 to Co. Rd. 89 and north to trail center.

No Minnesota Ski Pass required

(218) 475-2401 or (800) 232-1384 (Grand Portage Lodge and Casino)

MAPS: At trail center

LEVEL OF DIFFICULTY: Easy, more difficult, and most difficult

UP THE GUNFLINT TRAIL

The Gunflint Trail region has 180K of groomed, signed, and tracked trails. Maps are available at lodges adjacent to the trails for a minimal charge. Call the Gunflint Trail Association at (800) 338-6932 or one of the resorts listed below for more information.

GEORGE WASHINGTON MEMORIAL PINES TRAIL

3.3K ungroomed; a gentle, level loop amid Norway pines, along the edge of the Elbow Creek, and through a beautiful stand of cedar. Perfect for learning skiers.

From Highway 61 in Grand Marais, go north on the Gunflint Trail (Co. Rd. 12) for eight miles to parking on west side.

(218) 387-1750 (Gunflint Ranger Station)

LEVEL OF DIFFICULTY: Easy

CENTRAL GUNFLINT TRAILS

70K with single or double track, and 36K of skating lanes. Trails are maintained to perfection. Uncrowded wilderness skiing features longer loops with rest shelters and trails that skirt the edge of the Boundary Waters Canoe Area Wilderness over spruce-covered hills and across frozen lakes, with breathtaking cliff overlooks. Beginners will want to ski the 5K Summer Home Road loop, the 5.2K Ox Cart Trail, or either lodge's 1K lit trail. The remainder of the loops are primarily intermediate, featuring hills and curves, with two advanced loops. The 8K (plus 2K access) Bear Cub World Cup loop is designed to test the most advanced skier with 300-foot elevation changes, making for steep climbs and fast, fast, fast downhills.

$10 per day or $7.50 per half-day for nonguests; season passes available

Golden Eagle Lodge: (218) 388-2203 or (800) 346-2203; Bearskin Lodge: (218) 388-2292 or (800) 338-4170

TRAILHEADS: At Golden Eagle Lodge, 25.5 miles up the Gunflint Trail and 2.5 miles in, and at Bearskin Lodge, 27 miles up the Gunflint Trail and 1 mile in

LEVEL OF DIFFICULTY: Easy, more difficult, and most difficult

AMENITIES: Ski lessons and rentals at lodges

BANADAD SKI TRAIL

43K tracked. A 29K connecting trail between the Central and Upper Gunflint trail systems penetrates the Boundary Waters Canoe Area Wilderness; skiers can access the trail from any of the yurts. A short way in from the Trail Center trailhead are some small loops and the ungroomed, advanced 8K Caribou Lake loop. The moderate 5K Lace Lake loop skirts the BWCAW to connect with the Banadad Trail and the Poplar Creek Trail (about 8K back to Bearskin). (A yurt is a Mongolian-style hut that's designed and built expressly for the purpose of weathering cold and snowy winter conditions. *Banadad* is Ojibwe for "lost." Hmmm ...) The 5K lake crossing is a moderate ski from the Banadad to Old Northwoods Lodge.

Minnesota Ski Pass required

Boundary Country Trekking: (218) 388-4487 or (800) 322-8327, or boundarycountry.com

TRAILHEADS: At Boundary Country Trekking, 32 miles up the Gunflint Trail, 1 mile east on the Lima Grade, and 1 mile on Little Ollie Road.

LEVEL OF DIFFICULTY: More to most difficult

AMENITIES: Boundary Country Trekking offers yurt-to-yurt skiing packages, rentals, and lodging.

UPPER GUNFLINT TRAILS

90K single- or double-tracked, with 24K of skating lanes. The easiest trails are near lodges, which offer short, electric-lit or lantern-lit trails. Lots of easy to more difficult trails loop across the Gunflint Trail, through moose yards and the surrounding forested hills. More experienced skiers will like the 9.7K South Rim trail and the 6.5K (plus access) Highlands trail with Wipeout Hill, a big S-curve descending 120 feet to the Cross River.

No Minnesota Ski Pass is required, but a Gunflint Trail Pass is required. Passes, available at lodges, are $5 for one day, $10 for three days, or $25 for seven days.

Gunflint Lodge: (218) 388-2294 or (800) 328-3325; Gunflint Pines: (218) 388-4454 or (800) 533-5814; Heston's Lodge: (218) 388-2243 or (800) 338-7230

TRAILHEADS: At Gunflint Lodge, Gunflint Pines, and Heston's Lodge, all on South Gunflint Lake Road

LEVEL OF DIFFICULTY: Easy, more difficult, and most difficult

AMENITIES: At lodges

LODGE-TO-LODGE SKIING

To experience the best of the trail systems and lodging, consider a lodge-to-lodge ski package available from Tofte to Pincushion and up the Gunflint Trail. You can literally ski from lodge to lodge (with car transfer provided), or you can ski a variety of loops and shuttle part of the way. Packages include lodging, breakfast, trail lunch, and dinner. Yurt-to-yurt ski packages are a wonderful winter adventure. The yurts are warm and cozy, complete with a dining area, gas stove and oven, dishes and utensils, bunks and sleeping bags, wood stove, outhouse, and, if you'd like, a hut host to tend to the fire and cook. The Poplar Creek yurt even has a sauna!

boundarycountry.com

Boundary Country Trekking: (218) 388-4487 or (800) 322-8327

SKIING IN CANADA

For conditions and trail information, call (807) 625-5075, or nordictrails-tb.on.ca.

KAMVIEW NORDIC SKI CENTRE
28K tracked and skating lane, with 5.5K lit.
> Off Canada Highway 61 just past Neebing Road House on the 20th Side Road
> A fee is charged. $4 to $11 Canadian.
> (807) 475-7081
> LEVEL OF DIFFICULTY: Easy to most difficult
> AMENITIES: Chalet with services

KAKABEKA FALLS
13K tracked and skating lane; challenging, lit trails; sauna and showers.
> From Canada Highway 61, go west on Highway 11/17 past the falls to Highway 590, then turn left on Harstone Road.
> A fee is charged.
> (807) 475-1535
> LEVEL OF DIFFICULTY: Easy to most difficult

LAPPE NORDIC CENTRE
11K tracked and skating lane, with 5K lit; great for beginners to advanced; groomed daily.
> From Canada Highway 61, go west on Arthur Street, north on Mapleward Road, west on Concession Rd. 4 to chalet.
> A fee is charged.
> (807) 767-2423
> LEVEL OF DIFFICULTY: Easy, more difficult, and most difficult
> AMENITIES: Chalet with sauna and other services

MINK MOUNTAIN
8K tracked; 4 loops, including an easy 2K loop with views of Lake Superior.
> From the U.S.-Canada border, north on Highway 61 14 miles, east on Sturgeon Bay Road.
> (807) 622-5004 or (888) 616-6465
> LEVEL OF DIFFICULTY: Easy to more difficult

SLEEPING GIANT PROVINCIAL PARK
80K tracked and skating lane.

From Canada Highway 61, take Highway 11/17, then go south on Highway 587 to visitors center.

A fee is charged.

(807) 475-7081

LEVEL OF DIFFICULTY: More to most difficult

AMENITIES: Chalet, open weekends

Midwest Mountain Skiing

THE NORTH SHORE'S VERTICAL RISE, LAKE-EFFECT SNOW, diverse runs, and breathtaking vistas make for the Midwest's premier alpine skiing. Spirit Mountain and Lutsen Mountains take advantage of the ascending elevations along the shoreline. At the base of this range sits Lake Superior, a massive source of moisture contributing to roughly nine feet of snow per winter season. Since Lake Superior rarely freezes, water temperatures remain above 32°F. This means the lake warms cold winter days and cools spring days, resulting in a ski season that extends from November into April.

The prolonged season means you'll have ample time to work on your technique and become acquainted with the numerous runs the area has to offer. Duluth's Spirit Mountain features 24 runs on the south face of the hillside. At Lutsen Mountains 85 runs drop down the faces of four interconnected peaks. Gorgeous ridgetop panoramas fool the viewer's eye, requiring a second look to determine where the sky ends and the lake begins.

Superb snowmaking equipment and state-of-the-art groomers ensure quality snow conditions regardless of weather variations. Other amenities include rentals, lessons, children's centers, restaurants and lounges, and the Ski Patrol.

Spirit Mountain and Lutsen Mountains both offer a variety of rates and lodging packages. Prices given here are based on the 2003 season and may change. Two smaller alpine centers in the Duluth area – Chester Bowl and Mont Du Lac – offer an enjoyable skiing experience at bargain prices.

SPIRIT MOUNTAIN
From I-35, take exit 249 and follow the signs.

> Open 10 A.M. to 9 P.M. Monday through Friday, and 9 A.M. to 9 P.M. on Saturday, Sunday, and holidays
> Rates for adults and kids (7 to 12) and seniors (over 65). Flex 4 tickets are $35/$25; Flex 8 tickets are $40/$30; Extended tickets are $45/$35; and Night (5 P.M. to 9 P.M.) tickets are $20/$10. Flex 4 is for four hours of

skiing from your arrival time, Flex 8 is eight hours of skiing, and with an Extended lift ticket, you can ski from open to close. With the purchase of two regularly priced adult tickets, kids 18 and under ski for $15 each. Season passes are available for about $200. The price doubles after November 1.

(218) 628-2891 or (800) 642-6377

spiritmt.com

RUNS: The longest run is 5,400 feet, and the vertical drop is 700 feet; 24 runs with 7 beginner, 9 intermediate, and 8 expert. Big Air Terrain Park for snowboarders has two full-size half-pipes.

LIFTS: 5 chairlifts, one covered quad, one quad, two triple, one double, and a handle tow on the beginner run and at the tubing park

CROSS-COUNTRY SKIING: 22 kilometers of trails groomed daily; trails are double-tracked, with skating lanes. Rentals are available. See the cross-country section ("Skinny Skiers Rejoice!") for additional information.

SNOWSHOEING: Snowshoe through the woods; daily rentals available for $12.

TUBING: Blizzard Fun Park, Spirit Mountain's great tubing park, has three serpentine twists and a milder run for kids under six. The ride to the top is on an easy-to-use handle tow. Tickets are 10 for $5.

LODGING PACKAGES: At any of the 21 participating hotels, kids 18 and under sleep and ski free with the purchase of two adult lift tickets. Midweek (Sunday through Thursday, except holidays), with each night's lodging, you can receive two free adult Flex 8 tickets. Prices begin around $69. Inquire when making your lodging reservation.

CHILDREN'S CENTER: Supervised child care and meals are provided for children six months and older for $5 per hour, with reduced rates for each additional child in the family.

SKI SCHOOL: Spirit Mountain participates in the children's SKIwee and MINIrider ski school programs for youth 4 to 12. Adults 12 and older can take private, semiprivate, or group lessons.

RENTALS: Children's and adult equipment; shaped and specialty skis; snowboard equipment

LUTSEN MOUNTAINS
From Highway 61 in Lutsen, go north on the Ski Hill Road.
Open 9:30 A.M. to 4 P.M. Monday through Friday, 9 A.M. to 4:30 P.M. Saturday, Sunday, and holidays

Rates are $36 for kids ages 6 to 12 and $46 for 13 and older; children five and under ski free with paid family member anytime. Half-day discount is $5. Multiday discounts are given for two or more days of skiing. Seniors receive a $10 discount on their tickets. Season passes are $159 to $259 for children, $289 to $389 for adults, and $229 to $329 for seniors.

(218) 663-7281 or (800) 260-SNOW (recorded snow conditions)

lutsen.com

RUNS: The longest run is 2 miles, and the vertical drop is 1,008 feet; 85 runs on four mountains: Moose, Mystery, Ullr, and Eagle.

LIFTS: Gondola from the main chalet to Moose Mountain, seven double chairlifts, and a rope tow on the beginner run

CROSS-COUNTRY SKIING: 27 kilometers of trails, all groomed for traditional and skate skiing. Rentals are available.

GONDOLA RIDES: Nonskiers can enjoy a gondola ride for $5 child, $8 senior, and $9.50 adult. The Mountain Top Deli is open on Moose Mountain.

LODGING PACKAGES: Packages currently include Thanksgiving Ski Week, Christmas Countdown, $99 Getaways, Easter Weekend, and Spring Fling. Inquire when making your lodging reservation.

SKI SCHOOL: Lutsen Mountain's Childrens Center has three offerings for kids: Snowbunnies is for potty-trained through 3-year-olds and includes indoor and outdoor play; Kinderschool is for 4- and 5-year-olds and includes skiing on the rope tow and play time; Mountain Rangers are 6- and 12-year-old skiers. Rates are $40 for a half day and $58 for a full day with lunch. Adults can take private, semiprivate, or group lessons for skiing or snowboarding.

RENTALS: Children and adult equipment; shaped and specialty skis; snowboard equipment

CHESTER BOWL SKI AREA

Part of the Duluth city parks system, Chester Bowl offers seven alpine runs with a double chairlift, three kilometers of cross-country skiing, three ski jumps, and a speed skating oval. A small chalet provides an area for warming up and sells refreshments. The chairlift-serviced runs are beginner to intermediate and a great bargain. ♿ accessible restrooms.

From I-35, go north on Mesaba Avenue, then east on Skyline Parkway.

Open 4:30 P.M. to 8:30 P.M. Tuesday, Thursday, and Friday, 11 A.M. to 4:30 P.M. Saturday, Sunday, holidays, and school breaks

$3.50 per day per ticket
(218) 724-9832

LUTSEN REC, INC.
Excellent winter rentals from entry-level to high-performance downhill ski equipment, snowboards, ski boards, showshoes, and cross-country skis. High-quality rentals and a dedicated staff; sales and clothing, too.
From Highway 61 in Lutsen, midway up the Ski Hill Road
(218) 663-7863
lutsenrec.com

MONT DU LAC SKI AREA
Mont Du Lac has seven runs serviced by a double chairlift and a beginner area with a rope tow. The adjacent chalet has a cafe, rental shop, accessory shop, fireside lounge, and deck. Mont Du Lac has great rates and reasonable ticket and rental packages.
From I-35 exit west at Highway 23 and follow the signs.
Open 5:30 P.M. to 9 P.M. Tuesday through Friday, 10 A.M. to 9:30 P.M. Saturdays, and 10 A.M. to 5:30 P.M. Sunday; tubing is open 6 P.M. to 9 P.M. Tuesday through Friday, noon to 10 P.M. Saturday, and noon to 6 P.M. Sunday
Rates are for youth (12 and under) and adults (13 and older); kids under the age of 5 ski free with an adult ticket: night tickets are $6/$10, half-day tickets are $11/$17, full-day tickets are $15/$20; seniors (65 and older) can ski anytime for $10; and tubing is $12 for 2 hours. Season passes are available for about $100 through mid-December, then the price increases to $140. Family-rate tickets are based on 2 regularly priced adult tickets with all kids under the age of 18 skiing for $7.
(218) 636-3797
skimontdulac.com
RENTALS: Children's and adult equipment; shaped and shorty skis; snowboards and boots; helmets, snowshoes, and child safety harnesses

THUNDER BAY
Loch Lomond Ski Area: (807) 475-7787 or lochlomond.ca
Mount Baldy Ski Area: (807) 683-8441

Snowmobiling Up North

WHETHER YOU ARE LOOKING TO PLAY IN THE POWDER, SKIM across frozen lakes, or tour first-class trails, snowmobiling is intrinsic to winter up north. Riding provides the opportunity to explore the spectacular Lake Superior shoreline, adjacent ridges, lakes, forests, and towns.

Rugged terrain is tamed by the 146-mile North Shore State Corridor Trail. Leaving Duluth, the trail carves a lateral path through the backwoods and cliffs rising out of Superior until it reaches its final destination, Grand Marais. Numerous side trails break off the Corridor Trail, providing the rider with access to river banks, waterfalls, overlooks, wilderness loops, and small pockets of civilization.

Connecting trails from lakeshore communities also act as entry points to the Corridor Trail, which is a year-round, multi-use trail. The trail features maintained rest areas, parking lots, overlooks, and bridges and is groomed in its entirety on a weekly basis. Gas, food, lodging, repairs, and other services are offered by private businesses on many of the spur trails. Check local maps and visitors centers for specifics on the availability of services.

Trails cross private and public land and are developed and maintained through a Minnesota Department of Natural Resources Grant-in-Aid program. Local snowmobile groups act in conjunction with the state to create, groom, and maintain area trailways. Snowmobiling is free of charge as long as your snowmobile is registered in your home state or province. A speed limit of 50 miles per hour is in effect unless otherwise posted.

MAPS, TRAIL CONDITIONS, AND GENERAL INFORMATION

MINNESOTA DEPARTMENT OF NATURAL RESOURCES DIVISION OF TRAILS AND WATERWAYS
Maps and regulations: (888) MINN-DNR, (651) 296-6157, or (800) 657-3929 TDD

MINNESOTA OFFICE OF TOURISM TRAVEL INFORMATION CENTER
General guides: (800) 657-3700

NORTH SHORE TRAIL HEADQUARTERS
Trail conditions and updates: (218) 834-6626

DULUTH CONVENTION AND VISITORS BUREAU
Local services: (800) 438-5884 or (218) 722-4011

DULUTH DEPARTMENT OF PARKS AND RECREATION
Local maps: (218) 723-3337

TWO HARBORS/LAKE COUNTY VISITOR INFORMATION CENTER
Trail conditions, local maps, services: (800) 554-2116 (Lake County) or (800) 777-7384 (Two Harbors)

SILVER BAY AREA (WHISPERING PINES MOTEL)
Trail conditions, local maps, services: (218) 226-4712

GRAND MARAIS VISITORS CENTER
Trail conditions, local maps, services: (888) 922-5000

GUNFLINT TRAIL ASSOCIATION
Trail conditions, local maps, services: (800) 338-6932

NORTH SHORE VISITOR
Up-to-date trail conditions and listings of services: northshorevisitor.com

ENTRY POINTS TO THE CORRIDOR TRAIL

Described here are entry points to the North Shore State Corridor Trail and other groomed trails you may want to explore. In addition, abandoned railroad grades and unplowed forest service roads offer adventure in more remote areas.

WILLARD MUNGER STATE TRAIL
A 70-mile multiseason trail leading to Jay Cooke State Park (about 15 miles south) on past Carlton, Minnesota. A spur leads north to the Hermantown Missing Link Trail, from which you can pick up additional Duluth trails.

DULUTH CROSS TOWN TRAIL (WEST)
Ride the skyline ridge, around Spirit Mountain, and the forests behind the zoo. The trail is about 33 miles and connects with the Willard Munger State Trail.
From I-35, take Highway 23 west to 72nd Avenue West parking area.

DULUTH CROSS TOWN TRAIL (EAST)
From the North Shore State Trail (NSST), snowmobile through city woodlands, into the Hawk Ridge Valley and toward Lake Superior into Lester Park. Trail is about 12 miles and can also be accessed on Lester River Road,
From Highway 61 in Duluth, go north on 61st Avenue East, which turns into Lester River Road when you cross Superior Street.

DULUTH TO TWO HARBORS (MILE MARKER [MM] 0 TO 38)
From the trailhead, ride east to a scenic overlook at Amity Creek and on to the Lester River (6 miles). At the 19-mile mark is the intersection to the vast

48-mile Reservoir Riders Trail system (north and west of Duluth) and 5 miles further is a shelter at the Sucker River intersection with the Pequaywan Hoyt Lakes Trails (north to the Iron Range). It's another 14 miles to the Two Harbors trails.

> From I-35 go north on 21st Avenue East, northeast on Woodland Avenue, east on Martin Road, then turn at sign on Eagle Lake Road to parking area.

TWO HARBORS (MM 38)

The Two Harbors Corridor Trails lead 9 to 12 miles from the NSST into town.

> From Highway 61, go north on Co. Rd. 2 about 8.5 miles to the trailhead and parking area.

TWO HARBORS TO GOOSEBERRY FALLS STATE PARK (MM 38 TO 44.5)

A 13.5-mile connector trail leaves Two Harbors, crosses over the Gooseberry River (shelter), and goes on to connect with the trail leading into the park past the old CCC-built Interpretive Center.

> At Gooseberry, from Highway 61, on the northeast side of the Gooseberry River; ride 3 miles through the state park and 6 miles more to reach the NSST.

GOOSEBERRY TO BEAVER BAY, SILVER BAY, AND TETTEGOUCHE STATE PARK (MM 44.5 TO 64)

Riding the ridgeline and through the woods, you will come to a shelter at the east Split Rock River, access to Silver Bay alongside scenic Forest Highway 11, and a shelter at the intersection with the Red Dot Trail. Ride the Red Dot 9 to 10 miles into Beaver Bay, Silver Bay, or Tettegouche State Park. Take in the scenic overlook of Palisade Valley, and keep an eye open for wildlife.

> Pick up the Red Dot Trail on Highway 61 in Beaver Bay, off Highway 61 on Outer Drive in Silver Bay, or via Tettegouche State Park; ride 9 to 10 miles to the NSST.

TETTEGOUCHE TO FINLAND (MM 64 TO 76)

Ride up away from the shoreline through the town of Finland and east to the access point.

> From Highway 61 in Illgen City, go north on Minnesota 1 to Finland, or northwest on Co. Rd. 6 out of Little Marais to Finland; in Finland go east on Co. Rd. 7 about 1.5 miles to parking area.

FINLAND TO SCHROEDER/TOFTE (MM 76 TO 106)

This ride includes several scenic overlooks and crosses a handful of rivers. About 17 miles in, the NSST intersects with the Tomahawk Trail (north to Ely area – consider a 4-mile ride to Crooked Lake Resort, a favorite gathering spot for snowmobilers) and at 24 miles meets the 5-mile Schroeder Trail. In the next 6 miles you enter and exit Temperance River State Park and connect with the 5-mile Tofte Trail. A 31-mile trail system including the access trails runs between Schroeder and Tofte.

At Highway 61 and the Cross River in Schroeder; from Highway 61 in Tofte, go north on the Sawbill Trail about 4.5 miles to the parking area, or access the trail just east of the AmericInn; ride north about 5 miles to the NSST.

TOFTE TO LUTSEN (MM 106 TO 121.5)

A complex network of trails crisscrosses the woods between the NSST and Highway 61 in this area. Trails access resorts and the Lutsen ski area. The state trail runs behind the ridgeline to a shelter at Barker Lake.

From Highway 61 in Lutsen, go north on the Caribou Trail about 5 miles to the parking area.

LUTSEN TO GRAND MARAIS AND THE GUNFLINT TRAIL SYSTEM (MM 121.5 TO 146)

This section of the trail meanders back north past Pike Lake, through the woods, to two intersection points with the Gunflint Trail system: one past the west end of Devil Track Lake and one at Devil Track Lodge on the east end of the lake.

From Highway 61 in Grand Marais, go north on the Gunflint Trail to Co. Rd. 7, then east a few blocks to parking near 3rd Avenue West.

GUNFLINT TRAIL SYSTEM

At the west end of Devil Track Lake, you can pick up the Expressway, a 24-mile western trail leading past Two Island Lake, Twin Lakes, and the Mushquash Trail (which bisects the main trail and the Expressway) to the intersection with the main trail. Folks also ride the Clearwater Spur to Clearwater Lake, on Leo and Hungry Jack Lakes, on Poplar Lake, Gunflint Lake, and Saganaga Lake.

At Devil Track Lodge, 8 miles from Grand Marais (north on the Gunflint Trail, then east on Co. Rd. 8). Via the Gunflint Trail, drive north on the Gunflint to South Brule River parking, to Poplar Lake lodges, South Gunflint Lake Road, or to Saganaga Lake.

GRAND PORTAGE AREA

Nine to ten loops wind around the inland area at and behind the ridgeline parallel to Lake Superior.

From Highway 61, 25 miles north of Grand Marais, take Old Highway 61 northeast to Co. Rd. 17 and go north to the trail center. From Rydens Border Store, you ride the long, scenic Teal Lake Trail to the main cluster of trails. The Skyline Trail leads from Grand Portage Lodge and Casino east and north to connect with the trail system as well.

LOOKING FOR TRAILS IN CANADA?

Call the North of Superior Snowmobile Association in Ontario at (800) 526-7522.

RENTALS

Snowmobile rental and repair are procurable on a limited basis. Rentals at this time include the following establishments:

Willard Munger Inn in Duluth: (218) 624-4814 or (800) 982-2453
Castle Danger Sports: (218) 834-4646
Beaver Bay Sports: (218) 226-4666
Steve's Sports in Grand Marais: (218) 387-1835
Big Lake Marine in Grand Marais: (218) 387-2230
Windigo Lodge on the Gunflint: (218) 388-2222 or (800) 535-4320

Blades of Silver

ICE SKATING

WHAT BETTER PLACE TO HAVE JACK FROST NIPPIN' AT YOUR nose than a skating rink? If your pleasure is casually carving out a figure eight or a pickup game of hockey, lace up your skates and hit the ice. Duluth maintains more than 60 rinks plus a speed skating oval.

Even if you're not much of a skater, you can be a spectator. On any given weekend in Duluth you'll find hockey leagues of all levels playing, and at Chester Bowl you can watch local youth practice at the speed skating oval.

Noted below are public rinks. They are free of charge. Most rinks are open midweek afternoons and evenings, and all day on weekends. Those with restrooms tend to also sell refreshments. Pioneer Hall at the Duluth Entertainment and Convention Center, (218) 722-5573 ext. 123, has some open-skating times, but there is a fee. It is best to bring your own skates, since rentals are few and far between.

DULUTH RINKS

FOND DU LAC REC AREA
Pleasure skating with warming house and restrooms.
Highway 23 and 131st Avenue West

GARY REC AREA
Pleasure skating, warming house, and restrooms.
Filmore Street and 101st Avenue West

MORGAN PARK COMMUNITY CENTER
Pleasure skating and hockey, warming house, and ♿ accessible restrooms.
1243 88th Avenue West

RIVERSIDE REC CENTER
Pleasure skating, warming house, and restrooms.
  Manitou and Cato Street (81st Avenue West)

NORTON PARK REC CENTER
Pleasure skating, hockey, warming house, and restrooms.
  Coleman and 81st Avenue West

IRVING REC CENTER
Pleasure skating, two hockey rinks, warming house, and restrooms.
  20 South 57th Avenue West

MEMORIAL
Pleasure skating, warming house, and ♿ accessible restrooms.
  5315 Grand Avenue

MERRITT
Pleasure skating, hockey, warming house, and restrooms.
  4017 West 7th Street

LINCOLN PARK AND REC CENTER
Pleasure skating, warming house, and ♿ accessible restrooms.
  4th Street and 25th Avenue West

PIEDMONT COMMUNITY CLUB
Pleasure skating, two hockey rinks, warming house, and ♿ accessible restrooms.
  2302 West 23rd Street

DULUTH HEIGHTS COMMUNITY CLUB
Pleasure skating, hockey, warming house, and ♿ accessible restrooms.
  33 West Mulberry

OBSERVATION PARK
Pleasure skating and hockey, warming house, and restrooms.
  3rd Street and 9th Avenue West

HARBORVIEW
Pleasure skating, warming house, and ♿ accessible restrooms.
  11th Street and Lake Avenue

CENTRAL HILLSIDE COMMUNITY CENTER
Pleasure skating, warming house, and ♿ accessible restrooms.
    4th Street and Lake Avenue

HILLSIDE SPORT COURT
Pleasure skating, hockey, warming house, and restrooms.
    408 East 8th Street

BAYFRONT PARK
Pleasure skating.
    5th Avenue West and Harbor Drive

LAFAYETTE SQUARE
Pleasure skating and hockey, warming house, and restrooms.
    3026 Minnesota Avenue

GRANT (CENTRAL FIELD)
Pleasure skating, warming house, and restrooms.
    11th Street and 9th Avenue East

LOWER CHESTER
Pleasure skating and two hockey rinks on a refrigerated outdoor ice sheet, warming house, and ♿ accessible restrooms.
    5th Street and 15th Avenue East

CHESTER BOWL
Speed skating oval, ♿ accessible restrooms, alpine and nordic skiing, and ski jumps.
    1800 Skyline Parkway

WOODLAND COMMUNITY CLUB
Pleasure skating, two hockey rinks, warming house, and ♿ accessible restrooms.
    3211 Allendale Avenue

LESTER PARK
Pleasure skating, two hockey rinks, warming house with a fireplace, and ♿ accessible restrooms.
    Lester River Road north of Superior Street

PORTMAN SQUARE
Pleasure skating and hockey.
    McCulloch Street and 46th Avenue East

CONGDON PARK
Pleasure skating, two hockey rinks, warming house, and restrooms.
   Congdon Park Drive and Superior Street

RINKS ALONG THE NORTH SHORE

ODEGARD PARK
Lighted pleasure skating, hockey, warming house, and ♿accessible restrooms.
   In Two Harbors, on 13th Avenue near the water tower

FRANK RUKAVINA SILVER BAY ARENA (INDOOR)
Pleasure skating, hockey, warming house, and restrooms.
   In Silver Bay, across from the high school
   (218) 226-4214

FINLAND AREA REC CENTER
Skating rink with warming house and restrooms.
   2 miles east of Finland on Co. Ed. 7

BIRCH GROVE ELEMENTARY
Skating rink with restroom use during weekdays.
   On Highway 61 in Tofte

DOWNTOWN GRAND MARAIS
A number of locals flood the level area that is becoming Harbor Park.
   Downtown Grand Marais

COOK COUNTY COMMUNITY CENTER (OUTSIDE, WITH OCCASIONAL INDOOR)
Pleasure skating, hockey, warming house, and ♿ accessible restrooms. Indoor skating at the adjacent Curling Club is available on occasion.
   In Grand Marais, on Co. Rd. 7, one block east of the Gunflint Trail
   (218) 387-3015

GOLDEN EAGLE LODGE
Pleasure skating on Flour Lake; amenities at the lodge.
   25 miles up the Gunflint Trail and 2.5 miles east on the Clearwater Road
   (218) 388-2203 or (800) 346-2203
   golden-eagle.com

Many Places to Stay

THERE'S THIS ONE PARTICULAR HARBOR,
SO FAR BUT YET SO NEAR,
WHERE I SEE THE DAYS AS THEY FADE AWAY
AND FINALLY DISAPPEAR.

Jimmy Buffet, "One Particular Harbor"

Choosing where to stay can be the most important part of your travels. Your lodging must have the desired amenities, fit within your budget, and be a place you want to go back to at the end of a great day or, more important, at the end of an awful day. Check out Web sites to get a better sense of the lodging establishment, or call and ask to have a brochure sent.

Whenever you are planning a stay in Duluth or on the North Shore, it is always best to make a reservation. Weekends from Memorial Day through fall color season are often booked in advance. Holidays, key weekends, and dates of major events, like Grandma's Marathon, can fill in advance. Remember that some of the cabins and smaller resorts along the North Shore are seasonal only, open mid-May through mid-October. Many accommodations have a minimum night stay policy on busy weekends and peak times. Typically, cash or credit card deposits are required to hold a reservation.

Rate ranges are indicated and are as accurate as possible, but always call for exact prices and ask about specials and packages. Rate ranges are general and based on double occupancy. In general, lodging places along the Shore offer more than one type of accommodation and have several rate seasons throughout the year.

For quick access to North Shore lodging and current lodging specials, visit northshorevisitor.com. You can sign up to have news and specials e-mailed to you.

Rates

$	$49 or less per night
$$	$50 to $100 per night
$$$	$100 to $150 per night
$$$$	Over $150 per night

Credit Cards

AE	American Express
CB	Carte Blanche
D	Discover
DC	Diner's Club
MC	MasterCard
V	Visa

Duluth Hotels and Motels

LODGING CHOICES IN DULUTH INCLUDE FAMILY-OWNED AND easily recognized franchise motels, a historic inn, and mountain villas. Accommodations are clustered at Spirit Mountain, in west Duluth as you enter from I-35, downtown, heading north on Miller Trunk Highway, and in east Duluth as you travel toward the North Shore.

WEST DULUTH

ALLYNDALE MOTEL
Exceptionally clean, attractive rooms; set on a quiet five acres, eight minutes to downtown; microwaves and fridges.
510 North 66th Avenue West
$–$$
AE/D/DC/MC/V
(218) 628-1061 or (800) 806-1061
NUMBER OF ROOMS: 21
POOL: No
PETS: Negotiable
LAKESHORE: No
CONTINENTAL BREAKFAST: No

COMFORT INN OF DULUTH
Jacuzzi suites; indoor pool, sauna, whirlpool; meeting room; cable TV with Showtime.
3900 West Superior Street
$$–$$$
AE/CB/D/DC/MC/V
(218) 628-1464 or
(national) (800) 228-5150
comfortinn.com
NUMBER OF ROOMS: 81
POOL: Yes
PETS: No
LAKESHORE: No
CONTINENTAL BREAKFAST: Yes

DULUTH MOTEL

Ma-and-Pa motel; neat and clean; some fridges; cable TV; five minutes to zoo and Spirit Mountain or downtown and Canal Park area.
4415 Grand Avenue
$–$$
AE/D/MC/V
(218) 628-1008
NUMBER OF ROOMS: 21
POOL: No
PETS: No
LAKESHORE: No
CONTINENTAL BREAKFAST: No

GRAND MOTEL

Cable TV with Showtime; refrigerators. Near bike trail, Spirit Mountain, shops, and dining.
4312 Grand Avenue
$
MC/V
(218) 624-4821
NUMBER OF ROOMS: 13
POOL: No
PETS: No
LAKESHORE: No
CONTINENTAL BREAKFAST: No

MOTEL 6

Affordable; three miles to Canal Park, five miles to Spirit Mountain; cable TV, free HBO; nonsmoking rooms.
I-35 and 27th Avenue West
$–$$
AE/CB/D/DC/MC/V
(218) 723-1123 or
(national) (800) 4MOTEL6
NUMBER OF ROOMS: 99
POOL: No
PETS: Yes, attended
LAKESHORE: No
CONTINENTAL BREAKFAST: Coffee

SUPER 8 MOTEL OF DULUTH

2001 "Pride of Super 8" winner; remodeled; new Serta mattresses; cable with Showtime; free coffee; guest laundry; a few minutes to all of Duluth's attractions.
4100 West Superior Street
$–$$
AE/CB/D/DC/MC/V
(218) 628-2241 or
(national) (800) 800-8000
stayinduluth.com/super8
NUMBER OF ROOMS: 59
POOL: Whirlpool and sauna
PETS: No
LAKESHORE: No
CONTINENTAL BREAKFAST: Yes

WILLARD MUNGER INN

Brick inn with whirlpool and kitchen studios, fireplace suites, and affordable rooms; near Spirit Mountain (ski packages), zoo, and hiking and snowmobile trails; snowmobile rentals.
7408 Grand Avenue
$–$$
MC/V/AE/D
(218) 624-4814 or (800) 982-2453
mungerinn.com
NUMBER OF ROOMS: 22
POOL: No
PETS: No
LAKESHORE: No
CONTINENTAL BREAKFAST: Yes

SPIRIT MOUNTAIN AND THOMPSON HILL

MOUNTAIN VILLAS

Only on-site lodging at Spirit Mountain ski area; villas have wraparound views, living room with fireplace, two bedrooms, two baths, and kitchen; some with Jacuzzi tubs.
9525 West Skyline Parkway
$$$-$$$$
MC/V/D
(218) 624-5784 or (800) 688-4552
mtvillas.com
NUMBER OF VILLAS: 14
POOL: Yes
PETS: No
LAKESHORE: No
CONTINENTAL BREAKFAST: No

SPIRIT MOUNTAIN TRAVELODGE

Northwoods setting; efficiencies, extended-stay, and whirlpool suites; conference rooms; game room; cable TV. 24-hr restaurant and gas station adjacent, ski packages. Snowmobile trails.
9315 Westgate Boulevard
$-$$$$
AE/D/MC/V
(218) 628-3691 or (800) 777-8530
duluth.com/travelodge
NUMBER OF ROOMS: 100
POOL: Yes and sauna and whirlpool
PETS: Yes
LAKESHORE: No
CONTINENTAL BREAKFAST: Yes

SUNDOWN MOTEL

Air-conditioning; color TV with Showtime; eight minutes to downtown; next to Spirit Mountain; 10 minutes to Mall; clean!
5310 Thompson Hill Road
$
MC/V/D
(218) 628-3613
NUMBER OF ROOMS: 8

POOL: No
PETS: No
LAKESHORE: No
CONTINENTAL BREAKFAST: No

AMERICINN MOTEL AND SUITES OF DULUTH/PROCTOR

Northwoods lobby with stone fireplace; whirlpool and fireplace suites; family suites with kitchenettes, dining rooms, king beds, and private balconies; extended-stay suites. Blackwoods Grill, Bar, and Conference Center.
185 Highway 2, one mile off I-35
$$-$$$$
AE/CB/D/DC/MC/V
(218) 624-1026 or
(national) (800) 634-3444
visitduluth.com/Americinn
NUMBER OF ROOMS: 68
POOL: Yes
PETS: Yes, attended
LAKESHORE: No
CONTINENTAL BREAKFAST: Yes

COUNTRY INN AND SUITES

Rooms, suites, and Jacuzzi suites; spacious lobby with fireplace; adjacent to snowmobile trails; near Spirit Mountain and Black Bear Casino.
9330 West Skyline Parkway
$$-$$$$
AE/CB/D/DC/MC/V
(218) 628-0688 or
(national) (800) 456-4000
countryinns.com/duluthmn_south
NUMBER OF ROOMS: 70
POOL: Yes
PETS: No
LAKESHORE: No
CONTINENTAL BREAKFAST: Yes

DOWNTOWN DULUTH

BEST WESTERN
In downtown Duluth and near sky-walk system; 7 blocks to Canal Park.
131 West 2nd Street
$-$$$
AE/CB/D/DC/MC/V
(218) 727-6851 or
(national) (800) 528-1234
NUMBER OF ROOMS: 45
POOL: No
PETS: Yes
LAKESHORE: No
CONTINENTAL BREAKFAST: No

FITGER'S INN
Stunning rooms and suites overlooking Lake Superior, some with double whirlpools, fireplaces, and balconies; only AAA 4-diamond rating in northern Minnesota; originally a brewery in 1857, includes restaurants and shops.
600 East Superior Street
$$-$$$
AE/CB/D/MC/V
fitgers.com
(218) 722-8826 or (800) 726-2982
NUMBER OF ROOMS: 62
POOL: No
PETS: No
LAKESHORE: Yes
CONTINENTAL BREAKFAST: Yes

HOLIDAY INN HOTEL AND SUITES
In the heart of downtown; restaurants, lounges, and shopping complex. Deluxe rooms, 2-room suites, and kid suites, all with great amenities; Family Attractions Package.
200 West 1st Street
$$-$$$$
AE/CB/D/DC/MC/V
(218) 722-1202 or
(national) (800) 477-7089
holidayinnduluth.com
NUMBER OF ROOMS: 353

POOL: Yes – two
PETS: Attended
LAKESHORE: No
CONTINENTAL BREAKFAST: Yes

RADISSON HOTEL DULUTH HARBORVIEW
Overlooks the harbor and downtown area; Top of the Harbor revolving restaurant; skywalk connects you to everything.
505 West Superior Street
$$-$$$$
AE/CB/D/DC/MC/V
(218) 727-8981 or
(national) (800) 333-3333
radisson.com/duluthmn
NUMBER OF ROOMS: 286
POOL: Yes
PETS: Yes
LAKESHORE: No
CONTINENTAL BREAKFAST: No

VOYAGEUR LAKEWALK INN
Romantic whirlpool lodge rooms with fireplaces, and a penthouse suite with full kitchen, fireplace, deck, and floor-to-ceiling windows overlooking Lake Superior. Walk everywhere!
333 East Superior Street
$-$$$
AE/MC/V
(218) 722-3911 or (800) 258-3911
voyageurlakewalkinn.com
NUMBER OF ROOMS: 41
POOL: No
PETS: No
LAKESHORE: No
CONTINENTAL BREAKFAST: Yes

CANAL PARK

COMFORT SUITES OF DULUTH ♿

All 1-room suites have refrigerators, coffeemakers, and sofa sleepers; Jacuzzi suites; conference center; great location – closest to Aerial Lift Bridge and piers!
408 Canal Park Drive
$$–$$$
AE/CB/D/DC/MC/V
(218) 727-1378 or
(national) (800) 228-5150
duluth.com/comfortsuites
NUMBER OF ROOMS: 82
POOL: Yes
PETS: No
LAKESHORE: Yes
CONTINENTAL BREAKFAST: Yes

INN ON LAKE SUPERIOR ♿

On the Lakewalk in the heart of Canal Park; rooms and suites, many with lakefront balconies. Indoor and outdoor pools; evening campfire; make-your-own Belgian waffles.
350 Canal Park Drive
$$–$$$
AE/CB/D/DC/MC/V
(218) 726-1111 or (888) 668-4352
zmchotels.com
NUMBER OF ROOMS: 175
POOL: Yes
PETS: No
LAKESHORE: Yes
CONTINENTAL BREAKFAST: Yes

HAMPTON INN HOTEL

Walk to it all! Featuring whirlpool suites, lakeview rooms; deluxe continental breakfast; fitness room; meeting space.
310 Canal Park Drive
$$–$$$$
AE/D/DC/MC/V
(218) 720-3000 or
(national) (800) HAMPTON
duluth.com/hampton/

NUMBER OF ROOMS: 103
POOL: Yes
PETS: No
LAKESHORE: Yes
CONTINENTAL BREAKFAST: Yes

SOUTH PIER INN ON THE CANAL

New waterfront hotel at the foot of the Aerial Lift Bridge. Great views; upscale rooms and villas sleep up to 8; Jacuzzis, fireplaces, decks, private shoreline!
701 Lake Avenue South
$$–$$$$
AE/D/MC/V
(218) 786-9007 or (800) 430-7437
southpierinn.com
NUMBER OF ROOMS: 30
POOL: No
PETS: No
LAKESHORE: Harbor and Pier
CONTINENTAL BREAKFAST: No

CANAL PARK INN

In downtown Duluth's historic Canal Park; restaurant, lounge, and meeting rooms.
250 Canal Park Drive
$$–$$$$
AE/D/DC/MC/V
(218) 727-8821 or (800) 777-8560
NUMBER OF ROOMS: 144
POOL: Yes
PETS: Yes
LAKESHORE: Yes
CONTINENTAL BREAKFAST: Yes, for adults

HAWTHORN SUITES ♿

All-suite hotel includes a kitchen in every unit; choose from studio, one- and two-bedroom, Jacuzzi, and honeymoon suites; overlooks the *William A. Irvin* in the Minnesota Slip. Inside walk to restaurants.
325 Lake Avenue South
$$–$$$$
AE/CB/D/DC/MC/V
(218) 727-4663 or (800) 527-1133
hawthornsuitesduluth.com
NUMBER OF ROOMS: 107
POOL: Yes
PETS: Yes
LAKESHORE: On the Minnesota Slip
CONTINENTAL BREAKFAST: Yes

SUITES AT WATERFRONT PLAZA

New! Luxury 2- and 3-bedroom suites hotel. Fireplaces, whirlpool baths, laundry, and full kitchen. Excellent location.
325 Lake Avenue South
$$–$$$$
AE/CB/D/DC/MC/V
(218) 722-2143 or (877) 766-2665
waterfrontsuites.com
NUMBER OF ROOMS: 30
POOL: No
PETS: Some
LAKESHORE: On the Minnesota Slip
CONTINENTAL BREAKFAST: Yes

MILLER HILL AND SKYLINE

BUENA VISTA MOTEL AND RESTAURANT

Some rooms with fireplaces and waterbeds; beautiful Lake Superior view; restaurant and lounge; one mile from downtown.
1144 Mesaba Avenue
$-$$
AE/D/MC/V
(218) 722-7796 or (800) 569-8124
visitduluth.com/buenavista
NUMBER OF ROOMS: 28
POOL: No
PETS: Some
LAKESHORE: No
CONTINENTAL BREAKFAST: Coffee

FAIRFIELD INN BY MARRIOTT

Located near shopping, theaters, and the airport; indoor pool and spa; rooms and business suites; 4 miles from airport.
Across from the Miller Hill Mall
$$-$$$
AE/CB/D/DC/MC/V
(218) 723-8607 or (800) 228-2800
fairfieldinn.com
NUMBER OF ROOMS: 62
POOL: No
PETS: No
LAKESHORE: No
CONTINENTAL BREAKFAST: Yes

DAYS INN

Clean and reasonable, four new Jacuzzi rooms; spa and exercise area; free HBO; with senior, government, military, and business discounts.
Across from the Miller Hill Mall
$-$$$
AE/CB/D/DC/MC/V
(218) 727-3110 or
(national) (800) DAYSINN
NUMBER OF ROOMS: 86
POOL: No
PETS: Some

LAKESHORE: No
CONTINENTAL BREAKFAST: Yes

ECONOLODGE AIRPORT

Near Miller Hill Mall dining and shopping. New indoor pool, game room, and fitness room. Clean and quiet; nonsmoking rooms available; senior and AAA discounts.
4197 Highway 53
$-$$$
AE/CB/D/DC/MC/V
(218) 722-5522 or (800) 922-0569
econolodgeduluth.com
NUMBER OF ROOMS: 88
POOL: Yes
PETS: Yes
LAKESHORE: No
CONTINENTAL BREAKFAST: Yes

SKYLINE COURT MOTEL

Nice, affordable rooms; same family owners for years; walk to theaters, bowling, and restaurants. RV sites.
4880 Miller Trunk Highway
$-$$
AE/D/MC/V/DC
(218) 727-1563 or (800) 554-0621
visitduluth.com/Skyline/
NUMBER OF ROOMS: 17
POOL: No
PETS: Yes
LAKESHORE: No
CONTINENTAL BREAKFAST: Coffee

AIRLINER MOTEL

Near malls and airport; free HBO; some units have fully equipped kitchenettes.
5002 Miller Trunk Highway
$-$$
AE/D/MC/V
(218) 729-6628 or (800) 777-8478
NUMBER OF ROOMS: 16
POOL: No
PETS: No
LAKESHORE: No
CONTINENTAL BREAKFAST: No

EAST DULUTH

BEST WESTERN EDGEWATER EAST

Playground; nine-hole miniature golf and putting green; indoor pool and rec area; lakeside balcony rooms; complimentary cocktail hour; overlooking Lake Superior; on the Lakewalk; business center.
2400 London Road
$$–$$$
AE/CB/D/DC/MC/V
(218) 728-3601 or (800) 777-7925
zmchotels.com
NUMBER OF ROOMS: 220
POOL: Yes
PETS: Attended
LAKESHORE: No
CONTINENTAL BREAKFAST: Yes

BEST WESTERN EDGEWATER WEST

Overlooking Lake Superior; near restaurants and lounge.
2211 London Road
$$–$$$
AE/CB/D/DC/MC/V
(218) 728-3601 or (800) 777-7925
zmchotels.com
NUMBER OF ROOMS: 64
POOL: No
PETS: Attended
LAKESHORE: No
CONTINENTAL BREAKFAST: Yes

CHALET MOTEL

Eighteen blocks to downtown; non-smoking rooms available; lake view; sun deck.
1801 London Road
$–$$
MC/V/D
(218) 728-4238 or (800) 235-2957
NUMBER OF ROOMS: 34
POOL: No
PETS: Attended
LAKESHORE: No
CONTINENTAL BREAKFAST: No

Bed and Breakfast

DULUTH AND THE NORTH SHORE

MORE THAN TWO DOZEN BED-AND-BREAKFAST ESTABLISH-ments, from beautiful historic homes to stunning modern lakeshore houses, are available to the traveler. To get a good idea of the B&B you are interested in, visit their website or call for a brochure. B&BS include a full breakfast, from hearty northwoods spreads to gourmet fare, and most are intended for adults only. When making reservations, ask whether children are accepted. In addition to unique surroundings, B&BS are renowned for their hospitality, so be sure to ask your hosts for their area recommendations. All B&BS are smoke-free.

DULUTH

SOLGLIMT, A LAKESHORE B&B

On Park Point, 1 block south of Aerial Lift Bridge. Two second-floor suites; one with a double steam-shower, one with a private deck. King beds, sitting room, robes, and beach towels.
828 Lake Avenue South
$$–$$$$
MC/V
(218) 727-0590 or (877) 727-0596
solglimt.com
NUMBER OF ROOMS: 2
PRIVATE BATHS: 2
LAKESHORE: Yes

STANFORD INN BED & BREAKFAST

Well-preserved 1886 brick Victorian home with sauna; gourmet breakfast; two blocks from the Duluth Rose Garden and Lakewalk; gay-owned, serving gay and straight clientele since 1988.
1415 East Superior Street
$$
AE/D/MC/V
(218) 724-3044
visitduluth.com/stanford
NUMBER OF ROOMS: 4
PRIVATE BATHS: 1
LAKESHORE: No

THE A. CHARLES WEISS INN

1895 Victorian home features antiques in parlor, library, dining room; near Lakewalk; 5 rooms, 1 with fireplace and double whirlpool; 3-room fireplace suite.
1615 East Superior Street
$$–$$$
D/MC/V
(218) 724-7016 or (800) 525-5243
visitduluth.com/acweissinn
NUMBER OF ROOMS: 6
PRIVATE BATHS: 6
LAKESHORE: No

MATHEW S. BURROWS 1890 INN

Adult getaway in a restored Victorian masterpiece; gas fireplaces, parlor, and music room; very nice wraparound front porch.
1632 East 1st Street
$$–$$$
AE/D/MC/V
(218) 724-4991 or (800) 789-1890
visitduluth.com/1890inn
NUMBER OF ROOMS: 5
PRIVATE BATHS: 5
LAKESHORE: No

THE ELLERY HOUSE

Elegant 1890 home with balconies, fireplaces, lake views, and sleeping porch; children welcome; near Lakewalk. Full 3-course breakfast.
28 South 21st Avenue East
$$–$$$
AE/MC/V
(218) 724-7639 or (800) ELLERYH
visitduluth.com/elleryhouse
NUMBER OF ROOMS: 4
PRIVATE BATHS: 4
LAKESHORE: No

IMMIGRANT HOUSE B&B AND MEETING HOUSE

Renovated 1890s home with two rooms and meeting/retreat area for small groups. Lovely gardens. Convenient location.
2104 East Superior Street
$$
V/MC
(218) 724-3090
NUMBER OF ROOMS: 2
PRIVATE BATHS: 2
LAKESHORE: No

FIRELIGHT INN ON OREGON CREEK

Luxury historic brick home on a secluded street. All suites with fireplaces, and three with double Jacuzzis. Breakfast delivered to your suite. Enjoy the huge glass-enclosed porch and digital baby grand piano.
2211 East 3rd Street
$$$–$$$$
AE/MC/V/D
(218) 724-0272 or (888) 724-0273
firelightinn.com
NUMBER OF ROOMS: 5
PRIVATE BATHS: 5
LAKESHORE: No

MANOR ON THE CREEK INN

1907 early Craftsman-style mansion on two wooded acres overlooking a creek. Lovely little path and footbridge. Two rooms and six suites, some with whirlpool, fireplace, and porch. Afternoon refreshments, too.
2215 East 2nd Street
$$$–$$$$
D/MC/V
(218) 728-3189 or (800) 428-3189
man225onthecreek.com
NUMBER OF ROOMS: 8
PRIVATE BATHS: 8
LAKESHORE: No

THE COTTON MANSION

Romantic retreat with seven distinctively appointed rooms; queen beds; some with fireplaces and in-room whirlpools. Gourmet breakfast. Sunroom, library, living room, too.
2309 East First Street
$$$–$$$$
AE/MC/V
(218) 724-6405 or (800) 228-1997
cottonmansion.com
NUMBER OF ROOMS: 7
PRIVATE BATHS: 7
LAKESHORE: No

THE OLCOTT HOUSE BED & BREAKFAST INN

1904 Georgian Colonial brick mansion with a wonderful porch, library, music room with a baby grand, and private 4-room romantic carriage house. Working fireplaces and private porches. Spacious rooms.
2316 East 1st Street
$$–$$$
D/MC/V
(218) 728-1339 or (800) 715-1339
olcotthouse.com
NUMBER OF ROOMS: 6
PRIVATE BATHS: 6
LAKESHORE: No

LORD FRAZER HOUSE HISTORIC B&B INN

Your home away from home with 4 large, comfy rooms; 1 with a 2-person steam shower. Business travelers will appreciate the Lion's Den office. Sitting room, sunroom, and dining room.
2426 Superior Street
$$$
V/MC
(218) 728-1889 or (866) 567-3341
lordfrazer.com
NUMBER OF ROOMS: 4
PRIVATE BATHS: 4
LAKESHORE: No

A.G. THOMSON HISTORIC HOUSE B&B INN

1909 Dutch Colonial home on an acre of parklike land in a quiet neighborhood. Seven rooms, all with fireplaces and A/C; two with in-room double whirlpool; one with a private terrace and clawfoot tub. New private deluxe suite. Seven blocks to Lakewalk.
2617 East Third Street
$$$–$$$$
AE/D/MC/V
(218) 724-3464 or (877) 807-8077
thomsonhouse.biz
NUMBER OF ROOMS: 7
PRIVATE BATHS: 7
LAKESHORE: No

ALONG SCENIC 61

SPINNAKER INN BED & BREAKFAST

Relaxing atmosphere; hearty North Shore breakfast; close to Duluth; extended-stay discounts.
5427 Scenic 61
$$
D/MC/V
(218) 525-2838 or (800) 525-2838
cpinternet.com/~spinninn
NUMBER OF ROOMS: 2
PRIVATE BATHS: 2
LAKESHORE: Across road

EMILY'S 1929 EATERY, INN, AND DELI

Enjoy great food and old-fashioned hospitality in this 1929 inn. Breakfast at the Eatery is included.
Scenic 61 on Knife River
$$
credit cards not accepted
(218) 834-5922
emilyseatery.com
NUMBER OF ROOMS: 2
PRIVATE BATHS: 2
LAKESHORE: Knife River

TWO HARBORS

LIGHTHOUSE B&B

Fully restored, historic lighthouse keeper's quarters; 3 tasteful rooms with common bath; living and dining rooms. Scandinavian breakfast. Great grounds!
On the harbor at 1 Lighthouse Point
$$
MC/V
(218) 834-4814 or (888) 832-5606
lighthousebb.org
NUMBER OF ROOMS: 3
PRIVATE BATHS: 0
LAKESHORE: Yes, on the harbor

LITTLE MARAIS

STONE HEARTH INN B&B

Warmth without pretense on Lake Superior's shores. Six guest rooms with private baths in main house. Boathouse with large lakefront room and 1-bedroom condo. Carriage House has 2 guest rooms. Boathouse and Carriage House guests all receive continental breakfast; units include gas fireplaces and whirlpools. Great yard, beach, and big front porch!
Highway 61

$$–$$$$
MC/V/D
(218) 226-3020 or (800) 206-3020
stonehearthinn.com
NUMBER OF ROOMS: 10
PRIVATE BATHS: 10
LAKESHORE: Yes

GRAND MARAIS

DREAM CATCHER B&B

Northwoods B&B set amid 27 acres of birch and spruce, with overlooks of Lake Superior. Hearty breakfast. Great room with fireplace. A few minutes to Grand Marais, hiking, canoeing, and cross-country skiing.
Co. Rd. 7, five miles west of Grand Marais
$$
D/MC/V
(218) 387-2876 or (800) 682-3119
dreamcatcherbb.com
NUMBER OF ROOMS: 3
PRIVATE BATHS: 3
LAKESHORE: No

RUNNING WOLF B&B

Quiet secluded B&B 5 miles west of Grand Marais; spectacular views of Lake Superior; rooms and suites; large deck; forested setting; for those 14 years of age and older.
Co. Rd. 48, 5 miles west of Grand Marais
$$
MC/V
(218) 387-9653 or (877) 786-9653
NUMBER OF ROOMS: 4
PRIVATE BATHS: 2
LAKESHORE: No

MACARTHUR HOUSE
BED & BREAKFAST
Built to be a B&B; spacious rooms, some have 19-foot cathedral ceilings, sitting areas; common-area fireplace and Jacuzzi; 1 whirlpool suite. Full tasty breakfast.
520 West 2nd Street
$$–$$$
MC/V
(218) 387-1840 or (800) 792-1840
macarthurhouse.com
NUMBER OF ROOMS: 5
PRIVATE BATHS: 5
LAKESHORE: No

SNUGGLE INN II B&B
Four cozy rooms with own bath. Quick walk to harbor and downtown. Local art, nice deck, and gardens.
8 7th Avenue West
$$
AE/CB/D/DC/MC/V
(218) 387-2847 or (800) 823-3174
snuggleinnbb.com
NUMBER OF ROOMS: 4
PRIVATE BATHS: 4
LAKESHORE: No

ANTLER INN B&B
Charming bungalow features 5 bedrooms with comfy beds, 3 bathrooms; available as a whole house rental. Antiques, wood floors, hearty breakfasts – it feels like home. 2 blocks to harbor and downtown.
$$
(218) 387-3131 or (877) 388-3131
antlerinn.net
NUMBER OF ROOMS: 5
PRIVATE BATHS: 0
LAKESHORE: No

BALLY'S B&B AND
BOARDING HOUSE
Built in 1912 as a boarding house to accommodate teachers, forestry and government workers, it's open again to guests. Four bedrooms with private baths; full breakfast. Quick walk around town.
121 East 3rd Street
$$
(218) 387-1817 or (888) 383-1817
NUMBER OF ROOMS: 4
PRIVATE BATHS: 4
LAKESHORE: No

SUPERIOR OVERLOOK B&B
Relaxing home on a bluff overlooking Lake Superior; sauna; whirlpool suite. Full breakfast. Family room.
Highway 61, two miles east of Grand Marais
$$–$$$
MC/V
(218) 387-1571 or (800) 858-7622
boreal.org/a-superior-overlook
NUMBER OF ROOMS: 2
PRIVATE BATHS: 2
LAKESHORE: Yes

JAGERHAUS GERMAN B&B
A German retreat on a bluff with spectacular Lake Superior views. This "Hunters House" features a great hall with fireplace, 2 rooms, a suite, German decor, and breakfast.
184 Co. Rd. 14
$$–$$$
(218) 387-1476 or (877) 387-1476
jagerhaus.com
NUMBER OF ROOMS: 3
PRIVATE BATHS: 1
LAKESHORE: No

ON THE GUNFLINT TRAIL

PINCUSHION B&B

Set on the Sawtooth ridgeline on 44 wooded acres that extend to the Devil Track River Valley and offer views of Lake Superior; at the trailhead to excellent cross-country skiing in the winter and hiking and biking trails in the summer. Fireplace in common area; sauna; full breakfast.

Two miles up the Gunflint Trail on B&B Road
$$–$$$
MC/V
(218) 387-1276 or (800) 542-1226
pincushionbb.com
NUMBER OF ROOMS: 4
PRIVATE BATHS: 4
LAKESHORE: No

CLEARWATER CANOE OUTFITTERS AND LODGE

The lodge is on the National Register of Historic Places. Three B&B rooms, two suites, and six lakeside cabins; beach; sauna. Open May to September.

28 miles up the Gunflint Trail and 4 miles in on Clearwater Lake Road
$–$$
D/MC/V
(218) 388-2254 or (800) 527-0544 or (winter) (317) 578-8541
canoe-bwca.com
NUMBER OF ROOMS: 5
PRIVATE BATHS: 2
LAKESHORE: Yes

POPLAR CREEK GUESTHOUSE B&B

A secluded, peaceful Mission guesthouse in the woods on Little Ollie Lake and Poplar Creek. Hike, bike, canoe, ski, relax. Two B&B rooms with firelit common area with deck and kitchenette; 1 with a double shower, 1 with a double whirlpool. One-bedroom condo with private entrance; fireplace in living area; kitchen and deck.

30 miles up the Gunflint Trail and 2 miles west
$$–$$$
AE/D/MC/V
(218) 388-4487 or (800) 322-8327
poplarcreekguesthouse.com
NUMBER OF ROOMS: 3
PRIVATE BATHS: 3
LAKESHORE: Yes

OLD NORTHWOODS LODGE

Classic French-Canadian lodge with massive stone fireplace, Yelena's Gallery, dining room and bar, and 3 quiet guest rooms (for adults) with private baths and great Poplar Lake views; 1 with a double whirlpool bath. Hike, fish, ski, relax, and enjoy tasty meals. Cabins, too!

32 miles up the Gunflint Trail and a quarter-mile in.
$$–$$$
AE/MC/V
(218) 388-9464 or (800) 682-8264
oldnorthwoods.com
NUMBER OF ROOMS: 3
PRIVATE BATHS: 3
LAKESHORE: Yes

MOOSEHORN LODGE, CABINS, AND B&B

Lakeshore B&B on Gunflint Lake offers a B&B room and a suite with a fireplace; a 2-bedroom villa with full kitchen and living room; 4 cabins with 2 to 4 bedrooms, kitchen, fireplace, deck with BBQ, and use of canoe. Lodge has a firelit gathering room. Sauna. Boats and motors and pontoons for rent.
47 miles up the Gunflint Trail and 2 miles in on North Gunflint Lake
$$–$$$
MC/V
(218) 388-2233 or (800) 238-5975
moosehorn.com
NUMBER OF UNITS: 7
LAKESHORE: Yes

GRAND PORTAGE AREA

SWEETGRASS COVE GUESTHOUSE AND BODYWORK STUDIO

One suite with a loft bedroom, cozy living area, private bath, and bodywork studio on the edge of Lake Superior. Use wood-fired sauna, outdoor hot tub, and deck; great lakeshore. Day spa services include massage, sea salt scrub, and herbal wraps.
6880 East Highway 61
$$–$$$
(218) 475-2421 or (866) 475-2421
sweetgrasscove.com
NUMBER OF ROOMS: 1
PRIVATE BATHS: 1
LAKESHORE: Yes

North Shore Lodging

ODGING CHOICES ALONG THE SHORE VARY FROM SMALL, RUSTIC cabins to deluxe, full-amenity shoreside resorts. Some of the smaller motel and cabin complexes are open seasonally and offer fewer on-site amenities but are near activities and towns. The largest resorts are destinations in themselves, offering on-site dining, lounges, gift shops, kids' and nature programs, pools and recreation areas, hiking, fishing, and so on. Resorts along the Gunflint Trail are geared toward outdoor vacations or R & R in the woods, with a full variety of lodging options. I have listed lodging in order from southwest to northeast.

SCENIC 61 TO TWO HARBORS

These lodgings are all located on Scenic 61, the drive that begins at the eastern edge of Duluth and travels to just southwest of Two Harbors. Portions of the road have other names, but remember – it is all the same road!

NORTH SHORE COTTAGES

Overlooks Lake Superior; six side-by-side cabins from lake-view rooms to 1-bedroom cabins; simple, clean and reasonable; some cabins have fireplaces. Two-bedroom cottage with kitchen and gas fireplace. Open year-round.
7717 Congdon Boulevard
$–$$$
MC/V
(218) 525-2812
northshorecottages.com
NUMBER OF CABINS: 13
LAKESHORE: Across road
PETS: In some units

THE INN ON GITCHE GUMEE

Lake Superior view; northwoods-themed suites, some with fireplaces, whirlpools, kitchens; lounging area, decks, and patios; fresh flowers. Open year-round.
8517 Congdon Boulevard; 4 miles northeast on Scenic 61
$$–$$$
MC/V/AE/D
(218) 525-4979 or (800) 317-4979
innongitchegumee.com
NUMBER OF ROOMS: 10
LAKESHORE: Across road
PETS: No

LAKE BREEZE MOTEL RESORT

Quiet family resort overlooking Lake Superior on 11 wooded acres; heated outdoor pool; sauna; 4 motel rooms, 1 with a whirlpool; 11 suites with kitchens and some fireplaces; and a 3-bedroom duplex. Firepit, large play area, and nautical gift shop. Open year-round.
9000 Congdon Boulevard; 4 miles northeast on Scenic 61
$$
D/MC/V
(218) 525-6808 or (800) 738-5884
lakebreeze.com
NUMBER OF ROOMS: 4
NUMBER OF UNITS: 12
LAKESHORE: Across road
PETS: Some

GARDENWOOD MOTEL AND CABIN COURT

Twelve cabins and 4 motel rooms, some with kitchenettes; play area, game room, picnic tables, and grills. Reasonable. Motel open year-round.
5107 Scenic 61; 5 miles northeast on Scenic 61
(218) 525-1738 or (888) 950-8036
$-$$
D/MC/V/AE
NUMBER OF ROOMS: 4
NUMBER OF CABINS: 12
LAKESHORE: Across road
PETS: Yes

HEINZ'S BEACHWAY MOTEL AND CABINS

Quiet setting; great lake views; housekeeping cabins with kitchenettes; six standard and two deluxe motel rooms; senior discounts Sunday to Thursday. Weekly rates. Playground/park next door. Open May to October.
5119 Scenic 61; 5+ miles northeast on Scenic 61
$-$$
AE/D/MC/V
(218) 525-5191
lakesuperiorresorts.com
NUMBER OF ROOMS: 8
NUMBER OF CABINS: 6
LAKESHORE: Across road
PETS: No

LAKEVIEW CASTLE MOTEL AND DINING

Motel, restaurant, and lounge on Lake Superior. Open year-round.
5135 Scenic 61; 5+ miles northeast on Scenic 61
$-$$
AE/D/MC/V
(218) 525-1014
NUMBER OF ROOMS: 18
LAKESHORE: Across road
PETS: With permission

SHORECREST SUPPER CLUB AND MOTEL

Supper club and motel with wide-open lake views; swimming pool; one- and two-bedroom units, with or without kitchens. Motel open seasonally.
5593 Scenic 61; 9 miles northeast on Scenic 61
$-$$
AE/D/MC/V
(218) 525-2286
NUMBER OF ROOMS: 16
LAKESHORE: Across road
PETS: With permission

DODGE'S LOG LODGES

Great Lake Superior shoreline log cabins! Lakeside decks and grills, kitchens, and wood-burning fireplaces; well equipped. New 3-bedroom, 2-story Buchanan House with floor-to-ceiling lakeside windows. Open year-round.

5852 Scenic 61; 13 miles northeast on Scenic 61

$$–$$$$

MC/V

(218) 525-4088

dodgelog.com

NUMBER OF CABINS: 7

LAKESHORE: Yes

PETS: No

ISLAND VIEW RESORT

Hillside resort overlooking Lake Superior and Knife Island; clean, cozy cabins, some with decks or porches; walk to deli, marina, lakeshore, and local smoked fish shop. Open year-round.

Scenic 61, Knife River; 15 miles northeast on Scenic 61

$–$$

MC/V

(218) 834-5886

islandviewresortmn.com

NUMBER OF CABINS: 11 (1 year-round)

LAKESHORE: No

PETS: No

BIG BLAZE CAMPGROUND AND CABINS

Campground; 2 cabins on Lake Superior, both 1-bedroom kitchenettes; and a 1-bedroom condo away from the lake; picnic tables and grills.

560 Big Blaze Circle; 16 miles northeast on Scenic 61

$$$

(218) 834-2512

bigblaze.com

NUMBER OF CABINS: 3

LAKESHORE: Yes

PETS: No

STONEGATE ON SUPERIOR

Immaculately renovated 1930s log cabins and new log cottages; 1 and 2 bedrooms, kitchens, fireplaces, log furniture, down comforters. One cabin accessible; 3 cabins open year-round.

Box 411–412 Scenic Drive; 16+ miles northeast on Scenic 61

$$–$$$

MC/V

(218) 834-3355

stonegatesuperior.com

NUMBER OF CABINS: 8

LAKESHORE: Yes

PETS: No

BARTHELL'S CABINS

Log cabins in the woods on Superior's rocky shores. Lake view, kitchens, picnic tables. One cabin available year-round.

Scenic 61; 17 miles northeast on Scenic 61

$–$$

credit cards not accepted

(218) 834-2518

pamscards.com/resort

NUMBER OF CABINS: 8

LAKESHORE: Yes

PETS: With permission

BARTHELL'S RESORT

Well-kept 1930s log cabins, one on the shore. Open seasonally.

Scenic 61; 17 miles northeast on Scenic 61

$$

credit cards not accepted

(218) 834-3251

NUMBER OF CABINS: 3

LAKESHORE: Yes

PETS: With permission

BREEZY POINT ON LAKE SUPERIOR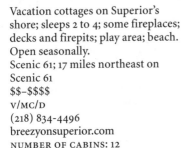

Vacation cottages on Superior's shore; sleeps 2 to 4; some fireplaces; decks and firepits; play area; beach. Open seasonally.
Scenic 61; 17 miles northeast on Scenic 61
$$–$$$$
V/MC/D
(218) 834-4496
breezyonsuperior.com
NUMBER OF CABINS: 12
LAKESHORE: Yes
PETS: No

BOB'S CABINS ON LAKE SUPERIOR

Quaint, cheery cabins; quiet retreat; spotlessly clean; 1,000 feet of rocky shoreline; no smoking. Open seasonally.
Scenic 61; 17.5 miles northeast on Scenic 61
$$
D/MC/V
(218) 834-4583
duluth.com/bobscabins
NUMBER OF CABINS: 16
LAKESHORE: Yes
PETS: No

RADOSEVICH'S EARTHWOOD INN

Motel rooms, family restaurant, and separate bar. Open year-round. Fun and friendly.
Scenic 61; 18 miles northeast on Scenic 61
$–$$
MC/V
(218) 834-3847
NUMBER OF ROOMS: 9
LAKESHORE: No
PETS: No

TWO HARBORS

AMERICINN LODGE AND SUITES

Close to all that Two Harbors has to offer; fireplace, whirlpool, and family suites; sauna, whirlpool, and pool. Deluxe continental breakfast; laundry. Open year-round.
Highway 61
$$–$$$
AE/D/DC/MC/V
(218) 834-3000 or
(national) (800) 634-3444
NUMBER OF ROOMS: 46
LAKESHORE: No
PETS: With permission

VIKING MOTEL

Near corner store, restaurants, and gas stations; double beds; one unit has a kitchenette. Nonsmoking available. Drive-ins only. Open seasonally.
Highway 61
$
D/MC/V
(218) 834-2645
NUMBER OF ROOMS: 10
LAKESHORE: No
PETS: No

VOYAGEUR MOTEL

A reasonable room at a reasonable rate. Open year-round.
Highway 61
$
D/MC/V
(218) 834-3644
voyageur-motel.com
NUMBER OF ROOMS: 8
LAKESHORE: No
PETS: Yes

COUNTRY INN ♿

A cozy stay at a comfortable price; Jacuzzi and specialty suites; pool; continental breakfast; AAA rating. Open year-round.
Highway 61
$–$$$
AE/D/DC/MC/V
(218) 834-5557
NUMBER OF ROOMS: 46
LAKESHORE: No
PETS: No

MOTEL TWO HARBORS

Cable and color TV; air-conditioned; walking distance to shops and restaurants; continental breakfast. Open year-round.
Highway 61
$
AE/D/MC/V
(218) 834-5171
NUMBER OF ROOMS: 16
LAKESHORE: No
PETS: Fee charged

SUPERIOR SHORES RESORT AND CONFERENCE CENTER ♿

A half-mile of shoreline; motel and lake homes with Jacuzzi, fireplace, and deck; delicious meals in the restaurant; lounge; continental breakfast; pool. Open year-round. Watch for a new development of lake homes and amenities.
Highway 61, one mile east of Two Harbors
$$–$$$
AE/CB/D/DC/MC/V
(218) 834-5671 or (800) 242-1988
superiorshores.com
NUMBER OF ROOMS: 57
NUMBER OF SUITES: 42
NUMBER OF TOWNHOMES: 42
LAKESHORE: Yes
PETS: Attended

FLOOD BAY MOTEL

Comfortable nonsmoking rooms with a lake or woodland view. Across from Flood Bay Wayside, an excellent agate-hunting area. Open late May to October.
Highway 61, one mile east of Two Harbors
$–$$
AE/MC/V
(218) 834-4076
NUMBER OF ROOMS: 10
LAKESHORE: Across road
PETS: No

TWO HARBORS TO GOOSEBERRY FALLS

THE GRAY GULL MOTEL AND CABINS

Very private, small resort; friendly folks; in-room fridges, coffee and tea. Open seasonally.
Highway 61, 3.5 miles east of Two Harbors
$–$$
credit cards not accepted
(218) 834-3372
NUMBER OF ROOMS: 4
NUMBER OF UNITS: 1
LAKESHORE: Yes
PETS: With permission

SILVER CLIFF MOTEL

Vintage motel with extraordinary Lake Superior views; one queen or two full beds; nonsmoking; pebble beach. Open seasonally.
Highway 61 at Silver Cliff, 4.25 miles east of Two Harbors
$–$$
credit cards not accepted
(218) 834-4695
NUMBER OF ROOMS: 7
LAKESHORE: Yes
PETS: No

CLIFF 'N SHORE RESORT

Seven motel rooms (2 with kitchens) and three fireplace cabins at Superior's edge with Silver Cliff views; serene spot. Open year-round.
Highway 61 at Silver Cliff, 4.25 miles east of Two Harbors
$-$$
credit cards not accepted
(218) 834-4675
NUMBER OF ROOMS: 7
NUMBER OF CABINS: 3
LAKESHORE: Yes
PETS: Cabins only

HALCYON HARBOR CABINS

Four year-round cabins and a cliff-side beach house on a Lake Superior bluff, all fully furnished with fireplaces; 2 beaches; off-season midweek discounts; cross-country ski rentals. Open year-round.
Highway 61, 5.25 miles east of Two Harbors
$$-$$$
AE/D/MC/V
(218) 834-2030
halcyoncabins.com
NUMBER OF UNITS: 5
LAKESHORE: Yes
PETS: Some

NORTHERN RAIL

Sleep in a renovated train car! Extending out from either side of the "depot" is a row of train car suites connected by a protected walkway. Themed suites with sitting areas, 3 with a separate living area (sleep up to 8), some with fridge and microwave. Deluxe continental breakfast.
1730 Highway 3; north of Highway 61 at the Stewart River
$$-$$$$
AE/MC/V
(218) 834-6084
northernrail.net
NUMBER OF SUITES: 17
LAKESHORE: No
PETS: No

GOOSEBERRY PARK MOTEL AND CABINS

Motel suites and kitchenettes, with separate living areas; lakeshore cabins with decks or porches, some with fireplaces. Clean and comfy. Across the road from the Rustic Inn Cafe and Gift Shop and snowmobile rentals. Open year-round.
Highway 61 in Castle Danger
$-$$$
MC/V
(218) 834-3751 or (800) 950-0283
gooseberryparkcabins.com
NUMBER OF ROOMS: 5
NUMBER OF CABINS: 6
LAKESHORE: Yes
PETS: No

GRAND SUPERIOR LODGE

Lakeshore log cabins and luxury 4-bedroom log lake homes with fireplaces, large decks, TV, VCR, and full kitchens. Main lodge with rooms and suites, restaurant, lounge, and gifts. Massage therapy; meetings and groups; huge cobblestone beach for rock hounding, canoeing, and bonfires; very near Gooseberry Falls State Park. Open year-round.
Highway 61 in Castle Danger
$$-$$$$
MC/V/AE/D
(218) 834-3796 or (800) 627-9565
grandsuperior.com
NUMBER OF ROOMS: 25
NUMBER OF CABINS: 6
NUMBER OF LAKEHOMES: 16
LAKESHORE: Yes
PETS: Some

GOOSEBERRY CABINS

Quiet family resort offering cozy cabins to spacious lakeside units; some fireplaces and decks; smoke-free; four year-round cabins; enjoy the cobblestone beach! Open year-round. One mile off Highway 61 just south-west of Gooseberry Falls State Park
$$
MC/V
(218) 834-3873
webpages.mr.net/karotime
NUMBER OF UNITS: 9
LAKESHORE: Yes
PETS: No

CASTLE HAVEN CABINS

Secluded housekeeping cabins on Lake Superior. Winterized cabins have fireplaces. One mile to Goose-berry Falls State Park.
One mile south of Highway 61
$$
(218) 834-4303
LAKESHORE: Yes
PETS: No

GOOSEBERRY TRAILSIDE SUITES

Romantic two-bedroom suites with hardwood floors, fully-equipped kitchens and wood-burning fire-places; adjacent to the state park; private lake-view deck with grill; sauna; no smoking. Open year-round.
Highway 61, just northeast of Goose-berry Falls State Park
$$–$$$
AE/D/MC/V
(218) 226-4966 or (800) 715-1110
http://members.aol.com/gtrailside
NUMBER OF ROOMS: 4
LAKESHORE: No
PETS: No

J. GREGER'S INN

Rustic, homestyle lodging; 2-room cabin with fireplace, and a homey inn with four "state park" rooms, one with a fireplace, all with microwave and fridge; no smoking; large back-yard with kids' playhouse, swing, and hammock. Breakfast for $5. On Gitchi Gami Trail. Open year-round.
Highway 61, just northeast of Goose-berry Falls State Park
$$
D/MC/V
(218) 226-4614 or (888) 226-4614
jgregersinn.com
NUMBER OF ROOMS: 4
NUMBER OF CABINS: 1
LAKESHORE: No
PETS: No

SPLIT ROCK CABINS

Modern housekeeping cabins on Lake Superior; 2 open all year. Boat ramp and dock; river and lake fish-ing; nearby hiking, biking, and cross-country ski trails.
3668 Highway 61; 16 miles northeast of Two Harbors
$$
D/MC/V
(218) 226-9735
NUMBER OF CABINS: 10
LAKESHORE: Yes
PETS: Some

BEAVER BAY

COVE POINT LODGE

Scandinavian lodge and 2-bedroom cottages on secluded cove; cozy and relaxing lake-view rooms and suites with Jacuzzis and fireplaces; great hall with fireplace; lakeside dining room and lounge; pool; senior discount. Open year-round.
Highway 61 in town
$$–$$$$
AE/D/DC/MC/V
(218) 226-3221 or (800) 598-3221
covepointlodge.com
NUMBER OF ROOMS: 45 + cottages
LAKESHORE: Yes
PETS: No

WINDSONG COTTAGES

New Windsong Cottages, a luxury home/rental development, is being built on Cove Point's 150-acre site. Plans include stunning lodging and a restaurant up the hill near Highway 61.

NORTHLAND TRAILS GUESTHOUSE

Private retreat in a onetime model log house; fully furnished 3-level home sleeps up to 8; master bedroom, loft bedroom, and two living areas. Perfect for families and groups. Near all the trails and parks.
Highway 61 in Beaver Bay
$$$–$$$$
(218) 226-4199
northlandtrails.com
NUMBER OF CABINS: 1
LAKESHORE: No
PETS: Inquire

BEAVER BAY INN AND MOTEL

Clean, reasonable motel rooms and two family loft units that sleep six, one with a full-sized whirlpool; full restaurant and small bar; center of town, next to local playground. Open year-round.
Highway 61 in town
$–$$$$
AE/MC/V
(218) 226-4351 or (800) 226-4351
innatbeaverbay.com
NUMBER OF ROOMS: 30
LAKESHORE: No
PETS: With permission

SILVER BAY TO SCHROEDER

MARINER MOTEL

Motel rooms including family two- and three-bedroom units with kitchenettes and saunas; clean; reasonable rates. Nonsmoking rooms. Open year-round.
Just off Highway 61 in Silver Bay
$–$$
AE/CB/D/MC/V
(218) 226-4488 or (800) 777-8452
NUMBER OF ROOMS: 28
LAKESHORE: No
PETS: Some

AMERICINN OF SILVER BAY

Brand new! A splash adventure AmericInn featuring a fabulous indoor water slide and pool, children's waterslide and pool, sauna, and spa. A great family getaway centrally located near hiking, state parks, skiing, snowmobiling, fishing, and the best of the Shore.
Just south of Highway 61 in Silver Bay
$$–$$$
AE/D/MC/V
(800) 634-3444
NUMBER OF ROOMS: 61
NUMBER OF UNITS: 15
LAKESHORE: No
PETS: Inquire

WHISPERING PINES MOTEL

Surrounded by Tettegouche State Park; 8 motel rooms and 1 walk-out unit with kitchenette; fridges, microwaves, in-room coffee; playground; clean and comfy! Open year-round.
Highway 61 in Illgen City
$–$$
AE/D/MC/V
(218) 226-4712 or (800) 332-0531
whisperingpinesmotel.com
NUMBER OF ROOMS: 9
NUMBER OF UNITS: 1
LAKESHORE: No
PETS: Some

BETTY'S CABINS

One- to three-room red log cabins on the Baptism River; friendly folks and relaxing atmosphere. No smoking. Open June to mid-October.
From Highway 61, go 2.5 miles north on Minnesota 1.
$–$$
credit cards not accepted
(218) 353-7362
lakesuperiorcabins.com
NUMBER OF CABINS: 4
LAKESHORE: No
PETS: No

SPIRIT OF GITCHE GUMEE

Gift shop, coffee house, and lodge with 4 cozy rooms. Complimentary espresso and scones in the morning.
Highway 61 in Little Marais
$–$$
AE/D/MC/V
(218) 226-6476
gitchegumee.net
NUMBER OF ROOMS: 4
LAKESHORE: No
PETS: No

LITTLE MARAIS
LAKESIDE CABINS

Eight water's-edge cabins and one between the shore and highway; two cozy one-room cabins, three one-bedroom, and four two-bedroom cabins; some with fireplaces, all with kitchens. Big grassy yard. Open seasonally.
Highway 61 in Little Marais
$$–$$$
D/MC/V
(218) 226-3456
superiorlakesidecabins.com
NUMBER OF CABINS: 9
LAKESHORE: Yes
PETS: Yes

FENSTAD'S RESORT

Secluded lakeshore cabins with fireplaces and kitchens; sauna; playground; hiking and cross-country ski trails; boat and motor rental, boat ramp and dock; cross-country ski and snowshoe rentals. Open year-round.
Highway 61 in Little Marais
$$–$$$
credit cards not accepted
(218) 226-4724
NUMBER OF CABINS: 17
LAKESHORE: Yes
PETS: No

CROOKED LAKE RESORT

Comfy, lakeside/lake-view 1- to 3-room cabins in the woods: no running water in cabins; central sauna/shower building; boat and motor rental. Camper spaces for $10 per night.
From Finland go northeast on Co. Rd. 7 for 20 miles.
$–$$
(218) 220-0211
NUMBER OF CABINS: 11
LAKESHORE: Yes
PETS: Yes

THE LODGE AT NINE MILE LAKE

Rustic 1- to 4-room cabins on/near lake; porches; limited electricity; no running water. Lodge has toilets, showers, pizza, sandwiches, beer, and setups.
From Finland, go northeast on Co. Rd. 7 for 16 miles.
$$–$$$
MC/V
(218) 220-0308
thelodgeatninemile.com
NUMBER OF CABINS: 7
LAKESHORE: Yes
PETS: Some

WILDHURST LODGE AND CAMPGROUND

Two well-kept log camping cabins, 3 sleeping rooms (1 with a fridge and microwave), 17 tent and 4 RV sites; canoe rental. Open year-round.
From Finland, go north on Minnesota 1 for 4.5 miles.
$
MC/V
(218) 353-7337 or (888) 353-7337
wildhurstlodge.com
NUMBER OF UNITS: 5 + camping
LAKESHORE: No
PETS: Yes

SCHROEDER

SATELLITE'S COUNTRY INN

Two- and three-bedroom cabins and motel-type rooms plus family restaurant; open May through November.
Highway 61 southwest of Schroeder
$–$$
(218) 663-7574
LAKESHORE: No
PETS: Some

SUPERIOR RIDGE

Motel or condo units with fireplaces and kitchenettes; vaulted, knotty pine interiors; gas fireplaces and saunas in some. Open year-round.
Highway 61
$–$$$
AE/MC/V/D
(218) 663-7189 or (800) 782-1776
superiorridge.com
NUMBER OF ROOMS: 6
NUMBER OF CONDOMINIUMS: 6
LAKESHORE: No
PETS: With permission

LAMB'S RESORT AND CAMPGROUND

Spacious secluded log cabins overlook Cross River or Lake Superior; half-mile beach on 60 acres; 100 secluded and lakeshore campsites; gift shop; walk to bakery; river hiking trails. Open seasonally.
Highway 61
$$
MC/V
(218) 663-7292
boreal.org/lambsresort
NUMBER OF CABINS: 14
LAKESHORE: Yes
PETS: With permission

TEMPERANCE TRADERS CABINS

New 1- and 2-bedroom cabins with full kitchens, living area, and decks; close to Temperance River State Park. Liquor store and gift shop.
Highway 61 in Schroeder
$$–$$$$
MC/V
(218) 663-0111
northshorecabins.com
NUMBER OF CABINS: 5
LAKESHORE: No
PETS: Some

TOFTE

SURFSIDE CABINS AND MOTEL

Seven lakeside cabins and six economical roadside motel units; quiet, clean, and comfortable; antique and card shop. Nonsmoking. Open seasonally.
Highway 61 in Tofte
$–$$
D/MC/V
(218) 663-7206 or (800) 352-7576
NUMBER OF ROOMS: 6
NUMBER OF CABINS: 7
LAKESHORE: Yes
PETS: No

SUGAR BEACH RESORT

Remodeled log cabins from small, clean, economical to stunning; 1500 sq. ft. lakeshore log cabins; decks and some with fireplaces; private, secluded surroundings. Open year-round.
Highway 61 in Tofte
$–$$$$
credit cards not accepted
(218) 663-7595
toftesugarbeach.com
NUMBER OF CABINS: 15
LAKESHORE: Yes
PETS: No

AMERICINN

Upscale motel rooms including whirlpool suites and a 2-bedroom apartment with full kitchen; indoor pool, sauna, and whirlpool; spacious firelit lobby with great continental breakfast; near trails/on snowmobile trail. Open year-round.
Highway 61
$–$$$
D/MC/V/AE
(218) 663-7899 or (800) 625-7042
americinntofte.com
NUMBER OF ROOMS: 51
LAKESHORE: No
PETS: Some

BLUEFIN BAY ON LAKE SUPERIOR

Townhome units rent as one entire unit or as a studio, a studio with loft, or a guest room. Lakeshore units feature fireplaces, balconies, private in-room whirlpools, full kitchen and dining areas, and spectacular views. Two restaurants, a lounge and indoor spa-pool-sauna complex, four-season outdoor pool and whirlpool; kids' play area; group meeting facilities; Coho Cafe Bakery and Deli. Open year-round.
Highway 61
$$–$$$$
D/MC/V/AE
(218) 663-7296 or (800) BLUEFIN
bluefinbay.com
NUMBER OF ROOMS: 80
LAKESHORE: Yes

COBBLESTONE CABINS

Vintage cabins for characters and common folk; reasonable; kids' play area; on Lake Superior with a beach; clean and cozy; sauna. Open mid-May through October.
Highway 61
$-$$
credit cards not accepted
(218) 663-7957
NUMBER OF CABINS: 8
LAKESHORE: Yes
PETS: No

CHATEAU LEVEAUX

Deluxe lakeside condominiums, 1-bedroom or 1-bedroom with sleeping loft, with fireplaces, kitchenettes, and patios or balconies, some with whirlpools; spacious motel rooms; all overlook Lake Superior; Jacuzzi-sauna-pool complex. Open year-round.
Highway 61
$$-$$$$
AE/MC/V/D
(218) 663-7223 or (800) 445-5773
chateauleveaux.com
NUMBER OF CONDOMINIUMS: 31
LAKESHORE: Yes
PETS: In some units

AT LUTSEN MOUNTAINS

THE MOUNTAIN INN

Motel rooms, mini- and king suites near Lutsen Mountains and Superior National golf course; continental breakfast; whirlpool. Open year-round.
$$-$$$
AE/MC/V/D
(218) 663-7244 or (800) 686-4669
lutsenlodgingcompany.com
NUMBER OF ROOMS: 30
LAKESHORE: No
PETS: Some

LUTSEN LODGING COMPANY

Renting a variety of properties including:
LUTSEN LOG LODGES: Private 3-bedroom log lodges with living area and fireplace, complete kitchen, and master bedroom with Jacuzzi. On the Ski Hill Road; $$$$; smokefree; no pets.
HIDDEN COVE CONDO: On Lake Superior; 2 bedrooms, kitchen, living room with fireplace, and wraparound deck. Off Highway 61; $$$-$$$$.
CLEARVIEW HOUSE: All the comforts of home; above Clearview on Highway 61; $$-$$$$.
MELISSA'S COASTAL RETREAT: Carefully renovated, beautiful 2-bedroom home on Lake Superior; weekly rentals; AE/D/MC/V; (218) 663-7244 or (800) 686-4669; lutsenlodgingcompany.com

CARIBOU HIGHLANDS LODGE AT LUTSEN MOUNTAINS

Family lodging; spectacular views; luxury condos, townhomes, executive lodges, Poplar Ridge homes, and main lodge rooms; some with fireplaces, whirlpools, saunas, and balconies; all have full amenities. Restaurant, vaulted lobby, towering stone fireplace, bakery, and gift shop. Family activities, kids' camp, and naturalist on site; indoor pool, sauna, and whirlpool; outdoor pool; spa building; near Superior National at Lutsen golf course; group meeting facilities; a ski-in, ski-out resort. Open year-round.
$$-$$$$
MC/V/AE/D
(218) 663-7241 or (800) 642-6036
caribouhighlands.com
NUMBER OF ROOMS: 27
NUMBER OF CONDOMINIUMS: 43
NUMBER OF TOWNHOMES: 37
NUMBER OF POPLAR RIDGE HOMES: 7
LAKESHORE: No
PETS: No

EAGLE RIDGE

A ski-in, ski-out resort; trailside location for mountain bike park, hiking, gondola rides, and alpine slide. Studios to three-bedroom condos, all with mountain views; indoor-outdoor pool with Jacuzzi and spa. Open year-round.
$$-$$$$
MC/V/AE/D
(218) 663-7284 or (800) 360-7666
eagleridgeatlutsen.com
NUMBER OF UNITS: 75

LUTSEN TO GRAND MARAIS

BEST WESTERN CLIFF DWELLER AND GULL HARBOR CONDOMINIUMS

Lake-view rooms with balconies or condominiums with fireplaces; whirlpool and sauna building at Gull Harbor. Open year-round.
Highway 61 in Lutsen
$-$$$
AE/D/DC/MC/V
(218) 663-7273 or (800) 223-2048
NUMBER OF ROOMS: 22
NUMBER OF CONDOMINIUMS: 5
LAKESHORE: Yes
PETS: With permission

LUTSEN RESORT AND SEA VILLAS

Scandinavian main lodge and Cliff House guest rooms, two-bedroom log cabins, and sea villa townhomes with one bedroom and a loft or two bedrooms; townhomes and cabins have fireplaces and decks; firelit dining room and lobby. Adjacent to Superior National golf course; large indoor pool; Jacuzzi and sauna building attached to main lodge; conference and meeting area. Second indoor pool complex in Sea Villa/log cabin area. Luxury Poplar Ridge condos along the east side of the Poplar River. Open year-round.
Highway 61 in Lutsen
$$-$$$$
AE/CB/D/DC/MC/V
(218) 663-7212 or (800) 258-8736
lutsenresort.com
NUMBER OF ROOMS: 49
NUMBER OF TOWNHOMES: 50
NUMBER OF CONDOS: 16
NUMBER OF LOG HOMES: 6
LAKESHORE: Yes
PETS: In Sea Villas

SOLBAKKEN RESORT

Lake Superior hillside kitchenette motel rooms, shoreline cabins, deluxe lake homes, and hillside lodge suites with kitchens; whirlpool and sauna; fireplaces in six units; comfortable beds; great bookshop and fireside lobby. Open year-round.
Highway 61 in Lutsen
$$–$$$
AE/D/MC/V
(218) 663-7566 or (800) 435-3950
solbakkenresort.com
NUMBER OF ROOMS: 9
NUMBER OF CABINS: 9
LAKESHORE: Yes
PETS: With permission

KOENEKE SHOREDGE

Rustic, modern log cabins on Caribou Point, Lake Superior; cabins accommodate two to seven people; two 2-bedroom and three housekeeping, 1 with a loft, 1 rustic, and 1 available daily. Open seasonally.
Highway 61 in Lutsen
$$–$$$
credit cards not accepted
(218) 663-7588
shoredge.com
NUMBER OF CABINS: 4
LAKESHORE: Yes
PETS: Yes

KAH-NEE-TAH COTTAGES AND GALLERY

Cottages with full kitchens and baths; cobblestone fireplaces; lake view. Open year-round.
Highway 61 in Lutsen
$$–$$$
D/MC/V
(218) 387-2585 or (800) 216-2585
kahneetah.com
NUMBER OF CABINS: 3
LAKESHORE: No
PETS: Yes

CASCADE LODGE AND RESTAURANT

Historic main lodge rooms, some with whirlpools; cabins (some log) with fireplaces and some with kitchens; four-unit motel; adjacent lodge-style restaurant. Nestled in the woods adjacent to Cascade State Park across from Lake Superior; hiking and cross-country ski trails right out the door. Open year-round.
Highway 61 at Cascade River
$–$$$
AE/D/MC/V
(218) 387-1112 or (800) 322-9543
cascadelodgemn.com
NUMBER OF ROOMS: 15
NUMBER OF CABINS: 10
NUMBER OF HOMES: 1
LAKESHORE: Across road
PETS: No

SUPERIOR PROPERTIES

Privately-owned homes along Lake Superior and Inland Lakes in Lutsen, Grand Marais, and along the Gunflint Trail. From quaint 1-room cabins with gas lights and no running water to luxury lake homes and everything in between. Renting almost 50 cabins, townhomes, and homes on a daily and weekly rate; some allow pets.
(800) 950-4361
Offices in Lutsen and Grand Marais
northofnorth.com/rentals.html

THOMSONITE BEACH INN AND SUITES

On Lake Superior; three 2-bedroom fireplace units with kitchens and sundecks for up to 6 people; three deluxe units with kitchens, 1 with a loft; and four spacious standard rooms. Great grounds; ledge-rock shore; picnic tables; gallery and gift shop featuring thomsonite jewelry. Open year-round.
Highway 61 between Lutsen and Grand Marais
$$–$$$
AE/D/MC/V
(218) 387-1532
thomsonite.com
NUMBER OF ROOMS: 8
NUMBER OF UNITS: 2
LAKESHORE: Yes
PETS: No

BALLY CREEK CABINS

Nestled in the woods with hiking and cross-country trails out the door; rustic cabins with outhouses; no smoking. Bring your own linens and cooking/eating utensils. Open year-round.
On Bally Creek Road 6 miles from Grand Marais
$$–$$$
D/MC/V
(218) 387-1162 or (800) 795-8068
bear-track.com
NUMBER OF CABINS: 5
LAKESHORE: No
PETS: Yes

GRAND MARAIS

Lodging is listed in alphabetical order.

ASPEN LODGE

The only place in Grand Marais with a swimming pool, whirlpool, and sauna; rooms and family suites; in-room fridges; sundeck; fireside lobby with cards and games; continental breakfast. Open year-round.
Highway 61 in town
$–$$$
AE/D/MC/V
(218) 387-2800 or (800) 247-6020
gmhotel.net
NUMBER OF ROOMS: 51
LAKESHORE: Yes
PETS: With permission

BEST WESTERN SUPERIOR INN AND SUITES

On Lake Superior in downtown; luxurious rooms and suites with refrigerators; luxury suites with fireplaces and Jacuzzis; thick bathrobes; all face Lake Superior. Private cobblestone beach; large whirlpool; continental breakfast; kids stay free. Open year-round.
Highway 61 in town
$$–$$$
AE/D/MC/V
(218) 387-2240 or (800) 842-VIEW
bestwestern.com/superiorinn
NUMBER OF ROOMS: 57
LAKESHORE: Yes
PETS: Limited

EAST BAY HOTEL

Historic hotel in downtown Grand Marais on Lake Superior. Motel rooms, deluxe suites, and top-floor suites with in-room Jacuzzis and fireplaces. Lounge, dining room, summer seating on the deck; sauna; large, open shoreline right out the door. Open year-round.
Main Street at the east bay
$–$$$
D/MC/V
(218) 387-2800 or (800) 414-2807
eastbayhotel.com
NUMBER OF ROOMS: 41
LAKESHORE: Yes
PETS: Yes

ELSIE'S LAKEVIEW CABINS

Super-clean log cabins on Lake Superior a few miles east of Grand Marais; 2 to 3 bedrooms, small living area, kitchenettes, and shoreline. Open seasonally.
On the Croftville Road
(218) 387-2029

GRAND MARAIS INN AND TOMTEBODA CABINS

Great family motel; Nordic lodge suites and classic log cabins set off the bike trail and Highway 61. Motel is clean, comfortable, and affordable. Nordic lodge is 4 spacious rooms with an over-sized deck. Cabins range from a 1-room honeymoon to classic 2-bedroom with fireplace and kitchen. Wood-fired oven and grill.
Highway 61 in Grand Marais
$-$$
AE/D/MC/V
(218) 387-1585 or (800) 622-2622
grandmaraisinn.com
NUMBER OF ROOMS: 17
NUMBER OF NORDICS: 4
NUMBER OF CABINS: 4
LAKESHORE: No
PETS: Some, attended

GRAND MARAIS SUPER 8

Sunlit spa room opens to sundeck; guest laundry; in-room fridges; continental breakfast. Open year-round.
Highway 61 in town
$-$$$
AE/D/MC/V
(218) 387-2488 or (800) 257-6020
gmhotel.net
NUMBER OF ROOMS: 35
LAKESHORE: No
PETS: Yes, limited

GUNFLINT MOTEL

Old World hospitality; modern, comfortable suites, 4 with kitchens; wood interiors and cathedral ceilings. Open seasonally.
Gunflint Trail in town
$-$$
credit cards not accepted
(218) 387-1454
gunflintmotel.com
NUMBER OF ROOMS: 5
LAKESHORE: No
PETS: Yes

HARBOR INN MOTEL AND RESTAURANT

Tastefully decorated rooms overlooking Grand Marais harbor; in-room fridges; balconies. Free continental breakfast or half-off breakfast at the restaurant. Open year-round.
Main Street
$-$$
AE/D/MC/V
(218) 387-1191 or (800) 595-4566
bytheharbor.com
NUMBER OF ROOMS: 10
LAKESHORE: Across road
PETS: No

LARSEN'S LAKEVIEW CABINS

Housekeeping cabins on Lake Superior or across the road. Modernized, clean log cabins; great beach.
On the Croftville Road a few miles east of town
(218) 387-2710
NUMBER OF CABINS: 5
LAKESHORE: Yes
PETS: Yes

LUND'S MOTEL AND COTTAGES

Motel with six spacious rooms; view of harbor and marina; near public pool complex. Charming housekeeping cottages, four with fireplaces. In serene wooded setting; family-owned since 1937. Open year-round.
Highway 61 in town
$–$$
D/MC/V/AE
(218) 387-2155 or (218) 387-1704
NUMBER OF ROOMS: 6
NUMBER OF COTTAGES: 8
LAKESHORE: No
PETS: Yes, in cottages

MANGY MOOSE MOTEL

Family motel in town; convenient to shopping, shoreline, and dining; reasonable. New owners! Open year-round.
Highway 61 in town
$–$$
D/MC/V
(218) 387-2975 or (800) 796-2975
NUMBER OF ROOMS: 9
LAKESHORE: No
PETS: No

NELSON'S TRAVELER'S REST CABINS

Set among mature pines in parklike setting; views of Lake Superior from five cabins; HBO in every cabin; grills, picnic tables, and firepits; quick walk to downtown; playground. Open May to October.
Highway 61 in town
$$
D/MC/V
(218) 387-1464 or (800) 249-1285
travelersrest.com
NUMBER OF CABINS: 11
LAKESHORE: No
PETS: No

RUSSELL'S COTTAGES

Four cottages and a log cabin, 2 suites, and a 3-bedroom home with fireplace, deck, and Lake Superior view. One block up from the Grand Marais harbor. Open May to October.
Gunflint Trail in town
$–$$$$
credit cards not accepted
(218) 387-1108
NUMBER OF HOMES: 1
NUMBER OF COTTAGES: 5
LAKESHORE: No
PETS: No

SAWTOOTH CABINS AND MOTEL

Two spacious motel rooms with two double beds; clean, comfortable housekeeping cabins; fireplaces; long-term rentals in the off-season. Nonsmoking. Open May to October.
Gunflint Trail in town
$$
MC/V
(218) 387-1522
NUMBER OF ROOMS: 2
NUMBER OF CABINS: 6
LAKESHORE: No
PETS: Limited

SEAWALL MOTEL

Vintage downtown motel with 15 clean, comfortable rooms; beautiful view of harbor. Open seasonally.
Highway 61 in town
$–$$
AE/D/MC/V
(218) 387-2095 or (800) 245-5806
NUMBER OF ROOMS: 15
LAKESHORE: Across street
PETS: Inquire

THE SHORELINE

Downtown near Artist Point; fireside, lake-view lobby; water's-edge sundeck; gifts; coffee and donuts served each morning. Open year-round.
Broadway
$$–$$$
AE/D/MC/V
(218) 387-2633 or (800) 427-6020
gmhotel.net
NUMBER OF ROOMS: 30
LAKESHORE: Yes
PETS: No

TIMBERLUNDS

Quaint cottages 1 mile west of Grand Marais, most on a bluff with great lake views. Include kitchen, bath, sleep up to 4, decks, grills, firepits. Reasonable; discounts for week stays. Open May to October.
Highway 61 just west of Grand Marais
$–$$
(218) 387-1147
NUMBER OF CABINS: 7
LAKESHORE: No
PETS: Ask

TRAILSIDE MOTEL AND CABINS

Eight modern motel units with microwaves and fridges; six cozy, clean completely furnished cabins; quiet wooded setting; lake view. Fabulous quilt shop. Quilters, plan a retreat! Open seasonally.
Highway 61 in town
$–$$
credit cards not accepted
(218) 387-1550 or (800) 525-2792
NUMBER OF ROOMS: 8
NUMBER OF CABINS: 6
LAKESHORE: No
PETS: Yes

GRAND MARAIS TO CANADIAN BORDER

ANDERSON'S NORTH SHORE RESORT

Clean, airy cabins, some on Lake Superior shoreline; 1 to 3 bedrooms. Full kitchens; decks, grills, and beach. Open year-round.
Croftville Road, two miles east of Grand Marais
$$–$$$
credit cards not accepted
(218) 387-1814
andersoncabins.com
NUMBER OF CABINS: 7
LAKESHORE: Yes
PETS: No

WEDGEWOOD MOTEL

Small, vintage motel with clean rooms, hospitable hosts, and coffee in the office. Senior discounts. Open year-round.
Highway 61, three miles east of Grand Marais
$–$$
credit cards not accepted
(218) 387-2944 or (877) 808-8902
NUMBER OF ROOMS: 5
LAKESHORE: No
PETS: Yes, dogs

OUTPOST RESORT MOTEL

Nice lake-view motel rooms and kitchenette suites; near Kadunce River Wayside picnic area and hiking trails; walk across road to cobblestone beach; smoke-free. Open year-round.
Highway 61 in Colvill, eight miles east of Grand Marais
$-$$
D/MC/V
(218) 387-1833 or (888) 380-1333
outpostmotel.com
NUMBER OF ROOMS: 12
NUMBER OF UNITS: 3
LAKESHORE: Across road
PETS: With permission

NANIBOUJOU LODGE AND RESTAURANT

Historic 1920s lodge with amazing Native American decor, solarium, and wonderful grounds; some rooms with fireplaces; great restaurant; high tea in the solarium. Open seasonally and weekends.
Highway 61, 13 miles east of Grand Marais
$$-$$$
D/MC/V
(218) 387-2688
naniboujou.com
NUMBER OF ROOMS: 24
LAKESHORE: Yes
PETS: No

HOLLOW ROCK RESORT

Private lodging overlooking Hollow Rock on Lake Superior; deluxe suite with kitchenette, 10-sided room with lots of windows; 5 private vacation cottages from 1-room open concept to 2-bedroom, all with decks and fireplaces, some with kitchens; all well-equipped (3-night minimum); 2 nightly rooms, 1 open with a kitchen/living/dining area for 2, 1- or 2-bedroom with fridge, microwave, and coffee. Also rent the 2-bedroom Skora House near Grand Marais; fireplace, gardens, deck, outdoor hot tub.
Highway 61, 35 miles northeast of Grand Marais, 3 miles southwest of Grand Portage
$$-$$$$
MC/V
(218) 475-2272
hollowrockresort.com
NUMBER OF UNITS: 9
LAKESHORE: Yes
PETS: No

GRAND PORTAGE LODGE AND CASINO

Casino action including blackjack, slots, keno, and bingo; restaurant; lounge; pool, whirlpool, and sauna. Open year-round.
Highway 61 in Grand Portage
$$-$$$
AE/D/MC/V
(800) 232-1384; (218) 475-2401
grandportagemn.com
NUMBER OF ROOMS: 100
LAKESHORE: Yes
PETS: With permission

GUNFLINT TRAIL

DEVIL TRACK LODGE

Great condos, guest rooms, and lake homes at the east end of Devil Track Lake. Restaurant, lounge, large hot tub room, patio, deck, pontoon, and fishing boats. Good fun all year-round.

3.6 miles north on the Gunflint Trail, 4 miles west on Co. Rd. 8
$$–$$$$
AE/D/MC/V
(218) 387-9414 or (877) 387-9414
deviltracklodge.com
NUMBER OF ROOMS: 5
NUMBER OF CONDOS: 3
NUMBER OF LAKE HOMES: 6
LAKESHORE: Yes
PETS: Some, ask

DEVIL TRACK LAKE HOME

Open, airy, move-right-in lake home on the south shore of Devil Track Lake; 3 bedrooms, separate double Jacuzzi room, sunroom with wood stove and futons, well-equipped kitchen, living/dining room, thick fluffy robes, deck, patio, grill. Kayak, canoe, cross-country ski, snowmobile. Open year-round.

3.6 miles north on Gunflint Trail, 2.6 miles west on Co. Rd. 8, 1.75 miles west on South Shore Road
$$$
AE/D/MC/V
(218) 387-1314
northshorevisitor.com/vacation-rentals/devil-track.html
NUMBER OF LAKE HOMES: 1
LAKESHORE: Yes
PETS: No

DEVIL TRACK CABINS

One-, two-, and four-bedroom cabins on the lake; kitchen and bath; canoe, dock space, boat rental. Hike, bike, fish, relax; 3 miles to restaurant and convenience store. Open seasonally.

3.6 miles north on the Gunflint Trail, 7+ miles west on Co. Rd. 8
$$
(218) 387-2194
NUMBER OF CABINS: 4
LAKESHORE: Yes
PETS: No

TROUT LAKE RESORT

Only resort on Trout Lake; small family resort with private modern cabins that sleep up to 11 people. Excellent trout fly-fishing; boat, motor, and canoe rental; sauna and beach. Open year-round.

789 Trout Lake Road, 12 miles up the Gunflint Trail and 4 miles in
$$–$$$
D/MC/V
(218) 387-1330 or (800) 258-7688
troutlakeresort.com
NUMBER OF CABINS: 7
PETS: Yes

GOLDEN EAGLE LODGE AND NORDIC SKI CENTER

Only resort on Flour Lake; four-season family resort. Modern housekeeping cabins; 2-bedroom, 2-bedroom deluxe, 3-bedroom, and suites. Boat, motor, and canoe rental; sauna and beach; 66K of excellent cross-country ski trails. Open year-round.

468 Clearwater Road, 25 miles up the Gunflint Trail and 2.5 miles in
$$–$$$$
AE/D/MC/V
(218) 388-2203 or (800) 346-2203
golden-eagle.com
NUMBER OF CABINS: 11
PETS: Summer only

BEARSKIN LODGE AND CROSS-COUNTRY SKI RESORT

Only resort on East Bearskin Lake; comfort in the wilderness; 11 cabins; private dock; private "Hot Tub Hus"; wonderful dining (by reservation only). 66K of sensational cross-country ski trails; boat, motor, and canoe rental; beach; partial outfitting services. Open year-round.
124 East Bearskin Road, 27 miles up the Gunflint Trail and 1 mile in
$$–$$$$
AE/D/MC/V
(218) 388-2292 or (800) 338-4170
bearskin.com
NUMBER OF CABINS: 15
PETS: No

ADVENTUROUS CHRISTIANS

Providing ministry in a wilderness environment; lodge has kitchen and dining area, living area, and a loft for overflow sleeping; 2 cabins with outhouses; 1 with 4 bunkrooms (sleeps up to 27), kitchen, and living area; 1 with 2 bedrooms, lofts (sleeps up to 12), kitchen, and living area, and running cold water.
Off the Gunflint Trail on the Bow Lake Road
(218) 388-2286 or (800) 392-1501
adventurouschristians.org

LITTLE OLLIE LODGING

Look in the B&B chapter for information about Poplar Creek Guesthouse. Little Ollie Cabin is a modern 2-bedroom log cabin that sleeps up to 7; equipped kitchen, free-standing fireplace, and bath with sauna and shower. On the edge of the BWCAW. Canoeing, mountain biking and hiking, and cross-country skiing. Two BWCAW wintertime yurts (see yurt-to-yurt skiing), each on its own small lake. Open year-round.
Off the Gunflint Trail, 1 mile west on the Lima Grade and 1 mile drive on Litle Ollie Road
$–$$$
AE/D/MC/V
(218) 387-4487 or (800) 322-8327
littleollielodging.com
NUMBER OF CABINS: 1
NUMBER OF YURTS: 2
PETS: Yes

HUNGRY JACK CANOE OUTFITTERS AND CABINS

On Hungry Jack Lake; 2 lakeside cabins; cute, well-kept, sleep 4+; use of canoe or boat; full-service outfitter shares knowledge and experience; clean, private bunkhouses; boat, motor, and canoe rental; beach. Open seasonally.
318 South Hungry Jack Road, 28 miles up the Gunflint Trail and 2 miles in
$–$$
D/MC/V
(218) 388-2275 or (800) 648-2922
hjo.com
NUMBER OF CABINS: 2
PETS: No

HUNGRY JACK LODGE

On Hungry Jack Lake; beautiful log lodge; cozy to deluxe housekeeping cabins with decks and docks; bar, lounge, and dining room. Marina, dock, bait and tackle; sauna and beach; boat, motor, and canoe rental; partial outfitting. Open year-round.
318 South Hungry Jack Road,
28 miles up the Gunflint Trail and 2 miles in
$$
MC/V/D/AE
(218) 388-2265 or (800) 338-1566
hungryjacklodge.com
NUMBER OF CABINS: 13
PETS: Yes

NOR'WESTER LODGE

On Poplar Lake; 10 cabins and town-homes with 1 to 4 bedrooms; fire-places, decks, patios, and all the amenities; five RV campsites. Gift shop; sauna, whirlpool, and beach; boat and motor rentals; personal-ized, complete canoe outfitting. Open year-round.
7778 Gunflint Trail, 30 miles up the Gunflint Trail
$$-$$$
D/MC/V
(218) 388-2252 or (800) 992-4FUN
boreal.org/norwester
NUMBER OF CABINS: 10
PETS: Inquire

TRAIL CENTER LODGE

On Poplar Lake; open, airy cabin home overlooking south end of lake; cute lakeshore cabins with decks; great hosts. Main lodge has fun restaurant and bar, gifts and books, and groceries and supplies. Boat, motor, and canoe rental; beach. Open year-round.
7611 Gunflint Trail, 30 miles up the Gunflint Trail
$$
MC/V
(218) 388-2214
trailcenterlodge.com
NUMBER OF CABINS: 3
PETS: Yes

WINDIGO LODGE

On Poplar Lake; 6 classic log and pine cabins, and 3 lodge villas; dining, lounge, and liquor store. Sauna; beach; partial outfitting with boat and motor rental. Open year-round.
7890 Gunflint Trail, 32 miles up the Gunflint Trail
$$-$$$
MC/V
(218) 388-2222 or (800) 535-4320
windigolodge.com
NUMBER OF CABINS: 10
PETS: Yes

OLD NORTHWOODS LODGE

On Poplar Lake; laid-back, north-woods atmosphere; beautifully renovated original cabins; sauna and beach; see B&B chapter for guest room info. Partial outfitting, plus boat and motor rental. Gourmet northwoods restaurant serving breakfast 7 A.M. to 1 P.M.; handmade pizza and dinner 5:30 P.M. to 9 P.M.; guest chefs. Trading Post and Yelena's Gallery. Open year-round.
7969 Gunflint Trail, 32 miles up the Gunflint Trail and a quarter-mile in
$$–$$$
AE/MC/V
(218) 388-9464 or (800) 682-8264
oldnorthwoods.com
NUMBER OF CABINS: 5
PETS: No

ROCKWOOD LODGE
AND OUTFITTERS

On Poplar Lake; rustic lodge with private dining and lounge; trading post; bunkhouse; very nice one- to three-bedroom cabins; deluxe cabins on Austin's Island; sauna and beach; complete outfitters. Open seasonally.
50 Rockwood Road, 33 miles up the Gunflint Trail and a quarter-mile in
$–$$$
D/MC/V
(218) 388-2242 or (800) 942-2922
rockwoodbwca.com
NUMBER OF CABINS: 7
PETS: No

LOON LAKE LODGE

Only resort on Loon Lake; cozy 1920s resort with modernized rustic 1- to 3-bedroom housekeeping cabins; beach; boat, motor, and canoe rental. Meals, conveniences, and souvenirs in lodge. Open seasonally (May through fall).
65 Loon Lake Road, 40 miles up the Gunflint Trail and a half-mile in
$$–$$$
D/MC/V
(218) 388-2232 or (800) 552-6351
boreal.org/loonlake
NUMBER OF CABINS: 8
PETS: Yes

GUNFLINT LODGE

On Gunflint Lake; third-generation innkeepers; the Gunflint Trail's largest resort; *all* the amenities, including conference center, massage therapist, pontoons, fishing boats, kayaks, mountain bikes, cross-country skis, snowshoes; loads of wonderful packages; adept wedding hosts, complete outfitters, guide service, excellent dining, saunas and spas, and programs. Open year-round.
143 South Gunflint Lake, 45 miles up the Gunflint Trail and three-quarters of a mile in
$$–$$$$
AE/D/MC/V/DC/CB
(218) 388-2294 or (800) 328-3325
gunflint.com
NUMBER OF CABINS: 23
PETS: Yes

GUNFLINT PINES

On Gunflint Lake; 20 campsites, 4 with camping cabins; and 4 modern, private A-frames; 3 cottages; firelit lodge with gifts, quick foods (8 A.M. to 8 P.M. seasonally); beach area; sauna; boat, 15-hp 4-stroke motor, canoe, snowshoe, and snowmobile rental. Open year-round.

217 South Gunflint Lake, 45 miles up the Gunflint Trail and 1 mile in

$–$$$

AE/D/MC/V

(218) 388-4454 or (800) 533-5814

www.gunflintpines.com

NUMBER OF CABINS: 7

PETS: Yes!

HESTON'S LODGE AND COUNTRY STORE

On Gunflint Lake; modern or rustic cabins in secluded virgin pine stands; country store with espresso; sauna and beach; boat, motor, and canoe rental. New observatory with view platform and resource room; new wood-fired communal oven. Open year-round.

579 South Gunflint Lake, 45 miles up the Gunflint Trail and 3 miles in

$$–$$$

D/MC/V

(218) 388-2243 or (800) 338-7230

hestons.com

NUMBER OF CABINS: 8

PETS: No

MOOSEHORN LODGE CABINS AND B&B

Two-bedroom villa with full kitchen and living room; 4 cabins with 2 to 4 bedrooms, kitchen, fireplace, deck with grill, and use of canoe. Lodge has a firelit gathering room and 2 B&B rooms. Sauna; pontoon, boats, and motors. Open year-round.

47 miles up the Gunflint Trail and 2 miles in on North Gunflint Lake

$$–$$$

MC/V

(218) 388-2233 or (800) 238-5975

moosehorn.com

NUMBER OF CABINS: 5

PETS: No

TUSCARORA LODGE AND OUTFITTERS

On Round Lake; 5 housekeeping cabins on lake; 2 to 3 bedrooms, include use of canoe; bunkhouse accommodations include shower and bathroom facilities; each sleeps 10; sauna and beach; full-service outfitters for trips into BWCAW, plus tow service on Saganaga Lake. Open seasonally.

193 Round Lake Road, 48 miles up the Gunflint Trail and 1 mile in on Round Lake

$–$$

MC/V

(218) 388-2221 or (800) 544-3843

tuscaroracanoe.com

NUMBER OF CABINS: 5

PETS: No

SEAGULL CREEK FISHING CAMP

Cabins and a bunkhouse on Seagull Creek; family beach and picnic area. Excellent fishing guides; boat and motor rental. Open year-round.
12056 Gunflint Trail, 55 miles up the Gunflint Trail
$$
credit cards not accepted
(218) 388-9929 or (800) 531-5510
seagullcreekfishingcamp.com
NUMBER OF CABINS: 3
PETS: Yes

SEAGULL CANOE OUTFITTERS

On Seagull Lake; complete outfitters rent five cabins on Seagull and Saganaga Lakes; all cabins are complete with kitchens, bathrooms, and bedrooms; some have decks and fireplaces.
12208 Gunflint Trail, 55 miles up the Gunflint Trail
(218) 388-2216 or (800) 346-2205
seagulloutfitters.com
NUMBER OF CABINS: 5

SPIRIT OF THE LAND AYH HOSTEL

On an island on Seagull Lake; lake transportation is available. Two cabins, one for men and one for women, each sleeps six; common lounge with kitchen and dining area; showers and outhouses nearby. From $17 to $19 per person per night.
12477 Gunflint Trail, 55 miles up the Gunflint Trail
(218) 388-2241 or (800) 454-2922
wildernesscanoebase.org
NUMBER OF CABINS: 2
PETS: No

BOUNDARY WATERS ADVENTURES LOG CABIN RENTAL

Wonderful 75-year-old log cabin on Seagull Lake; walk-in cabin sleeps up to 4; 1-room cabin with screen porch and bunkhouse; very well equipped – modern conveniences, yet rustic; queen bed, fireplace, grill, lawn chairs, hammock, canoe, 16' x 16' floating dock. Open Memorial Day to Labor Day.
(800) 894-0128
members.aol.com/gunflint/bwa
NUMBER OF CABINS: 1
PETS: Some

VOYAGEUR CANOE OUTFITTERS

On Seagull River. Across the river are two cabins, 1 deluxe riverside cabin and 1 rustic secluded cabin (walk to bath/shower house for facilities), bunkhouses that sleep up to 4; toilet/shower facilities. On the mainland side are 2 deluxe loft condos available year-round, bunkhouses, and a bathhouse. Open year-round.
189 Sag Lake Trail, 55 miles up the Gunflint Trail and 1 mile in
$-$$$
AE/D/MC/V
(218) 388-2224 or (800) 777-7215
canoeit.com
NUMBER OF CABINS: 2
NUMBER OF CONDOS: 2
PETS: Inquire

WAY OF THE WILDERNESS GULL CHALETS

On Seagull River; two bunkhouse chalets, each with sleeping lofts, kitchen, bathroom, and deck. Trail End Cafe serves breakfast through dinner, beer, and pizza 8 a.m. to 8 p.m. daily; trading post. Hosts for adjacent Trail's End Campground and Iron Lake and Kimball Campgrounds. Open seasonally.
12582 Gunflint Trail, 56 miles up the Gunflint Trail
$$
MC/V
(218) 388-2212 or (800) 346-6625
wayofthewilderness.com
NUMBER OF CABINS: 2
PETS: Some

Daylight in the Swamps!

CAMPGROUNDS

COURTS AND CAMPS ARE THE ONLY PLACES
TO LEARN THE WORLD IN.

Earl of Chesterfield, October 2, 1747

THE MAJORITY OF NORTHEASTERN MINNESOTA IS PUBLIC
forest. The Superior National Forest covers more than three million
acres, including the million-acre Boundary Waters Canoe Area
Wilderness (BWCAW). Add to this the thousands of acres of state park and
state forest land, plus privately held preserves. Welcome to the north woods.

The attractions here for campers include virgin pine, roaring waterfalls,
rare orchids, noble timber wolves, and, always, the adjoining expanse of Lake
Superior. Accessibility is relative. The more primitive, solitary spots are typically farthest from the hubs along the shore. Several privately operated
campgrounds are clustered on the outskirts of Duluth, along Scenic 61, near
the villages along Superior's coast, and up the Gunflint Trail. Every state park
but one is a step off Highway 61.

Although camping is allowed anywhere in the Superior National Forest
except where posted otherwise, the ranger stations maintain a number of
designated campgrounds. All have picnic tables, fishing, fire grates, toilets,
and drinking water (unless otherwise noted). All have RV-accessible sites (no
hookups, though), and all sites are first-come, first-served. Fees vary; the
2003 rates are given below. For additional information, stop by the Tofte or
Gunflint Ranger Stations, or call them at (218) 663-7280 and (218) 387-1750,
respectively.

To protect the integrity of the BWCAW, permits are required for entry and each entry point has a daily quota. See the bwcaw chapter ("Our Back-yard") for additional information.

U.S. FOREST SERVICE CAMPGROUNDS IN COOK COUNTY

NINEMILE LAKE CAMPGROUND
Tucked back in the woods with several of its 23 sites along the lake, this campground features a boat launch, an area for large groups, and a five-mile hiking trail. Rates are $9 per night.

From Highway 61 in Schroeder, go north on Co. Rd. 1 for 10 miles, then east on Co. Rd. 7 for 4 miles.

FOUR MILE AND TOUHEY LAKES (RUSTIC)
Nice little wooded sites! No drinking water; picnic tables and outhouse; 4 sites and a dock at Four Mile, 5 sites at Touhey. Fish for walleye and northern.

From Highway 61 in Schroeder, go north on the Temperance River Road, west on Forest Rd. 166, north on the Richey Lake Road, west on The Grade where you will come first to Four Mile, then Touhey Lake.

TEMPERANCE RIVER CAMPGROUND
This campground is just far enough off the highway for you to feel like you are in the woods, but still close enough to get fresh rolls and lattes in the morning. Some of the nine sites are on the Temperance River. The rate is $10 per night.

From Highway 61 in Tofte, go north on the Sawbill Trail (Co. Rd. 2) for 12 miles; the campground is on the west.

SAWBILL LAKE CAMPGROUND
This big campground has lots to do! Check out the barrier-free fishing pier, interpretive nature trail, large-group area, and picnic area. In addition, it is an entry point for the bwcaw, which adds to its popularity – have a backup campground in mind. Nearby Sawbill Outfitters has canoe rentals, firewood, permits, gifts, and some sundry and grocery items. The 50 sites cost $10 per night.

From Highway 61 in Tofte, go north on the Sawbill Trail (Co. Rd. 2) for 25 miles; the campground is on the west.

BAKER LAKE (RUSTIC)

This backcountry campground offers five secluded spots, a boat launch, and access to the BWCAW. No drinking water is available, and no fee is charged.

From Highway 61 in Tofte, go north on the Sawbill Trail (Co. Rd. 2) for 16 miles, then east on Forest Rd. 170.

CRESCENT LAKE CAMPGROUND

A nice, spread-out, midsize campground, Crescent Lake has a barrier-free fishing pier and campsite, a boat launch, and large-group facilities. Catch crawfish, jig for walleye, and hike the shoreline trails. The 33 sites are available for $10 per night.

From Highway 61 in Tofte, go north on the Sawbill Trail (Co. Rd. 2), then east on Forest Rd. 170; or from Highway 61 in Lutsen, go north on the Caribou Trail (Co. Rd. 4), then west on Forest Rd. 165.

WHITE PINE LAKE (RUSTIC)

Three backcountry sites are set near the boat launch and barrier-free fishing pier. No drinking water is available, and no fees are charged.

From Highway 61 in Lutsen, go north on the Caribou Trail (Co. Rd. 4) for seven miles, then west on Forest Rd. 164 for three miles.

CLARA LAKE (RUSTIC)

Clara Lake and White Pine are similar – three quiet, backcountry spots without much traffic. Clara also has a boat launch, but is quieter. No drinking water is available, and no fees are charged.

From Highway 61, go north on the Caribou Trail (Co. Rd. 4) for nine miles, then west on Forest Rd. 340 for three miles.

CASCADE RIVER (RUSTIC)

This pretty little area has four campsites and a day-use picnic area on the river. No drinking water is available, and no fees are charged.

From Highway 61, go north on the Caribou Trail (Co. Rd. 4) for 20 miles, then east on Forest Rd. 170, and south on Forest Rd. 158 to the junction with Co. Rd. 57.

DEVIL TRACK LAKE CAMPGROUND

Devil Track is a great family spot. It is close to Grand Marais and has a swimming beach, carry-down boat access, a picnic site, berry picking, and a boat launch a half-mile east. The 16 sites are $12 per night.

From Highway 61 in Grand Marais, go north on the Gunflint Trail (Co. Rd. 12) for four miles, then west on Co. Rd. 8 for eight miles.

TWO ISLAND LAKE CAMPGROUND

Two Island appeals to anglers, with some of the 38 sites along this fishing lake, a boat launch, and other fishing lakes nearby. A $12 per night fee is charged.

From Highway 61 in Grand Marais, go north on the Gunflint Trail (Co. Rd. 12) for four miles, west on Co. Rd. 8 for six miles, and north on Co. Rd. 27 for four miles.

KIMBALL LAKE CAMPGROUND

Kimball is a designated trout lake, which means you are required to purchase a trout stamp for your fishing license. This is a nice little campground with 10 sites and a trail around the lake, and nearby Mink Lake has a barrier-free fishing pier and swimming beach. A $12 to $14 per night fee is charged.

From Highway 61 in Grand Marais, go north on the Gunflint Trail (Co. Rd. 12) for 11 miles, then east on Forest Rd. 140 for 2 miles.

TWIN LAKES (RUSTIC)

Three primitive drive-in sites set between East and West Twin Lakes. Picnic table, outhouse, fire ring. No fees charged. Fish and swim!

From Highway 61 in Grand Marais, go north on the Gunflint Trail, 6 miles west on the South Brule Road, and 4 miles south on the Lima Grade.

EAST BEARSKIN LAKE CAMPGROUND

Camp adjacent to the BWCAW! The 33 sites are in the woods and along the shores of the lake, which is partially within the Boundary Waters. To boat on that portion of the lake, a permit is required, and motor size is limited to 25 hp. A $12 per night fee is charged.

From Highway 61 in Grand Marais, go north on the Gunflint Trail (Co. Rd. 12) for 25 miles, then east on Forest Rd. 146 for 1 mile.

Reservations accepted: call (877) 444-6777, or reserveusa.com

FLOUR LAKE CAMPGROUND

The 35 sites at Flour Lake campground are spread out. Hike the nearby Honeymoon Bluff trail (see hiking chapter for more info), or enjoy an evening of fishing. A fee of $12 to $14 per night is charged.

From Highway 61 in Grand Marais, go north on the Gunflint Trail (Co. Rd. 12) for 27 miles, then east on Clearwater Road (Co. Rd. 66).

Reservations accepted: call (877) 444-6777, or reserveusa.com

BIRCH LAKE (RUSTIC)

Take the steep carry-down access to 1 primitive site on this rainbow and lake trout lake. Outhouse. No fees.

From Highway 61 in Grand Marais, go north on the Gunflint Trail to the Birch Lake access sign; go east to parking.

IRON LAKE CAMPGROUND

Iron Lake offers seven secluded forest sites and carry-down boat access. The campground is a few miles off the Gunflint Trail and feels very deep in the woods. A $12 to $14 per night fee is charged.

From Highway 61 in Grand Marais, go north on the Gunflint Trail (Co. Rd. 12) for 36 miles, then south on Old Gunflint Trail for 2 miles to the camp entrance.

Reservations accepted: call (877) 444-6777, or reserveusa.com

TRAILS END CAMPGROUND

This popular campground is the final destination of the Gunflint Trail. Many people use it as a starting point for trips into the BWCAW, Quetico Provincial Park, and Saganaga Lake. The 33 sites are spread out, with some very nice sites on the ridge overlooking the Seagull River. Features include two boat launches; two boat accesses; nearby phone, gas, groceries, and sundry items; Trail's End Cafe; some water hookups; and ideal wildlife viewing. A fee of $12 to $16 per night is charged.

From Highway 61 in Grand Marais, go north on the Gunflint Trail (Co. Rd. 12) for 56 miles to the campground entrance.

Reservations accepted: call (877) 444-6777, or reserveusa.com

DEVILFISH, CHESTER, AND ESTHER LAKES (RUSTIC)

Secluded primitive campsites north of Hovland in the Grand Portage State Forest. Devilfish has 2 drive-in sites, a dock, swimming, fishing, picnic tables, and an outhouse. Chester has 1 drive-in site with a picnic table and outhouse; designated trout lake; good swimming. Esther has 3 drive-in sites on a small, beautiful lake; fish, swim; picnic tables and outhouse; no fees charged.

From Highway 61 in Hovland, go north on the Arrowhead Trail 11 miles, west on the Esther Lake Road 5½ miles to Devilfish Lake, 6 miles to Chester Lake, and 7 miles to Esther Lake.

MCFARLAND LAKE (RUSTIC)

At the end of the Arrowhead Trail; 2 drive-in campsites, 2 picnic sites; a dock, fishing, swimming, picnic tables, and outhouses. Access to the BWCAW and Border Route hiking trail.

> From Highway 61 in Hovland, go north on the Arrowhead Trail almost 18 miles to McFarland Lake.

FINLAND STATE FOREST CAMPGROUNDS

SULLIVAN LAKE CAMPGROUND

Most of the 11 sites at this small, secluded campground are along Sullivan Lake. The campground features a boat launch, 2 nature trails, 4 day-use picnic sites, fire rings, picnic tables, outhouses, and drinking water. Sites are available first-come, first-served, and a fee of $10 per night is charged.

> From Highway 61 in Two Harbors, go north on Co. Rd. 2 for 26 miles, then east on Co. Rd. 15 for 0.5 mile.
>
> (218) 226-6377 (Split Rock Lighthouse State Park)

ECKBECK CAMPGROUND

Eckbeck often serves as an overflow area for campers who haven't found a spot along Superior's shores. Located on the Baptism River, the campground has 30 drive-in sites. Six very nice sites are along the river. The campground has 4 day-use picnic sites, fire rings, picnic tables, outhouses, and drinking water from a flowing well. Sites are available first-come, first-served, and a fee of $10 per night is charged.

> From Highway 61 in Illgen City, go north on Minnesota 1 for three miles.
>
> (218) 226-6365 (Tettegouche State Park)

FINLAND CAMPGROUND

Finland offers 39 drive-in campsites spread out along the Baptism River and tucked in the woods. A great picnic site is available across the river. You can get to it from Minnesota 1 – watch for signs. The campground has 4 day-use picnic sites, fire rings, picnic tables, outhouses, and drinking water from a flowing well. Sites are available first-come, first-served, and a fee of $10 per night is charged.

> From Highway 61 in Illgen City, go north on Minnesota 1 for six miles to Finland, then east on Co. Rd. 6 for 0.25 mile.
>
> (218) 226-6365 (Tettegouche State Park)

STATE PARK CAMPGROUNDS

State park campgrounds offer 24 to 80 sites each, including rustic, backpack, cart-in, and modern sites. Refer to the state park chapter for details.

PRIVATE AND MUNICIPAL CAMPGROUNDS IN DULUTH

BUFFALO VALLEY CAMPGROUND

This campground has more than 100 tent and RV sites with hookups and is located at the midpoint of the Willard Munger State Trail, so campers can take advantage of the excellent hiking and biking opportunities. Hot showers; off-sale beer and ice. Full restaurant and bar on site, plus volleyball and softball areas. Rates range from $20 to $26.

> 2590 Guss Road
> (218) 624-9901
> buffalohouse.com

SPIRIT MOUNTAIN CAMPGROUND

Overlooking Duluth, the St. Louis River, and Lake Superior are 73 pull-through or secluded tent and RV sites. Guests often hike the cross-country ski trail system. Rates are $15 to $25.

> At Spirit Mountain
> (218) 624-8544 or (800) 642-6377 x544
> spiritmt.com

FOND DU LAC CAMPGROUND

Primarily used by anglers during the opener and early fishing season, Fond du Lac is on the St. Louis River. They offer toilets, picnic tables, fire rings, and drinking water and charge $15 to $18 per site, or $1 to park and $3 to use the boat launch. No reservations, first-come, first-served.

> 134th Avenue West and Highway 23
> (218) 749-5388
> members.aol.com/launch8000/camp.htm

INDIAN POINT CAMPGROUND

Indian Point is on the St. Louis River and has 70 wooded tent and RV sites, some with hookups. Showers, laundry, ice, firewood, snacks, arcade, playground; canoe and bike rentals. The campground is adjacent to the Western

Waterfront Trail and Willard Munger state hiking and biking trail. Rates range from $17 to $23 daily and $119 to $161 weekly.

75th Avenue West and Grand Avenue/Highway 23

(218) 624-5637 or (800) 982-2453

indianpointcampground.com

RIVER PLACE CAMPGROUND

Full hook-up sites on city water and sewer; on the St. Louis River. Boat launch, docks, bait. By the night, week, month, or season. Call for rates.

From I-35, take Highway 23 south just past Boy Scout Landing.

(218) 626-1390

LAKEHEAD BOAT BASIN

On Park Point, especially for boaters; 30 blacktop RV parking sites, 12 with full hook-ups. Bathrooms, showers, laundry, dump station, boat dockage; $15 to $34 per night.

1000 Minnesota Avenue, 3 blocks south of Aerial Lift Bridge

(218) 722-1757 or (800) 777-8436

lakeheadboatbasin.com

THE PARK

A few RV sites with full hook-ups north of the Miller Hill Mall area. Great deli.

5109 Miller Trunk Highway

(218) 729-5087

SNOWFLAKE CENTER

Secluded, wooded winter cross-country ski site offers primitive, walk-in tent sites with picnic tables and fire rings. Chalet has restrooms and showers, phone, snacks, firewood. $10 to $13 per night. Alcohol- and tobacco-free. 18-hole disc golf course.

4348 Rice Lake Road (¼ mile north of Arrowhead Road)

(218) 726-1550 or (218) 724-9022

skiduluth.com

ISLAND BEACH CAMPGROUND AND RESORT

Deluxe campground on Island Lake, 20 miles north of downtown Duluth. Rates for the 47 primitive and RV hookup sites are $16 to $17, with weekly rates from $96 to $102. Four cabins are available at up to $100 per night. Activities center on the lake and include swimming and fishing. The on-site store sells gas, bait, and licenses and rents boats, motors, canoes, and paddleboats. Docking space is available near the boat launch. Other amenities include hot shower and laundry facilities, a game room, volleyball, basketball, and horseshoes.

6640 Fredenberg Lake Road
(218) 721-3292
northwoods.net

CAMPGROUNDS ON SCENIC 61 TO TWO HARBORS

DULUTH TENT AND TRAILER
Near Duluth, the 54 sites are set among beautiful large pines. Primitive and RV hookups are available for $17 to $19 per night. Clean washrooms, shower, and laundry.

8411 Congdon Boulevard
(218) 525-1350

KNIFE RIVER CAMPGROUND
Located on the western side of Knife River near the marina; 30 tent and trailer sites with full hookups; cobblestone Lake Superior beach, the community of Knife River, and local hiking and biking trails. Primarily a fishermen's destination. Children's play area. From $19 per night.

Scenic 61 at Knife River
(218) 834-5044

BIG BLAZE CAMPGROUND AND CABINS
Right on Lake Superior's shores, Big Blaze has 40 tent and RV sites with hookups for $24 to $35 per night. Most sites are somewhat wooded. Besides enjoying the big lake, you can hike and bike in the area.

560 Big Blaze Circle
(218) 834-2512
bigblaze.com

WAGON WHEEL CAMPGROUND
Lake Superior shoreline campsites. Most are RV sites with full hookups, but they do offer six tent sites. Rates are $21 to $24 per night.

552 Old North Shore Road
(218) 834-4901

PENMARALLTER CAMPSITES
Open-area campground between Highway 61 and Scenic 61 with spacious, pull-through sites with full hook-ups, firepits, and picnic tables; showers and toilets.

725 Scenic Drive

(218) 834-4691

BURLINGTON BAY CAMPSITE
Explore Two Harbors from this Lake Superior coastal campground. Twenty tent sites and 91 trailer sites with full hookups stretch along the shore and inland, just across from the golf course and adjacent to the local visitors center.

Highway 61 in Two Harbors at Burlington Bay

(218) 834-2021 and off-season (218) 834-5631

CAMPGROUNDS FROM BEAVER BAY TO GRAND MARAIS

NORTHERN EXPOSURE CAMPGROUND
Some open, some semi-wooded RV and tent sites with some hook-ups; picnic tables, fire rings. Shower/bath house with convenience items.

On Highway 61 a few miles northeast of Silver Bay

(218) 226-3324

CROOKED LAKE RESORT, THE LODGE AT NINE MILE LAKE, AND WILDHURST LODGE AND CAMPGROUND
See the lodging chapter for info on these Finland-area campgrounds.

LAMB'S CAMPGROUND AND RESORT
Lamb's offers 100 private tent and RV sites tucked in the woods or along a half-mile of cobblestone beach. Amenities include hookups, showers, hiking, fishing, plus 15 log housekeeping cabins. This scenic campground showcases the Cross River. Enjoy the gift shop!

In Schroeder, on the Cross River and Lake Superior

(218) 663-7292

boreal.org/lambsresort

GRAND MARAIS CAMPGROUND AND REC AREA

The campground has more than 300 tent and trailer sites, including water-front sites. Rates range from $14 to $20. The full-service Rec Area is walking distance to downtown shops, attractions, and restaurants and features a picnic area, pavilion, playground, public boat launch and docks, plus an indoor Olympic-size swimming pool, children's pool, Jacuzzi, and sauna. Ask about their wooded hillside sites and lakeside sites!

On the Grand Marais harbor

(218) 387-1712 or (800) 998-0959

CAMPGROUNDS ON THE GUNFLINT TRAIL

OKONTOE FAMILY CAMPSITES AND HORSE CAMPING

32 tent and trailer sites, most lakeside or lake view on the shores of Bow Lake and River. Amenities include hiking trails, a swimming beach, fishing, a playground, and small camp store. 13 spacious horse sites (up to 50' x 90') with 30' by 7' high stationary cable stakeout with space for 4 horses; bring proof of cogging test within last 6 months. Rates start at $20.

On Bow Lake

(218) 388-2285

okontoe.com

GOLDEN EAGLE LODGE

Nine tent and RV campsites in a wooded area. Each site has electric, water, picnic table, and fire ring. Enjoy all the lodge amenities! New shower house. Rates from $22.

On Flour Lake

(218) 388-2203 or (800) 346-2203

golden-eagle.com

HUNGRY JACK LODGE AND CAMPGROUND

Twelve tent and RV sites with hookups, dump station, fishing, rentals, swimming, hiking, a playground, and lodge. Rates are $25 per night.

On Hungry Jack Lake

(218) 388-2265 or (800) 388-1566

hungryjacklodge.com

NOR'WESTER LODGE
Nor'wester offers five RV campsites with hookups, a sand beach, and a playground, plus cabins, villas, a gift shop, and complete outfitters.

7778 Gunflint Trail on Poplar Lake

(218) 388-2252 or (800) 992-4FUN

boreal.org/norwester

WINDIGO LODGE
Windigo has 10 campsites in addition to their cabins, villas, and main lodge. Rates start at $22.

7890 Gunflint Trail on Poplar Lake

(218) 388-2222 or (800) 535-4320

windigolodge.com

GUNFLINT PINES CAMPGROUND AND RESORT
Gunflint Pines combines the best of camping with all the amenities of a resort. The campground has 20 campsites, 7 premium lakefront, 2 lakefront tent-only, 7 water and electric, and 4 camping cabins that sleep up to 5; camping cabins are new buildings with bunks, a food prep area, electricity, and an outdoor water spigot so you can cook/camp outside and sleep inside. A dump station; clean bathhouse; lodge serving quick foods 8 A.M. to 8 P.M., a gift shop, and groceries; fishing with boat and motor rental; swimming; a playground; and hiking. Rates start at $20 per night. Seven modern housekeeping cabins are also available.

217 South Gunflint Lake

(218) 388-4454 or (800) 533-5814

gunflintpines.com

ISLE ROYALE

Refer to the Isle Royale chapter ("National Parks and Monuments") for information on camping on the island.

Out and About

CRUISIN' AND PLAYIN' THE RADIO,
WITH NO PARTICULAR PLACE TO GO.

Chuck Berry

Good Eats

DINING

I WOULD GLADLY PAY YOU TUESDAY
FOR A HAMBURGER TODAY.

Wimpy

WHERE SHOULD YOU EAT? THAT ALL DEPENDS. WHAT DO you like to eat? Are you looking for good food, or good food and an experience? I've got suggestions for both. Let's begin with my favorite dining stops in Duluth.

DULUTH

In the Mood for Charbroiled Steaks and Great Service

PICKWICK RESTAURANT
Menu selections feature delicious charcoal-broiled meats and seafoods, including their famous pepper cheeseburger. This place really hops, so be prepared to tip back a frothy, dark draft beer while you wait, or make a reservation, not accepted Friday or Saturday night. Their only downfall is they are wise enough to take a day off – Sundays.

508 East Superior Street, downtown
(218) 727-8901

Looking for Fresh Ingredients and a Gourmet Flair

BENNETT'S BAR AND GRILL
Bennett's produces distinctive handmade entrees using the freshest possible ingredients. They serve a delectable Sunday brunch, which is rounded off with a panoramic view of Lake Superior.
  Fitger's Complex, downtown
  (218) 722-2829

LAKE AVENUE CAFE
Lake Avenue has wonderfully seasoned, appealing lunch and dinner entrees, and they often offer a vegetarian entree.
  Dewitt-Seitz Marketplace, Canal Park
  (218) 722-2355

Something Not So Scandinavian

TASTE OF SAIGON
They have a variety of Chinese and Vietnamese specialties and an excellent choice of vegetarian entrees.
  Dewitt-Seitz Marketplace, Canal Park
  (218) 727-1598

HACIENDA DEL SOL
Savor hand-prepared authentic meals or a la carte items served as spicy as you like. The summer patio is a remarkably secluded place to sip a cool beer or chat over sangria. They have a kids' menu, too!
  319 East Superior Street, downtown
  (218) 722-7296

THAI KRATHONG
Spicy, peanutty, delicious Thai entrees served for lunch and dinner. Beer and wine offered.
  114 West First Street, downtown
  (218) 733-9774

INDIA PALACE
A large variety of authentic Indian dishes. Sample several at the daily lunch buffett (11:30 A.M. to 2 P.M.) or choose from the menu at dinner (5 P.M. to close).

319 West Superior Street, downtown
(218) 727-8767

A Little Italian and a Lot of Wine

BELLISIO'S ITALIAN RESTAURANT

Bellisio's offers the best wine selection and the only flights of wine north of the Twin Cities. The entrees made with all fresh ingredients are excellent.

405 Lake Avenue South in Canal Park

(218) 727-4921

I've Got a Hankering for a Coney Island

You can't beat a coney island hot dog from either place.

THE ORIGINAL CONEY ISLAND

105 East Superior Street, downtown

(218) 723-7861

CONEY ISLAND DELUXE

112 West 1st Street, downtown

(218) 722-2772

Miller Hill Mall

(218) 722-5403

Breakfast with a View

BUENA VISTA

Watch ship activity from this hilltop restaurant. Ask for a window seat and enjoy the start to your day.

1144 Mesaba Avenue, on the hill above downtown Duluth

(218) 722-9047

A Slow-Spinning Sunday Brunch

TOP OF THE HARBOR

Enjoy an oversized Sunday brunch in this revolving carousel restaurant atop the Radisson Hotel.

505 West Superior Street, downtown

(218) 727-8981

Sandwich with a View

SIR BENEDICT'S ON THE LAKE
A renovated service garage on the National Register of Historic Places, Sir Ben's makes sandwiches to order. They also offer a vast beer selection, wine, and outdoor seating with unobstructed views of Lake Superior.
805 East Superior Street, downtown
(218) 728-1192

All Cream, All Natural Ice Cream

PORTLAND SQUARE MALT SHOP
Ice cream fanatics will drop their cones in delight.
Just east of the Fitger's Complex, downtown

Summertime Deck Dining (Wintertime Deck Dining Never Took Off)

GRANDMA'S SALOON AND GRILL
Wave at sailors from exotic ports! Lunch, dinner, and cocktails at the foot of the Aerial Lift Bridge.
522 Lake Avenue South, Canal Park
(218) 727-4192

A Really Good Beer

FITGER'S BREWHOUSE AND GRILL
Tip back a fresh, hand-crafted ale; to go with it they have burgers, sandwiches, soups, vegetarian entrees, and salads. Live entertainment.
600 East Superior Street, in Fitger's Complex
(218) 726-1392

Where to Eat When You're Back for a Visit to the Old Neighborhood

CHESTER CREEK CAFE
Small, artsy, innovative menu for lunch and dinner. Beer and wine. Espresso drinks and baked items from At Sara's Table.
1902 East Eighth Street, near UMD
(218) 724-6811

BIXBY'S BAGELS
Big selection of tender bagels and tasty toppings, espresso bar, and light menu served lunch and dinner.
16002 Woodland Avenue, near UMD
(218) 724-8444

BULLDOG PIZZA
Good food, friendly folks, beer and wine. Watch 'em make pizzas! Nearby yarn shop and Mount Royal branch of the library make this a good rainy day stop.
Mount Royal Shopping Center, off 1600 Woodland Avenue
(218) 728-3663

A Really Good Pizza

PIZZA LUCÉ
All your favorite traditional 'zas plus great gourmet variations; appetizers, pasta, hoagies, salads, vegan and vegetarian specialties. Lunch, dinner, and late night. Eat in, take out, delivery.
340 Lake Avenue South, downtown
(218) 727-7002

Really, We'd Love to Bring Dinner

The following offer very tasty soups, salads, entrees and dessert. Grab a bottle of wine and you're done!

COCOS TO GEAUX
320 West Superior Street, downtown
(218) 740-3039

SAVORIES FINE FOODS TO GO
5 South 13th Avenue East, near the Rose Garden east of downtown
(218) 625-5555

GALLAGHERS CAFE D'WHEELS
Homemade meals like Mom used to make!
5231 East Superior Street, east Duluth
(218) 729-7100

NORTH SHORE PICKS

Since dining options can be limited along the North Shore, I will make my
suggestions and list the additional establishments. My favorites on the Shore,
in geographical order, are New Scenic Cafe, anytime; Russ Kendall's Smoke
House for snacks, beer, and conversation; Vanilla Bean Cafe and Bakery for
lunch and dinner; Kamloops for dinner; Rustic Inn for breakfast and pie; bread
and wine at Coho Cafe; holiday brunch at Lutsen Resort; seafood deli items at
Dockside Fish Market; pastries and dinner at Victoria's Bakehouse; mussels
at the Harbor Inn; Sven and Ole's for beer, peanuts, and a Vild Vun pizza; East
Bay Hotel for Scandinavian coffee and raisin rye toast; the Java Moose for cafe
lattes; Gunflint Tavern for a beer and great soup and sandwiches; Trail Center
anytime; and Naniboujou Lodge for high tea and Sunday brunch.

ALONG SCENIC 61

LAKEVIEW CASTLE DINING ROOM
Breakfast, lunch, and dinner; Greek specialties; food served in the lounge, too.
5135 Scenic 61
(218) 525-1014

SHORECREST SUPPER CLUB
Delightful vintage supper club featuring steak and seafood.
5593 Scenic 61
(218) 525-2286

NEW SCENIC CAFE
Fresh food with flair! Creative menu items, specials, and desserts; nice beer
and wine list; hearty breakfasts; kids' menu; no smoking; great lake view.

5461 Scenic 61
(218) 525-6274
sceniccafe.com

RUSS KENDALL'S SMOKE HOUSE
Smoked fish is a topic of great debate at our house. I am a Russ Kendall devotee, and my husband Bill is a Mel's man. Russ's fish is moist and exudes the subtle smoky flavor. Russ also stocks cheese and crackers, homemade jerky, draft beer, and antiques.
Scenic 61 at Knife River
(218) 834-5995

EMILY'S 1929 EATERY, INN, AND DELI
Pick up your picnic supplies here. Traditional fish boils on Fridays from February through October. Great breakfasts. Hearty lunches.
Scenic 61 at Knife River
(218) 834-5922
emilyseatery.com

MEL'S FISH HOUSE
I'll admit it's pretty tasty smoked fish. Open seasonally.
Scenic 61 at Knife River
(218) 834-5858

TWO HARBORS

BLUEBERRY HOUSE BAKERY
Muffins and gooey sweets.
Highway 61
(218) 834-5726

VANILLA BEAN BAKERY AND CAFE
The bakery has a nice assortment of flavorful breads, rolls, buns, focaccia, sticky buns, not-so-sticky buns, donuts, and the like. The cafe offers a nice alternative menu with some favorite standbys for breakfast, lunch, and dinner. Specials and new menu items!
Highway 61
(218) 834-3714

THE LANDING
Sports bar and restaurant.
> Highway 61
> (218) 834-5191

JUDY'S CAFE AND BAKERY
Fresh baked goods, homemade meals, and hospitable service.
> Highway 61
> (218) 834-4802

SUPERIOR'S CHOICE FISH MARKET
Fresh and smoked fish from a fourth-generation commercial fisherman; lots
of other goodies, too.
> Highway 61
> (218) 834-3719
> superiorschoicefish.com

BLACKWOODS BAR AND GRILL
Breakfast, lunch, and dinner, with hardwood grill specialties. Full lounge
with great beer selections and appetizers.
> Highway 61
> (218) 834-3846

AMERICAN LEGION CLUB POST 109
Lunch, dinner, and lounge. Burgers, sandwiches, and specials.
> 614 1st Avenue
> (218) 834-4141

LOU'S FISH 'N' CHEESE HOUSE
Smoked fish, jerky, and cheese. Daily fish dinner. Deep-fried cheese curds
and cheese sticks. Cool faux-log paint job!
> Highway 61
> (218) 834-5254

KAMLOOPS
Tasty, tasty, tasty! The menu has variety and showcases local fish. Restaurant
and lounge. Breakfast, lunch, and dinner.
> Highway 61 in Superior Shores Resort
> (218) 834-5671

FAST-FOOD FRANCHISES
McDonald's, Subway, Pizza Hut, Dairy Queen, Hardee's
> Highway 61

TWO HARBORS TO GRAND MARAIS

BETTY'S PIES
Famous pies and short-order menu. Beer and wine.
> Highway 61, east of Two Harbors
> (218) 834-3367

RUSTIC INN CAFE
Log cafe with happy staff; large, tasty breakfasts plus lunch, dinner, and the best made-from-scratch pies.
> Highway 61 in Castle Danger
> (218) 834-2488
> rusticinncafe.com

SPLASHING ROCK RESTAURANT
Lakeside and deck dining and lounge; open breakfast, lunch, and dinner. Classic American entrees with a gourmet twist. Take-out pizza on Friday and Saturday nights.
> At Grand Superior Lodge, Highway 61 in Castle Danger
> (218) 834-3796 or (800) 627-9565
> grandsuperior.com

COVE POINT LODGE DINING ROOM
Continental breakfast for lodge guests only. Lunch served seasonally and dinner year-round; both are open to the public. Gourmet dining in a semi-formal, intimate setting.
> Highway 61 in Beaver Bay
> (218) 226-3231 or (800) 598-3221
> covepointlodge.com

WINDSONG CAFE AND DELI
A new cafe and deli featuring dine-in and take-out menu items morning 'til evening. Stop by to sample the new menu!
> Highway 61 in Beaver Bay
> (218) 226-3231

NORTHERN LIGHTS RESTAURANT
> Open for lunch and dinner, including soup and salad bar, and
> occasionally a waffle bar.
> Highway 61 in Beaver Bay
> (218) 226-3012

BEAVER BAY INN

Full menu breakfast through dinner. Homemade items, daily specials, and a lounge.

Highway 61 in Beaver Bay

(218) 226-4351

innatbeaverbay.com

LEMON WOLF CAFE

Something just a little different and quite tasty; breakfast, lunch and dinner.

Highway 61 in Beaver Bay

(218) 226-7225

DAIRY QUEEN AND BRAZIER

96 Outer Drive in Silver Bay

NORTHWOODS CAFE

Local coffee klatch hangout. Daily specials.

Shopping center in Silver Bay

(218) 226-3699

SATELLITE COUNTRY INN

Breakfast, lunch, and dinner made by mom or someone just like her. Famous for fishcakes!

Highway 61, west of Schroeder

(218) 663-7574

SUPERIOR BAKERY

Baked sweets, bread, and espresso bar; sandwiches and lunch items.

Highway 61 in Schroeder

BREAKERS BAR AND GRILLE AND BLUEFIN RESTAURANT

The Breakers Bar and Grille serves a casual lunch and dinner menu in the lakeside lounge. The Bluefin offers lakeside dining for breakfast, lunch, and dinner. Excellent menu variety, including unexpected treats. Kids' menu.

Highway 61 in Tofte

(218) 663-6200

bluefinbay.com

COHO CAFE BAKERY AND DELI

Fresh bakery with excellent breads; incredible desserts; dine-in or take-out breakfast, lunch, and dinner at the deli; award-winning pizza.

Highway 61 in Tofte
(218) 663-8032
bluefinbay.com

LOCKPORT MARKET AND DELI
Breakfast, lunch 'til late and espressos every day of the year; sandwiches and baked treats; groceries and sundry items, too. Big, hearty, tasty pasties!

Highway 61 in Lutsen
(218) 663-7548

LUTSEN RESORT
Stunning Scandinavian architecture and large stone fireplaces accent meals in this lakeside dining room. Breakfast, lunch, and dinners, which feature gourmet entrees. Kids' menu. Poplar River Pub has a casual menu and complete list of spirits.

Highway 61 in Lutsen
(218) 663-7212
lutsenresort.com

TRACKS
Casual dining with wildlife sightings and mountainside views. Breakfast, lunch, dinner, and cocktails. Kids' menu. Black angus steaks. Pizza.

At Caribou Highlands Lodge at Lutsen Mountains
(218) 663-7316
caribouhighlands.com

CARIBOU CROSSING BAKERY AND DELI
Fresh baked pastries and sweets; sandwiches made to order; gourmet coffees and frozen yogurt.

At Caribou Highlands Lodge at Lutsen Mountains
(218) 663-7241
caribouhighlands.com

ROSIE'S CAFE AND MOUNTAIN TOP DELI
Short-order food served cafeteria-style. Rosie's is in the main chalet, and the Mountain Top Deli is atop Moose Mountain, accessible by gondola.

At Lutsen Mountains
(218) 663-7281

PAPA CHARLIE'S
Slopeside; new fine dining room, casual family dining; serving northwoods-

inspired lunch and dinner menu daily, with live entertainment in the expanded bar on weekends. Great deck overlooking Moose Mountain Valley.

At Lutsen Mountains

(218) 663-7800

CASCADE LODGE

Distinctive family restaurant serving meals throughout the day in a vintage lodge setting, overlooking Lake Superior.

Highway 61 at the Cascade River

(218) 387-2911

cascadelodgemn.com

GRAND MARAIS

THE PIE PLACE

Full menu of homemade pies and baked sweets, with changing menu for breakfast, lunch, and dinner.

Highway 61, west of Grand Marais

(218) 387-1513

HARBOR LIGHT

Informal fine dining specializing in steaks, fish, chicken, and seafood. Great burgers and more. Serving beer, wine, and cocktails.

Highway 61, west of Grand Marais

(218) 387-1142

BIRCH TERRACE

1800s home overlooking harbor; supper club menu for dinner; full fireside lounge with deck and bar menu. Kids and senior menu.

Highway 61

(218) 387-2215

DOCKSIDE FISH MARKET

Smoked fish, cheese, crackers, seafood, and fish soups and wraps and snacks. Sells local and fresh-frozen fish and seafood, too.

Highway 61 in town

(218) 387-2906

ANGRY TROUT CAFE

Fresh, tasty products, including organic and locally produced foods. Indoor and outdoor dining. Tasty pasta, fresh fish, appetizers, salads, sandwiches, and scrumptious desserts. Seasonal.

Highway 61 in town
(218) 387-1265

VICTORIA'S BAKEHOUSE AND DELI

Divine pastries! Plus fresh bread, rolls, and cookies, made-to-order sandwiches. Delicious innovative dinners. Beer, wine, espresso bar. Inside or on the deck.

Highway 61 in town
(218) 387-1747

DAIRY QUEEN AND BRAZIER

Enjoy your favorite DQ Cool Treats and Brazier Hot Eats at this great northwoods DQ. Fast, clean, and friendly.

Highway 61 in town
(218) 387-1741

SOUTH OF THE BORDER CAFE

Reasonably priced, diner breakfast and lunch served from 5 A.M. to 2 P.M.

Highway 61 in town
(218) 387-1505

MY SISTER'S PLACE

Family dining with lots of burgers, hot dogs, homemade soup and chili, appetizers, and other tasty stuff. Opens at 11 A.M. daily. Beer and wine served. *Her* sister's place is another great restaurant, Trail Center on the Gunflint Trail.

Highway 61
(218) 387-1915

HARBOR INN RESTAURANT

New innovative menu! Good food, breakfast, lunch, and dinner. When you're looking for something different. Beer and wine. Homemade pies. Overlooking the harbor.

Main street
(218) 387-2095
bytheharbor.com

GUN FLINT TAVERN
Healthy fare, eclectic menu featuring fabulous soups, wonderful sandwiches and wraps, appetizers, and desserts. Great selection of draft microbrews and small, well-selected wine menu. Live jazz and blues. Smoke-free.

Main street in town
(218) 387-1563
gunflinttavern.com

BLUE WATER CAFE
Short-order menu with homemade chili and soups. Breakfast, lunch, and dinner.

Main street in town
(218) 387-1597

SVEN AND OLE'S

Ideal family spot. Pizza, subs, salads, burgers, fries, soup, muffins, and frozen yogurt. Upstairs peanut bar, The Pickle Herring Club, offers a full bar and the Shore's largest selection of domestic and imported beer.

Main street in town
(218) 387-1713
svenandoles.com

WORLD'S BEST DONUTS
Fresh donuts, sweet rolls, and their famous Skizzle. Open seven days a week from late May through early October.

Main street in town
(218) 387-1345

EAST BAY HOTEL RESTAURANT
Traditional Scandinavian fare; steaks, fresh Lake Superior fish, and from-scratch baked goods are served breakfast, lunch, and dinner. The dining room sits on the edge of the east bay of Lake Superior. The lounge has huge carved wooden Viking dragon heads – something you don't see every day. Enjoy your favorite espresso drink with or without spirits at Breezy on the Porch.

Main street in town
(218) 387-2800

JAVA MOOSE

Two locations: Summertime java stop on the Trading Post boardwalk. Year-round espresso cafe serving hot drinks, cool beverages, sandwiches, soups, fruit, muffins, salads, cookies, and specials.

On the Lake Superior Trading Post boardwalk in town
(218) 370-1150
At the junction of Highway 61 and main street
(218) 387-9400

GUNFLINT TRAIL

BEARSKIN LODGE

Dinner by reservation only; set-price entree of the day, sirloin steak, or vegetarian choice; kids' menu, too.

124 East Bearskin Road
(218) 388-2292 or (800) 338-4170
bearskin.com

HUNGRY JACK LODGE

Family-style breakfast and dinner. Pizza anytime. Beer, wine, and set-ups.

318 South Hungry Jack Road
(218) 388-2265 or (800) 338-1566
hungryjacklodge.com

TRAIL CENTER

I like the Trail Center. I like it enough to make the 60-mile round-trip for a meal, and it's always our breakfast stop on our way fishing at Sag. They put together a great atmosphere, good variety of tasty food, and reasonable prices. Plus you can get a beer or a drink and catch up on who's doing what up the Trail.

7611 Gunflint Trail at Poplar Lake
(218) 388-2214
trailcenterlodge.com

WINDIGO LODGE
Burgers and sandwich menu for lunch and dinner. Beer and wine. Pizza, too!
7890 Gunflint Trail at Poplar Lake
(218) 388-2222 or (800) 535-4320
windigolodge.com

OLD NORTHWOODS LODGE
Hearty gourmet breakfasts from 7 A.M. to 1 P.M.; handmade pizzas; gourmet dinners 5:30 P.M. to 9 P.M. Visiting chefs. Full bar.
Old Northwoods Road on Poplar Lake
(218) 388-9464
oldnorthwoods.com

LOON LAKE LODGE
Reservations required; family-style meals, breakfast to dinner.
65 Loon Lake Road
boreal.org/loonlake
(218) 388-2232

GUNFLINT LODGE
Outstanding dinner selections include the Walleye Pistachio Nut Sausage appetizer and Roast Stuffed Pork Tenderloin with Blackberry Sauce. If at all possible, go slightly off-season to fully appreciate the food, the lodge, and the view. Open for breakfast and lunch, too. And ask about the *Gunflint Lodge Cookbook,* which includes recipes for that divine meal you just ate.
143 South Gunflint Lake
(218) 388-2294 or (800) 328-3325
gunflint.com

GUNFLINT PINES
Serving snacks, pizza, hot dogs, and quick foods all day in the summer and limited in the winter.
217 South Gunflint Lake
(218) 388-4454 or (800) 533-5814
gunflintpines.com

HESTON'S COUNTRY STORE
An espresso bar in a classic little store served up by friendly folks.
840 South Gunflint Lake
(218) 388-2243
hestons.com

TRAIL'S END CAFE

Serving a diner breakfast, lunch, dinner, and pizzas, 8 A.M. to 8 P.M. daily in the summer. Beer and snacks, too.

At the end of the Gunflint Trail
(218) 388-2217
wayofthewilderness.com

GRAND MARAIS
TO CANADIAN BORDER

NANIBOUJOU LODGE

Amazing lodge with Native American decor. Wonderful Sunday brunch, plus savory menu choices breakfast through dinner. Make the extra 20-minute drive from Grand Marais to eat at Naniboujou; I know you'll like it.

Highway 61 at the Brule River
(218) 387-2688
naniboujou.com

GRAND PORTAGE LODGE

Serving from early morning till late evening in the dining room overlooking Grand Portage Bay. Traditional menu highlighted by the unexpected.

Highway 61 in Grand Portage
(218) 475-2401
grandportagemn.com

RYDEN'S BORDER STORE AND CAFE

The last American diner. Open March through October, from early morning until 8 P.M.

Highway 61 at the Canadian border
(218) 475-2330

Local Wares

SHOPPING

LOOKING AND TOUCHING AND BROWSING AND SAMPLING AND
oohing and aahing and buying and enjoying. Everyone shops.
Maybe a sweatshirt for that cool breeze off the lake. How about that
birchbark picture frame for the den back home? Did you see that print? The
most distinguishing feature of the local shops is that they offer unique items.
Several shops showcase local paintings, prints, and crafts.

Duluth's retail shops are clustered in eight areas throughout the city. The
most popular area is Canal Park. Shops and antique stores line Canal Park
Drive and Lake Avenue, which lead to the Dewitt-Seitz Marketplace. A
beautiful brick building on the National Register of Historic Places, Dewitt-
Seitz (dewitt-seitz.com) houses retail shops, restaurants, and a candy store.
All facilities are accessible – ask a shopkeeper for aid with the elevator. The
cornerstone of DeWitt-Seitz is the Blue Heron Trading Company featuring
kitchen gadgets, gourmet foods, and funky gifts. Inquire within about cooking classes and their annual cheesecake competition. Across the way, visit
the Art Dock, representing more than 150 regional artisans. Down the hall is
the Lake Avenue Cafe, and upstairs J. Skylark has specialty toys, cards, and
games for kids of all ages.

Downtown Duluth is another retail stronghold, and most of the shops are
connected by the extensive skywalk system. On Superior Street between
Second and Third Avenues West sits the Holiday Center, with forty shops
and restaurants. Down Superior Street to the east is Fitger's Brewery Complex, a renovated 1857 brewery that overlooks Lake Superior and now houses
restaurants and specialty shops. On your walk from the Holiday Center to
Fitger's, stop in at the Electric Fetus for their excellent variety of CDs and
gifts and at Global Village to enjoy their collection of ethnic clothing, crafts,
gifts, and jewelry.

At the top of the hill sits the Miller Hill Mall and surrounding shopping centers. This is Duluth's big franchise shopping hub. Miller Hill Mall has more than a hundred stores and restaurants – I especially like Espana for their coffee.

In West Duluth, between Nineteenth and Twenty-Second Avenues West, is the West End Mall area, with fifty-four shops and restaurants. I suggest stopping at Minnesota Surplus Outfitters, provider of outdoor supplies, clothing, and shoes and boots, and Carr's Hobbies, which boasts an incredible array of model trains, planes, and cars. A bit farther west is the Valley Center Mall, a neighborhood shopping center on Central Avenue and I-35. Three other neighborhood shopping centers are the Plaza at Twelfth Avenue East and Superior Street, Kenwood on Kenwood Avenue and Arrowhead Road, and the Lakeside-Lester business area on Superior Street between Forty-Third and Sixty-First Avenues East.

Gift shops and antique stores along Scenic 61 are intermingled with eating establishments and some great picnic sites. The shops mostly feature products with a regional flair – loon, moose, and wolf items, maple syrup, wilderness stationery, books, and such. Shops include Once upon a Time, the Corner Cupboard, Brad Nelson's Designs, Loon Landing, Playing with Yarn, Practicals Collectibles and Antiques, the Scenic Gift Shop, and Tom's Logging Camp, a logging museum and shop. The Stewart River Boatworks, makers of classic wooden canoes and kayaks, is near Knife River. Admire the handiwork and ask about classes.

Entering Two Harbors, you will find lots of shops right along Highway 61, but be sure to take a right at the first or second stoplight and drive downtown. A pleasant waterfront area includes museums, shops, and restaurants.

Be sure to stop at the Superior Hiking Trail store for books, maps, and Granite Gear. Agate City has excellent science and nature toys and agates, too. For real maple syrup, try Buddy's Wild Rice. Souvenir hunters shop at Sawtooth Mountain Trading Post, Weldon's Gifts, and the Sailor's Outlet. For antiques, try Home Sweet Home and Second Chance Antiques. Specialty shops include Glory Bee's Bible and Book, Avalanche Cycle, Jo-El's Apple Barrel, North Shore Botanicals, The Oldest Sister, Louise's Place, Mimi's, and Wings by the Bay.

Northeast of Two Harbors, at Castle Danger, is the Pioneer Crafts Co-op. Stop here. They have a great mix of local arts and crafts. Next door you will find the Rustic Inn Gift Shop adjacent to the cafe. Across the highway are gifts at Grand Superior Lodge and in the Gooseberry Falls State Park visitors center.

The small community of Beaver Bay sports an eclectic mix of interesting shops, all on Highway 61. Park the car and make a walking tour of the Cedar Chest, Christmas Up North, the Quilt Corner, the Beaver Bay Agate Shop, and Bay Antiques. You will be pleased!

From Minnesota 1 to Co. Rd. 6 on Highway 61 are Lake Superior Paintings with local watercolors and oils by Richard DeLuge, A Fish Out of Water with a gallery, gifts, and wonderful Scandinavian items, the Eagle's Nest with a superb mix of regional merchandise, gifts at Tettegouche State Park, and the Spirit of Gitche Gumee with gifts, furniture, tasty treats, and coffee.

In Silver Bay, head to the shopping center where you will find Dianna's Hallmark and Flowers, Julie's Variety, and Vicki's Corner Store. These gals have the corner on the local market.

In Schroeder, pull into Lamb's Resort to browse their shop. Most resorts in the Tofte-Lutsen area have shops, including Antiques and Gifts at Surfside Resort, Bluefin Gifts at Bluefin Bay, WatersEdge Trading Company in Tofte, Caribou Crossing at Caribou Highlands Lodge, the Lutsen Resort gift shop, and Cascade Lodge's gift shop. Solbakken Resort has a great selection of books. In Schroeder stop by the Temperance Traders gift shop and liquor store. Also in Tofte are Ye Olde Store on the Shore, Birch Tree Gifts, the Tall Tale Yarn Shop, stocking fine yarns, threads, patterns, and related products, and Sawtooth Outfitters with gear for the outdoor enthusiast. The North Shore Market and Liquor Store is just that plus a great meat shop.

Up the Ski Hill Road are Lutsen Rec, with souvenirs and ski-related items, and the Lutsen Mountain Gift Shop. On Highway 61 in Lutsen, stop at Lockport for groceries, convenience items, gifts, espresso and meals, and handmade furniture. At the Clearview Mall you can take care of all your needs at Clearview General Store, Great Gifts, Heavy Duty Sewing, CT Liquors, and the post office.

Local artisans' work can be found at Kah-Nee-Tah Gallery. Thomsonite Beach Museum has a stunning collection of thomsonite stones; jewelry featuring the semiprecious gemstone is for sale. In Grand Marais, you can find regional artists represented at Sivertson Gallery, Eight Broadway, and Betsy Bowen's Studio.

Grand Marais is a shopper's paradise! You will find quite the variety, from exquisite one-of-a-kind pieces of art to T-shirts to refrigerator magnets to birchbark baskets to dazzling jewelry to regional books to outdoor clothing to gifts. Walk from shop to shop, with delightful stops for coffee, lunch, and cocktails. Most shops are located on the highway, the main downtown street, and side avenues. On the way into town, stop at Blue Moose for unique artisan wares and a garden nursery. Across the road is Crystal's Log Cabin Quilts, a quilter's paradise. A new antique store is open on the highway, TLC Antiques, open seasonally.

Don't miss Magpie Antiques near the Best Western on Lake Superior. Stop into Beth's Fudge and Gifts (take a right off the main street onto Broadway) to sample the heavenly fudge and browse the store for gifts for all ages. Also visit the Birchbark Gallery Books and Gifts, which has an extensive collection of regional books and national best-sellers, and the Lake Superior Trading Post, a Grand Marais landmark. Another Grand Marais fixture is Joynes Ben Franklin, a little bit of everything and a fun place to visit. Nearby, tucked inside the Fireweed Building, is Lady Slipper Floral. Three fun stores, all in a row, are Northern Lights Jewelry with fine and unique casual jewelry, the Shirt Outfitters where you absolutely will find the T-shirts to take home, and Gunflint Mercantile, everything Gunflint in town plus fudge. Next door is the king daddy of all Grand Marais antique stores, Lake Superior Collectibles. Up the block and across the highway are the Arrowhead Pharmacy and the Viking Hus with outstanding European imports. Across the avenue are Creative Nature with art and music supplies, the Florist, and Rosebush Antiques, a lot of finds in a little space.

Back downtown, visit The Attic, full of treasures, and White Pine North, with northwoods gifts, stunning clothing, and gourmet foods and coffee. On the corner is The Market, a collection of international items. At the end of main street on the East Bay is Drury Lane Books, with hand-picked books and reader and writer events.

All the lodges and resorts along the Gunflint Trail have gift shops. Make a day of shopping and learn about each of these great places to stay. Midway, right along the Gunflint Trail, are gifts and souvenirs at Loon's Nest Gifts, Trail Center with a selection of northwoods, sundry, and food items, and the Nor'wester Lodge's gift shop, which is a jewel. Merchandise runs the gamut from northwoods to jewelry to baskets to books.

Between Grand Marais and the Canadian border are a few unassuming shops. Naniboujou has a small area with souvenirs. Native American jewelry and handwork are featured at the Grand Portage Lodge gift shop. Finally, Ryden's Border Store is a massive souvenir and gift shop that carries a huge line of cowboy boots for women, men, and children. Have your picture taken with the black bear at the bar!

Museums and Historic Sites

INTERESTED IN THOSE WHO CAME BEFORE YOU? VISIT THE FOL-
lowing museums and sites for a glimpse at the past. Many feature
exhibits and presentations about the history of the people who now live
in Duluth and the North Shore.

MUSEUMS IN DULUTH

LAKE SUPERIOR MARINE MUSEUM
AND MARITIME VISITORS CENTER

To learn more about the history of Lake Superior shipping, visit the Maritime Center. Operated by the U.S. Army Corps of Engineers, the museum
houses actual-size replicas of a ship cabin, pilothouse, and massive steam
engine. Exhibits and displays include several scale ship models, a working
radar, and video presentations. Kids, try to move the ship through the model
Soo Locks. Cool!

In Canal Park at the piers

Open daily 10 A.M. to 9 P.M. in the summer (beginning the third week
   of May); shorter hours in the spring (beginning the third week of
   March); and 10 A.M. to 4:30 P.M. Friday through Sunday in the
   winter

Free admission

(218) 727-2497

lsmma.org

WILLIAM A. IRVIN GREAT LAKES SHIP
AND THE LAKE SUPERIOR TUG

Be amazed at the sheer size of this ship! And at 610 feet, it's a little one com-
pared to the 1,000-footers you'll see pass under the Aerial Lift Bridge. The
William A. Irvin sailed for more than 40 years and was the flagship of U.S.
Steel's Great Lakes fleet. Tours take you from bow to stern exploring the

massive cargo holds, crew quarters, pilothouse, and formal dining room. Canvassing the *Irvin* gives a whole new meaning to boat watching.

Docked next to the *Irvin* is the *Lake Superior* tugboat. Originally a World War II tug, it towed ammunition across the English Channel and was sunk near the end of the war. It was raised and recommissioned for work on the St. Lawrence Seaway, Lake Superior, and Duluth harbor. You can take a self-guided tour of just the tug, but it is included, at no extra cost, when you tour the *Irvin*.

> 350 South 5th Avenue West
>
> Open late April through October; tours (one hour) depart every 20 minutes.
>
> Package tours (*Irvin* and *Lake Superior* tug) cost $6.75 for adults, $5.75 for students and seniors, and $4.50 for kids 3 to 12. Admission for *Lake Superior* tug only is $3 for adults and $2 for kids 3 to 12. A package including admission for the *Irvin* and the *Lake Superior* tug and a pass to the Duluth OMNIMAX theater is $11.00 for adults, $10.00 for students and seniors, and $8.00 for children 3 to 12.
>
> (218) 722-7876 in season; (218) 722-5573 out of season
>
> williamairvin.com

THE DEPOT

Fusing heritage and history with world culture and art, The Depot is a splendid combination of museums and performing arts. Built in 1892, the original railroad station served as many as 55 trains per day. Railway decline led to its closing in the 1960s. A 1977 renovation updated the station to house the St. Louis County Heritage and Arts Center, or as the locals say, The Depot.

Within the grand confines of The Depot are four museums, an art institute, and the headquarters of five regional performing arts associations. The heritage of Minnesota's early loggers and fur traders is explored in the exhibits of the St. Louis County Historical Society. Learn about French explorers, American Indian cultures, and immigrants to the region.

Natural history and world culture are the focus of the Duluth Children's Museum. Kids explore the cultures of the world through wonderful exhibits and programs like the two-story Habitat Tree.

It wouldn't be The Depot without the world-class collection of vintage locomotives and railroad equipment in the Lake Superior Museum of Transportation. Climb aboard giant locomotives and century-old cars. Watch the model train exhibit. Listen to the train whistles blow.

The nearby Depot Square museum is an accurate reconstruction of 1910

Duluth shops and storefronts. Throughout the summer you can take a free trolley ride and savor a Bridgeman's ice cream cone.

Accenting the walkways in Theater Hall and the Balcony Galleries are works from the Duluth Art Institute. The Institute highlights the creations of local, national, and international artists in all types of media. But you needn't restrict yourself to studying still art. Check the schedules of the Minnesota Ballet, Duluth Playhouse, Duluth-Superior Symphony Orchestra, Matinee Musicale, and Arrowhead Chorale for various performing arts events.

5th Avenue West and Michigan Street

Open 9:30 A.M. to 6 P.M. daily Memorial Day to Labor Day; 10 A.M. to 5 P.M. Monday through Saturday and 1 P.M. to 5 P.M. Sunday the remainder of the year

Adults $8.50, children (6 to 11) $5.25, family (2 parents and 2 children under 13) $23.50; special group and senior rates by arrangement – call (218) 733-7503.

(218) 727-8025; recorded hot line: (888) 733-5833

duluthdepot.org

LAKE SUPERIOR & MISSISSIPPI RAILROAD COMPANY

Hop aboard and cruise the shores of the St. Louis River in a vintage train featuring an open Safari Car. Enjoy a great ride at a reasonable price! This nonprofit is run by volunteers dedicated to the preservation of railroad history and the restoration of railroad artifacts.

Freemont Street and Grand Avenue (across from the Zoo behind the Little Store)

Saturdays and Sundays from mid-June through early October; tours (90 minutes) depart at 10:30 A.M. and 1:30 P.M.

Adults $8, children (under 12) $6

(218) 624-7549

lsmrr.org

FITGER'S BREWERY MUSEUM

Highlights the history of the brewery including great artifacts and memorabilia. A fun way to learn a little history.

600 East Superior Street

Open 10 A.M. to 5 P.M. Monday through Friday, 11 A.M. to 4 P.M. Saturday, and noon to 3 P.M. Sunday

Free admission

(218) 722-8826

fitgers.com

KARPELES MANUSCRIPT MUSEUM
Karpeles is dedicated to the preservation of original, handwritten letters and documents of the women and men who have shaped and changed history. This amazing museum houses changing displays that have included the original manuscripts of the Bill of Rights, the Emancipation Proclamation, Handel's *Messiah,* and others.

902 East 1st Street

Open daily from noon to 4 P.M., except closed on Mondays from Labor
   Day through Memorial Day

Free admission

(218) 728-0630

rain.org/~karpeles/dul.htm

GLENSHEEN
Built at the turn of the century by Chester Congdon, this magnificent estate is situated on 7.6 acres on Lake Superior's shoreline in East Duluth. The 39-room Congdon mansion has been preserved in its original state and sits at the center of beautiful formal gardens and manicured grounds. Tours showcase the fine woodwork, stained glass, and original furnishings on the first two floors and include the carriage house and grounds, where portions of the movie *Guess Who's Coming to Dinner?* were filmed. Tours of the third floor and attic can be added, and Glensheen is available to rent for weddings and special occasions. If you are visiting during the Christmas holiday season, be sure to include Glensheen in your plans. Wonderful Old English holiday decorations and musicians give Glensheen an especially festive air. Glensheen is also offering dining on a trial basis on Tuesdays in June through August. On alternate weeks they offer either fine dining or a traditional family fish boil. Call for information.

3300 London Road

Open daily from 9:30 A.M. to 4 P.M. in May through October, Friday
   through Sunday from 11 A.M. to 2 P.M. in November through April

Adults $9.50, juniors (12 to 15) and seniors $7.50, children (6 to 11) $4.50

(218) 726-8910

d.umn.edu/glen

MUSEUMS ALONG THE SHORE

TOM'S LOGGING CAMP

Families love this authentic re-creation of a 1900s logging camp and North West Company fur trading post. A nature trail, Hell's Creek, and eight museum buildings are spread under the shade of a thick conifer forest. Buildings include the Old North West Company Trading Post, museum, harness shop, shoemaker's shop and horseshoeing stall, horse barn and blacksmith shop, bunkhouse and cook's shanty, and a Finnish sauna. Tom also has tame deer, a rainbow trout pond, bunnies, and pygmy goats.

Scenic 61 about 16 miles northeast of Duluth
Open seasonally
Adults $3, children (6 to 15) $2, 5 and under free
(218) 525-4120
tomsloggingcamp.com

THE LITTLE RED SCHOOL HOUSE AT LARSMONT

This historic schoolhouse now serves as a community building.

Scenic 61 in Larsmont

LAKE COUNTY HISTORICAL SOCIETY MUSEUMS AND SITES

lakecountyhistoricalsociety.org

1892 TWO HARBORS LIGHT STATION

Tour the oldest operating lighthouse in Minnesota; on the National Register of Historic Places. Visit the Fog Horn Building, which focuses on fishing and shipwrecks, and a pilot house from the iron ore ship *Frontenac*. The keeper's quarters are now a B&B (see related chapter for more information).

Lighthouse Point, Two Harbors waterfront
Open 9 A.M. to 7 P.M. Monday through Saturday, 10 A.M. to 3 P.M. Sunday
Adults $3, youth (ages 9 to 17) $1, under 9 free

CRUSADER II FISHING VESSEL

This renovated 1939 fishing craft was used off Knife River for years and was originally christened by the then crown prince of Norway. She now sits on the waterfront ground available for inspection.

3M MUSEUM

Showcases the history of the company in the 1902 office; features photos, artifacts, documents, a lab area and hands-on interactive program; on the National Register of Historic Places.

> downtown Two Harbors
> Open 12:30 P.M. to 5 P.M. daily
> Free admission

1907 DEPOT MUSEUM

A regional museum including the John Beargrease Room, Children's Room, a porcelain doll collection, butterfly collection, a toys-through-the-years exhibit, Veterans' Room, and a hands-on kids' area.

> Two Harbors waterfront in the old Duluth & Iron Range Railroad
> headquarters
> Open 9 A.M. to 5 P.M. Monday through Saturday and 10 A.M. to 3 P.M.
> Sunday
> Adults $2, youth (ages 9 to 17) $1, under 9 free

EDNA G. TUGBOAT

Board this Two Harbors icon and visit the captain's quarters, engine room, crew's quarters, galley, and pilothouse. The *Edna G.* was built in 1896 and was the last coal-fed, steam-powered tug in operation on the Great Lakes; a National Historic Site.

> Two Harbors waterfront
> Open 9 A.M. to 5 P.M. Monday through Saturday and 10 A.M. to 3 P.M.
> Sunday
> Adults $2, youth (ages 9 to 17) $1, under 9 free

3 SPOT ENGINE AND CABOOSE AND MALLET STEAM ENGINE

The trains are available for viewing under a covered canopy. The 1883 3 Spot engine and caboose were transported from Philadelphia to Duluth via rail and towed on a scow to Two Harbors. She almost didn't make it when she was hit by an unusual July nor'easter off Knife River. The Mallet is one of the largest locomotives ever made and was donated to the historical society by the Duluth Missabe & Iron Range Railroad.

R. J. HOULE VISITORS CENTER

The Civilian Conservation Corps (CCC) originally built this log building as a residence for the fire ranger at the fire tower on Cloquet Lake in the Isabella

Ranger District. The building was moved to Two Harbors in 1977 and is graced by Peter Toth's hand-formed Native American totem pole.

Open late May through October

Highway 61 in Two Harbors at Burlington Bay

(218) 834-5431 or (800) 554-2116

NORTH SHORE HISTORICAL MUSEUMS

1910 SPLIT ROCK LIGHTHOUSE, SIGNAL BUILDING, TRAM STATION, AND HISTORICAL CENTER

Refer to the state parks chapter for additional information.

Highway 61 about 20 miles northeast of Two Harbors

BAY AREA HISTORICAL SOCIETY

A small center open to the public for information and perusal of artifacts.

Silver Bay, on the corner of Outer Drive and Davis

Open 10 A.M. to 4 P.M. Tuesday through Saturday, Memorial Day through Labor Day

(218) 226-4534

FINLAND HISTORICAL SOCIETY

This center is still being developed at the time of this writing (summer 2003) and will depict early life in Finland, Minnesota.

On Co. Rd. 6 in Finland

Open 11 A.M. to 4 P.M. daily late June through Labor Day

(218) 353-7380

CROSS RIVER HERITAGE CENTER

Sponsored by the Schroeder Historical Society, the center features exhibits and collections from the early logging days of Schroeder. Stop by, they often have hands-on projects going on.

On Highway 61 in Schroeder at the Cross River

Open 9 A.M. to 4 P.M. Monday, Thursday, and Friday, and 11 A.M. to 4 P.M. Sunday in the winter; open 9 A.M. to 5 P.M. Monday through Friday, 9 A.M. to 4 P.M. Saturday, and 11 A.M. to 4 P.M. Sunday in the summer

(218) 663-7706

NORTH SHORE COMMERCIAL FISHING MUSEUM

Built across the bay from the original site of the twin fish houses, the museum is a replica of the Tofte brothers' and Hans Engelsen's 1905 fish house. Displayed within the museum are many relics, photos, and artifacts that were passed down by the Tofte and Engelsen families. This great little museum tells the story of commercial fishing along the Shore and at Isle Royale. Watch for their events and special exhibits. The Lutsen Tofte Visitors Center is also located here.

Highway 61 in Tofte

(218) 663-7804

commercialfishingmuseum.org

COOK COUNTY HISTORICAL SOCIETY MUSEUM
The museum was the light keeper's home in the 1880s. An assortment of local artifacts, pictures, and exhibits tell the story of Grand Marais. The new fish house building on the harbor at the marina replicates an important aspect of local history. Often, the volunteer on duty can tell a pretty good story, too.

From Highway 61 in Grand Marais at the stoplight, go south two and a half blocks; across from Beth's Fudge Shop.

(218) 387-2883

JOHNSON HERITAGE POST
This log gallery and museum stands on the site of the original Johnson Trading Post. The west wing features historical info and paintings by Anna Johnson.

Downtown Grand Marais

(218) 387-2314

ST. FRANCIS XAVIER CATHOLIC/CHIPPEWA CHURCH
The area where the church sits was once known as Chippewa City. The local Ojibwe and missionaries built the church in 1896. Stop by the Cook County Historical Society museum for information.

Highway 61 in east Grand Marais

HISTORIC SITES IN DULUTH

A number of additional sites are noted in the history chapter, "In Days of Old."

1858 MINNESOTA LIGHTHOUSE
At the end of Park Point, hike the trail past the airport.

1870 LAKE SUPERIOR & MISSISSIPPI RAILWAY DEPOT
13308 West 3rd Street

1889 MASONIC TEMPLE OPERA HOUSE
2nd Avenue East and Superior Street

1889 KITCHI GAMMI CLUB
9th Avenue East and Superior Street

1890 TOWNHOMES
1210 to 1228 East 1st Street

1890 BENJAMIN WELLS HOME
48th Avenue East and London Road

1891 FIRST PRESBYTERIAN CHURCH
300 East 2nd Street

1892 UNION DEPOT
5th Avenue West and Michigan Street

1892 FIRE HOUSE NO. 1
1st Avenue East and 3rd Street

1892 DULUTH CENTRAL HIGH SCHOOL
Lake Avenue and 2nd Street

1892 SACRED HEART CATHEDRAL AND CATHEDRAL SCHOOL
206 and 211 West 4th Street

1897 LAKEWOOD PUMPING STATION
Scenic 61, north of Brighton Beach

1899 DULUTH MISSABE & IRON RANGE RAILWAY DEPOT
100 Lake Place (now the Waterfront Visitors Center)

1900 A. FITGER BREWHOUSE
600 East Superior Street

1905 AERIAL LIFT BRIDGE
Canal Park

HISTORIC SITES ALONG THE SHORE

SCENIC 61 DRIVE
Follows the path of the original road up the Shore, which was established about 1919.

1856 BUCHANAN WAYSIDE
Site of the first North Shore post office and an early community.
　Scenic 61, five miles northeast of Knife River

1856 DULUTH & IRON RANGE RAILROAD DEPOT
Includes a museum.
　On the waterfront in Two Harbors

1883 ORE DOCK #1
The ore dock closest to shore.
　On the waterfront in Two Harbors

1883 3 SPOT TRAIN
Next to the 3 Spot is the Mallet Engine.
　On the waterfront in Two Harbors

1892 TWO HARBORS LIGHT STATION
Includes a museum.
　On the waterfront in Two Harbors

1896 *EDNA G.* TUG
The tug was in service until 1981.
　On the waterfront in Two Harbors

1896 SUNKEN SHIP *SAMUEL P. ELY*
In the water in Two Harbors near the western breakwall

R. J. HOULE VISITORS CENTER
Civilian Conservation Corps (CCC) log building and totem pole.
　Highway 61 in Two Harbors at Burlington Bay

VIRGIN PINE AND CEDAR AT ENCAMPMENT FOREST
Drive by this virgin forest, but remember, it is all private property, so please exercise respect.
　Highway 61 northeast of Two Harbors

1930S CCC BUILDINGS AT GOOSEBERRY FALLS STATE PARK
Includes the old Interpretive Center on Highway 61 and some beautiful buildings near the river's mouth.

Highway 61, 12 miles northeast of Two Harbors

1900S PILINGS AT THE MOUTH OF THE SPLIT ROCK RIVER
Pilings from the Merrill & Ring Lumber Company's railway.

Highway 61, about 19 miles northeast of Two Harbors

BEAVER BAY CEMETERY
Final resting spot of some of the original settlers of Beaver Bay, the oldest (1856) community along the North Shore.

Highway 61 in Beaver Bay

GRAVE OF CHIEF JOHN BEARGREASE
Beargrease ran mail up and down the Shore via dogsled. The Beargrease Sled Dog Race is named after him.

From Highway 61 in Beaver Bay, go north one block behind the Holiday Station.

1910 TETTEGOUCHE CAMP ON MIC MAC LAKE
Hike or bike in; you can rent these cabins.

In Tettegouche State Park

FATHER BARAGA'S CROSS
Father Frederic Baraga was an early missionary from Austria, who frequently traveled aboard the American Fur Company's boats. In 1846, Baraga was stationed at St. Joseph's Church in La Pointe, Michigan, and was headed to an outpost on the North Shore. The wind picked up, and the waves battered the small boat. It was doubtful they would survive, much less reach their destination. After a harrowing night, the group safely beached the boat off the mouth of the Cross River. In gratitude for their safe arrival, Father Baraga erected a wooden cross on the beach. A symbolic granite cross has been placed in remembrance of Baraga's journey.

Off Highway 61 in Schroeder; follow the trail at the public launch parking area.

LUTSEN RESORT
The resort was established in the 1880s; the main lodge was built in the 1940s.

Off Highway 61 in Lutsen

1880S BREAKWALL AND LIGHTHOUSE
In Grand Marais; parking adjacent to Artist Point

1903 EAST BAY HOTEL
In Grand Marais, where the main street hits the east bay

ST. FRANCIS XAVIER CATHOLIC/CHIPPEWA CHURCH
Inquire about visiting hours at the Cook County Historical Museum.
  Highway 61 in Grand Marais, about a half-mile past the stoplight

FIVE-MILE ROCK
Used as a distance marker by early travelers.
  Highway 61, five miles east of Grand Marais

NANIBOUJOU LODGE
Highway 61, about 15 miles northeast of Grand Marais

GRAND PORTAGE NATIONAL MONUMENT
Off Highway 61 about 36 miles northeast of Grand Marais, go south one mile
and follow the signs.

SUNKEN SHIP *AMERICA*
The bow is in a few feet of water in the North Gap; you can view the ship if
you ride the *Wenonah* out to Isle Royale.
  In the North Gap between Isle Royale and Thompson Island

REMAINS OF COPPER MINES ON ISLE ROYALE
Refer to the park map you receive when landing on the island.

Arts and Culture

CREATIVITY IS ... SEEING SOMETHING
THAT DOESN'T EXIST ALREADY.
YOU NEED TO FIND OUT HOW
TO BRING IT INTO BEING AND
THUS BE A PLAYMATE WITH GOD.

Michele Shee

THROUGHOUT THE AGES DULUTH AND THE NORTH SHORE
have inspired a diverse group of artists. Remnants of Dakota and
Ojibwe beadwork, weavings, and pictographs reveal age-old inter-
pretations of living with this land. Ethnic songs, dances, and rituals were and
are imparted to each new generation.

It is the receptiveness of each generation that has allowed the continuation and growth of arts. At the turn of the century, Duluth became an established city, and notable artists began taking up residency. Important painters
who lived in Duluth include Eastman Johnson, Peter Lund, David Erickson,
and Knute Heldner. Sinclair Lewis, the first American to win a Nobel prize
for literature, and Margaret Culkin Banning, a popular fiction writer, also
lived in Duluth.

DULUTH GALLERIES

TWEED MUSEUM OF ART   ♿

The finest all-around display can be seen at the Tweed Museum of Art, located on the campus of the University of Minnesota, Duluth (UMD). The Tweed intends to "supplement student education and to inform, educate, entertain and enlighten the general viewer." Permanent collections are housed in four of the nine galleries, and the remaining five galleries display 40 or more annual exhibits.

The permanent collection features a cross section of European, American, and contemporary art. For more than two decades, from the 1950s to the 1970s, the Tweed Museum sponsored a summer visiting artist program. Contributions from the guest artists are also part of the permanent collection. In the European art collection are 15th-century Italian religious pieces, 16th- and 17th-century old master paintings from the Dutch and Netherlandish schools, 19th-century Barbizon school works, and early-20th-century works from Germany, France, and Spain. American Impressionist paintings are a major focus of the American art collection of 19th- and 20th-century pieces. A share of this display emphasizes artists who have lived and taught in Duluth. Almost 1,600 of the museum's 4,000 pieces are housed in the remaining gallery's contemporary art collection.

On the campus of the University of Minnesota, Duluth
Open Tuesdays from 9 A.M. to 8 P.M., Wednesday through Friday from 9 A.M. to 4:30 P.M., and weekends from 1 P.M. to 5 P.M. Guided tours are available by calling at least one week in advance.
Admission is by suggested donation: families $5, individual $2, seniors/students $1
(218) 726-8222
(218) 726-6319 (store)
d.umn.edu/tma

ART DOCK
DeWitt-Seitz Marketplace, Canal Park
(218) 722-1451

BLUE LAKE GALLERY
308 South Lake Avenue, Park Point
(218) 725-0034

ART OPTIONS
132 East Superior Street, downtown
    (218) 727-8723

DECKER'S ART AND FRAMING
1402 East 1st Street, downtown area
    (218) 728-2717

DULUTH ART INSTITUTE
At The Depot
    (218) 733-7560
    duluthartinstitute.com

FRAME CORNER GALLERY
323 West Superior Street, downtown
    (218) 722-7174
    artduluth.com

LIZZARD'S ART GALLERY
38 East Superior Street, downtown
    (218) 722-5815
    lizzards.com

LOOSE MOOSE
2311 Woodland Avenue, near UMD
    (218) 728-0112

OLDE TOWNE GALLERIES
Village Mall, near Miller Hill Mall
    (218) 722-9676

SIVERTSON GALLERY
361 Canal Park Drive
    (218) 723-7877
    sivertson.com

WATERS OF SUPERIOR
395 Lake Avenue South, Canal Park
    (218) 786-0233
    watersofsuperior.com

SCULPTURES IN DULUTH

ALBERT WOLSON
Avrad Fairbanks/bronze
  Adjacent to Marine Museum

A DETERMINED MARINER
Richard Salews/bronze
  Morse Street and Canal Park Drive

SPIRIT OF LAKE SUPERIOR
Kirk St. Maur/bronze
  Southeast corner of Buchanan and Canal Park Drive

FOUNTAIN OF THE WIND
Douglas Freeman/bronze, stainless steel, and glass
  Southwest corner of Buchanan and Canal Park Drive

IMAGE WALL
Mark Marino and Kent Worley/mosaic tiles
  Canal Park Drive

LAKE SUPERIOR FOUNTAIN
Ben Effinger/black granite
  Canal Park Drive and Superior Street

STENEN (THE STONE)
Kenneth Johansson/red granite
  At Lake Place Plaza

DULUTH LEGACY
Donna Dobberfuhl/brick (ironstone)
  Canal Park Drive

MAN, CHILD AND GULL
Sterling Rathsack, Jr./bronze
  Canal Park Drive

GREEN BEAR
Leo Lankinen and Valter Soini/bronze
  At Lake Place Plaza

PERFORMING ARTS IN DULUTH

DULUTH PLAYHOUSE
At The Depot
(218) 733-7555
duluthplayhouse.org

DULUTH-SUPERIOR ENTERTAINMENT LEAGUE
Schedules touring performances.
(218) 722-2000 or (800) 622-2003
entertainmentleague.com

DULUTH-SUPERIOR SYMPHONY ORCHESTRA
Performs 7 masterworks and 3 pop programs at the Duluth Entertainment
and Convention Center.
Office at The Depot
(218) 733-7575
dsso.com

LAKE SUPERIOR CHAMBER ORCHESTRA
Summer festival orchestra performs on 5 Wednesday evenings in June
and July.
Mitchell Auditorium at St. Scholastica
(218) 724-5231

MINNESOTA BALLET
Office at The Depot
(218) 529-3742
minnesotaballet.org

RENEGADE COMEDY THEATRE
404 West Superior Street
(218) 722-6775
renegadecomedy.org

CITY OF DULUTH MUSIC IN THE PARKS
Glensheen Concerts by the Lake: Wednesdays in July at 6:30 P.M.
Live at Lake Place Park: Fridays throughout summer, 12:15 to 12:45 P.M.
Bayfront Fridays: Late June through late August; call for times.
Chester Creek Concerts at Chester Bowl: Tuesday evenings, early June
    through early August

Fitger's Music in the Courtyard: Saturdays throughout summer, 5 to 8 P.M.
Free admission!
(218) 722-4011

ART AND MUSIC EVENTS IN DULUTH AND ALONG THE SHORE

PARK POINT ART FAIR
Juried event. 110 artists and craftsmen.
5000 Minnesota Avenue in Duluth
Fourth weekend in June
parkpoint.org/html/art_fair.html

GRAND MARAIS ART FAIR
Juried show.
Downtown Grand Marais
Second weekend in July
grandmaraisartcolony.org/arts_festival.htm

MINNESOTA SHAKESPEARE FESTIVAL AT GRAND MARAIS
Performances, street events, music, classes. Canceled for 2004.
At the Arrowhead Center for the Arts and throughout Grand Marais
10 days, last weekend in June through first weekend in July
(218) 387-1284

TWO HARBORS FOLK FESTIVAL
Concerts, a children's tent, dancing, jam sessions, artisans, workshops,
storytelling, and food.
On the lakefront in Two Harbors
Third weekend in July
(218) 834-2600 or (800) 777-7384
thff.org

DULUTH INTERNATIONAL FOLK FESTIVAL
Celebrating diversity through the arts! The festival showcases dancers,
musicians, entertainers, craftspeople, and food booths reflecting the region's
diverse ethnic backgrounds.
Leif Erikson Park on Superior Street

First Saturday in August 10:30 A.M. to 5 P.M.
(218) 722-7425
ymcaduluth.org/event_folk.html

BAYFRONT BLUES FESTIVAL
Darn good music all weekend long! More than 20 national performers play
on two concert stages, plus blues bands perform at 25 local nightclubs. The
Bayfront Blues Festival is one of the largest blues festivals in the Midwest.
Bayfront Park in Duluth
Middle weekend in August
(715) 394-6831
bayfrontblues.com

ARTS ORGANIZATIONS AND
GALLERIES ALONG THE SHORE

ARROWHEAD CENTER FOR THE ARTS
This is the performing arts center in Grand Marais and home to the Grand
Marais Art Colony, North Shore Music Association, WTIP, and Grand Marais
Playhouse. The nationally recognized Art Colony was established in 1947 by
Minneapolis School of Art instructor Birney Quick. The "Grand Marais
Outdoor School of Painting" operated in conjunction with the Minneapolis
School of Art. It gave students time and inspiration to practice their tech-
nique and gave Birney time to fish. Birney had friends who liked to fish, too.
He brought up pals from the Minneapolis Symphony to give benefit concerts
throughout the 1950s and 1960s and was instrumental in bringing jazz musicians to the area. The community and visiting urbanites were receptive to
the cultural events.

When the Minneapolis School of Art evolved into the Minnesota College
of Art and Design in the early 1960s, they made a corporate separation from
the Colony, but a mutually supportive relationship continued. The Colony
became a private business and moved into the old St. John's Catholic Church
in 1961, where it offered summer workshops. In 1986, the Art Colony became
a nonprofit organization, and in the summer of 1998, they moved their
offices to the Grand Marais Art Center.

Adult workshops are given throughout the year, with the majority offered
between June and October. Most of the week-long workshops lean toward
individualizing the artist and thus are personal creativity sessions. About a

third of the classes are instruction-oriented and are aimed at improving technical ability.

The Grand Marais Playhouse produces a number of shows throughout the year, including plays, readings, and musical events.

From Highway 61 in Grand Marais, go north on the Gunflint Trail (Co. Rd. 12), then east on Co. Rd. 7 for two blocks; the center is located in the school campus.

ACA: (218) 387-1284; Grand Marais Art Colony: (218) 387-2737, grandmaraisartcolony.org; Grand Marais Playhouse: (218) 387-1036, grandmaraisplayhouse.com

NORTH SHORE MUSIC ASSOCIATION

The association brings a number of regional and national performers to the Shore each year.

(218) 387-1284

boreal.org/music

JOHNSON HERITAGE POST ART GALLERY

This is the stunning log structure overlooking the Grand Marais harbor. The Gallery came into being through the generosity of Lloyd Johnson, who donated the funds to build the gallery as well as the land, which was the site of his family's trading post at the turn of the century. The works of painter Anna Carolina Johnson, Lloyd's mother, are permanently displayed in the west wing. The great room and east wing display rotating exhibits of area and regional artists.

115 West Wisconsin Street; from Highway 61 in Grand Marais, take the main street downtown.

(218) 387-2314

PLAYING WITH YARN

Scenic 61 at Knife River

(218) 391-0516

SILVER CREEK STUDIO

Near Two Harbors

(218) 834-0756 or (800) 963-8785

coldsnap.com

SILVER CREEK GIFTS AND GALLERY
Highway 61 northeast of Two Harbors
(218) 834-4995
silvercreekgifts.com

COOTER POTTERY
Off Lake Co. Rd. 3, north of Highway 61 at the Stewart River
(218) 834-5424

PIONEER CRAFTS CO-OP
Highway 61 in Castle Danger
(218) 834-4175
pioneercrafts.com

QUILT CORNER
Highway 61 in Beaver Bay
(218) 226-3517

A FISH OUT OF WATER
Highway 61 near Little Marais
(218) 226-3680

KAH-NEE-TAH GALLERY
4210 West Highway 61, in Lutsen
(218) 387-2585
kahneetah.com

BETSY BOWEN STUDIO
In the Old Playhouse north of downtown Grand Marais
(218) 387-1992
woodcut.com

BLUE MOOSE
On Highway 61 as you enter Grand Marais (seasonal)
(218) 387-9303

CRYSTAL'S LOG CABIN QUILTS
On Highway 61 as you enter Grand Marais
  (218) 387-1550

FARM AND CRAFT MARKET
Downtown Grand Marais, Saturdays in the summer

EIGHT BROADWAY STUDIOS
Downtown Grand Marais
  (218) 387-9079

SIVERTSON GALLERY
Downtown Grand Marais
  (218) 387-2491
  sivertson.com

Beyond the Border

THUNDER BAY AND CANADA

WHERE U.S. HIGHWAY 61 ENDS, CANADIAN HIGHWAY 61 begins. Continuing your travels along the North Shore naturally brings you into Ontario, Canada. The remainder of the North Shore of Lake Superior is a 465-mile road along wild shoreline from Pigeon River to Sault Sainte Marie. You will find plenty of sight-seeing opportunities in the 37-mile trip from the border to Thunder Bay. I have provided the basics for crossing the border and some of my favorite destinations on the other side.

CUSTOMS AND CROSSING THE BORDER

Below is a review of Canadian customs regulations. Crossing the border usually involves a few quick questions and takes a minute or two. Boaters entering Canadian waters must check with Customs at the proper port of entry. For answers to specific questions or an update on regulations, call Pigeon River Canadian Customs and Immigration at (807) 964-2093.

Remote Area Border Crossing Permits

If you plan to cross the international border in a remote area without a Customs office, you will need to acquire a Remote Area Border Crossing (RABC) permit. This is relevant to anyone who wants to enter Quetico Provincial Park from the Boundary Waters Canoe Area Wilderness, especially those who used to check through Customs on Saganaga Lake (that office is now closed). To obtain an RABC permit, call Immigration at (807) 964-2093 and request an application. The process via mail takes a minimum of four weeks, so plan accordingly. Your other option is to drive to Pigeon River between 7 A.M. and 11 P.M. Central Standard Time and complete the application. The permit costs $30 Canadian or $22 U.S. funds and covers a family unit for one year.

Proof of Citizenship

Citizens of the United States must provide a driver's license, passport, or birth certificate. Children need a birth certificate, and children other than your own need a signed letter of permission from their parent or guardian. Visitors from countries other than the United States require a passport and/or a visitor's visa. Those with a criminal record should contact Customs before crossing the border.

Allowances for Overnight Visitors

Allowances for overnight visitors are as follows: Each traveler is allowed a two-day supply of food. Each vehicle can carry a full tank of gas plus six gallons; any additional fuel is subject to tax and duties. Each person 18 years of age or older may take one carton of cigarettes and 50 cigars. Each person 19 years of age or older may take a case of beer, 40 ounces of spirits, or 1.5 liters of wine duty-free. Allowances for day visitors vary and are ordinarily less.

Firearms and Ammunition

Each person 18 years of age or older may carry a hunting rifle or shotgun and up to 200 rounds of ammunition, provided the firearm is for sporting or competition use only. Guns carried for sporting purposes are allowed only during open hunting seasons. Fully automatic weapons and guns less than 26 inches long are prohibited. Absolutely no handguns are allowed.

Pets

Pets must be in good health or they can be denied access. Dogs and cats 3 months or older must have a certificate from a vet verifying up-to-date rabies vaccination.

Driving

A valid driver's license from any country is good in Canada for up to three months. Seat belt use is mandatory in Canada. Speed limits are posted in kilometers per hour.

Time Change

The portion of Ontario I will be referring to is in the Eastern time zone, which is one hour ahead of the Central time zone.

MONEY EXCHANGE

Ryden's Border Store on the Minnesota side of the border offers excellent exchange rates. Banks and credit unions will also exchange currency. Credit cards give the standard exchange rate for the day.

GENERAL SALES TAX (GST) EXEMPTION

Non-Canadian residents who spend $100 (Canadian) or more on accommodations or goods may receive a refund of the General Sales Tax they paid. You must have original receipts, certain items are not included, and restrictions apply. Pick up a brochure and application at the border.

HAVING A GOOD TIME IN CANADA

Sometimes the fun is just going to another country. And as long as you're there, consider touring a few of the places mentioned here. Multicultural Thunder Bay blends urban services with rural friendliness. The city was two towns until 1970, when Fort William and Port Arthur merged. Fort William was established in 1717 and became a fixture on the lake in 1802 when it became the headquarters of the North West Company, which had moved north from Grand Portage. Next door, Port Arthur handled shipping business and grew to be the world's largest grain-handling port. For a complete guide to Thunder Bay, contact Thunder Bay Tourism at (800) 667-8386 or tourism.city.thunder-bay.on.ca or Ontario Tourism at (800) ONTARIO or nosta.on.ca, or stop by the visitors center on Highway 61 at the Grand Marais Inn/Tomteboda Cabins in Grand Marais or just over the Canadian border at the Pigeon River visitors center, open June through mid-September. The sites I recommend are listed in sequential order from the border through Thunder Bay.

MIDDLE FALLS PROVINCIAL PARK

Located along the Pigeon River, this park features a picnic and recreation area with a shelter and trails leading to the wide, scenic Middle Falls and Pigeon, or High, Falls. The High Falls drop 120 feet. A fine picnic spot. More info at the Pigeon River visitors center.

A few miles past the border on your left on Provincial Road 593
Open June to September
(807) 473-9231
ontarioparks.com/english/pige.html

THUNDER OAK CHEESE FARM

A working dairy and cheese-making enterprise. Stop by for a tour and watch cheese making at 10 A.M. on Mondays, Wednesdays, and Fridays. Specializing in Gouda.

Off Highway 61 less than a mile on Boundary Drive
Open 9 A.M. to 5 P.M. Monday through Saturday
(807) 628-0175

GAMMONDALE FARMS

This pick-your-own strawberry farm has a huge hayloft with a tire swing, a barn full of friendly animals, pony rides, refreshments, picnic tables, and tasty strawberries. Each fall they are open for Applefest with hayrides, caramel apples, and an inventive corn-husk maze. A family Christmas celebration is held in December featuring a Nativity with live animals.

About 28 miles past the border and north on McCluskey Road for
3 miles.
(807) 475-5615
gammondalefarm.com

KAKABEKA FALLS PROVINCIAL PARK

Another great picnic site, the park has a visitor information center that offers hikes, kids' programs, sing-alongs, and films. Multiple viewing platforms provide a variety of views at the 128-foot "Niagara of the North." Two adjacent campgrounds have 169 sites.

20 miles west of Thunder Bay on Highway 11/17
Open year-round, limited in winter
(807) 473-9231 or (807) 475-1535 winters
ontarioparks.com/english/kaka.htm

OLD FORT WILLIAM

Stop here! This is the world's largest reconstruction of an early 1800s fur trading post and is hosted by costumed staff reenacting daily life. The fort includes 42 historic buildings, a mammoth wharf and canoe landing, a working farm, and a native camp. Rendezvous Place houses exhibits, video presentations, gifts, artwork, and both heritage-style and contemporary dining. Located on the Kaministiquia River, the fort includes a visitors center, trading post, and cantina.

From Thunder Bay, on Highway 61, follow the signs.
Open mid-May through mid-October from 10 A.M. to 5 P.M. daily
(807) 577-8461
oldfortwilliam.on.ca

MOUNT MCKAY SCENIC LOOKOUT

Part of the Nor'Wester Mountain Range, Mount McKay peaks at 975 feet above the city and harbor of Thunder Bay. Halfway up is a memorial chapel honoring Native Americans killed in World War II. The parkway is on reservation land, and a toll is collected.

Take Highway 61B off Highway 61 and follow the signs.

(807) 622-3093

WATER CRUISES ON *PIONEER II*

Take a sight-seeing cruise aboard this 52-foot, passenger vessel that features indoor panoramic views, snack bar, and restrooms. The 2-hour tour travels through the harbor and mouth of the Kaministiquia River.

Marina Park at the Thunder Bay Harbor

Summers; ask about charters and dinner cruises; adults $15, seniors $13, child to age 12 $7.50

(807) 623-BOAT

SAILING CRUISES

Day charters, lessons, bareboat tours, and luxury charters from Sailboats Ontario (807-767-1972) and Sail Superior (807-628-3333 and sailsuperior. com).

THUNDER BAY RECREATIONAL TRAIL

This 34K multipurpose paved trail connects the southern and northern portions of Thunder Bay, with access to dining, shopping, and attractions. Pick up a map at the visitors center at the border.

CANADA GAMES COMPLEX

A humdinger of a swimming pool! A monster of a water slide! Plus a huge kiddie pool, a heated swirlpool, indoor track, squash, fitness equipment, babysitting, and a restaurant.

Winnipeg Avenue

Call (807) 684-3311 for fees and directions.

gamescomplex.com

THUNDER BAY MUSEUM

The museum showcases 10,000-year-old prehistoric Ojibwe and Cree artifacts and relics from the fur trading, mining, and shipping industries in Ontario.

From Highway 61, take a right on Arthur one block to May Street, and
  right on May; museum is on your left.
Open daily from mid-June through Labor Day from 11 A.M. to 5 P.M.
  and the rest of the year on Tuesday through Sunday from 1 P.M. to
  5 P.M.
(807) 623-0801

CENTENNIAL CONSERVATORY
Stop and smell the flowers. This is an especially nice stop on cold, blustery
days. The main room features permanent, multitiered plant exhibits from
around the world, while the east wing showcases changing floral displays,
and the cacti house is loaded with succulents.
  Off Balmoral Street at 1601 Dease Street
  Open 1 P.M. to 4 P.M. daily
  Free admission
  (807) 622-7036

HOITO IN FINN TOWN
Downstairs from the Finlandia Club of Port Arthur, Hoito serves up Finnish
fare the way mom used to make it.
  314 Bay Street
  (807) 345-6323

BREW PUB AND BRASSERIE
Belly up for a mug of this microbrewery's excellent home brew. If you ask
nicely, they may even give you a tour.
  Off Highway 61 on Red River Road
  (807) 767-4415

THUNDER BAY AGATE MINE
This recently (1998) discovered agate mine is the only one in Canada and
one of three in the entire world. Agates are usually found in gravel deposits,
so this mine is a rarity! You can mine your own agate and view the largest
agate in North and South America.
  Drive through Thunder Bay on Highway 11/17 to Highway 527 and head
    north one mile.
  Open mid-May through mid-October daily from 10 A.M. to 6:30 P.M.
  (807) 683-3595 (seasonal)
  agatemine.com

CENTENNIAL PARK AND BUSHCAMP MUSEUM
In Canada, you don't say "woods," you say "the bush." As in, "I've been out in the bush cutting wood all day." And that's why you would be bushed. This bushcamp is a 1910 logging camp museum on a 147-acre park, featuring a blacksmith shop, bunkhouse, sauna, cookhouse, petting zoo in the barn-yard, Trowbridge Falls Campground, hiking/cross-country ski trail, and Muskeg Express train.

Drive all the way through Thunder Bay and west on the Current River Road.

Camp open June through September; park open year-round

(807) 683-6341

ART GALLERIES AND STUDIOS
For a guide to working studios in northern Ontario, see studiosnorth.com.

CHIPPEWA PARK
Beach, park, campground, and cabins, wonderful turn-of-the-century carousel, amusement rides, and 10-acre wildlife exhibit with raised walkway and observation platforms.

East of Highway 61, at the end of City Road

Park open year-round; exhibit and rides June through Labor Day

(807) 623-3972 (campground)

SLEEPING GIANT PROVINCIAL PARK
Legend has it that Nanabosho, the Giant, son of the west wind, led the Ojibwe to their new home on Superior's North Shore, safe from their Dakota enemies. One day, while sitting by the lake, Nanabosho scratched a rock and discovered a rich silver mine. Silver was worthless to the Ojibwe, but Nana-bosho was frightened that the white man would find the silver and take away their new homeland. Nanabosho's leader, the Great Spirit, swore his people to secrecy, and for a while they all lived peacefully. However, vanity eventu-ally got the best of one of the chiefs, who made himself some silver weapons. It came to pass that the chief was warring with some Dakota and died. A few days later, Nanabosho spotted a Dakota leading white men across Superior to the silver mine. Frightened and wanting to protect his people, Nanabosho disobeyed the Great Spirit and caused a huge storm, which sank the canoe and killed the men. The Great Spirit was angered by Nanabosho, and as a punishment, turned him to stone. The Sleeping Giant can be seen at the end of the Sibley Peninsula, a part of the Sleeping Giant Provincial Park.

Hike the rugged backcountry past inland lakes and streams to amazing overlooks of Lake Superior. The park features a visitors center, hiking and cross-country ski trails, a campground, picnic areas, beaches, lookouts, and a bird observatory.

About 26 miles past Thunder Bay and a few miles south on Highway 587
(807) 977-2526
ontarioparks.com/english/slee.html

General Information and Services

VISITOR INFORMATION IN DULUTH

DULUTH CONVENTION AND VISITORS BUREAU
Endion Station, 100 Lake Place Drive
   Open 9 A.M. to 5 P.M., Monday through Friday, year-round
   (218) 722-4011 or (800) 438-5884 (4DULUTH)
   visitduluth.com

WATERFRONT TOURIST INFORMATION CENTER
Harbor Drive at the Vista Fleet dock
   Open daily May through October
   (218) 722-6024

THOMPSON HILL STATE INFORMATION CENTER
I-35, exit 249
   Open daily year-round, from 8 A.M. to 6 P.M. in summer and from
      9 A.M. to 5 P.M. in winter
   (218) 723-4938

VISITOR INFORMATION ALONG THE NORTH SHORE

northshorevisitor.com

NORTH SHORE VISITORS CENTER
Highway 61 and Lester River
   Open daily from late May into October

R. J. HOULE WAYSIDE REST AND INFORMATION CENTER
Highway 61 in Two Harbors
> Open daily from late May to mid-October and from 9 A.M. to 1 P.M. on
> > Wednesday through Saturday from mid-October through early May
> (218) 834-4005 or (800) 554-2116
> lakecnty.com

BEAVER BAY TOURIST INFORMATION CENTER
Highway 61 in Beaver Bay
> Open daily from late May through September

SILVER BAY/EAST LAKE COUNTY CHAMBER OF COMMERCE
Covering Silver Bay, Beaver Bay, Finland, Isabella, and Little Marais.
> Outer Drive in Silver Bay
> Open daily late May through September
> (218) 226-4870 or (888) 634-5210

LUTSEN-TOFTE TOURISM ASSOCIATION
Highway 61 in Tofte in the twin red fish houses
> Open year-round
> (218) 663-7804 or (888) 61NORTH
> 61north.com

GRAND MARAIS VISITOR INFORMATION CENTER
From Highway 61 at the stoplights in Grand Marais, go south one and a half
blocks.
> (218) 387-2524 or (888) 922-5000
> grandmarais.com

GUNFLINT TRAIL ASSOCIATION
Where Highway 61 and main street meet in Grand Marais
> (800) 338-6932
> gunflint_trail.com

TOURISM THUNDER BAY
Highway 61 in Grand Marais at Grand Marais Inn/Tomteboda Cabins
> Open daily in summer, shorter hours in winter
> tourism.city.thunder-bay.on.ca and northshorevisitor.com

VISITOR INFORMATION FOR ADJACENT AREAS

SUPERIOR/DOUGLAS COUNTY, WISCONSIN VISITOR INFORMATION CENTER
Highway 2 in Superior at entrance to Barker's Island
    Open daily in summer and Monday through Saturday in winter
    (715) 392-2773 or (800) 942-5313
    visitsuperior.com

NORTHERN LIGHTS TOURISM ALLIANCE SERVING NORTHEAST MINNESOTA
    wildnorth.org

MINNESOTA OFFICE OF TOURISM
Open 8 A.M. to 4:30 P.M. Monday through Friday; at other times, recorded information is available via touchtone telephone.
    (800) 657-3700 or (651) 296-5029 (Twin Cities)
    exploreminnesota.com

OTHER HELPFUL PHONE NUMBERS AND WEB SITE ADDRESSES
U.S. Forest Service General Information: (218) 626-4300
Superior National Forest Web site: superiornationalforest.org
Tofte Ranger Station: (218) 663-7280
Gunflint Ranger Station: (218) 387-1750
Minnesota DNR: (888) MINNDNR or (651) 296-6157
Minnesota DNR Web site: dnr.state.mn.us
BWCAW: (877) 550-6777 or BWCAW.ORG

EMERGENCY SERVICES

All areas mentioned in the book are covered by 911.

DULUTH
Duluth Police Department, nonemergency: (218) 723-3434;
    TDD, (218) 723-3293
Duluth Fire Department, nonemergency: (218) 723-3219
St. Louis County Sheriff (Duluth): nonemergency (218) 726-2340

Lake County Sheriff (Two Harbors): (218) 834-8385
Two Harbors Police Department: (218) 834-5566
Silver Bay Police Department: (218) 226-4486
Schroeder Fire Hall: (218) 663-7559
Tofte Fire Hall: (218) 663-7619
Cook County Sheriff (Grand Marais): (218) 387-3030
Grand Marais Law Enforcement: (218) 387-3030
Grand Portage Fire Department: (218) 475-2401

MEDICAL CARE

CLINICS IN DULUTH
The Duluth Clinic: 400 East Third Street; (218) 786-8364/786-6000 Urgent
  Care
Duluth Clinic – West: 4325 Grand Avenue; (218) 786-3500
Duluth Clinic – Lakeside: 4621 East Superior Street; (218) 786-3550
Family Practice Center: 330 North 8th Avenue East; (218) 723-1112

EMERGENCY ROOMS IN DULUTH
St. Mary's/Duluth Clinic: 407 East 3rd Street; (218) 786-4357 or
  TTY (218) 786-4333
St. Luke's Hospital: 915 East 1st Street; (218) 726-5616 or TTY (218) 726-5463

HOSPITALS IN DULUTH
St. Mary's Medical Center: 407 East 3rd Street; (218) 786-4000 or
  TTY (218) 726-4333
St. Luke's Hospital: 915 East 1st Street; (218) 786-5555 or TTY (218) 726-5480
Miller-Dwan Medical Center: 502 East 2nd Street; (218) 727-8762

HOSPITALS AND EMERGENCY ROOMS ALONG
THE NORTH SHORE
Lake View Memorial Hospital: 325 11th Avenue in Two Harbors;
  (218) 834-7300
Cook County North Shore Hospital: At Co. Rds. 12 and 7 in Grand Marais;
  (218) 387-3040

CLINICS ALONG THE NORTH SHORE
Superior Health Medical Group: 1010 4th Street in Two Harbors;
  (218) 834-7200

Bay Area Health Center: 50 Outer Drive in Silver Bay; (218) 226-4431
Sawtooth Mountain Clinic: At Co. Rds. 12 and 7 in Grand Marais;
   (218) 387-2330
Sawtooth Mountain Clinic, West End Branch: Highway 61 in Tofte;
   (218) 663-7263

AUTO SERVICE AND TOWING

Listed here are sources for automotive towing in Duluth and along the North Shore and auto repair and parts businesses located along the Shore. Since Duluth has a large number of repair services and parts suppliers, they are not listed here – refer to the Yellow Pages for these. Gas can be purchased in Two Harbors, Beaver Bay, Silver Bay, Tofte, Lutsen, Grand Marais, seasonally midway up the Gunflint Trail, and at the U.S.-Canadian border.

DULUTH GENERAL
Twin Ports Towing: (218) 591-0658

WEST DULUTH
Dieryck's Service: 5608 Cody Street; (218) 624-9039
Thompson's Freeway Amoco: 27th Avenue West and I-35; (218) 722-0005

DOWNTOWN DULUTH
Jack's Mobil Service: 1130 East 4th Street; (218) 724-1965
Lake City Towing: Duluth; (218) 722-7781
Like New II Towing: 2220 Michigan Street; (218) 722-8111 or (218) 343-1335

WOODLAND
KJ Auto Service/AAA: 4002 Woodland Avenue; (218) 728-4429
Humes Towing Pros: 4779 West Arrowhead Road; (218) 726-0336 or (218)
   722-3330

NORTH SHORE
Auto Parts Pro (parts): 501 7th Street in Two Harbors; (218) 834-2191
Nord Auto Supply (parts): 122 Waterfront Drive in Two Harbors;
   (218) 834-2277 or (800) 637-5142
Two Harbors Amoco: (218) 834-3844
Blazer's Towing: Highway 61 in Beaver Bay;
   (218) 226-4447

Palisade Bumper-to-Bumper Auto Parts (parts): 99 Outer Drive in Silver
   Bay; (218) 226-3321
Nelson Auto Parts and Towing: Highway 61 in Tofte; (218) 663-7475
Grand Marais Standard/Towing: Main Street in Grand Marais;
   (218) 387-1646
NAPA Auto Parts (parts): Highway 61 in Grand Marais; (218) 387-2304
Steve's Sports and Auto (parts and repair): Highway 61 in Grand Marais;
   (218) 387-1835
Wally's Towing: Grand Marais; (218) 370-0740
Wrecking J's Towing: 4 miles east of Grand Marais on Co. Rd. 58;
   (218) 387-1018

ROAD CONDITIONS

When traveling through Duluth and along the North Shore, keep in mind
that Highway 61 is a curving, two-lane, scenic highway. In peak seasons
(holidays, weekends, and July and August), plan on traveling 50 miles per
hour. Take special care when passing. Due to the popularity of earlier editions of this book and the subsequent increase in traffic, road construction
continues over the next several years to improve both the safety and the road
design of Highway 61.

I suggest obtaining a Minnesota road map (available at service stations)
and county maps (from tourist information centers) for your travels through
Duluth and along the North Shore.

For road conditions on Minnesota state highways, call (218) 723-4866 or
511 on any phone except those on the Verizon plan.

CLIMATE

Lake Superior keeps the shoreline cooler in the summer and warmer in the
winter. Winter temperatures shown here do not take into account the wind-
chill factor. Snowfall averages seven to ten feet per year, with the first flakes
dropping in late October and the last flurry in April. For travelers in this
area, I recommend layering clothing to adjust for the varying temperatures.
Temperatures given are an average. Near Duluth, temperatures will be
slightly higher, and near the Canadian border, they will be cooler. Don't
forget about the lake effect!

AVERAGE HIGH TEMPERATURE (IN FAHRENHEIT)

Jan	Feb	Mar	Apr	May	Jun	Jul	Aug	Sep	Oct	Nov	Dec
23°	27°	33°	47°	54°	62°	72°	72°	61°	51°	39°	26°

AVERAGE LOW TEMPERATURE (IN FAHRENHEIT)

Jan	Feb	Mar	Apr	May	Jun	Jul	Aug	Sep	Oct	Nov	Dec
1°	13°	18°	31°	38°	43°	56°	56°	47°	38°	27°	10°

MILEAGE FROM DULUTH

Thunder Bay, Ontario: 186 miles
Canadian Border: 146 miles
Grand Marais, MN: 110 miles
Lutsen, MN: 92 miles
Silver Bay, MN: 55 miles
Two Harbors, MN: 26 miles
Minneapolis/St. Paul, MN: 156 miles
Des Moines, IA: 402 miles
Milwaukee, WI: 392 miles
Chicago, IL: 465 miles
Fargo, ND: 255 miles

BANKING

When you leave Duluth to travel up the North Shore, keep in mind that automatic cash machines can be found in Two Harbors, Silver Bay, Tofte, Lutsen, Grand Marais, and Grand Portage. Most banks are open Monday through Friday, with limited hours on Saturday mornings. For a full listing of Duluth credit unions, refer to the Yellow Pages. Ryden's Border Store at the U.S.-Canadian border gives one of the best rates of exchange on American and Canadian currency and is open seven days a week.

DULUTH BANKS

Beacon Bank: 401 West Superior Street; (218) 722-0238
North Shore Bank of Commerce: 131 West Superior Street (Main Office);
    (218) 722-4784
Wells Fargo Duluth: 230 West Superior Street (Main Office);
    (218) 723-2600

Pioneer National Bank: 331 North Central Avenue West; (218) 624-3676
Republic Bank: 306 West Superior Street (Main Office); (218) 733-5100
Western National Bank, 57th Avenue and Grand Avenue; (218) 723-5100

NORTH SHORE BANKS AND CREDIT UNIONS

Lake Bank: At Super One in Two Harbors; (218) 834-2111
Wells Fargo: 622 1st Avenue in Two Harbors; (218) 834-2151
Two Harbors Federal Credit Union: 626 2nd Avenue in Two Harbors;
 (218) 834-2266
Lake Bank: 88 Outer Drive in Silver Bay; (218) 226-4957
North Shore Federal Credit Union: 85 Outer Drive in Silver Bay;
 (218) 226-4401
North Shore Federal Credit Union: Highway 61 in Lutsen; (218) 663-7665
Security State Bank: Main Street in Grand Marais; (218) 387-1000
Grand Marais State Bank: Highway 61 in Tofte; (218) 663-7891
Grand Marais State Bank: Highway 61 in Grand Marais; (218) 387-2441
North Shore Federal Credit Union: Highway 61 in Grand Marais;
 (218) 387-1312

CHURCHES

Since churches and services are limited up Highway 61, they are listed below.
Ask about special mass sites, since a few parishes add extra services during
the summer at locations other than the church. A full listing of places of worship and worship times for the Duluth area can be found in the phone book.

ASSEMBLIES OF GOD

Living Waters Fellowship in Two Harbors: (218) 834-4545
Beaver Bay Assembly of God Church: (218) 226-3014

BAPTIST

First Baptist Church in Two Harbors: (218) 834-4738
Grace Baptist in Two Harbors : (218) 834-3255
Silver Bay Baptist Church: (218) 226-4202
Palisade Baptist Church: (218) 226-3039
First Baptist Church in Grand Marais: (218) 387-2090

CATHOLIC

Holy Spirit Catholic Church in Two Harbors: (218) 834-4313

St. Mary's Church in Silver Bay: (218) 226-3691
St. John's Church in Grand Marais: (218) 387-1409
Holy Rosary Catholic Church in Grand Portage: (218) 387-1409

COMMUNITY
Mount Rose Community Church in Grand Portage: (218) 475-2300

EVANGELICAL
Evangelical Free Church in Two Harbors: (218) 834-2606
Evangelical Free Church in Grand Marais: (218) 387-1565

INTERDENOMINATIONAL
United Protestant Church in Silver Bay: (218) 226-3973

JEHOVAH'S WITNESSES
Silver Bay: (218) 353-7451
Grand Marais: (218) 387-1318

LUTHERAN
French River Lutheran: (218) 525-5659
Knife River Lutheran: (218) 834-5172
Emmanuel Lutheran in Two Harbors: (218) 834-4736
Our Savior's Lutheran Church in Two Harbors: (218) 834-5383
Bethlehem Lutheran in Two Harbors: (218) 834-4158
Hope Lutheran (Missouri Synod) in Two Harbors: (218) 834-5345
Faith Lutheran in Silver Bay: (218) 226-3908
Sychar Lutheran Church ELCA in Silver Bay: (218) 226-4424
Zion Lutheran Church of Finland: (218) 353-7369
Zoar Lutheran Church in Tofte: (218) 663-7925
Lutsen Lutheran Church in Lutsen: (218) 663-7494
Bethlehem Lutheran Church in Grand Marais (ELCA): (218) 387-2227
North Shore Recreation Ministry in Grand Marais: (218) 387-1064
Trinity Lutheran Church in Hovland: (218) 387-2227

UNITED CHURCH OF CHRIST
First Congregational Church in Grand Marais: (218) 387-2113

PRESBYTERIAN
United Presbyterian Church of Two Harbors: (218) 834-4257

GROCERY STORES

Several large supermarkets can be found in the Duluth area. I have chosen to list specialty food shops in Duluth and all groceries and food shops along the Shore.

SPECIALTY FOOD STORES IN DULUTH
Amazing Grace: DeWitt-Seitz Marketplace in Canal Park; (218) 723-0075
Bay Side Market: 1901 Minnesota Avenue; (218) 727-7635
European Bakery (breads): 109 West 1st Street; (218) 722-2120
Fichtner's Sausages and Meats: 134 West 1st Street; (218) 722-2661
First Oriental Grocery of Duluth: 323 East Superior Street; (218) 726-0017
Great Harvest Bread Co.: 13th Avenue East and Superior Street;
    (218) 728-9560
Italian Village: 301 North Central Avenue; (218) 624-2286
The Park Bench: 5105 Miller Trunk Highway; (218) 729-5089
Positively 3rd Street Bakery: 1202 East 3rd Street; (218) 724-8619
Whole Foods Co-op: 1332 East 4th Street; (218) 728-0884

GROCERY STORES ALONG THE NORTH SHORE
Russ Kendall's Smokehouse: Scenic 61 at Knife River; (218) 834-5995
Mel's Fish: Scenic 61 at Knife River; (218) 834-5858
Lou's Fish House: Highway 61 in Two Harbors; (218) 834-5254
Vanilla Bean: Highway 61 in Two Harbors; (218) 834-6964
Two Harbors Super One: Just off Highway 61 in Two Harbors; (218) 834-5651
Zup's Big Dollar: Silver Bay Shopping Center; (218) 226-4161
Finland Cooperative: Highway 61 in Finland; (218) 353-7389
Coho Cafe and Deli: Highway 61 in Tofte; (218) 663-8032
North Shore Market: Highway 61 in Tofte; (218) 663-7288
Lockport Market and Deli: Highway 61 in Lutsen; (218) 663-7548
Clearview General Store: Highway 61 in Lutsen; (218) 663-7478
Cook County Whole Foods Co-op: in Grand Marais; (218) 387-2503
Dockside Fish Market: Highway 61 in Grand Marais; (218) 387-2906
Victoria's Bakehouse and Deli: Highway 61 in Grand Marais; (218) 387-1747
Gene's IGA: Highway 61 in Grand Marais; (218) 387-1212
Johnson's Big Dollar: Highway 61 in Grand Marais; (218) 387-2480

LIQUOR STORES

There are a number of liquor stores in Duluth. I have listed a few that are centrally located. Many deliver throughout Duluth. In Minnesota, all liquor stores are closed on Sundays and major holidays.

DULUTH
Canal Park Liquors: 302 Lake Avenue South; (218) 733-0850
Good Times Liquor Store: 32 West 1st Street; (218) 727-1424
Lake Aire Bottle Shoppe: 2530 London Road; (218) 724-8818
Lake Superior Liquors: 31 East 1st Street; (218) 722-3518
Last Chance Liquor and Wine Cellar: 619 East 4th Street; (218) 727-6825
Loiselle Liquor: 413 East 4th Street; (218) 722-6590
Hermantown Liquor Store: Miller Trunk and Haine Road; (218) 723-1616
Mount Royal Bottle Shop: 1602 Woodland Avenue; (218) 728-6168
Fitger's Wine Cellars: Fitger's Complex; (218) 733-0792

NORTH SHORE
Two Harbors Liquor Store: Highway 61 in Two Harbors; (218) 834-3745
The Green Door Liquor Store: Highway 61 in Beaver Bay; (218) 226-9963
Silver Bay Municipal Liquor Store: 95 Outer Drive in Silver Bay;
    (218) 226-3106
Temperance Traders Liquor Store: Highway 61 in Schroeder; (218) 387-0111
North Shore Market and Bottle Shop: Highway 61 in Tofte; (218) 663-7288
CT Liquors: Highway 61 in Lutsen; (218) 663-7370
Grand Marais Municipal Liquor Store: Off Highway 61 in Grand Marais;
    (218) 387-1630

PHOTO DEVELOPING

Duluth Camera Exchange and Northern Photo offer camera repair, although it may take a week for estimates, since the work is often sent out. Photo finishing along the Shore is usually overnight.

DULUTH
CPL, Custom Photo Lab: 405 East Superior Steet; (218) 722-6759
Duluth Camera Exchange/One Hour: 321 West Superior Street,
    (218) 727-2225; 1405 Miller Trunk Highway, (218) 727-5626; and
    215 North Central Avenue, (218) 628-2325

Express Lane Photo/One Hour: 1717 Mall Drive; (218) 722-1335
First Photo/One Hour: 326 East Central Entrance; (218) 722-9567
Great Prints 35 Minute Photo: Miller Hill Mall; (218) 727-1060
Northern Photo/One Hour: Downtown Holiday Mall; (218) 722-2708
True Colors One Hour Photo Finishing: 625 West Central Entrance;
    (218) 722-7696
Walgreen Drug Stores: Valley Center, (218) 628-2377; Miller Hill Mall,
    (218) 727-8387; and 1 South 13th Avenue East, (218) 724-8551
Wal-Mart: 4740 Mall Drive; (218) 727-1228

NORTH SHORE
Pamida: Off Highway 61 in Two Harbors; (218) 834-2889
Wings by the Bay: 601 1st Avenue, Two Harbors; (218) 834-5111
SnapShots One Hour Photo Developing: Highway 61 in Grand Marais;
    (218) 387-2563
Arrowhead Pharmacy: Highway 61 in Grand Marais; (218) 387-1133
White Pine North: main street in Grand Marais; (218) 387-1695

POST OFFICES (AND ZIP CODES)

55609	Knife River: On Scenic 61 at Emily's; (218) 834-3433
55616	Two Harbors: On the corner of 6th Street and 1st Avenue; (218) 834-3430
55601	Beaver Bay: On Highway 61 in Beaver Bay; (218) 226-4129
55614	Silver Bay: At the shopping center in Silver Bay; (218) 226-3700
55613	Schroeder: On Highway 61 in Schroeder; (218) 663-7568
55615	Tofte: On Highway 61 in Tofte; (218) 663-7985
55612	Lutsen: On Highway 61 in Lutsen; (218) 663-7323
55604	Grand Marais: On Highway 61 in Grand Marais; (218) 387-1020
55606	Hovland: On Arrowhead Trail, just north of Highway 61 in Hovland; (218) 475-2286
55605	Grand Portage: 101 Store Road; (218) 475-2303

Suggested Reading

GENERAL NATURAL HISTORY AND NATURE WRITING

Alin, Erika. *Lake Effect: Along Superior's Shores*. Minneapolis: University of Minnesota Press, 2003.

Anderson, Scott. *Distant Fires*. Duluth: Pfeifer-Hamilton, 1990.

Breining, Greg. *Wild Shore: Exploring Lake Superior by Kayak*. Minneapolis: University of Minnesota Press, 2002.

Cary, Bob. *Root Beer Lady: The Story of Dorothy Molter*. Minneapolis: University of Minnesota Press, 1993.

———. *Tales from Jackpine Bob*. Duluth: Pfeifer-Hamilton, 1996.

Cook, Sam. *Camp Sights*. Minneapolis: University of Minnesota Press, 2002.

———. *Friendship Fires*. Minneapolis: University of Minnesota Press, 2003.

———. *Quiet Magic*. Minneapolis: University of Minnesota Press, 2002.

———. *Up North*. Minneapolis: University of Minnesota Press, 2003.

Crowley, Kate, and Mike Link. *Boundary Waters Canoe Area Wilderness*. Stillwater, Minn.: Voyageur Press, 1987.

Drabik, Harry. *The Spirit of Canoe Camping*. Minneapolis: Nodin Press, 1981.

Gruchow, Paul. *Boundary Waters: The Grace of the Wild*. Minneapolis: Milkweed Editions, 1997.

Heinselman, Miron. *The Boundary Waters Wilderness Ecosystem*. Minneapolis: University of Minnesota Press, 1996.

Henricksson, John. *A Wild Neighborhood*. Minneapolis: University of Minnesota Press, 1997.

———, editor. *North Writers: A Strong Woods Collection*. Minneapolis: University of Minnesota Press, 1991.

———, editor. *North Writers II: Our Place in the Woods*. Minneapolis: University of Minnesota Press, 1997.

Hoover, Helen. *The Gift of the Deer*. Minneapolis: University of Minnesota Press, 1998.

————. *The Long-Shadowed Forest.* Minneapolis: University of Minnesota Press, 1998.

————. *A Place in the Woods.* Minneapolis: University of Minnesota Press, 1999.

————. *The Years of the Forest.* Minneapolis: University of Minnesota Press, 1999.

Humphries, Jeff, and Betsy Bowen. *Borealis.* Minneapolis: University of Minnesota Press, 2002.

Jaques, Florence Page. *Canoe Country and Snowshoe Country.* Minneapolis: University of Minnesota Press, 1999.

Ojakangas, Richard W., and Charles L. Matsch. *Minnesota's Geology.* Minneapolis: University of Minnesota Press, 2001.

Olson, Sigurd F. *Listening Point.* Minneapolis: University of Minnesota Press, 1997.

————. *The Lonely Land.* Minneapolis: University of Minnesota Press, 1997.

————. *The Meaning of Wilderness: Essential Articles and Speeches.* Minneapolis: University of Minnesota Press, 2001.

————. *Of Time and Place.* Minneapolis: University of Minnesota Press, 1998.

————. *Open Horizons.* Minneapolis: University of Minnesota Press, 1998.

————. *Reflections from the North Country.* Minneapolis: University of Minnesota Press, 1998.

————. *Runes of the North.* Minneapolis: University of Minnesota Press, 1997.

————. *The Singing Wilderness.* Minneapolis: University of Minnesota Press, 1997.

————. *Spirit of the North: The Quotable Sigurd F. Olson.* Minneapolis: University of Minnesota Press, 2004.

Slade, Andrew. *White Woods, Quiet Trails: Exploring Minnesota's North Shore in Winter.* Two Harbors, Minn.: Ridgeline Press, 1997.

Sutter, Barton. *Cold Comfort: Life at the Top of the Map.* Minneapolis: University of Minnesota Press, 2000.

Tester, John R. *Minnesota's Natural Heritage: An Ecological Perspective.* Minneapolis: University of Minnesota Press, 1995.

Waters, Thomas F. *The Streams and Rivers of Minnesota.* Minneapolis: University of Minnesota Press, 1977.

————. *The Superior North Shore.* Minneapolis: University of Minnesota Press, 1987.

HISTORY

Backes, David. *A Wilderness Within: The Life of Sigurd F. Olson*. Minneapolis: University of Minnesota Press, 1997.

Bolz, J. Arnold. *Portage into the Past: By Canoe along the Minnesota-Ontario Boundary Waters*. Minneapolis: University of Minnesota Press, 1960, 1999.

Furtman, Michael. *Magic on the Rocks: Canoe Country Pictographs*. Cambridge, Minn.: Birch Portage Press, 2000.

Havighurst, Walter. *The Long Ships Passing: The Story of the Great Lakes*. Minneapolis: University of Minnesota Press, 2002.

Kerfoot, Justine. *Woman of the Boundary Waters*. Minneapolis: University of Minnesota Press, 1994.

King, Frank A. *Minnesota's Logging Railroads*. Minneapolis: University of Minnesota Press, 2003.

———. *The Missabe Road: The Duluth Missabe and Iron Range Railway*. Minneapolis: University of Minnesota Press, 2003.

Nute, Grace Lee. *Lake Superior*. Minneapolis: University of Minnesota Press, 2000.

———. *The Voyageur*. St. Paul: Minnesota Historical Society Press, 1931, 1976.

———. *The Voyageur's Highway: Minnesota's Border Lake Land*. St. Paul: Minnesota Historical Society Press, 1941, 1976.

Raff, Willis H. *Pioneers in the Wilderness: Minnesota's Cook County, Grand Marais, and the Gunflint in the 19th Century*. Grand Marais, Minn.: Cook County Historical Society, 1981.

Sivertson, Howard. *The Illustrated Voyageur*. Mount Horeb, Wis.: Midwest Traditions, 1994.

Workers of the Writer's Program of the WPA. *The WPA Guide to the Minnesota Arrowhead Country*. St. Paul: Minnesota Historical Society Press, 1988.

SHIPWRECKS

Hancock, Paul. *Shipwrecks of the Great Lakes*. San Diego: Thunder Bay Press 2001.

Holden, Thom. *Above and Below: A History of Lighthouses and Shipwrecks of Isle Royale*. Houghton, Mich.: Isle Royale Natural History Association, 1985.

Marshall, James R., editor. *Shipwrecks of Lake Superior*. Duluth: Lake Superior Port Cities, Inc., 1986.

Stonehouse, Frederick. *The Wreck of the Edmund Fitzgerald.* Marquette, Mich.: Avery Color Studios, 1995.

Thompson, Mark L. *Graveyard of the Lakes.* Detroit: Wayne State University Press, 2000.

Wolff, Julius. *The Shipwrecks of Lake Superior.* Duluth: Lake Superior Marine Museum Association, Inc., 1979.

ISLE ROYALE

Cochrane, Timothy, and Hawk Tolson. *A Good Boat Speaks for Itself: Isle Royale Fishermen and Their Boats.* Minneapolis: University of Minnesota Press, 2002.

Gale, Thomas P., and Kendra L. Gale. *Isle Royale: A Photographic History.* Houghton, Mich.: Isle Royale Natural History Association, 1995.

Peterson, Rolf Olin. *The Wolves of Isle Royale: A Broken Balance.* Minocqua, Wis.: Willow Creek Press, 1995.

Simonson, Dorothy. *The Diary of an Isle Royale School Teacher.* Houghton, Mich.: Isle Royale Natural History Association, 1988.

Sivertson, Howard. *Once upon an Isle: The Story of Fishing Families on Isle Royale.* Mount Horeb, Wis.: Wisconsin Folk Museum, 1992.

———. *Tales of the Old North Shore.* Duluth: Lake Superior Port Cities, Inc., 1996.

Stonehouse, Frederick. *Isle Royale Shipwrecks.* AuTrain, Mich.: Avery Color Studios, 1983.

DINING AND COOKING

Berg, Ron. *Northwoods Fish Cookery.* Minneapolis: University of Minnesota Press, 2000.

Berg, Ron, and Sue Kerfoot. *The Gunflint Lodge Cookbook: Elegant Northwoods Dining.* Minneapolis: University of Minnesota Press, 1997.

Gauerke, Richard. *Something Wild Cookbook.* Cambridge, Minn.: Adventure Publications, 1990.

Kreag, Judy. *Savor Superior.* Kuttawa, Ky.: McClanahan Publishing, 1993.

Legwold, Gary. *The Last Word on Lefse.* Cambridge, Minn.: Adventure Publications, 1992.

Marrone, Teresa. *The Back-Country Kitchen: Camp Cooking for Canoeists, Hikers, and Anglers.* Minneapolis: Northern Trails Press, 1996.

———. *The Seasonal Cabin Cookbook.* Cambridge, Minn.: Adventure Publications, 2001.

Swanson, Bonnie Jean. *Dining in the Spirit of Naniboujou: Recipes Collected*

from Naniboujou Lodge, Grand Marais, Minnesota. Grand Marais,
Minn.: Tim and Nancy Ramey, 1999.

FISHING

Breining, Greg. *Fishing Minnesota: Angling with the Experts in the Land of
10,000 Lakes.* Minneapolis: University of Minnesota Press, 2003.

Furtman, Michael. *A Boundary Waters Fishing Guide.* Minocqua, Wis.:
NorthWord Press, 1990.

Perich, Shawn. *Fishing Lake Superior: A Complete Guide to Stream, Shoreline, and Open-Water Angling.* Minneapolis: University of Minnesota
Press, 1994.

———. *Fly-Fishing the North Country.* Duluth: Pfeifer-Hamilton, 1995.

TRAVEL GUIDES

Beymer, Robert. *The Boundary Waters Canoe Area.* 6th ed. Berkeley, Calif.:
Wilderness Press, 2000.

———. *Superior National Forest.* Seattle: The Mountaineers, 1989.

Dahl, Bonnie. *The Superior Way: A Cruising Guide to Lake Superior.* 2nd ed.
Duluth: Lake Superior Port Cities, Inc., 1992.

Dregni, Eric. *Minnesota Marvels: Roadside Attractions in the Land of Lakes.*
Minneapolis: University of Minnesota Press, 2001.

Fenton, Howard. *50 Circuit Hikes: A Stride-by-Stride Guide to Northeastern
Minnesota.* Minneapolis: University of Minnesota Press, 1999.

Furtman, Michael. *Canoe Country Camping.* Minneapolis: University of
Minnesota Press, 2002.

Johnson, Steve. *Mountain Biking Minnesota.* Guilford, Conn.: Falcon Press,
2002.

Newman, Bill, Sarah Ohmann, and Don Dimond. *Guide to Sea Kayaking
on Lakes Superior and Michigan: The Best Day Trips and Tours.* Old Say-
brook, Conn.: Globe Pequot Press, 1999.

Olsenius, Richard. *Minnesota Travel Companion.* Minneapolis: University
of Minnesota Press, 2001.

Perich, Shawn. *The North Shore: A Four-Season Guide to Minnesota's
Favorite Destination.* Duluth: Pfeifer-Hamilton, 1992.

Superior Hiking Trail Association. *Guide to the Superior Hiking Trail.* Two
Harbors, Minn.: Ridgeline Press, 2001.

Tornabene, Ladona, et al. *Gentle Hikes: Minnesota's Most Scenic North Shore
Hikes under 3 Miles.* Cambridge, Minn.: Adventure Publications, 2002.

THE OJIBWE

Gilman, Carolyn. *The Grand Portage Story.* St. Paul: Minnesota Historical Society Press, 1992.

Hart, Joanne, and Hazel Belvo. *Witch Tree: A Collaboration.* Duluth: Holy Cow! Press, 1990.

Kegg, Maude. *Portage Lake, Memories of an Ojibwe Childhood.* Minneapolis: University of Minnesota Press, 1993.

Kohl, Johann Georg. *Kitchi Gami: Life among the Lake Superior Ojibway.* St. Paul: Minnesota Historical Society Press, 1985.

Morton, Ron, and Carl Gawboy. *Talking Rocks: Geology and 10,000 Years of Native American Tradition in the Lake Superior Region.* Duluth: Pfeifer-Hamilton, 2000.

Nichols, John D., and Earl Nyholm. *A Concise Dictionary of Minnesota Ojibwe.* Minneapolis: University of Minnesota Press, 1995.

Northrup, Jim. *The Rez Road Follies: Canoes, Casinos, Computers, and Birch Bark Baskets.* Minneapolis: University of Minnesota Press, 1999.

Peacock, Thomas D., and Marlene Wisuri. *Ojibwe Waasa Inaabidaa: We Look in All Directions.* Afton, Minn.: Afton Historical Society Press, 2002.

Van Laan, Nancy, with illustrations by Betsy Bowen. *Shingebiss: An Ojibwe Legend.* Boston: Houghton Mifflin, 1997.

Warren, William W., and W. Roger Buffalohead. *History of the Ojibway People.* St. Paul: Minnesota Historical Society Press, 1984.

NATURE GUIDES

Bates, John. *Trailside Botany: 101 Favorite Trees, Shrubs, and Wildflowers of the Upper Midwest.* Duluth: Pfeifer-Hamilton, 1995.

Chartrand, Mark. *Audubon Society Field Guide to the Night Sky.* New York: Alfred A. Knopf, 1991.

Erickson, Laura. *For the Birds, An Uncommon Guide.* Duluth: Pfeifer-Hamilton, 1994.

Green, John C. *Geology on Display: Geology and Scenery of Minnesota's North Shore State Parks.* St. Paul: Minnesota Dept. of Natural Resources, 2000.

A Guide to Minnesota's Scientific and Natural Areas. St. Paul: Minnesota Dept. of Natural Resources, Section of Wildlife, Scientific and Natural Areas Program, 1999.

Hazard, Evan B. *The Mammals of Minnesota.* Minneapolis: University of Minnesota Press, 1982.

Moyle, John B., and Evelyn W. Moyle. *Northland Wildflowers: The Comprehensive Guide to the Minnesota Region.* Revised ed. Minneapolis: University of Minnesota Press, 2001.

National Audubon Society Field Guide to North American Wildflowers: Eastern Region. Ed. John W. Thieret, William A. Nierling, and Nancy C. Olmstead. New York: Alfred A. Knopf, 2001.

Peterson, Roger Tory. *A Field Guide to the Birds of Eastern and Central North America.* 5th ed. Boston: Houghton Mifflin, 2002.

Stensaas, Mark. *Canoe Country Flora: Plants and Trees of the North Woods and Boundary Waters.* Duluth: Pfeifer-Hamilton, 1996.

———. *Canoe Country Wildlife.* Duluth: Pfeifer-Hamilton, 1993.

———. *Rock Picker's Guide to Lake Superior's North Shore.* 2nd ed. Duluth: Kollath-Stensaas, 2002.

Stensaas, Mark, and Rick Kollath. *Wildflowers of the BWCA and the North Shore.* Duluth: Kollath-Stensaas, 2003.

Strangis, Jay Michael. *Birding Minnesota.* Helena, Mont.: Falcon Press, 1996.

Tekiela, Stan. *Birds of Minnesota.* Cambridge, Minn.: Adventure Publications, 1998.

———. *Trees of Minnesota.* Cambridge, Minn.: Adventure Publications, 2001.

Weber, Larry. *Butterflies of the North Woods.* Cambridge, Minn.: Adventure Publications, 2001.

———. *Spiders of the North Woods.* Duluth: Kollath-Stensaas, 2002.

PICTORIAL

Blacklock, Craig. *Horizons.* Moose Lake, Minn.: Blacklock Nature Photography, 2002.

———. *The Lake Superior Images.* Moose Lake, Minn.: Blacklock Nature Photography, 1993.

Blacklock, Craig, and Nadine Blacklock. *The Duluth Portfolio.* Duluth: Pfeifer-Hamilton, 1995.

Blacklock, Nadine, and Craig Blacklock. *Gooseberry.* Duluth: Pfeifer-Hamilton, 1994.

Gruchow, Paul. *Travels in Canoe Country.* Boston: Little, Brown, 1992.

Steinke, Jay. *Gunflint Territory.* Duluth: Tea Table Books, 1993.

———. *Superior's North Shore: Wild Places.* Duluth: Tea Table Books, 1993.

CHILDREN'S

Arnosky, Jim. *Every Autumn Comes the Bear.* New York: G. P. Putnam's Sons, 1993.

Bauer, Marion Dane, with illustrations by Allen Garni. *When I Go Fishing with Grandma.* Mahwah, N.J.: BridgeWater Books, 1995.

Beskow, Elsa. *Peter in Blueberry Land.* London: Floris Books, 1987.

Bowen, Betsy. *Antler, Bear, Canoe: A Northwoods Alphabet Year.* Boston: Houghton Mifflin, 2002.

———. *Gathering: A Northwoods Counting Book.* Boston: Houghton Mifflin, 1999.

———. *Tracks in the Wild.* Boston: Houghton Mifflin, 1998.

Butler, Dori Hillestad. *M Is for Minnesota.* Minneapolis: University of Minnesota Press, 1998.

Casanova, Mary. *One-Dog Canoe.* New York: Melanie Kroupa Books, 2003.

Climo, Shirley. *Stolen Thunder: A Norse Myth.* New York: Clarion Books, 1994.

Erickson, Laura. *Sharing the Wonder of Birds with Kids.* Minneapolis: University of Minnesota Press, 2002.

Holling, Clancy. *Paddle to the Sea.* Boston: Houghton Mifflin, 1941.

Lunge-Larsen, Lise, and Mary Azarian. *The Race of the Birkebeiners.* Boston: Houghton Mifflin, 2001.

Lunge-Larsen, Lise, and Margi Preus. *The Legend of the Lady Slipper: An Ojibwe Tale.* Boston: Houghton Mifflin, 1999.

Peacock, Thomas, and Marlene Wisuri. *The Good Path: Ojibwe Learning and Activity Book for Kids.* Afton, Minn.: Afton Historical Society Press, 2002.

Peterson, Roger Tory. *A Field Guide to the Birds Coloring Book.* Boston: Houghton Mifflin, 1982.

———. *A Field Guide to Wildflowers Coloring Book.* Boston: Houghton Mifflin, 1982.

Stong, Phil, and Kurt Wiese. *Honk the Moose.* Duluth: Trellis, 2001.

Van Laan, Nancy, and Betsy Bowen. *Shingebiss: An Ojibwe Legend.* Boston: Houghton Mifflin, 1997.

Index

Nina A. Simonowicz grew up in Duluth and now lives outside Grand Marais with her husband, Bill, and son, Max. She is the owner of Nina Works!, a marketing company specializing in North Shore tourism and Web sites, including her northshorevisitor.com.

Betsy Bowen is author and illustrator of *Antler, Bear, Canoe: A Northwoods Alphabet Year, Tracks in the Wild,* and *Gathering: A Northwoods Counting Book.* She illustrated *Borealis,* a collection of poems by Jeff Humphries (Minnesota, 2002). She works out of Betsy Bowen's Studio in Grand Marais.